AF657673

HISTORIANS AND HISTORIOGRAPHY OF ORISSA

A Study in Perception and Appropriation of Orissan History

HISTORIANS AND HISTORIOGRAPHY OF ORISSA

A Study in Perception and Appropriation of Orissan History

by

Laxmikanta Mishra

Sitakanta Mishra

Kaveri Books

New Delhi - 110002

First Published in 2005
ISBN: 978-81-7479-052-1

Published by
Kaveri Books
4832/24, Ansari Road
New Delhi-110002 (India)
Tel: 011-23288140, 47072321
E-mail : info@kaveribooks.com
E-mail : kaveribooks@gmail.com
Website: www.kaveribooks.com

Typeset at
Delta Book World, New Delhi - 110 002.

PRINTED IN INDIA

Transliteration

The system of transliteration to be followed in the book is given below :

English	Oriya	Hindi
ā	ଆ	आ
ī	ଈ	ई
ū	ଊ	ऊ
ṛ	ଋ	ऋ
ṅ	ଙ	ङ्
ch	ଚ	च्
chh	ଛ	छ्
ñ	ଞ	ञ
ṭ	ଟ	ट्
ṭh	ଠ	ठ्
ḍ	ଡ	ड्
ḍh	ଢ	ढ्
ṇ	ଣ	ण
ś	ଶ	श्
sha	ଷ	ष
ksh	କ୍ଷ	क्ष
Jñ	ଜ୍ଞ	ज्ञ्

The whole work has been broadly divided into two parts. In the first part there is an analytical attempt to grasp the exhilarating history writing methods of English historians who contrived the broad contours of Orissan historiography. And in the second part we have tried to draw the threads together and spin out the strand of the history of Orissa

In the course of discourses on the historiography of Orissa, four distinct trends have emerged. These are colonialist, nationalist, biased and sober historiography. Whereas there had been on the one hand denigration of Orissan polity, economy, society and religion by the British colonialist, Evangelical and utilitarian historians, there has been, on the other hand, sincere and committed attempts by some of the Bengali historians of 19th century to dismember Oriya identity. Emphasis had also been given to contrive a clear picture of Orissan history by studying the sober historiography. Among all the historians discussed in the work, notable mention may be made of Andrew Stirling, William Wilson Hunter, John Beames and George Toynbee of the Orientalist-colonialist category; Pyarimohan Acharya, Jagabandhu Singh, Nilakantha Dash, Krupasindhu Mishra and Birupakshya Kar of the nationalist category; Rajendra Lal Mitra and Bijoy Chandra Majumdar who carried some bias against the Oriyas in their historical writings on Orissa; and Manmohan Chakraborty, Bishen Swarup, Manmohan Ganguly, Rakhal Das Banerjee, Benimadhav Barua, Binayak Mishra and Nirmal Kumar Bose who attempted to write sober history.

The work is divided into several chapters. Chapter one gives an introduction to the present study on Orissan historiography in the backdrop of different trends so far identified and noticed in the study of Indian history. Chapter two makes a comprehensive review of different trends noticed in the study of modern historiography of India. In chapter three, a broad outline of the nature of historiography of Orissa during the ancient, medieval and modern periods is provided. In analyzing modern Orissan historiography, a broad categorization of the historians has been made on the basis of their approaches and line of historical understanding. This categorization has been followed while evaluating the historical work on Orissa. In view of the importance of the Raj in the British articulation of Indian history, the nature and contour of the Raj syndrome and its influence on

Preface

The historiography of Orissa being a virgin field of study necessitates serious historical research and the present work is a humble attempt in this regard. Such a study has also assumed greater significance as historiography has of late been included in the post-graduate and M.Phil curricula of different colleges and universities. We are therefore happy to present to the enlightened elite, scholars of history and students alike this endeavour "*Historians and Historiography of Orissa—A Study in Perception and Appropriation of Orissan History*". This work is a pioneer venture to survey and assess the distinctive character of historians who had ventured to articulate the history of Orissa. Notwithstanding the compulsions of preparing a report, or recording a gazetteer, or writing something like history for the use and satisfaction of bureaucrats in their daily needs, the history of Orissa had come up through a length of cognizable existence.

In satisfying the current demand for historiography, the present work has modestly attempted a presentation, in all its comprehensiveness, of an account of the historical compositions on Orissa. It is thus a pioneering attempt on a hitherto unexplored field.

During the recent years, historical research has gone beyond mere fact finding and stresses have been laid on new interpretations, theorization and evaluation of historical compositions. Keeping in line with the recent trends in historical research, the present work provides a historical analysis of the historical compositions on Orissa available on record right from the ancient times.

historiography, has been discussed in chapter four. Chapter five which has been devoted to the Orientalist and colonialist historiography of Orissa has been further subdivided into five sub-chapters. Chapters six, seven and eight present an in-depth analysis of different historiographers as categorized there and summarily provide an account of their works from the point of view of historiography. In a nutshell the work is an exhaustive attempt at understanding the historiographical knowledge produced by the British and Bengali historians during the whole of the British rule on Orissa's cultural, social and political institutions and the response of Orissan historians to these articulations.

The present work is basically the outcome of our years of painstaking research on the subject leading to our doctoral degrees. We therefore express our deep indebtedness to Dr Umakant Subuddhi, Professor of History, Gangadhar Meher College, Sambalpur, Orissa and Dr Teertha Prakash Jena, Reader & Head of the Department of History, Government College, Phulbani, Orissa for not only supervising our work during research but also giving insightful suggestions at different stages of the work. Dr Himadri Banerjee, Professor of History (Guru Nanak Chair), Jadavpur University, Calcutta, had provided us extremely valuable academic support at every stage of the work. We sincerely acknowledge his help. Dr Prafulla Kumar Mohanty, Senior Lecturer in History, M.P.C. College, Baripada, Orissa, offered very informed and helpful suggestions for the development of the present work. We express our sincere gratitude to him. Dr Narendra Kumar Dash, Professor and Head of the Department of Indo-Tibetan Studies, has been of great help at the crunch time. We are extremely thankful to him. We are deeply indebted to our spouses, Binapani and Nirupama respectively, for their smiling faces both at hard and happy times and also for their lively and constructive criticism.

Finally we express our gratitude and special thanks to Shri Rakesh Goel, Proprietor, M/s Kaveri Books, without whose efforts this book would not have perhaps seen the light of the day. We sincerely hope that the book will earn appreciation from all corners.

Laxmikanta Mishra

Sri Gundicha **Sitakanta Mishra**

Contents

1

Introduction

Serious researches into the studies on modern historiography of India are a purely recent phenomenon. In fact efforts to trace out the distinct trends, approaches and intrinsic historical ideas of the historiographers of India began roughly half a century ago. This happened despite the fact that, starting from about the middle of the 19th century, the first hundred years saw a spate of writings on the history of India. Though modern historical writing started, of course, under the British auspices with a clear Europo-centric approach, the latter half of the 19th century and the first half of the 20th century marked definite progress in historical compositions and the application of new historical methods.

In order to evaluate the historical works from the parameters of historiography, it was all the more necessary to study the historical ideas and methodology current among those who made pioneering contributions to the progress of modern historical writings on India. The first ever such attempt was made in the School of Oriental and African Studies, University of London, in the year 1956 when a seminar was organized to evaluate the historical writings on India, Pakistan and Ceylon. The proceedings of the seminar were brought out in a comprehensive volume edited by Sir C.H. Phillips and entitled "*Historians of India, Pakistan and Ceylon*". Introducing this volume, the editor has significantly remarked that "historians of the people of the sub-continent have in the past operated rather like guerilla fighters in a jungle, often performing feats of individual brilliance but lacking discipline and often vaguely aware of the part they should play in a general campaign. The papers presented in the seminar have enabled us for the first time to survey the size and nature of the jungle itself, to establish and affirm the nature of our common discipline and to cut a few broad paths along which we may move with more certainty, direction and co-operation".[1] After this, lots of efforts have been made in India to make serious inroads into the study of modern Indian historiography, and a spate of writings explaining distinct trends, approaches and methodologies appeared.[2]

Such historiographical studies also prompted some historians in more advanced areas like Bengal, Maharashtra, Punjab, Tamilnadu and Karnataka to undertake similar studies in their regional perspectives. The historians in these areas had better acquaintance with the methods of historical research because of their better education in urban setting. And we have got a number of highly standard works on these regional histories. In fact all those who wrote on Indian historiography mainly belonged to these areas and naturally having their potential for historical research also wrote on regional historiography. Accordingly these historians portray the same historical tendencies that they exemplify in the national perspective, and distinct trends in regional studies have been identified.

Many regions of the country have been devoid of such historiographical investigations primarily because the studies in the political and cultural history of these regions remain incomplete and researchers tend to keep themselves busy in these areas of historical enquiry. Orissa presents a burning example of this as her political and cultural history is yet to be reconstructed on scientific lines. Orissa has remained a virgin area of study and the few articles we have in this area are purely piecemeal works and can hardly be seriously taken view of. It would not be an exaggeration to say that no research has been done so far on the historical writings of modern Orissa although history writing on Orissa in the modern times began since the 19th century and a score of standard historical works are available to warrant a historiographical study.

In the Orissan context we have altogether more than a dozen historians scholars who have contributed significantly to the modern historiography of Orissa. All these historians or scholars who have made fairly considerable contribution to Orissan historiography and are great scholars themselves in their own merit, have not yet been properly evaluated at the highest level. Their works on Orissan history or the combined works of those historians make a wealth of historical writing on Orissa's past. On the basis of their approach to the combined writing of Orissan history, the historians have, in the present book, been grouped together into four broad categories, namely:

(a) Orientalist-Colonialist historians;

(b) Nationalist historians;

(c) Some biased historians' writings; and

(d) Some sober historical writings.

While the first two groupings have been made directly in relation to their counterparts at the national level, the last two groups have pure regional orientations. While discussing the Orientalist-Colonialist historians, the trends of imperial perceptions and its bearings on the colonialist historiography of Orissa, a separate chapter has been devoted to the study of the concept of, the Raj. Since the concept of the Raj was central to the British administration of the Indian sub-continent, the broad parameters and intricate detours of the Raj syndrome discussed here include the multi-dimensional aspects of perceptions, the and sensibilities which denote the British attitude to Indian history and society.

The Raj was in fact the central piece of the British empire. It had enormous influence on the imperial strategy. The Raj syndrome denotes the imperial sensibility and psychology. It had its imprints on all the departments of imperial governance. The establishment, consolidation, expansion, administration of the Raj and the general behaviour of the imperial protagonists and the average Englishmen carried its reflections. The British scholarship throughout 17th, 18th, 19th and 20th century while appropriating India's past in order to justify and legitimize their rule over India, was also guided by the broad parameters of the Raj syndrome. In their understanding and contemplation of India, there had always been an enduring tension between two ideals, one of similarity and the other of difference. Again in contriving both the mercantilist and colonialist historiography of India, two conflicting perceptions were developed. While the imperialists and missionaries viewed India as an area of darkness and unredeemed barbarism, the conservatives and orientalists viewed India as a mature and great civilization. Utilitarians and liberals agreed wholly neither with the one, nor with the other, which meant that in parts they agreed with both.

The governing hypothesis or underlying ideological presupposition of the most influential works by the British historians was a belief in the unique superiority of the English and European heritage and a belief in the Indian inferiority. The British colonialist historiography had mostly been conformed to the broad parameters chalked out by James Mill, Henry Maine, J.F. Stephen, etc. The primary objective of the work is to weave a pattern for the historiography of Orissa developed by Andrew Stirling, James Prinsep, Markham Kittoe, J.R. Ousley, W.W. Hunter, J. Fergusson, John Beames, George Toynbee and others against the contours contrived by the colonialist historians of Indian history. Besides attempts have been made to finding the meaning of imperial sensibility in the appropriated history of Orissa. In view of the importance of the ideological moorings implicit in the Raj syndrome and its influence on the historiography, a chapter has been comprehensively devoted to the study of the concept of the Raj syndrome on the backdrop of general historiography before embarking on an in-depth analysis of the colonialist historians at their individual value.

While discussing the individual historians, a general typology has been adopted. This typology pointing out the scope and method of study is outlined below:

(a) a brief biographical sketch of the historian by way of a general introduction;

(b) an outline of the historians' major works or important writings on Orissan history.

(c) The historians' attitude and approach towards the sources of his work/works and their interpretation;

(d) Critical review of the historian's writings on Orissa.

(e) Methodology followed by the historian including his own ideas of history and bias, if any; and

(f) Shortcomings of the historian in his approach towards Orissan history.

In the modern historiography of India we come to know about discernible changes in the standard and nature of historical research and methodology essentially because of the increasing interaction amongst historians around the globe and the consequent adoption of new methodologies. So much so that till the middle of the 20th century Indian history was being looked into from two opposite angles, namely, colonialists otherwise called imperialists and nationalists.

Another approach, which gradually made inroads into historical research on India, was the adoption of the Marxist approach. The historical source materials and the long colonial domination provided the historians of this genre much grain for adopting this method. With the development of time and interdisciplinary researches these historians were prompted to adopt different social science techniques. In the eighties also Indian scholars at Cambridge University attempted to study the role of subaltern classes in the country's freedom struggle. These historians identified themselves with the subaltern school of historical studies. During these years scholars also studied the western perception on India, which till the middle of this century was considered as an imperialist standpoint. These scholars held an altogether different view of the western influences on Indian society and political imperatives. Professor Amartya Sen spearheads this group of historians. All these approaches have been comprehensively studied at length and the shortcomings and limitations of all these approaches have been highlighted in the subsequent chapters. It is needless to say that Amartya Sen's model has presented a fairly satisfactory and comprehensive method to analyse Indian history.

In Orissa, though the modern historical writings started under the efforts of the British historians, nevertheless the people of Orissa in early times exhibited a high sense of history in the form of inscriptions and literary texts. The Hathigumpha inscription of Kharavela not only maintained the concept of time but also chronologically discussed the life and achievements of emperor Kharavela of the first century B.C. Thereafter for a long time no complete work having any significant historical value emerged until Gangadhar Mishra wrote "Kosalānanda Kāvya" in 1664 A.D. This work depicts the history of Chauhan rule in western Orissa and also refers to the Bhoi rule and Muslim invasion of Orissa. Despite all limitations "Madāla Pañjī" (of doubtful dates) is, however, an attempt at writing the history of Orissa. Among the other accounts of such genre are "Jayachandrika" of Prahallad written in 1781; "Gangāvaṁsanucharitam" of Vasudev Ratha Somayajji and "Katakarajavaṁśāvalī" written some time around the middle of the 19th century; "Bhanjavaṁśāvallī" (of Ghumsar) of Suryamani Chyao

Patnaik written sometime in 1830 and two works on the Bhanjas of Mayurbhanj, namely, "Bhanja Vaṁśa Mallikā" and "Rājakula Vaṁśanu" written in the year 1801 and 1807 respectively. The authorship of the last two named accounts are unknown.

With the coming of the British in Orissa, the modern historical writings on Orissa began. Andrew Stirling who worked as Persian Secretary to the British Government in India wrote his "Account, geographical, statistical and historical of Orissa proper or Cuttack" in the pages of the *Asiatic Researches* in the year 1825. The work had severe limitations because of the paucity of source materials available to Stirling. He used the unreliable and much collated "Madāla Pañjī" as his source material. Sir William Hunter, who was the Director General of Statistics, published his famous two volume work "Orissa" in the year 1872. These two volumes were certainly an improvement upon the works of Stirling. John Beames who was contemporary of Hunter has significant achievements in the field of philosophy but his contribution to the field of Orissan history was equally significant. His "Notes on the History of Orissa under Mohemmadan, Maratha and British Rule" was published in the pages of the "*Journal of the Asiatic Society of Bengal*" in the year 1883. Beames also contributed many articles on some archaeological remains of Orissa. The works of these scholars despite all their ideological moorings contributed phenomenally to the Orissan historical studies because of their fact finding nature and unearthing of historical source materials. Among the other European scholars who have shown a keen interest on Orissan antiquities, mention may be made of Markham Kittoe and Beglar, who brought to light some important antiquities of Orissa by painstaking explorations undertaken by the former during 1836-38 and by the latter during the 60s of the last century.

During the latter part of the 19th century historical writings on Orissa by the native scholars moved in two parallel lines but with diametrically opposite intentions and directions. Rajendra Lal Mitra produced two splendid works on Orissan monuments. His "Antiquities of Orissa" in two volumes were published in 1875 and 1880 but the greatness of this work was overshadowed by the role Rajendra Lal Mitra played in the anti-Oriya language campaign spearheaded by some Bengali elite. Naturally this invited a reaction and some writers actuated by Oriya nationalism wrote on different aspects of the history of Orissa as a direct challenge to the colonialist and linguistic bias. This began with Pyarimohan Acharya's "Utkal Itihasa" published in the year 1880. During this time also Manmohan Chakraborty and John Faithful Fleet made significant research on the epigraphic sources available by that time and their works were published in the pages of the *Journal of Asiatic Society of Bengal*. Fleet edited the copper-plate inscriptions of the early Somavaṁśī kings and made attempts to determine their chronology. Manmohan Chakraborty contributed significantly to the studies of the inscriptions of the Gaṅgā kings. His "Chronology of the Eastern Gaṅgās of Kalinga" published in the *Journal of Asiatic Society of Bengal* in the year 1903 is indeed a brilliant piece of work and solved many problems concerning the political chronology of the period.

With the beginning of the 20th century there was a spurt in the writings on Orissan history. However, the parallel and the opposite forces that began in the previous century continued to dominate the historical thought process in Orissa. Nevertheless attempts at sober historical writings on Orissa also continued but the attention was more on the study of art and architecture. Two monumental works namely, Bishen Swarup's "Konark: Black pagoda of Orissa" appeared in the year 1910 while "Orissa and her remains" by Manmohan Ganguly was published in the year 1912. The spate of nationalistic historical works written more in traditional lines include "Utkal Itihasa" by Krupasindhu Mishra published in the year 1920 and "Prachina Utkala" by Jagabandhu Singh published in the year 1928. During this time nationalists like Nilakantha Dash and Birupakshya Kar also contributed significantly to Orissan historical research through their scholarly articles.

Bijoy Chandra Majumdar toed the line of Rajendra Lal Mitra. But unlike Mitra, he wrote political history in "Orissa in the making" published in the year 1925 which was heavily biased against the Oriyas.

Scholars like Rama Prasad Chanda, Rakhal Das Banerjee, Benimadhav Barua and Binayak Mishra wrote more works on scientific lines. Chanda excavated Biratgarh at Khiching in 1922 and made a thorough study of the monuments of Khiching and the history of Bhanja ruling family of Mayurbhanj. His "History of Mayurbhanj" however appeared in the year 1949.

In the "History of Orissa" running into two volumes and published in the year 1930 and 1931, Rakhal Das Banerjee made the first ever systematic study of the history of Orissa right from pre-historic times till the British period. Because of the comprehensiveness and the synthesis of archaeological, literary and archival data, this work continued to be referred to as a standard work on the history of Orissa even decades after the book made its first appearance. In this regard, Benimadhav Barua's contribution is no less significant. His "Old Brahmi inscriptions in Udaygiri and Khandagiri hills" appeared in the year 1929. Last among this group of historians was Binayak Mishra whose expertise in Sanskrit language helped him in the study of epigraphy. He threw sufficient light on the Bhaumakara kings of Orissa through his study of the inscriptions belonging to these rulers. His most important work "Orissa under Bhauma Kings" appeared in 1934. A work of similar nature the "Dynasties of Medieval Orissa" published in the year 1936 threw much light on the minor dynasties of medieval Orissa. Professor Nirmal Kumar Bose who focused his attention on art history produced his famous "Canons of Orissan architecture" in the year 1932. All the above historical compositions have been evaluated at length in the subsequent chapters.

References

1. C.H. Phillips (ed), *Historians of India, Pakistan and Ceylon,* 1961, London, p.3.
2. V.S. Pathak, *Ancient Historians of India,* 1966, New Delhi; J.N. Sarkar, *History of History Writing in Medieval India,* 1977, Calcutta; R.C. Majumdar, *Indian Historiography: Some Recent Trends*, 1968, Calcutta; S.P. Sen (ed), *Historians and Historiography of Modern India*, 1973, Calcutta.

Indian Historiography:
A Review

For long it has been maintained that the ancient Indians were ahistorical people and lacked a sense of history. Comparisons are made with the ancient Greeks whose history was recorded by a series of historians, and the Chinese who have traditionally maintained chronicles of various dynasties and rulers. The Indian tradition until the seventh century A.D. lacks any literature which can be specifically described as historical writing proper. Historical documents are embodied in various kinds of literature which are not historical documents per se. From the seventh to the twelfth centuries A.D. there are a number of historical biographies and some histories of kingdoms which can certainly be included in the category of historical literature. In this literature, the ancient Indians did keep records of those aspects which they felt were significant and worth preserving. It is true that most of these records do not deal with political events and activities. These are more in the nature of genealogies, legends and monastic chronicles—all legitimate constituents of historical tradition but not, unfortunately, very useful as a description of contemporary happenings. But many of these documents are not treated as serious historical documents since the required critical assessment of events is very often lacking, and, except on rare occasions, historical casualty is not frequently based on rational and empirical arguments.

A close and careful scrutiny of the Vedic, Buddhist, Jaina and other religious records wherein lists of teachers have been presented, would reveal that the people in ancient India were not totally lukewarm to the preservation of historical records. The earliest form of *'Itihāsa'* was found in the form of oral tradition which flourished from the early Vedic age as a floating mass of experiences, history and legends. This tradition gradually got formalised towards the end of the later Vedic age. This oral tradition assumed a fixed literary form during the period between c. 400 B.C. and c. 400 A.D.

The nearest equivalent term for history used in Sanskrit literature is *'Itihāsa'*—which literally means 'thus it was' or 'so it has been'. By extension the term came to refer to legends, history and accounts of past events. The purpose of 'Itihāsa' was to refer to the events of the past in such a manner as would relate them to the goals and purposes of the Hindu tradition. The historical tradition grew out of a variety of literary forms current during the Vedic period. Of these, the most significant were the *gāthās* (songs), *narasaṁśīs* (eulogies of heroes), *ākhyānas* (dramatic narratives) and *Purāṇas* (ancient lore). These were very often the compositions of the priest poets attached to the various tribes. The original tradition was oral and the compositions were recited at ceremonial gatherings. The written records of the tradition came considerably later.

The two epics the *Ramayana* and the *Mahabharata* include elements of the historical tradition which arose largely from attempts to provide antecedents in order to connect the origin of the tribes and geographical locations with the heroes of the epics and in geographical sections to indicate relationships at various levels between the Gods and the heroes.

The work of collecting this information and composing it in a literary form was the special function of the Sutas and the Magadhas, the bards and the chroniclers. They were probably originally drawn from the priest-poet families of the Vedic Period and were at this time accorded an important status. Their work was to preserve the genealogies of the Gods, the kings, the *ṛṣis* (seers) and the heroes and to compose the royal panegyrics and eulogies as the occasion demanded. In the context of new settlements and inter-tribal warfare the genealogies of kings became the nucleus of the historical tradition since these were maintained, among other things, for the functional purpose of proving legal rights and social status, not to mention the preservation of tribal identity. Throughout the period from the rise of the Mauryan empire in the 4th century B.C. to the establishment of the Gupta kingdom, there is virtually no evidence of any purely historical writing and this in spite of the fact that this period was germane to the evolution of major political and social institutions in ancient India. One can only assume that the Sutas, the Magadhas and the official archivists quietly pursued their activities. For it was the material which they collected and put into literary form which was incorporated into the Purāṇic texts which were compiled or rewritten from the time of the Gupta rule i.e. the 4th century A.D. The word '*Purāṇa*' literally means old and was used for a body of literature consisting largely of traditional history and aspects of social and religious life, which it was thought should be preserved. It was claimed by the authors of the Purāṇas that Purāṇic literature was handed down from very ancient times. The earliest surviving written evidence of at least a part of the '*Itihasa*' tradition such as is found in the Purāṇas therefore dates back to the 4th century A.D. This period is much later than that of the original composition and relates to a changed socio-cultural milieu. The original material must have undergone considerable modification in the process of being incorporated into the Purāṇas. In spite of the continuity, this was not a static tradition, for the form in which it was used over the centuries.

The Itihāsa-Purāṇa tradition had three main constituents-myth, genealogy and historical narrative. The remote past was described in the form of myths and probably fabricated genealogies. There is by far no means of checking the authenticity of these genealogies.The more immediate past was recorded almost entirely in the form of genealogies filled out with historical narrative. Some of these genealogies can be checked with other sources to establish their historical authenticity. The historical literature of the post-Gupta period is almost exclusively historical narrative but the authors of this literature show a familiarity with the Itihāsa-Purāṇa tradition, which is frequently used, as the source of references to myths and genealogies. Inscriptions of the post-Gupta period referring to the antecedents of local kings also make the connection with the Itihāsa-Purāṇa tradition.

In this tradition continuity was seen not in the sequence of political events but more often in the sequence of lineage. Political history was not therefore the point of the Indian historical tradition.

It, however, did gradually become important in the literature of the post-Gupta period.

The attribution of the authorship of the Purāṇas to the sages was justifiably an attempt to claim both antiquity and authority for the texts. This is further emphasized in the genealogical sections where the dynastic lists are given in the form of a prophecy using future tense. This has the advantage for us today for providing a rough clue as to the date of compilation of the Purāṇas since the prophecy would have to terminate with contemporary events. Although historical material is woven into the various sections of the Purāṇas, this is not done totally in an arbitrary manner. The format of the Purāṇas, does suggest a framework which reflects a fairly integrated view of the past, in spite of the fact that this view is somewhat obscured by mythology, cosmology and the unfolding of the Vaiṣṇavite tradition. This tradition was transmitted through the recitation of Ākhyānas and the kindred forms of narrative on religious and popular occasions. The recitation was generally accompanied by music and mime. Bāṇa Bhaṭṭa in his *Harṣa Charita* makes a reference to Pantomimic recitation (*Utsāha*). Further, the dramas and Itihāsa were so closely associated that this was regarded as similar ways of acquiring knowledge of the past. His close relation of dramaturgy and histrionics with Itihāsa influenced the nature of Ākhyāyikās. Besides drama and dramaturgy, Kathā also influenced the Ākhyāyika.

As long as the traditions remained oral, it would require professionally skilled memorizers. Once it was written down, the work of these bards became less valuable. Those with access to formal education, namely, branches took over the records.

From the seventh century onwards the historical tradition as expressed in the idea of Itihāsa and Purāṇa underwent a process of enlargement. The genealogical aspect of the tradition was not only maintained but also intensified in the various Vaṁśāvalīs or family chronicles maintained in many kingdoms. In addition, the tradition also gave rise to a new genre of historical writing, the historical biography. The emergence of small regional kingdoms led to the development of local loyalties and interests and more strongly defined association of a locality with its history. Together with this, the centre of historical interest had moved from the tribe to the king and his court. The heroic tradition had given way to the court and the focus of the court, the king. The Seta receded into the background and the court became central to the historical writings.

In this tradition, which developed roughly, between the period 600 B.C. and 120 A.D. we have three schools of historical writings. One such school flourished in the Kashmir region. This was directly derived from the old Vaṁśa tradition which, besides throwing many offshoots in India, Ceylon and Burma and in royal courts, monasteries and temples, blossomed into such works as the *Nṛpāvali* of Kshemendra, the *Partivavali* of Hilaraja, the eleven Rajakathas mentioned by Kalhana and several *Rājataraṅginīs*. The second school developed in Gujarat under the influence of the Jainas. The last school was mainly engaged in writing biographies, which started with the composition of '*Harśacharita*' by *Bāṇabhaṭṭa* in the seventh century A.D. Besides Bāṇa's writings, we have equally famous biographies as '*Vikramāṅkadeva Carita*' by Bilhana, the '*Kumārapāla Caritas*', and the '*Pṛthvīrāja Vijaya*' attributed to Jayanaka. Occasionally, biographies of important ministers were also written. These works were written within the frameworks of the Indian perspective on the world, emphasizing the values of chivalry, heroism and loyalty. A recognisable literary form, with well-defined phases of introduction and climax of the plot and the theme, was used. The authors being sophisticated court poets, did not hesitate on occasion to sacrifice historical veracity to an elegant turn of the phrases or to dramatic analogies. It was very often frankly admitted that the purpose of biography was eulogistic. The departure from the earlier historical tradition lay in the fact that these works focussed attention on a particular person or on a single dynasty and therefore covered a far smaller life span and concerned themselves with a precisely defined geographical area. The historical frame became much smaller but allowed greater detail. The link with both the Itihāsa and Purāṇa tradition was maintained indirectly. The court poets used these earlier texts as source material and more directly by associating the subject of biography with earlier heroes and legends. This was largely an attempt at literary ornamentation and at continuing the Itihāsa tradition.

The last of the major works in this survey is the famous history of Kashmir, the Rājataraṅginī by Kalhana in about 1149 A.D.

This work, which owes a great deal to the Itihāsa and Purāṇa tradition is nevertheless a departure from it. It covers the history of Kashmir from the mythical past to the 12th century A.D. and uses much more local religious and secular literature, inscriptions and historical remains from an earlier period. In the context of the evolution of historical writing in India, Rājataraṅginī appears well within the Indian tradition. If any influence on the work is to be found, it would perhaps be more worthwhile to consider the influence of the Buddhist traditions on Kalhana. Historical biographies in Sanskrit declined after the conquest of many parts of northern India by the Turks and Afghans.

The final categories of literature that can be discussed in this group are the Buddhist chronicles of Sri Lanka commonly known as the Pālī chronicles. These were mainly written in an area outside the geographical limits of India proper and, nevertheless, had their association with the Indian historical tradition. Of the many chronicles, the most pertinent are *Dīpavaṁśa* and *Mahāvaṁśa*.

Besides, ancient India had many historical materials in the form of lithic inscriptions, copper-plate grants, coins, etc., where the idea of time was mostly maintained.

The above discussion vividly explains that ancient Indians did not lack historical material or a historical sense. What was lacking was the proper enthusiasm or the ability to bind together the scattered new materials into a critical text with a proper historical setting.

The advent of Muslims in India brought with it a conscious form of historiographical expression. They introduced a great series of chronicles which were written by the men of affairs and contemporaries. The Muslim period marked a phenomenal increase in quantity and improvement in the quality of historiography in the country. Persian chronicles set a model for possible aspirants. There were many varieties of history which the Persian chroniclers in India wrote. Most of them were officially sponsored and, hence, were well organised eulogies. Some chroniclers did maintain a private account of happenings in the country. Some of the monarchs like Babar and Jahangir maintained their own diaries, which are as good as full-fledged histories. The earliest historical writing in India was *Chachnama* written in the 12th century A.D. This is a historical romance connected with the Arab conquest of Sind. This was followed by a spate of works in Persian. Alberuni's work closes a long series of accounts about ancient India. Besides, there are many masterpieces like Menaj-u-ddin Siraj's *Tabaqat-I-Nasiri*, Fakri Muzarate Mubarak Shah's *Susasahi Ausara Mubarakisahi*, Ziauddin Barani's *Tarikh-I-Firoz Shahi*, Abu Fazal's *Akbarnamah* and *Ain-I-Akbari*, etc.

Besides chronicles, we have official biographies, autobiographies of the rulers, official dispatches, and foreign travellers' accounts, which lend much to the historiography of the medieval period of Indian history.

Despite all the greatness of these works in terms of historical form and content, a significant aspect about the personal chroniclers is that they were all courtiers or were aspirants to that position. As such they were aligned with one faction of the court or the other. Thus the court was the focal point of their attention and the events they have narrated in their works are directly or indirectly related to it. Even the terminology they used is related to the particular context of the court history.

Secondly medieval Indian chroniclers wrote with a strong religious bias. They were obsessed with the superiority of Islamic faith and religion. Even those who wrote independently also suffered from racial pride and prejudice. They have all portrayed Muslim rulers as champions of Islam and they wrote very little about the life of the common people. Harbans Mukhia sums up the historiography of medieval Muslim chronicles as follows :

(1) The historians being courtiers and belonging to the nobility were only interested in preserving the status quo in the complexion and composition of the nobility and in the relationship between the ruler and the nobility.

(2) The terminology used by the contemporary historians is relevant only to the internal tensions and conflicts and compromises within the ruling class which consisted of both Hindus and Muslims. These conflicts within the ruling class are not reflections of conflicts at the social level.

(3) The subjective element in the works of the medieval rulers is very strong. Often they write not what had happened but what they wished to have happened.

Despite all the lacunae, the works of the medieval Muslim chroniclers remained very important. But for them the history of the Islamic India of that period would have remained totally unknown except in official papers. The Muslim period is fully recorded through completely in the background of Islamic orthodoxy, personal prejudice and fulsome flattery. They are certainly not inferior to the kind of history known to the Pre-Renaissance period in Europe. In medieval period many foreigners who visited India carefully observed, heard and noted down with frankness what they saw. The accounts of Marco Polo, Niccolo Conti, Nekitin, Abdus Razak, Fr. Monserrate, Bernier, Tavernier and many other Muslim and European travellers remained invaluable documents of medieval Indian history. The modern historiography in India began only with the advent of the British in India.

The historical writings produced by the European scholars beginning in the eighteenth century were formulated in terms of ideological attitudes then predominant in Europe and naturally these were significantly different from the indigenous tradition of India.

European ideologies entailed a set of attitudes towards India which were for the most part highly critical, though there were some sympathetic historians also. These ideologies continued to be influenced even after Indian scholars began to write. It has been only in recent years that the influence of ideologies on the interpretation of Indian history has been recognised. India was by no means a country unknown to Europe. In the post-renaissance period knowledge of and familiarity with India grew with the visit of merchants, ambassadors and missionaries from various parts of Europe to the Indian sub-continent. The accounts written by some of these visitors—such as those of Sir Thomas Roe, the ambassador of James I to the Royal Court of the Moghul Emperor Jahangir or the famous Bernier who visited India in 1668 and was associated with the Court of Louis XIV—became the basic European source of information on India in the seventeenth and eighteenth centuries. Some of these accounts were fairly reliable. Others were a mixture of observation and a large amount of fantasy.

The first serious study of India and its past began in the late 18th century with the work of the scholars who have since been described as Orientalists or Indologists. This study arose principally because the East India Company required that its officers, in order to administer properly the territories it acquired, should become familiar with the habits, laws and history of the people they were governing. Thus William Jones as a Judge in the Presidency of Bengal was able to devote time to the study of Sanskrit and Philosophy, of the Indo-European languages and to work on the pre-British legal terms. Nevertheless, scholars such as William Jones, Charles Wilkins, H.T. Colebrooke, and W.H. Wilson did also have genuine interest in the culture of India and would probably have sustained this interest without the incentive of being administrators in India. Because of this, their work took them beyond the codification of laws and into the realms of classical Sanskrit literature, and the study of religion, philosophy ,etc. In order to encourage this research and provide a focus on it, *The Asiatic Society* was founded at Bengal in 1748. By the middle of the 19th century orientalists were no longer merely the people who had direct contact with India through the East India Company. Interest in the ancient past of India had by then spread to many universities in Europe with scholars working on Sanskrit and related subjects.One of the best of such so called orientalists and Indologists who had never visited India was Max Mueller. Prof. Amartya Sen prefers to call the approaches of these scholars on India under investigative approaches. Professor Sen's study of the western perception of India will be discussed at length later in the course of this chapter. It was largely due to the efforts of the orientalists that translations of Indian literature and of the philosophical works became popular with the intellectuals in Europe and even in America. Much of this enthusiasm was, however, limited to literary circles and did not make the required impact on the historians.

The intellectual ferment thus created by the discovery of a large number of historical source materials neatly changed the course of historical research in India and thereby the reconstruction of the history of the ancient period. This enterprise being largely undertaken under the auspices of the British historians eventually became the ideological weapon for both the British and the Indian historians, both of whom used this to satisfy their respective ideological interests during India's struggle for independence.

Recently in a brilliantly written article in the *New Republic* (June 7, 1993) the entire text of which was reproduced in the *New*

Wave Prof. Amartya Sen says that unless one chooses to focus on the evolution of a specific conceptual tradition, internal consistency is precisely what is hard to find in the variety of Western preceptions of India. For there are several fundamentally contrary ideas and images of India and they have quite distinct roles in the Western understanding of the country and also influencing the manner in which Indians see themselves. Prof. Sen prefers to discuss the attempts from outside India to understand and to interpret the country's traditions in three distinct categories, viz, the exoticist, the magisterial and the investigative. The exoticist approach concentrates on the wondrous aspects of India. The focus here is on what is different, what is strange in a country that, as Hegel put it, has existed for millennia in the imagination of the Europeans. The magisterial approach deals with the notions of India as an imperial territory from the point of view of its governors. This outlook assimilated a sense of superiority and guardianhood needed to deal with a country that James Mill described as that great scene of British action. This of course is a British phenomenon but a great many British observers did not fall into this category and some non-British ones did. The investigative approach is the most catholic of all and covers various attempts to understand Indian culture and tradition from outside, without looking only for the strange and without being weighed down by the magisterial burden.

To begin with the investigative approach, the nature of investigation is not always guided an the impulse of curiosity and also does not remain completely innocent of the power and characteristic interests of the observer. The motivation for investigation and the nature of observations would indeed depend on the role and position of the observer vis-à-vis the object of investigation. An excellent example of investigative approaches understanding India can be found in Alberuni's Arabic "*Tariq-I-Hind*" or "*History of India*" written in early eleventh century. Alberuni first came to India with the marauding troops of Mahmud of Ghazni and became very much involved with India. Proceeded to master Sanskrit, he studied Indian texts on mathematics, natural sciences, literature, philosophy and religion, conversed with as many experts as he could and also observed social conventions and practices. His book presents a remarkable account of the intellectual traditions and social customs of India at the time. Alberuni's work was almost certainly the most impressive of such investigations but there are a great many examples of serious Arabic studies of Indian intellectual traditions around that time. Brahmagupta's pioneering Sanskrit treatise on Astronomy had been first translated into Arabic in the 8th century A.D.(Alberuni translated it three centuries later), several works on medicine, science and philosophy had Arabic rendering by 9th century and so on. It was through the Arabs, of course, that the Indian decimal system reached Europe, as did Indian writings on mathematics, science and literature in general. Alberuni was particularly aware of the difficulties of achieving an understanding of a foreign land and people and specifically warns the reader about it. While Arab scholarship on India provides plenty of examples of investigative approach, it is not unique in this respect. Quite a lot of early European studies on India must be put in this general category. A good example is that of the Italian Jesuit Roberto Nobili who went to South India in the early 17th century and whose remarkable scholarship in Sanskrit and Tamil permitted him to produce quite authoritative works on Indian intellectual discussions in Latin as well as in Tamil. Another Jesuit priest Pous from France produced a grammar of Sanskrit in Latin in early 18th century and also sent a collection of Indian manuscripts to Europe.

Still the real eruption of European interest in India took place a bit later, in direct response to British rather than Italian or French scholarship on India. A towering figure in this intellectual transmission was the redoubtable William Jones, the legal scholar and officer of the East India Company who came to India in 1783 and by the following year had established the *Asiatic Society of Bengal* with the active patronage of Warren Hastings. In collaboration with such scholars as Charles Wilkins and Thomas Colebrooke, Jones, the *Asiatic Society* did a remarkable job in translating a number of classic religious documents as well as legal treatises (particularly "*Manusmriti*") and literary works such as Kalidas's "*Shakuntala*". Jones knew India better than any other European. One can find many such examples of dedicated scholarship among British Officers in East India Company and there can be little doubt that the western perceptions of India were profoundly influenced by such investigations. Western scholarship in Indian studies had continued at a high level right into the present time. Although Europeans (British, German,

French, Russian and others) have been more occupied with the sub-continent than Americans have in recent years, there have been more interest in the United States of America as well, and a community of distinguished scholars with expertise on India has clearly emerged.

Turning to the magisterial approach, Prof. Amartya Sen writes that the task of ruling a foreign country does not go easily with seeing the objects as equal. It is quite remarkable that the early British administrators in India, even the controversial Hastings, were as respectful of the Indian traditions as in fact they were. The empire was still in its infancy and was being enlarged rather gradually and tentatively if not quite in a fit of absent-mindedness.

A good example of a magisterial approach to India is the classic book on India written by James Mill, published in 1817 on the strength of which he was appointed as an official of the East India Company. Mill's *History of British India* played a major role in introducing the British governors in India to a certain characterization of the country. Mill disputed and dismissed practically every claim ever made on behalf of Indian authors. He concluded that it was totally primitive and rude. This diagnosis fitted well with Mill's general position in favour of bringing a rather barbaric nation under the benign and reformist administration of the British empire. Consistent with his briefs, Mill was also an expansionist in dealing with the remaining independent states in the sub-continent, the obvious policy to pursue, he explained, was to make war on those states and subdue them. Mill chastised early British administrators (such as Jones) for having taken Hindus to be a people of high civilization, while they have in reality made but a few of the earliest steps in the progress of civilization. At the end of a comprehensive attack on all fronts, Mill came to the conclusion that the Indian civilization was at par with other inferior ones known to Mill very nearly the same as that of the Chinese, the Persian and the Arabians and he also put in this category for good measure subordinate nations, the Japanese, the Cochin-Chinese, Siamese and even Malayas and Tibetans.

Mill wrote the book without ever having visited India. It was also hard for him to be there in person and this was not only because he had not been to India personally. He knew no Sanskrit, no Persian, no Arabic and had practically no knowledge of any of the modern Indian languages, and so his reading of Indian material was most limited. Moreover, there was his inclination to distrust anything stated by native scholars, since they appeared to him to be liars. Perhaps some examples of Mill's treatment of particular claims of achievements may be useful to illustrate the nature of his extremely influential approach. The invention of the decimal system with place value and a zero, now used everywhere as well as the so-called Arabic numerals are generally known to be Indian developments. Alberuni had mentioned them in his eleventh century book on India and many European as well as Arab scholars had written on the subject. But Mill dismisses the Indian claim to priority altogether on the ground that the invention of numerical characters must have been very ancient and whether the signs used by the Hindus are so peculiar as to render it probable that they invented them or whether it is still more probable that they borrowed them are questions which for the purpose of ascertaining their progress in civilization are not worth resolving. He proceeds then to explain that the Arabic numerals are really hieroglyphics and that the claim on behalf of Indians and the Arabs reflect the confounding of the origin of ciphers or numerical characters with that of hieroglyphic writing. Mill's rather elementary error lies in not knowing what exactly a decimal or place value system is but his ill-informed smugness cannot be understood except in terms of his implicit unwillingness to believe that a really sophisticated invention could have been by such a primitive people.

Another interesting example is Mill's reaction to Indian astronomy and its prescient argument for a heliocentric view of the planetary system with a rotating Earth and a model of gravitational attraction. Āryabhaṭṭa who was born in 476 A.D. and investigated by, among others, Varāhamihira and Brahmagupta in 6th and 7th centuries proposed such a view. Their works were well known in the Arab world. Jones had been told about these works in India and he reported what he had learnt. But Mill expressed total astonishment at Jones's gullibility. After ridiculing the absurdity of this attribution and commenting on the pretensions and interests of Jones's Indian informants, Mill concludes that it was extremely natural that Sir William Jones whose Pandits had become acquainted with the idea of European philosophers respecting the system of the universe, should hear from them that those ideas were contained in their own books.

There are plenty of other examples of magisterial readings of India in Mill's history. This had some practical importance since the book was extremely influential in British administration and widely praised. It was described by Macaulay as on the whole the greatest historical work which has appeared in the English language since that of Gibbon. This view of the poverty of Indian intellectual traditions played a major part in the educational reforms in British India as was readily seen from the minutes of Indian Education. The impact of the magisterial view of India was not confined only to Britain towards India. Modern documents in the same tradition have been influential elsewhere including the United States of America.

Coming to the exoticist approach on India Professor Sen says, that India has often been stimulated on the observation of exotic ideas and view. Arrian's and Strabo's accounts of Alexander the Great's spirited conversation with various sages including the naked symnosophists of north west India may or may not be authentic but ancient Greek literature is full of uncommon happenings and thoughts attributed to India. There are various accounts of exotic Indian travels by ancient Greeks. This approach has many veridical weaknesses and an inescapable fragility that can be seen again and again. A wonderful thing is imagined about India and sent into a high orbit and then is brought crashing down.

Both the magisterial and exoticist approaches have asymmetrical effects. Magisterial criticisms tend to blast the rationalist and humanist aspects of India with the greatest force (this is true of Mill as of Mayo) whereas exoticist administrations tend to build up the mystical and extra—rational aspects with particular care. The result of the two taken together is to bias forcefully the understanding of the Indian culture away from its rational aspects. Indian traditions in mathematics, medicine, linguistics or epistemology may be well known to the western specialists but they play very little part in the general western understanding of India. Mysticism and exoticism by contrast have a more hallowed position in that understanding.

The European exoticists' interpretation and praise of India found a large welcoming audience in colonial India and to some extent it even had a political role in the nationalist movement for independence from Britain. The ecstatic appreciations were quoted again and again and the negative remarks by the same authors (Herder, Schelegel,

Goethe and others) were frequently enough systematically overlooked. In his *"Discovery of India"*, Jawaharlal Nehru comments on this phenomenon. "There is a tendency on the part of the Indian writers to which I have also partly succumbed to give selected extracts and quotations from the writings of European scholars in praise of old Indian literature and philosophy. It would be equally easy, and much easier to give other extracts giving an exactly opposite view point. "In the process of accepting the exoticist praise, the Indian interpretation of the past hastened to move in the direction of the objects of the exoticist praise, focussing more on the mystical and the anti-rationalist. That process was also fed by the negative critiques of Indian culture, coming particularly from magisterial views. In responding to those critics (this was too important for Indian nationalism) it was too easy to cite appreciation from other Europeans and gave the exoticist championing of the East further prominence.

All this, Prof. Sen believes, has helped to undermine an adequately pluralist understanding of the nature of Indian intellectual tradition within India itself.

Of these three approaches, Prof. Amartya Sen identified in the western perception of India, the most influential approach that affected the historical writing on India, particularly in fashioning the imperialist point from the angle of British administration of India was the magisterial readings of Indian history. This at the same time gave birth to the nationalist approach as a reaction against the imperialist challenge and the nationalists used the exoticist approach of western Indian perception for their own advantage.

The ideological presupposition that governed the hypothesis of the most influential works by the British historians during the period was a belief in the unique superiority of the Indian heritage. Histories by Indians and Europeans tended either to implicitly accept this hypothesis or were written in reaction against it. It is only during the post-independence period that a new voice begins to be heard among the historians of India, the one based on the analysis of change and social conflict.

There have been attempts by scholars to group the historians of India into different sets of schools. Romila Thapar broadly categorized these schools into three groups based on the trends they follow in historical research on India. These schools are : Orientalists, Utilitarians and the Nationalists. With these three, she adds the communalists and the modern scientific historians who attempted to incorporate into their work the findings and techniques of social science and archaeology.

Those who directly or indirectly supported the British interests in India dominated trends in Indian historiography prior to independence. These include the European historians who were mostly British and who attempted to justify the British imperialist aims and interests. Secondly there are those who opposed the British interests. During the early stages of British imperial expansion in the latter half of the 18th century, the main impediment to the British imperial consolidation was the lack of basic information about Indian culture. The Orientalists supplied this information. Although most of the early Orientalists were free from prejudices against Indian culture, willingly or unwillingly they served the British imperial needs and were very often directly sponsored by the British government in India.

Indeed the Orientalists performed their essential service to the British government by the mid-nineteenth century. The first serious attempt to study the history of India began soon after the Revolt of 1857-58. During this time the British rulers felt that the revolt was due to the lack of their knowledge of Indian religion, manners, customs, and history. Further, the people could not be won over to Christianity and consequently to the empire unless the missionaries acquired an idea of the vulnerable points in their social structure. Max Mueller had this Oriental revivalism. According to him, to the missionary, an accurate knowledge of the sacred books was as indispensable as the knowledge of the enemy's country to a General. The other German and European scholars who lent their hands in this enterprise include Franz Bopp, Otto Bothlingk, Rudolf Roth, Christian Lassen and Louis de la Valle Possin.

Also belonging essentially to the Orientalist School of this genre were a number of Indian nationalist historians including R.G. Bhandarkar, H.C. Raychoudhury, V.D. Savarkar, A.C. Ray and to some extent Ramesh Chandra Majumdar. The works of these later Orientalists are characterized by their meticulous concern for accuracy, and exhaustive collection of all available facts and an almost obsessive avoidance of systematic generalization and evaluation. Many of these later Orientalists displayed a genuine affection and enthusiasm for their subject. Nonetheless, the fact is that they worked exclusively with ancient materials and often in an obscurantist and tedious fashion. This rendered them relatively innocuous to imperial authorities who continued to extend to some limited financial support. Most important from the imperialist point of view was the very ideological mentality of these scholars. Virtually none of them even tend to mount an effective counter attack against the more popular imperialist interpretation of Indian history.

The orthodox imperialist notions on Indian history particularly directed their attention to Indian polity and tried to project the idea that first an Oriental rule was autocratic in character. Secondly, all oriental history is one unceasing record of valour, greatness, degeneration and decay. Third, the empires of the east were mainly tax-collecting institutions (which I feel is equally applicable to British interest). They exercise coercive power on their subjects of the most violent kind and do not impose laws as distinct from particular and occasional commands. And, fourthly, India never attained to the idea either of the state or of the fatherland and that it could not evolve any political institution and even in conception. Such a viewpoint about India's past history and polity was obviously dominated by imperialist ideology. Among these open imperialist interpretations three schools are distinctly identified. First, the Evangelists school which was popular only for a brief period and perhaps the only influential work of this school was that of Charles Grants' "observations on the state of society among the Asiatic subjects of Great Britain" . Second was closely allied with this school and is popularly called as utilitarian school. Its great masterpiece was that of James Mill's '*History of British India*'. This work became a textbook for the British Civil servants coming to India for more than a century. Even H.H. Wilson who was generally much more sympathetic to the early period of Indian history, was content to add a critical commentary in the form of two notes to a later edition of Mill's '*History of India*' and did not think it necessary to write a fresh work contradicting some of Mill's out-of-date statements. Mill was a radical in the British context and, as was the case with quite a few other radicals of this, period, he tended to exaggerate the conservatism and backwardness of India in order to accentuate his own radicalism. The utilitarians were not the only group who saw pre-British Indian history as being almost totally without virtue. Charles Grant had taken a similar position, although their motives (Evangelists) were different from those of the Utilitarians. Whereas, Mill was concerned with changing India through legislation, the Evangelists wished to do it through conversion to Christianity. Not unexpectedly, the Evangelists concentrated on trying to prove that the essential backwardness of India, as they saw it, was due to the Hindu religion. Both Grant and Mill believed that the translations of Sanskrit works and other materials available to them were sufficient to make any comprehensive evaluation of ancient Indian culture and society.

Mill's assertion that the Indian past had been that of an unchanging, static society dominated by despotic rulers was reflected in various philosophies of history current in the 19th century. The most influential of these with respect to Indian history were the works of Hegel. For him true history involved dialectical change and development. Indian history remained stationary and fixed and, therefore, outside the main stream of world history. The static character of Indian society because of its immutable pattern of villages with its concomitant despotic rulers has been the accepted truth of Indian history. The concept of Oriental despotism began to take shape.

The idea that the British administration brought to an end the tradition of oppressive despots is a basic belief in the writings of perhaps the best known of the administrator historian, Vincent Arthur Smith. In fact till his publication, '*Early History of India*', came out in the year 1904, no adequate political history of India did really appear. His work is virtually the only important ancient history of India written by what may most conveniently be called the mature Imperialist School of Indian Historiography. He devoted himself especially to the study of ancient India and combined in his scholarship both more advanced techniques of historical reconstruction and a clearly defined interpretation. Smith had a strong pro-Greek bias and this only showed his attempts to suggest that the finer qualities of Indian civilization were derived from Greece. Heroes and empires were the subject matter of history and furthermore only those who had survived successfully were worthy of consideration. Thus Ashoka, Chandragupta II and Akbar became heroes for him. Smith's depiction of the rise and fall of empires and the intervening dark ages did weaken the idea of a totally unchanging society even if the change was largely limited to the upper sections of the society. Vincent Smith and his contemporaries writing on India were in a sense reflecting the main trend of British historical writing of the time. Smith's works nevertheless presented a considerable advance over the earlier writings on the subject because a whole new body of evidence was now available. Still their main concern remained the writing of political and dynastic history of India for which fresh information was available from epigraphic and numismatic evidences.

Though this school dominated the field of modern Indian historiography after Smith, most of the work was written either by Orientalists or Nationalists. Indeed the Cambridge School of Historians down to the present day is still dominated by the idea that British rule was benevolent in India.

The imperialist ideology posed a serious challenge to Indian scholarship. Opposing the British imperialist interests in India, these historians were broadly identified as nationalists. These historians by virtue of their painstaking research on the manifold aspects of the past history of our country tried to build a strong and powerful case for the political and social progress of the country in their own times.

Even after independence, in fact, these historians were indeed remarkably few in number. For the history of British India, they were virtually non-existent unless one considers the anti-imperialist theoreticians and economic writers such as Karl Marx, Digby, Hobson, Nauroji and Ramesh Chandra Dutt. Notable mention can be made of Ramesh Chandra Dutt (*Early Hindu Civilization*, 1880), R.D. Banerji (*Age of Imperial Guptas*, 1933), K.P. Jayaswal (*History of India*, 1933) and Jawaharlal Nehru (*Discovery of India*, 1944). The fact that few of these writers were academic historians testify to the effective control exercised by the British government over both their own and Indian universities and to the threat of the imperial rule they represented. These historians are generally classed as Nationalists though, for the most part, the nationalism they professed in their works was of a necessarily timid and vicarious sort.

The initial Indian writers particularly R.G. Bhandarkar followed the British models because at that time the Indian historians did not have any new perspective on Indian history. But the impact of the nationalist movement was felt on the later generations of writers. Their interpretations were based clearly on the nationalistic point of view. There was an unashamed glorification of the ancient Indian past. This was in part a reaction to the criticism of Mill and other writers and in part a necessary step in the building of national self-respect. The glorious past was a compensation for the humiliating present. To some extent, the glorification of the past represented a revival of interest in the writing of the more sympathetic Orientalists and not surprisingly eulogistic quotations from Max Mueller, for instance, were given as a proof of the disinterested European opinion of India's past. This we have already examined in Prof. Amartya Sen's exoticist approach on the western perception of India earlier in this chapter.

These writers visualized ancient Indian society as a comparatively unchanging society over the period from 1000 B.C. to 1000 A.D. with a uniformly high quality of achievements. The basis of this stability was the ancient Aryan culture. It was felt that 19th century historians had belittled the important achievements of ancient India by denying its antiquity and suggesting that its achievements were borrowed mainly from Greece. There was an attempt therefore to place literary sources as early in time as was reasonably feasible and to prove that the more worthwhile aspects of Indian culture were entirely indigenous. To counter the argument that the Indian tradition lacked a concern for the rational and the pragmatic, it was maintained that Indian culture had an essentially spiritual quality which was totally opposed to that of the essentially materialistic western civilization. It followed that in essence Indian culture was superior. The nationalist historians of India also expressed the desire to stress the political unity of India right from earliest times.

Some of these generalizations appear to be self-contradictory but clearly they were not regarded so at that time. For example, whereas, on the one hand, non-violence was regarded as a distinguishing feature of Indian culture, there was, at the same time, a glorification of the military power. For some, Ashoka's policy of non-violence was his greatest achievement. Other historians found this the major criticism of him, arguing that he so weakened the defence of India that the northwestern part of the Indian sub-continent was conquered with ease by foreign invaders. The adulation of

Chandragupta Maurya or the flattering comparisons of Samudragupta with Napoleon the Great, were all based on pride in the military powers of these rulers. Similar is the case of the glorification of India's colonization of the South Eastern countries during the early and medieval ages. So much so that Professor Radha Kamal Mukherjee devoted a complete volume for this discussion on his famous work '*History of India's Maritime Shipping*'.

Historians such as Vincent Smith, W.W. Tarn and others came under attack because of their theories concentrating on the widespread influence of the Greeks on Indian culture. A determined attempt was made to prove that Indian civilization did not lack any of the laudable qualities ascribed to the Greeks. Thus, Kasi Prasad Jayaswal maintained that the political life of the ancient Indian Republics had been based on the concepts of democracy and representative government to the same degree, as had the political life of Greek city states. Alternatively, Ananda Coomarswamy argued against the aesthetic superiority of the Greek art, since the Greeks were obsessed with physical beauty whereas the Indian artists sought to express higher spiritual values in their work. It was this quality in Indian art which made it aesthetically unappealing to the western views.

The nationalist historians were writing at a time when the leaders of the national movement were demanding political rights and political representation in the government. Understandably, therefore, the political life and institutions of the past were probably the most sensitive areas of disagreement with the earlier historians. That is why a detailed analysis of Kautilya's "*Arthasastra*" was made and frequent comparisons of this text were made with the writings of Machiavelli and the ideas of Bismark, or for that matter, the comparison of the "*Mantriparishad*", as described by Kautilya with the Privy Council of Britain and the suggestion that the Kautilyan monarch was similar to that of the British crown. In matters relating to political history and institutions, the values current in European thought were accepted and their equivalents sought in the Indian past.

Prof. Ram Sharan Sharma sums up the merit and demerit of the revivalist and nationalist line of approach in the study of India's past as follows. First, by presenting an encouraging picture of the past it filled the people with great self-confidence that was needed for boosting the nationalist movement. This knowledge of ancient

India gave tongue to those who advocated the self-government and independence of India. Secondly, this ideology prnduced splendid research works and certain points regarding the prevalence of limited monarchy, republics and local self-government, and international law in ancient India came to be accepted by nearly all scholars in spite of the dissenting note of V.A. Smith that it was not safe to rely on the admonitions of early sages about the ideal king. One more positive outcome of both the imperialist and nationalist ideology is that both accepted the unity of Indian empire as a reality. Historiographically, this conscious opposition to the earlier writings forced the historians to take a fresh look at the sources. They raised controversies and naturally fresh debates began on the interpretation of sources. The recognition of an historian's conceptual framework became meaningful. The interpretation of Indian history was no longer based on a monolithic ideology deriving authority from the concept of Oriental despotism. Furthermore, the study of the ancient past began to have relevance for the present and historical writing had to be more than the antiquarian's collection of past relies. Although most of the historical writings were still confined to dynastic history, the debate on ancient political and cultural life necessitated the study of the social and economic history of India. As a result, a new stream of studies in history began to take shape.

From the historical point of view a more valuable offshoot of the nationalist school was the growth of interest in regional and local histories. Studies of regional histories of smaller geographical areas and states, such as histories of Bengal, Orissa, Maharashtra and various parts of the peninsula became more common. This was a useful departure from the current trend of historical writing because it corrected the tendency to generalize about the entire Indian sub-continent on the basis of the history of the Ganges heartland.

The limitations of the Nationalist School of history writing are, while it did serve the educated middle class against alien rule, it hardly touched conscious intellectuals interested in masses of peasants and workers who were being drawn into the nationalist struggle for independence from 1920 onwards. By fulsome adoration of ancient Hindu institutions, it tended to antagonize the Muslims though this was not done deliberately. It gave us a false sense of values. It glossed over the fact that whether it was monarchy or republic, the two upper varnas dominated the lower varnas who were generally excluded from all political offices. It also ignored the fact that one fundamental feature of our legislation was that it worked in the interests of the upper varnas. It did not pay attention to the fact that the ruling class consciously exploited religion for the promotion of their political interests. It never took into consideration the fact that wealth and political offices went hand in hand. In its craze for proving the superiority of the ancient institutions of India over those of the ancient west, it hardly tried to examine them in the light of the evolution of tribes as known from anthropology or in the light of the early institutions of the Indo-European people. Consciously or unconsciously, the nationalist historians hailed India's colonization of the South-East Asian countries as a great positive aspect of India's glorious history, a concept the nationalist leaders of India were fighting against.

After independence, radical changes in the political situation of the country brought about a consequent radical intellectual ferment in the historical research in India. English language histories of British India continue to be dominated by a modified pro-imperialist viewpoint, especially those written by British and American historians. The Cambridge School of historians also still goes with the imperialist ideology that British rule was benevolent. Prof. Bipin Chandra and others severely under attack by a new generation of radical anti-imperialist historians lead this group. Similarly in the field of ancient Indian studies, the Orientalist tradition continued uninterrupted, chiefly by the older generation of scholars. While others, tired of the endless accumulation of historical facts, have embarked upon the task of the re-evaluation of India's ancient heritage. Three scholars worthy of mention in this respect are Professor A.L. Basham, Professor D.D. Kosambi and Prof. Romila Thapar.

Relatively few scholars have focussed attention on cultural imperialism which the French considered as their prime mission in historical study. It is usually based on a curious mixture of genuine altruism and rationalizations and legitimization of colonial expansion. Cultural imperialism and its underlying psychological attitudes and ideological presuppositions are of central concern for the strongest influence of imperialism on the writing of Indian history. These attitudes indeed played a major role in the political and economic policy of the imperial powers as well as their cultural ones. In some respects, the arguments over the relative priority of the economic, political and cultural factors of imperial rule are beside the point since the three factors inevitably condition and modify each other. Bipin Chandra sums up these arguments as follows: "Thus when we say that colonisation is to be seen as a structure, we mean that colonial interests, policies, state and its institutions, culture and society, ideas and ideologies and personalities are to be seen as functioning within the parameters of colonial structure and they are out to be defended by their interrelationships as a whole". In other words, whatever the original or principal motivation for imperial expansion, once colonial rule is established, the political, economic and cultural policies of imperial power form a complex, mutually determined unified system. In a colonial system the needs and desires of the metropolitan state and its ruling class determine the economic, political and cultural policies of the metropolis.

In the case of Indian history this situation was most clearly illustrated by the remedies of Indian problems proposed by Evangelists and Utilitarians. For the former, the solution lay in western education and conversion to Christianity and for the latter, in education and constitutional and legal reforms. Both the Schools felt, these changes could only be implemented under permanent British rule. In so far as their policies are realized, however, they only served to hasten its downfall.

According to Hanna Arendt,[40] despite all ideological debates and presuppositions, all the foreign rulers at least share one thinking in common. That is, the habit of race thinking which in the latter half of the nineteenth century gradually evolved into full-fledged racism with the help of the doctrines of poly-genists and social Darwinism. Arendt prefers to define ideologies as systems based on a single opinion that proved showing enough to attract and persuade a majority of people and broad enough to lead them through the various experiences and situations of an average life. She argues that by about the end of the 19th century western world was dominated by only two such ideologies. These are ideologies, which interpret history as our economic struggle for classes, and ideology that interprets history as a natural fight of races. In the case of England, the latter ideology came to dominate through a complex series for political and intellectual events. In Arendt's veiw, one of the easiest and most important of these events was Edmond Burke's declaration that the liberties of Englishmen were an entailed inheritance derived to us from our forefathers. With this hypothesis Burke sought to discredit the rights of man propounded by the French Revolution and substitute the rights of Englishmen. Though this doctrine of the unique and superior cultural heritage of the English nation was not openly racist in its original formulation, it functioned very much the same way to legitimize the paramount subjugation of the colonial people who lacked this heritage. It paved the way for the eventual illogical but persuasive alliance of nationalism and racism, which forward the base of the mature imperialist ideology of the 20th century.

This idea of the unique superior cultural heritage of the English nation and a corresponding unique but inferior heritage of the Indian nation are repeatedly found in English writings on India from at least the time of Charles Grant's observations (1872).

Vincent Smith's "*Early History of India*" did belong to the oriental tradition of scholarship. He rarely indulged in the total condemnation of ancient Indian heritage in the manner of Grant and Mill. None the less his Europe-centric and imperialist bias clearly reveals itself in a number of incidental comments as in his emphasis on the general political instability of ancient India which he sees as broken only by a few relatively shortened major dynasties.

By the time Smith wrote, the concept of oriental despotism had become more ambiguous as a justification for imperial rule since the colonial government itself was inter-ceasingly being accused of being just such despotism. Smith solves this difficulty by turning the concept on its head lamenting India's reversion to her normal condition of anarchical autonomy after its temporary and partial unification under the wholesome despotism of Hars'avardhana.

The transition from pre to post-independence studies of India, is embodied in Professor A.L. Basham's discreetly popular text "*The Wonder that was India*"[41] published in the year 1954. Within its odd 500 pages he reviews with affection, a judicious sense and literary elegance, the major fronts of nearly 200 years of oriental scholarship on ancient Indian prehistory and history, literary, political and social ideas, religion and fine arts. What Professor Basham purposefully hesitated to do is to offer a radically new and speculative interpretation of the sources of change and conflict in ancient India, and of the inter-relation of economic, political and social structure and cultural values. What his work has done is that it laid a solid concise foundation for more efforts in this direction.

Prof. D.D. Kosambi, who was professionally a mathematician and served throughout his life as a Professor of Mathematics at the Tata Institute of Fundamental Research (TIFR) at Bombay, had no such hesitations. He followed Marxist ideas and developed a keen interest in the systematic study of social organization and economic and political institutions. He sped forth new ideas and provocative comments as if from a shotgun.

Although some of his ideas are very difficult to verify, many have opened up new paths for understanding and research. Most valuable has been his hypothesis of the breaking of India's political and economic development from about the 3rd century A.D. by the establishment of an economy based on largely autonomous villages settled by private enterprise.[42] Rather more confusing and equally fruitful are his speculations about the collapse of the Mauryan Empire, which he at times seems to attribute too much to the same factor. With these theories D.D. Kosambi reintroduces the autonomous villages and social stagnation aspects of oriental depotism but does so for a limited period and through Marxist, not imperialist ideology. One contemporary scholar who has continued and better systematized some of Kosambi's hypothesis is R.S. Sharma.[43] But these historians did not accept the scheme implicit in the theory of Asiatic mode of production. Their interpretations are derived more from the understanding of the principles of dialectical materialism and the historical philosophy of Karl Marx as has frequently been the case with Asian Marxists writing their own history.[44] At this point it will be worthwhile to light briefly upon the Marxist approach to history and to what extent it is relevant to apply this Marxist method to the interpretation of Indian history.

Marx's chief interest at all times was in Europe; his central concern was always to analyse and comprehend the bourgeois society of the 19th century which he saw around in Germany, France, Belgium and England and to the overthrow of which he dedicated his life. He studied other types of society mainly in order to find how the capitalism of his own day had come into being. India and the rest of the Orient had interest for him primarily in so far as they could throw light upon European development or offer an instructive contrast. The reason why Marx took India as his model for the earliest phase of European development is to be sought in the intellectual climate of the year in which he was writing. The relationship then recently discovered between Sanskrit and the Indo-Aryan languages led to the theory that India was the ancestral home of all Indo-Aryan-speaking peoples including Greeks and Romans, the Slavs, the Germans and the Celts. Similarly, it was felt that Indian origins could be found for many aspects of European social history, forms of the family, the kinship, the commune, etc. Henry Maine, for example, wrote in 1861 that institutions long dead in Europe were still very much alive in India.[45] Thus among the many kinds of tribalism, community forms or the primitive communism discussed by Marx, the pride of place went to these in India. The ancient villages represented the original, oldest and simplest forms of the country mode of production. The four modes of production, Karl Marx analyzed, represent essentially analytic type of relationships among the working producers and the controllers of the means of production. The four epochs are also the stages through which European history has actually passed. Yet we have no basis for taking them as periods following directly one upon the other. Nor is there a suggestion that the sequence is either universal for inevitable. Marx chalks out in the *Critique*[46] a rough sketch of the path, he believes, the social history of Europe had followed. He does go in to provide an exhaustive catalogue of the steps along the way. In the preface to the *Critique* Marx explains in detail what he meant by the mode of production. Broadly the different modes represent given levels of development of technique or stages in man's progressive control over the forces of nature. The property relations in a particular society merely give legal expression to the existing relations of social production. It is in these forms that Karl Marx characterizes the slave, the feudal and, above all, the bourgeoisie mode of production.But he never gives a specific content along these lines to the oriental or Asiatic modes of production. It is also not clear whether Marx was oriental broadly to cover all tribal, primary and community formations, or whether he entered it to refer exclusively to what he considered the simplest and oldest of these forms, the ancient Indian type. In either case he did not indicate in which areas and over what periods of time the Asiatic mode had predominated. We might say that he left open the question as to whether the Asiatic mode was entirely comparable to the slave, the feudal and bourgeoisie modes with a single characteristic set of legal, economic and political structures of whether it was more like a residual category of all other or all earlier societies. One must emphasize the lack of precision, in fact, the absence of many clear definitions of the Asiatic mode of production, since Marx never subsequently returned to this topic apart from a passing reference or two.[47]

Further, whether Karl Marx was right in his claim that communal ownership and cultivation had been characteristic of an earlier period, is doubtful. The further back we go into Indian history, the more difficult it becomes to establish any definite fact about the structure or functioning of the villages. Nevertheless the weight of scholarship which has been brought to bear on the subject in the years since Marx wrote on India suggests that Marx's simple form was perhaps a quite exceptional one. In his *"Agrarian System of Moghul India"*[48] Irfan Habib writes that in the sources he has consulted, he has not found the slightest suggestion that the peasant's right to land was ever held in common. He also argues against the concept of a village community that owned the land on behalf of all its members. No evidence exists for proving communal ownership of land or even a periodic distribution and redistribution of land among peasants. There is an element of paradox in Marx's emphasis on the primacy of India as the point of departure for European development. On the one hand, Marx insists that the ancient Indian form of common property as embodied in joint ownership and joint cultivation of the land by the entire village is the original form which all others evolved. On the other hand, he holds that these characteristic features of the ancient Indian village plus the tight union of agriculture and handicrafts provide the basis for the static, unchanging nature of the Asiatic Society. The self-same ancient Indian community shows why these later forms had failed to emerge in Asia.

An application of Marxian method in historical research, Marx was indeed illserved by some of his followers who insisted on a rigid universal periodisation of primitive communism-slavery-feudalism-capitalism and classifying all societies according to these successive formations[49] on the basis of relations of productions. Marxist historians tend to see all history as a succession of these social formations. It is extremely doubtful if this sequence can be of universal application. Unfortunately the evidence for ancient India is so difficult to arrange chronologically that the economic history of India is exceptionally hard to reconstruct. It is very difficult to establish that serfdom, an essential element of European feudalism, was prevalent in India. But taking land as the basis for the study of relations of production, these Marxist historians of India did try to put Indian history into Marx's rigid evolutionary framework. This explains these historians' inherent weakness for Marxism and their preconceived notion for its application. Moreover, the very basis of Marxism as available methodology for historical evolution can be questioned, for the Marxist concept itself makes room for breeding inequality. Further, a mere analysis of economic relations does not make it fit for the Marxist analysis.

In the works of Professor Romila Thapar[50] the influence of both A.L. Basham and D.D. Kosambi are clearly discernible. She has so far refrained from wide ranging theoretical speculations and generalisations but has also displayed an increasing dissatisfaction with the comparative unconcern for the study of social change and conflict in most orientalist scholarship. Her basic plea is for a history with social science techniques, to concentrate less on purely political events which have contributed to the evolution of Indian culture. Much of her work in fact consists of careful analysis and refutation of the ideological bias and generalisations of earlier historians. The generalisation she herself has so far been willing to make most successfully on ethics, religion, and social protest are well documented and cautions laws. What often one feels lacking in her works is a set of systematic theoretical generalizations to verify the whole thesis. A historical work which makes such generalizations risky, indeed, requires the formulation of an ideological bias but this after all provides much food for thought. No one today reads Grant or Mill or Nehru because of his historical accuracy. They remain important works precisely because of the ideological bias of authors.

There have been two recent interpretations [51] of the Indian national movement, which need mention here. First in English, Sir Loues Namier pioneered a kind of historiography which eminently suited the 18th century parliamentary politics of England. He sets the explicit pronouncements of public figures against their inner thoughts and personal interests as revealed in their private papers.

There is nothing objectionable in this. On the contrary, such a method can often serve to illuminate not only intentions but also casual relationships. The only difficulty is that by examining the trees in such a microscopic manner one runs the risk of forcing an erroneous picture of the records. Such dangers abound when practitioners who wish to appear revisionists or iconoclasts extend the Namierite method to the study of the nationalist movement. The school has its particular seat at Cambridge. Anil Seal's *"Emergence of Indian Nationalism"* probably represents its best and most representative product up-to-date. There may be no quarrel with the facts about the individuals as Anil Seal presents them. The main failure with Seal and of his Cambridge School colleagues generally is that it is not their facts but their setting that is wrong.

Another approach has become associated with Ranjit Guha and a band of like-minded younger historians who contribute to Guha's *Subaltern Studies*. These historians generally insist that peasants and workers, called as subaltern classes by these historians, had their spontaneous, traditional and generally more radical methods of resistance and these developed independent of the nationalist leadership which sought to suppress them into channels useful to the leadership. It seems that while the subaltern's anxiety to illuminate the struggles of workers, peasants and tribal people is welcome, their historical perspective is unacceptably narrow. The Subaltern School may be right in saying that a divergence of interest existed between mass struggle and the strategic and tactical objectives of the various segments of nationalist leadership, but it is not clear how a general condemnation of the elite leadership is more helpful or more refined than the Marxist comprehensions of the class alignments of the various sections of that leadership. Secondly, it does not seem justified to ignore the charges that took place in peasant consciousness by the transmission and absorption of ideas whose origins lay outside the peasant tradition. Therefore, while taken in isolation and in immediate terms, a peasant struggle might appear autonomous. The changes in consciousness that lay behind the struggle cannot be treated in isolation from the spread of ideas generated by the nationalist movement. Thus considered, the subaltern studies of India's national struggle for freedom virtually died down with Professor Ranjit Guha and his colleagues at Cambridge, for they could not clearly distinguish themselves from what the Marxist historians had to say of the nationalist movement.

These are the major trends that have so far been identified in the modern historiography of India. The basic premise behind the effort to trace out this historical consciousness among the people is the conception that history must be regarded as an eternal quest for truth. History is the fundamental basis – everything else that may be urged on this behalf is only secondary and subordinate to it. Both Neibuhr and Ranke, the two great commanding figures in modern historiography, laid this down as the first principle of history. "In laying down the pen", wrote Neibuhr, "we must be able to say in the sight of god, I have not knowingly nor without earnest investigation written anything which is not true". Ranke supplemented it by the following observation, "History has had assigned to it the task of judging the past, of instructing the present for the benefit of the ages to come." To such lofty functions this work does not aspire. Its aim is merely to show what actually occurred. This is all to mean that truth, nothing but the truth and the whole truth as far as it may be ascertained should form the steel frame of history on which one may build a structure according to different plans and patterns. In this exercise also moral judgement as well as various inferences are welcome and even necessary; only the facts are established with a scrupulous regard for truth alone without any influence of preconceived judgement and afford sufficient materials for forming judgment.

In this respect one cannot forget the high ideals taught by Kalhana, one of the great historians, ancient India could boast of. Kalhana held that the true historian must keep a detached mind and, like a judge should recast events after having discarded bias and prejudice. This lofty ideal was held up as a historian's motto by one of the greatest historians of modern India, Sir Jadunath Sarkar. He once said "I would not care whether truth is pleasant or unpleasant and in consonance with or opposed to current views, I would not mind in the least whether truth is or is not a blow to the glory of my country. If necessary I shall bear in patience the ridicule and the slander of friends and the society for the sake of preaching truth. But still shall seek truth, understand truth and accept truth. This should be the firm resolve of the historian."[52]

At this point also it would be worthy to note down the faults or defects of a historian. Ibn Kaldun the great Arab historian gives a long list of these defects which include a very common desire among the historians to gain the favour of those of high ranks, by praising them, by spreading their fame, by flattering them, by embellishing their doings, and interpreting in the most favourable way all their actions.[53] Ibn Khaldun then justly observed that all this gives a distorted version of the historical events. This characteristic is a growing menace to the historiography of modern India. We have of course made this point as well as our intentions amply clear at the neighing of this chapter. Since we only trace the distinct trends, approaches and historical perceptions among the modern historians of India, we intend to study and trace these trends in the modern historiography of Orissa in the following chapter.

References

1. Romila Thapar, *Past and Prejudice* (1975), p.3.
2. Romila Thapar, *Ancient Indian Social History* (1978), p.268.
3. *Ibid.*, p.270.
4. V.S. Pathak, *Ancient Historians of India*, (1966), p.21.
5. Romila Thapar, *op.cit.* (1978), p.271.
6. *Ibid.*, p.291.
7. *Ibid.*, p.291.
8. *Ibid.*, p.292.
9. *Ibid.*, p.275.
10. K.S. Lal, *Studies in Medieval Indian History*, (1966), New Delhi.
11. Harbans Mukhia, "Medieval Indian History and Communal approach" in *Communalism and Writing of Indian History*, Delhi, (1981), p.24-38.
12. Romila Thapar, *op.cit.* (1978), p.2.
13. The term 'Orientalist'was used in the wider sense of scholars interested in Asia and the term Indologist referred to those interested only in India. The more generally used term even for the latter was orientalists.
14. Professor Amartya Sen, "Distortions and its consequences—India and West" in *New Wave*, Vol.22, No.48 & 49, July 25 & Aug, 1, 1993, New Delhi.

15. Professor Amartya Sen, *op.cit.*, (1993).
16. *Ibid.*, p.8, No. 48.
17. *Ibid.*, p.8.
18. *Ibid.*, Vol.22, No. 48, p.8.
19. *Ibid.*, Vol.22, No. 48, p.9.
20. Amartya Sen, *op.cit.*, Vol. 49, p.9.
21. Romila Thapar, *Past and Prejudice* (1975), New Delhi.
22. Max Mueller, *A History of Sanskrit Literature*, 1917 (rep.), p.1.
23. D. Lorenzen, "Imperialism and the historiography of Ancient India" in S.N. Mukherjee (Ed.) *India : History and Thought*, 1982.
24. Beni Prasad, *State in Ancient India,* 1928, Allahabad, p.498.
25. Louis Senart, *Caste in Ancient India,* 1939, London.
26. Romila Thapar, *Ancient Indian Social History* (1978), p.5.
27. *Ibid.*, p.5.
28. Hegel, *Lectures on Philosophy of History*, 1837.
29. Vincent Smith, *Early History of India,* Oxford, 1904 and *Oxford History of India,* Oxford, 1919.
30. Romila Thapar, *op.cit.* (1978), p.9.
31. V.A. Smith, *Early History of India,* Oxford, 1924, p.442.
32. Romila Thapar, *op.cit.* (1978), p.9.
33. Irfan Habib, *Interpreting Indian History,* N.E. Hill University, Shillong, 1986.
34. D. Lorenzen, *op.cit.*, p.54.
35. *Ibid.*
36. R.C. Majumdar, *Corporate Life in Ancient India*, 1966, Poona, p.126-27.
37. R.S. Sharma, *Aspects of Political Ideas and Institutions in Ancient India,* Delhi 1959.
38. Romila Thapar, *Ancient Indian Social History* (1978), p.14.
39. *Ibid.*, p.16.
40. H. Arendt, *Imperialism,* 1988, New York, p.39.
41. A.L. Basham, *The Wonder that was India,* London, 1954.
42. D.D. Kosambi, *Introduction to Indian History,* 1956, Bombay.
43. R.S. Sharma, *Indian Feudalism,* 1965, Calcutta.

44. D.D. Kosambi, *Introduction to Indian History,* Bombay, 1956; R.S. Sharma, *Shudras in Ancient India,* Delhi, 1958; and D.R. Chanana, *Slavery in Ancient India,* New Delhi, 1960.
45. The classic work of Sir Henry Maine, *Ancient Law,* was first published in 1861. Also edited by Sir Frederic Pollock, London, 1907, See p.272-77.
46. Karl Marx, *Critique of Political Economy*, Chicago, 1904.
47. Daniel Thorner, *The Shaping of Modern India*, 1980, New Delhi, p.370.
48. Irfan Habib, *Agrarian System of Moghul India*, 1963 Bombay, P.119-123.
49. Irfan Habib, *Interpreting Indian History*, 1985, Shillong, p.12.
50. Romila Thapar, *Ashoka and Decline of Mauryas*, 1962, London; *Ancient India,* Vol. 1, 1966, London; *Ancient Indian Social History,* 1978, New Delhi.
51. Refer Irfan Habib, *Interpreting Indian History,* Shillong, 1985, p.53 & 57.
52. Ramesh Chandra Majumdar, 'Indian historiography: Some recent trends' presidential address at the 6th Annual Conference of the Institute of Historical Studies, held at Srinagar, in Oct. 1968, reprint in S.P. Sen (ed) *Historians and Historiography of Modern India,* Calcutta, 1973, pp.xix-xx.
53. Ibn Khaldun quoted in *Ibid.*

3

Historiography of Orissa

The historiography of Orissa could be discussed in two phases. These are : historiography in Ancient and Medieval Orissa; and historiography in modern Orissa. The basis behind this periodisation in the study of Orissan historiography is that it is only with the beginning of the full-fledged history writing in the late nineteenth and early twentieth centuries that we begin to trace distinct trends, perceptions and approaches in the art of writing history in Orissa. Historiography before that or, to be precise, during any periods of Orissa's history, remains restricted to the fact that we have to ponder over the available historical materials to trace out historical allusions in them and also to find out if at all these speak of the people's consciousness about the necessity of keeping and preserving historical records and the art of history writing proper.

To begin with the historiography in ancient Orissa, Orissa does not have any significant historical writing either in the form of bardic literature of northwestern India to testify the historical consciousness among the people of Orissa in the ancient days or any historical narrative of the order, magnitude and worth of Kalhana's *"Rājataraṅginī"*. Orissa did not have either the religious texts, like the Rāmāyana and the Mahābhārata or the Purāṇas which throw much light on the history, society and culture of India, got written in Oriya until Sarala Das wrote the *Mahabharata* in Oriya in 15th century. Some Purāṇas were also written after this period in Oriya. But before that we have a total absence of comprehensive historical works excepting a passing reference to some happenings in some Sanskrit works. But a major historical material we have in ancient Orissa is an inscription. This is the Hāthigumphā inscription of Maha-Meghavahana king Kharavela of Chedi dynasty of the 1st century B.C. The inscription, which contains 17 lines in all, depicts the king's ancestry, early career and achievements in a chronological order up to his reign. The inscription thus gives a short biography of Kharavela. It surprisingly maintains all the methods of historical writing. N.K. Sahu writes, the "Hāthigumphā" inscription cannot simply be regarded as a pan-eulogism and the spiritual stamp placed on it restricts the scope of high exaggeration. So unlike other panegyric writings, the Hāthigumphā inscription can be treated as a faithful and authentic record."[1] The inscription is extremely potent historically, for it maintains the appropriate historical methods adopted in the wrting of inscriptions. In India, the place, which is assigned to Kalhana's "*Rajatarangini*" among historical writings, is well described by the scribe of this inscription in the realm of epigraphy. It betrays a well-informed historical consciousness among Indians more than 2000 years ago. To use the terminology of Kautilya of '*Arthaśāstra*' fame, it is a *Prajñāpana lekha* (public notification) for the purpose of narrating "*ākhyānam*" the principal events of the king Kharavela and is endowed with all the six qualities of *Aretha Karma* (proper arrangement), *Sambandha* (relevancy) *paripūrṇata* (completeness) *mādhuryam* (sweetness), *anoryam* (dignity) and *spasthatvam* (lucidity). All these contribute to make a complete historical composition. While the Hāthigumphā inscription[2] of Kharavela maintains its greatness as a complete historiographical account in epigraphy in Orissa (more so in Indian the context). Orissa could not produce any other historical record of this magnitude during the ancient period.

As we move onto the medieval period, we have some *smruti* as well as Sanskrit works which make some historical allusions to different historical happenings. We have then nearly three identical works in *Madāla Pañjī*, the famous temple chronicle of Puri; 'Kataka rājavaṁśāvalī' and 'Gaṅgāvaṁśanucharitam' of Vasudeva Ratha Somayaji. Though evidenally written in different periods, these three are considered identical works. In all these three works, which are not complete works themselves, we have again only some historical allusions to different political happenings. The authenticity of historical references in these three works can be ascertained only after historical corroborations from other reliable historical source materials like inscriptions, coins, and other archaeological remains.

Though historians find many discrepancies in the Madāla Pañjī surrounding God Jagannātha and the battles fought by Orissan Kings during different times centering the Jagannātha shrine, the list is mainly a descriptive account. Historians do not agree either on the date or the historicity of the account particularly because a complete text of the *Pañjī* has so far not been available. Still the initial writers on history depended primarily on *Madāla Pañjī* as their main historical source material because the *Pañjī* has given an elaborate description of the kings and rulers of ancient Orissa right from the mythical Kali age. In the later age, the historicity of the *Madāla Pañjī* came to be seriously doubted. According to Man Mohan Chakraborty "the historical value of *Madāla Pañjī* has been very much over-rated. Then again the chronicle being on palm leaves, it had to be re-copied three or four times in a century and in re-copying many mistakes crept in particularly in figures. Lastly the *Sevā* (worship) was closed several times on account of Mohammedan raids on the Jagannātha shrine and many volumes must have been lost at that time. Hence, the text is found to be full of mistakes and cannot be relied upon unless corroborated by other evidences".[3]

Despite all interpolations, exaggerations and mistakes as regards dates and descriptions, still it contains many general historical source materials, for example, the activities of different kings, their conquests, administration, state boundaries, art, culture and society of their age, etc. That is why, K.C. Panigrahi attributes much significance to it as a rare historical source material. According to him *Madāla Pañjī* is one of the rarest historical documents written by the Hindus. That is why *Madāla Pañjī* holds a very significant position among the source materials in Orissan history. If any one neglects this *Pañjī* while writing on Orissan history, his knowledge on Orissan history will certainly be incomplete.[4]

Similarly the *'Kataka Rājavaṁśāvalī'*[5] is a Sanskrit work compiled in the early part of the nineteenth century from older records available probably in the archives of Jagannāth temple and/or with the functionaries like *Dheu (Tadhan) Karaṇa* and *Deula Karaṇa* who were responsible for keeping the records of various nature connected with the Jagannātha temple. The text describes the history of Orissa right from the beginning of the Kāli Age till the conquest of the province by the British. The text presents the traditional history of Orissa from the standpoint of the priests of Jagannātha Temple, though there is no denying the fact that very often significant historical facts not having any bearing upon the Jagannātha Temple have also been faithfully recorded. The text forms part of the corpus of literature broadly categorised as *Madāla Pañjī*. It presents a detailed chronology of the kings of Orissa from Kāli era till Rama Chandra Deva III of the Bhoi dynasty of Kurdha. Like the Purāṇic texts and other ancient texts of such nature, the Madāla Pañjī provides the chronology of the kings of the pre-Śaka period with unbelievably long reigning periods. Some rulers of the period have been given a ruling period as long as 757 years. The chronology of the kings of the Kesarī Dynasty can be attributed a fair degree of historicity though all the kings mentioned in the text cannot be historically ascertained. As such the historicity or historical accuracy of the text cannot be significantly vouchsafed.

"Gaṅgavaṁśanucharitam"[6] of Vasudeva Ratha Somayaji is a *Campu Kāvya* written in Sanskrit. The main aim of the book was to describe the history of the Gaṅgā dynasty. The author of the *Campu Kāvya,* Vasudeva Rahta Somayaji, was a court poet of Anangabhima Deva, a powerful and enlightened ruler of Khemundi Kingdom of South Orissa. The description of the Gaṅgās of Cuttack given in the text is found to be extremely traditional whereas the account of the royal families of Khurdha, Athagarh, Khallikote, Dharakote, etc., is more trustworthy and has got some historical value.

There are a few other works of the medieval period worth mentioning here. The poet Vidyādhara of the 13th century wrote a treatise on *alaṅkāra* or rhetorics in which he has sung the eulogy of his patron king Narasiṁgha Deva I, the powerful ruler of the Gaṅgā dynasty. This book gives some historical information regarding the expedition against *Yavana* or the Muslim kings of Bengal and the fight with Hemira, the Sultan of Delhi. The coronation and the reign of Narasimha Deva as well as his virtues and achievements have been depicted impressively.

'Śrikriśṇa bhakti vātsalya caritam' is a one act drama written by Gajapati Rāma Chandra Deva of Khurdha dynasty (1568-1600 A.D.). This work, though small, gives some information about the revival of Hinduism in Orissa after the Muslim onslaught.

Another work worth mentioning is the *"Kośalānaṅda Mahākāvya"* by the poet Gaṅgādhara Mishra written in 1664 A.D. This work narrates the history of the ruling Chauhan family of Kośala or present Bālangīr and Sambalpur areas.

There is another work named *'Bhaṅja-Mahodayam'* written by Nīlakaṅṭha Mishra in the light of *'Gaṅgāvaṁśanucharitam'.* In this we have narration about the genealogy of the ruling family of the Keonjhar state. Besides we have *'Jayacandrikā'* of Prahallād Dube written in 1781, *'Bhaṅja vaṁśāvalli'* and *'Rāyakula vaṁśānu'*, both of unknown authorship, written in 1801 and 1807 respectively. All these works certainly present some historical allusions but we need corroborations from more reliable sources to vouchsafe their historical veracity.

Like the modern historiography of India, the historiography and the discovery and reconstruction of the history of Orissa began during the British rule. In the case of modern Indian historiography the British writings on Indian history eventually served as the ideological weapon by both the imperialists and the nationalists. The underlying ideological presupposition of the most influential works by the British historians was a belief in the unique superiority of the English and the European cultural heritage and/or a belief in the consequent inferiority of the Indian heritage. Histories by Indian nationals and Europeans tended either to implicitly or explicitly accept this hypothesis or are written in reaction against it. Scholars have broadly categorized the historians of the pre-independence period into three distinct and opposite schools. These are the Orientalists, Imperialists and the Nationalists. This division has been made on the basis of the purpose with which these historians wrote the history of this country. On that backdrop, both the Nationalist and the Imperialist groups of historians wrote in opposite directions but largely to serve their respective interests. For the Imperialists, the purpose and the interest was to find out the logic for the continuance of the British rule and their imperial consolidation in India. To achieve that end, finding out the lapses and inferiorities of the Indian civilization and proving the superiority and all goodness of the British and for that matter European civilization were found to be the best methods the imperialist could choose to follow. On the other hand, the Nationalist historians set these Imperialists notions as their main target of attack and their purpose in writing the history of India lay largely in glorifying the Indian culture and civilization. In this process, however, both these groups of historians served the Indian nation a very large interest and purpose. Since this was the period of primary historical discoveries, these scholars, apart from holding their respective notions intact, helped in unearthing more and more historical source materials viz. inscriptions, numismatic evidences, literary texts and so on. This largely suffices to call these historians as Orientalists as well, though this should more appropriately be applicable to those European scholars working on Indian history.

It does not sound appropriate to fit this division of historians of India of the colonial period, in classifying the historians of Orissa of the same age i.e. the pre-independence colonial age. For, besides serving the ends of the nationalist struggle for independence, Orissa had to wage its own struggle for a separate statehood as well as establishing her own linguistic identity. Before Orissa was separated from the Bengal Presidency and was made into a separate state on 1st April 1936, Orissa sought for the state formation on linguistic basis for quite a large period and some of those who participated in this struggle also laid their hands upon writing the history of Orissa. Secondly, during the latter part of the nineteenth century Orissa had again to fight against another parochial outlook. This is the anti-Oriya stand by a group of scholars like Babu Rajendra Lal Mitra *et al.* The motive force behind this anti-Oriya stand was to disqualify the status of Oriya as an independent language. Such a stand can be broadly termed as a part of the efforts of the Bengali elite against the formation of Orissa as a separate province. A positive offshoot of this anti-Oriya attitude was an intellectual ferment in Orissa which resulted in a spate of writings in Oriya. Politically also this encouraged the Orissa people to demand for the amalgamation of all the Oriya-speaking tracts then lying scattered in different neighbouring provinces. During this time Pyarimohan Acharya wrote the first ever history of Orissa in Oriya language. Interestingly enough, the magisterial readings of British administrator-historian John Beames supported the cause of the Oriyas despite all his imperialist bias.

On the back drop of this general background of the colonialist period in Orissa, the historians of Orissa both British and Indian can be categorized into four broad categories. They are, first, the Orienalist-colonialists; second, the Nationalists; third, some historians biased against Oriya language and fourth, the historians who wrote a sober history of Orissa. All these historians can equally be Orientalist scholars in general for they were writing in the formative stage of modern Orissan historiography and, despite all their bias, they made certainly a significant contribution to the world of historical knowledge by unearthing as much historical source material as possible. In the light of the above discussion the Orientalists could be categorised as below:

(1) Colonialists – The British historians,

(2) Nationalists : the Oriya historians who took an Oriya Nationalist stand,

(3) Some historical writings biased against the Oriyas.

(4) Some sober historical writings on Orissa by a group of historians.

Among the British colonialist historians those who immersed themselves strongly into the study of Orissan history, three find special mention. They are Andrew Stirling, W.W. Hunter and John Beames. Andrew Sterling who came to India in 1813 to work as the Persian Secretary to Government of India and was posted in Orissa evinced some interest in history and pioneered historical investigations in Orissa. He wrote the work entitled *"An Account, Geographical, Statistical and Historical of Orissa proper or Cuttack"*, in the year 1825 which was published in the *Asiatic Researches* (Vol. 15). This effort of Andrew Stirling is certainly admirable not only for the time it was written but also for the fact that it was the pioneering work on Orissan history. The work has, however, severe limitations particularly because Andrew Stirling entirely depended on the unreliable *Madāla Paṅjī*, the temple chronicle of the Jagannātha Temple of Puri to present his work. We do not find much hard line imperialist thinking in his work. Some of his conclusions based on *Madāla Paṅjī* raised historical controversies and debates even after one hundred and fifty years he wrote the work. Mention here can be made of the celebration in the year 1989 of the millennium of the establishment of Cuttack city on the basis of the conclusions arrived at by Andrew Stirling that Cuttack was founded in the Year 989 A.D., which was debatably a wrong interpretation of the reference made to this effect in the *Madāla Pañjī*. The work seems to be a copy of the *Madāla Pañjī* in the form of a historical compilation. Still, his was the first attempt on the history of Orissa and can be dubbed as an Orientalist writing as far as modern historiography of Orissa is concerned.

Compared to Stirling's orientalist approach to Orissan history, W.W. Hunter and John Beames perceptibly took a hard line Imperialist approach largely intended to serve the British interest in India. William Wilson Hunter who served as the Director General of Statistics published his famous work *"Orissa"* in two volumes in the year 1872. In this work Hunter made humble efforts to analyse and understand the history and culture of Orissa as would conform to the requirements of sober history. But this was limited to the bare representation of historical facts political, social or economic. He had many source materials at his disposal for historical investigation. But his subjective interpretation of these facts was, however, largely directed towards the imperialist line of thinking. Hunter was essentially an Anglophile and admired every thing that was British. As a natural corollary to this line of thinking, Hunter took a completely utilitarian approach like that of J.S. Mill in his magisterial readings or Orissan history. He started with the basic premise that Orissa was primarily uncivilized and it was only through revolutions as first, the religious upheavals mainly Buddhism and Vaiṣṇavism and second, the British rule of Orissa that brought the rule of law to this Province. Hunter thus applied the utilitarian doctrines to his interpretations of the history of India and Orissa and viewed British rule in India as an interaction between Eastern and Western forces. As such Hunter took a keen interest in the study of Indian institutions and society. The British administrator-historians in India this time desired application of the utilitarian doctrines to the governance of India which required a good system of judicial procedure. The greatest exponent of this utilitarian doctrine in India, James Mill studied Indian history in this light and concluded that Hindus had failed in social justice and hence in the scale of civilisation they would not rise high. If the British too were to ignore this aspect, they too would be categorised as barbarians and would not prosper. Hunter went a step further and became the high priest of the kind of history whose purpose was glorification of the British rule in India. Hunter was thus an Anglophile and the founder of a school of historiography that believed in Pax-Britanica.[7] Besides Hunter also made significant contributions to historical research and knowledge by his daunting labours in comiling the *Imperial Gazetteer of India* and writing history also in the form of biographies, a task he took upon in a later age. His *'Annals of Rural Bengal'* also opened up a new line of historical investigations in the study of the history of rural regions of the country.

Jonh Beames was a contemporary of William Wilson Hunter who did valuable research on Orissa while serving as Collector of Balasore and also Commissioner of Orissa Division. John Beames belonged to those most privileged class of Halleyburian group of I.C.S. officers who occupied the most senior civilian posts under the British administration in India. Still there were instances when Beames stood by the people despite all his magisterial superiority. But ironically enough he also shared the prejudices of his peers and did not recognise Indian I.C.S. Officers as his academic and cultural equals. This largely influenced all his writings. He strongly detested the Bengali intelligentsia, which figured prominently in the anti-Oriya language campaigns. In the field of philology he was a pioneer who helped in contradicting the Bengali arguments against the independent and separate existence of the Oriya language. In his linguistic abilities he compares favourably with Robert Needham Cust who claimed to be able to use eight Asian and eight European languages. Beames had earned a medal in Persian and in Sanskrit at Halleybury. He picked up Bengali, Punjabi, Oriya and Hindi, not to mention Urdu. He knew quite a few other classical languages also and it is no wonder that he found gratification in oriental studies particularly on the philology. During the happiest year of his Collectorship 1872-79 he produced his magnum opus the three volumes of "*Comparative Grammar of the Modern Aryan Languages*". Beames himself wrote that this book favourably reviewed in English and Grammar paper and adopt as a text book in many universities. It won cosiderable reputation and fame.[8] John Beames is considered to have belonged to the highest class of gramarians for whom recognition came rather late. Barun De suggested that Beam may cite the work of George A. Grierson who in his Linguistic Survey acclaimed Beames as one of the finest authority in the field. Barun De for all his reservations placed Beames among the most brilliant scholars in the I.C.S.who endeavoured to learn all dialects of the languages of the district to which he was posted.[9]

But Beames never achieved the same kind of distinction in the field of historical writing, His *"Notes on the History of Orissa under Mohammedan, Marhatta and English rule"*[10] read like a chronicle and contain very little that is analytical. Yet his historical writings for the *Journal of Asiatic Society of Bengal, the Indian Antiquary and Indian Observer* have their value and particularly while at Balasore prevented him from perishing from ennui.[11] His *Manual of District of Balasore* remained unpublished because Sir Richard Temple pretended to find fault with it. At Cuttack earlier, he studied some Buddhist remains in greater detail.

Besides these three prominent English writers, among other European scholars who contributed somehow or other to the study of Orissa, mention may be made of Ewer whose Khurdha settlement report published in 1818 threw new light on the economic condition of the people and G. Toynbee whose *'History of Orissa'* published in 1828 gives an account of the early British land revenue administration in Orissa from 1803-1828.[12] Two famous archaeologists M. Kittoe and Beglar brought to light many important antiquities of Orissa by painstaking explorations undertaken by the former during 1836-38 and by the latter during the 60s of that century.

Significantly and strongly opposing this stand of the British Imperialist writers were the Nationalist historians who were equally called Orientalists considering the age they were writing in or about. In order to counteract the British Imperialist notions, these Nationalist historians took a different stand altogether. As far as modern historiography of Orissa is concerned, they assimilated the cause of Oriya nationalism in their writings. The notable features of their approach to Orissan history can be summed up as follows :

(1) Like the colonialists, these historians were also Orientalists. They laboured a lot to unearth and discover as many new historical materials as possible in order to suit their interests and specific approach with regard to the writing of the history of Orissa. In this process their contribution to Oriental scholarship lay in tracing out many historical source matierals for the furtherance of historical research in future.

(2) Their main approach towards Orissan history was to glorify the traditions, culutre and history of Orissa. That was perhaps the only way to counteract the British historians' inductive notion that Indian history and culture was inferior to that of the Europeans and that the Indians did not know the rule of law and that there was no order in the entire history of India besides some brief interludes. The British historians also tried to project the idea that the entire period of Indian history was a history of chaos and disorder and it was only the British who gave order to the country. The British historians of Orissa also project the same notion. The Nationalist historians took this approach only because the glorification of our indigenous cultures and the rejection of their arguments were perhaps the only way to counteract the imperialist attitude.

(3) Analogous to the point mentioned just before, the Nationalist historians took off with the basic idea of the existence of complete Indian nationhood, even though there was nothing like a united India before India got independence or well past some few years when all the states previously under colonial rule were amalgamated into the Indian Union. This premise is indeed necessary to project a sort of Indian nationalism amongst the Indian masses. The same thing occurred amongst the Nationalist historians of Orissa. Orissa was then fighting for achieving a separate identity of her own both in language and in statehood. The movement, which continued for over half a century, created an intellectual ferment resulting in spates of historical research and writings. History was the most important area of study for these intellectual nationalists. Obviously we have the Nationalist historical writings which took up this regional cause more. And we have all the Nationalist historians who were not historians by profession but devoted themselves for the cause of Oriyá nationalism as well as the national struggle for independence.

(4) While glorifying our ancient past the Nationalist historians knowingly or unknowingly made the mistake of acknowledging and glorifying the colonisation of Far-eastern and Southeast Asian countries by Hindu rulers. The people of ancient and medieval Orissa, having played a very significant role in this process of colonisation, found high glorification by the historians of Orissa. Indeed Orissa had a high tradition of overseas trade and maritime activity. Surprisingly this sounds quite ridiculous particularly because our national interest during the struggle for independence was to oppose the colonial rule and the Nationalist historians had the national task to project the ideological framework for creating a national consciousness against the colonial rule.

Among the historians of Orissa who broadly come under this group are: Pyarimohan Acharya, Jagabandhu Singh, Pandit Nilakantha Dash, Pandit Krupasindhu Mishra and Birupakshya Kar. The most significant aspect about this group of writers is that none of these historians were professionals. They did not have any kind of training in the methods of historical research. But they certainly had their role in the independence struggle of the country as well as in the movement for the formation of Orissa as a separate province and the amalgamation of all Oriya-speaking tracts. Further, since these scholar-statesmen were to fight the Bengali elite of the time on both counts first, for the recognition of Oriya as a separate language and second, the formation of Orissa as a province, their works on Orissan history mainly concentrated on taking a completely regional nationalistic stand which was all the more necessary for their purpose. They concentrated on everything that glorified Orissa's history, culture, tradition, and society in every possible manner and counteracted strongly the biased standings of some non-Oriya scholars. These nationalist historians of Orissa, who were completely non-professional in this field, took up the study of history as a matter of necessity and consequently suffered from many limitations. There were no objective interpretations of the historical source materials. Secondly, most of them mainly thrived on highly unreliable literary sources particularly *Madāla Pañjī* to present the history of Orissa. At this particular point it would be worthwhile to mention that, though Rakhal Das Banerji has been clubbed among the nationalist historians in the Indian context

(Age of Imperial Guptas), he had not taken any kind of nationalist approach while writing on Orissa history. Indeed, himself an archaeologist, Rakhal Das Banerji undertook a scientific line of approach in his study of Orissa. That is why we intend to discuss Rakhal Das Banerji in the category of sober historical writers on Orissa as far as the historiography of Orissa is concerned.

The third group of historians were a group of Bengali elite who were strongly biased in their writings on Orissa. Mainly belonging to this group are Babu Rajendra Lal Mitra of the fame of *'Antiquities of Orissa'* and Shri Bijoy Chandra Majumdar. Their main ideological presupposition was to oppose the separate identity of Oriya language and the creation of a separate Orissa Province. Babu Rajendra Lal Mitra who came to Orissa in the 1860s to work for his survey of antiquities in Orissa severely entangled himself in the anti-Oriya Language Movement and vehemently spoke against an independent existence of Oriya language. This role of Babu Rajendra Lal Mitra overshadowed all the merit of the scholarly work *"Antiquities of Orissa"* (1875) as being biased. Bijoy Chandra Majumdar took to the traditional line of approach and was heavily biased in his presentation of Orissan history. Chronologically Babu Rajendra Lal Mitra's writings came ahead of any of the nationalist writings, but for the purpose of the present analysis which is devoted to the study of trends in modern Orissan historiography, we intend to discuss this group of historians (primarily two) after the major historical trends, the imperialists and the nationalists.

With the beginning of the 20th century a spate of writing on Orissan history began with a somewhat scientific approach on the treatment of Orissan history and subscribed much to the requirements of sober history. Manmohan Chakraborty made intensive scientific research on the epigraphic sources available by that time. He edited and analysed the copper-plate records of the Eastern Gaṅgās of Kalinga. The brilliant works of Manmohan Chakraborty on the "*Chronology of Eastern Gaṅgā Kings of Orissa*" published in the *Journal of the Asiatic Society of Bengal* in 1903 solved many problems and paved the way of future research on the subject.

Many writers concentrated on the study of architecture as their theme because this gave them greater scope to treat scientifically their subject. We have the monumental works of Manmohan Ganguly *"Orissa and her remains"* which appeared in the year 1912. Two years before, Bishen Swarup had done a commendable work on *'Konark'*. We have got another commendable work in Professor Nirmal Kumar Bose's *Canons of Orissan Architecture' (1932).*

Though considered a Nationalist Rakhel Das Banerji is considered the front runner of the scientific line of research and his *History of Orissa* in two volumes was a systematic attempt to write the history of this land from the pre-historic times to the British period based on archaeological and archival data. Although this work is now completely outdated, Rakhel Das Banerjee stands unique among the scholars of Orissan history for advocating the scientific line of study from beginning to end. His *History of Orissa (1930)* was the first effort to deal comprehensively with the history of Orissa under different chapters and headings. R.D. Banerjee also contributed individually to studying many inscriptions, notable among them, being the Hathigumpha Inscription of King Kharavela. This solved many problems of the early history of Kalinga.

Dr. B.M. Barua also edited the Hathigumpha Inscription and some other fragmentary inscriptions of the Kharavelas time in his book *'Old Brahmi Inscriptions in Udayagiri Caves'*, published by the University of Calcutta in 1929. He made some restorations in the Hathigumpha text and provided a lengthy historical note on the rule of Kalinga by Kharavela and his successors. His work was a scientific study of the early history of Orissa during the rule of the Chedi dynasty of which Kharavela was the most prominent.

The last major scholar in this category is Pandit Binayak Mishra. Because of his phenomenal knowledge of Sanskrit, he could analyze many epigraphic sources of Orissan history and he brought to light the history of the Bhaumakara rulers of Orissa by compiling the inscriptions issued by the rulers of that dynasty in his famous work *Orissa under the Bhauma Kings* published in the year 1934. The other important work of Pandit Binayaka Mishra is *"Dynasties of Medieval Orissa"* which presents an account of some of the minor dynasties of early Medieval Orissa. All these scholars completely kept themselves separated from any kind of ideological moorings and restricted themselves to the scientific treatment of their topic.

Because of this line of approach adopted by them, we can conveniently group them as historians writing sober history.

References

1. N.K. Sahu, *History of Orissa*, 1964, p.355-56.
2. We have many translations of the text of the inscription.
3. M.M. Chakraborty, *Notes on Language and Literature of Orissa* in *Journal of Asiatic Society of Bengal*, Part II, 1898, p.336.
4. K.C. Panigrahi, *Itihasa o Kimbadanti*, 1963, p.53.
5. *Kataka rājavaṁśāvalī* was compiled and presented with translations by Dr. G.C. Tripathi and Dr. Herman Kulke under Indo-German Research Project on *"Sources of Orissan History"*. This also forms essentially a part of Col. Mackenzie's collection which was sent to London from Madras in early 1825. The collection was later taken over in the manuscripts stock of the India Office Library. The text bears close resemblance to the text *"Odradesa Vaṁśāvalī"* kept, in the Oriental Manuscript Library at Madras. The text was of exceptional importance for studies pertaining to Orissa. But K.C. Mishra has presented a translation of the text. However the text is hopelessly corrupt at many places and also contains large lacunae here and there.
6. A fairly good edition of the text is done by Pratima Misra, under the patronage of Dept. of Culture, Govt. of Orissa.
7. B. Sehikh Ali, *History: Its Theory & Method*, 1990, Madras, p.338.
8. John Beames Memoirs of Bengal Civilian, 1896 (rep.1984). New Delhi, p.215-16.
9. Barun De "Brajendranath De and John Beames – A Study in Reactions of Patriotism and Paternalism in the ICS at the time of Ibert Bill" in *Bengal Past and Present*, Vol. 81 (Jan-June 1962), p.15-16.
10. John Beames "Notes on the History of Orissa under Mohemmadans, Marhatta & English Rule in *Journal of Asiatic Society of Bengal*, 52 (1883), 231-37.
11. *John Beames Memoirs*, 1896 (1984), p.216.
12. *Orissa Historical Research Journal*, IX, 1 & 2; x, 1 & 2.

4

The Raj Syndrome and General Historiography

The daring voyage of Columbus in 1492, as a unique experiment in the history of mankind, set in motion a chain of consequences, changing the fate of the earth in different ways. Within six years of this experiment the "Vasco da Gama Epoch" in Indian history was inaugurated and in 1510 Alfonso Albuquerque conquered Goa. The destinies of Europe, South America, and Africa got intermeshed and interlocked with each other by the voyages of Columbus, Vasco da Gama and Albuquerque. Various colonizing, trading, merchandising and missionary activities of European enterprises based on the instinct for exploitation reached their apogee in the Nineteenth Century. The colonizing endeavour by the European enterprises in every part of the known world and that of the British in the Indian sub-continent remained in the incidental quest for the subordination of human societies and the launching of the project of inventing a new 'man'. Thus followed a series of technological and socio-political transformations.

The technological prowess of Europe in general and Britain in particular led to the development of the assumption of moral superiority. It was only Europe which mattered every other civilization, was seen either as a crude prelude to Europe or of no further relevance. Other civilizations might have their programmes, and it was deemed interesting but of little significance for the Europeans. For Europe its values were the only authentic ones; its art, music, architecture, ideas, social organizations, its ethnicity in short would become the only universal for all men, and world history was written to accommodate these assumptions. The socio-geography of other lands would be ploughed under and the new European seed would be sown therein.[1]

Europe, failing utterly in conversing directly with the subject races of the colonized nations, virtually created caricatures of the society it ruled. The vast and impressive corpus of literature was one of the European instruments of "Orientalism" for dominating, subjugating, restructuring and exercising authority over the 'Orient'.

In consonance with the European conquest of the people in the other world, the Raj started symbolizing the centrality of the British Empire and developed its imperial psychology and sensibility. It became syndromic in the course of its history and progress. "The Raj had sparked off its imperial stereotypes; fashioned the objects of its investigative modalities; tinted the imperial looking glass; ensued in official and public debates different strategic discussions; encouraged and applauded soldiers, administrators, publicists and missionaries, animated its extrovert troubadours and confronted its patient and plodding reconcilors".[2] The whole set of attitudes and perceptions so developed in justifying the Raj had been popularized as the Raj Syndrome.

The European dominance over its colonies was successfully effected through its literature, poetry, its recorded history, its parliamentary debates, and its sciences both natural and social and through propagation of its medical knowledge. This vast body of literature took the shape of sociology, history, anthropology, histories of science and technology ethics contained the language of imperialism clothed in the symbols of scholarly objectivity. The imperial propaganda swayed the whole British nation with a lot of ecstasy about its own expansion in the Indian sub-continent. The empire which had always remained a faith for an average Englishman, had become in due course of its progress the leitmotif of his daily life. The imperial euphoria was expressed in the plot of novels, flavoured the dialogues of the plays, set the rhythm of ballads, and constituted the inspiration of orators. Liptons' slogan "From tea garden to teapot" typified the force of the psychological propaganda for the empire.[3]

The information industry of the British Raj in India claiming for a complete moral and unimpaired ascendancy over the inarticulate masses had orchestrated the English behaviour in stimulating to fashion and foster an opprobrious perception of India and thereby a remarkable nostalgia for the Raj was developed.

British attitudes to Indian society were at no point of time one piece and had always remained either multilateral or multivariate. The perceptions were sharply divided and conflicting against each other. Imperialists and missionaries alike had viewed India as an area of darkness and of unredeemed barbarism. The Conservatives and Orientalists had viewed India as a mature and great civilization. The Utilitarians and Liberals with their ideas on liberty and the inviolable worth of the individual and human nature being intrinsically everywhere, failed to develop a set of coherent doctrines. A variety of views over a long period of social upheaval had influenced the liberals in early Victorian England. Because of the untenable position in the ideological framework in the Victorian England, the Liberals had failed to distinguish themselves distinctly from the imperialists as far as their understanding of India was concerned. Then from time to time the perceptions of India in each one of the groups were fluctuating.

The agenda of the Raj to change the traditional India into a scientific and rational modernity was itself a product of the larger intellectual framework of the eighteenth century philosophy of the Enlightenment, the most central issue of which was science and rationality versus faith and tradition. The study of India was part of a larger scholarly enterprise in which the Victorians, as children of the Enlightenment, sought rational principles that would provide a comprehensive and comprehensible way of fitting everything they saw in the world around them into ordered hierarchies.[4]

The term "Imperialism" is derived from the word 'imperial' referring to empire and emperor with a clear-cut ancient lineage indicating awesome, majestic or tyrannical systems—Imperial Rome, the Mughal empires, the Chinese dynastic empires—who enjoyed special status throughout the world. "In the 19th Century, while England was acquiring the greatest of all modern empires, many

Englishmen believed that its special quality distinguishing it from the lesser political orders laid on British leadership a responsibility of trusteeship and the welfare of mankind. In the North American Colonies before the demise of the first British empire, there was strong support for it as an institution through which the colonists could achieve their rights as Englishmen, Crown and Parliament willing".[5] Edmond Burke during the trial of the Governor-General Warren Hastings following his impeachment in 1787 for misconduct while holding office articulated a theory of colonial trusteeship. This was more forcefully argued because of the failure of British governance in North America. Subsequently in 1835, reiterating Burke's views on 'colonial trusteeship', the House of Commons through the report of the Aborigines Committee expressed that the British government was responsible for the welfare of its subject races even as it was responsible for the welfare of Englishmen.

In the initial years of emergence of Imperialism as an economic and political force during 19th century, it was well associated with the trusteeship and governing of colonies for human purposes and values. Victorian protagonists in the far reaches of the British Empire stunningly embodied these values. Lord Curzon, the Viceroy of India did not absolutely dissemble when he wrote, "In empire we have found not merely the key to glory and wealth but the call to duty and means of service to mankind".[6] Lord Cromer, the de facto ruler of Egypt from 1883 to 1906, while advocating the same view stated, "The British generally... possess in a very high degree the power of acquiring the sympathy and confidence of any primitive races with which they are brought into contact. Nothing struck me more than the manner in which the young men, fresh from British military college or University, were able to identify themselves with the interests of the wild tribes of Sudan and thus to govern them by sheer weight of character and without use of force".[7]

Imperialism has an aspect of general problem, namely, the use of force or coercion in social organization. Traditional analysis of imperialism laid stress on causal factors, while explaining the British governance of India in 19th century and the vigorous competition among the European powers for the territories in Sub-Saharan Africa during the last quarter of 19th Century. Some of them found the explanation in economic factors and others in non-economic factors. The agents of Imperialism invariably coerced subject peoples in varying degrees and thereby depressed the sense of well-being and freedom. Coercion is, however, an ubiquitous phenomenon, may be gratuitously random, or may be originated in the intimacy of personal relationships. There are many occasions for the use of coercion, which may be manifested in many ways from the physical threat to the life and limbs to the withdrawal of love or other highly regarded values. Imperialists usually coerce societies, which are mostly entangled in them, and the root of the coercion may be found in the scarcity of resources, which invariably affects all societies. In the vast body of Marxist, classical and neo-classical literature, the sketchy treatment of coercion in Imperialism is visibly expressed.

The classical, neo-classical and the Marxist theorists of Imperialism are without exception Western and knew little about the non-Western societies, which suffered from Western Imperialism. When the West began penetration into unknown terrains in the non-Western world, they developed the inclination of interpreting the non-Western societies and cultures through the conceptual and moral categories of their own societies.

Imperialism may also be viewed as a relationship in which one collective entity dominates, controls and coerces another and prevents it from acting in its own interests. England and India representing collective entities as countries, states or regions differ from one another in language, religion, ethnicity and political organization and in a potentially imperialist relationship between the two. When during 19th century England could acquire and accumulate greater wealth than India, maintain a strong military establishment, became more knowledgeable about the natural and social worlds around them, Indian people experienced the coercive impact of the imperialist conduct of Great Britain. This can very well be appreciated only by studying the inequalities and differences of the relationship in a concrete historical setting. Throughout the rise and fall of British imperialism in India, the imperial proconsuls endeavoured to create an environment in the Indian sub-continent in which the ordinary affairs of life could be carried on differently from what they otherwise would have been. Imperialism, however, is a very complex phenomenon, the impact of which is embedded in specific histories. So it is appropriate to recognize that there are imperialisms rather than a monolithic imperialism.

The political, constitutional and imperial history of British rule in India is a story about changing inequality, which began with the establishment and assertion of British imperialism in India and culminated in the Indian recapturing of its sovereignty. It is also a story of the changing, modifying and rethinking of systems of control. To rule India successfully the British had to devise and constantly to adjust a structure of bureaucratic and political institutions that would allow them to control the vital areas of government, while ensuring the co-operation or acquiescence of the bulk of their subjects. The Indian empire, which was put together by the conquests of the East India Company during the late eighteenth and early nineteenth centuries, was for the British unprecedented in its extent and character. As Thomas Macaulay exclaimed in wonder in his speech on the renewal of the Company's Charter in 1833, the Indian empire, 'the strongest of all political anomalies', was a state that 'resembled no other in history'.

In the first decade of the seventeenth century, England was not an imposing and subjugating power. William Hawkins came to India in 1608 not as a conqueror in quest of the Mughal throne, but as a supplicant seeking trading opportunities. In retrospect, his presence there manifested some strengths or assets that in time allowed England to assume the imperial mantle of the Mughal emperors. When the Mughal empire declined in the eighteenth century, the Company became a formidable competitor for political power that was initially acquired in Bengal at the end of the century.

With the rapid growth of Industrial Revolution in the nineteenth century, England asserted its interests in India with increasing effectiveness and the East India Company's commercial interests and ventures were minimized because the British assets grew relative to Indian assets. When the wealth, military power, knowledge, organizational capacity and ideology were combined together, the capacity of the British to achieve their private and public purposes were furthered. The British society that achieved industrial growth in the private sector at home became adept at attaining public and private purposes in India as well as in other colonized nations. British imperialism in India was obviously the outcome of India being unable, unwilling or uninterested in comprehending and asserting a common or public interest against the British interest in extending its rule there.

In pursuance of Britain's private and public purposes and objectives over the years, the information industry of the British Raj was stimulated to fashion and foster an opprobrious perception of India. Administrators, politicians and specialists had been earnest in highlighting the heterogeneous realities of the country, its peoples, its religions, castes, customs, languages and the fantastic variety of its natural surroundings. Over the years the endeavour of the civil servants had remained in claiming for the Raj complete moral and unimpaired ascendancy while the majority of the Indian people were committed to an uninterrupted continuity of the British rule, the so-called problems of self-determination had been vaunted to have been contrived and manipulated by a clamorous minority unconcerned of the interests of the inarticulate masses.

It had always remained the intent of the administrators, writers, elites, and missionaries to locate and scrutinize the unseemly Hindu practices and demolish their implicit social hegemony. In the British contemplation of India, there always existed an enduring tension between two ideals, one of similarity and the other of difference. This had on the other hand shaped differing strategies of governance for the Raj.The British vision of India was never at any point of time being informed by a coherent set of ideas. Rather the ideals that sustained the empire had always been shot through with contradictions and inconsistencies. "At sometimes and for some purposes the British conceived of Indians as people like themselves or as people who could be transferred into something resembling a facsimile of themselves, while at other times they emphasized what they believed to be enduring qualities of Indian difference. Sometimes indeed they simultaneously accommodated both the views in their thinking making it perilously difficult to discern any larger system at all".[8]

However, throughout the Raj, the ideas that most powerfully informed British conceptions of India and its people were those of India's difference. All the energies and skills of the nineteenth century

British scholarship were harnessed in developing a colonialist knowledge, whose function was to erect a past, that can be used as a pedestal on which the triumphs and glories of the colonizers and their instrument, the colonial state, could be displayed to the best advantage. "Indian history, assimilated thereby to the history of Great Britain, would henceforth be used as a comprehensive measure of difference between the peoples of these two countries. Politically that difference was spelt out as one between the rulers and the ruled; ethnically between a white Herrenvolk and blacks; materially between a prosperous Western power and its poor Asian subjects; culturally between higher and lower levels of civilization, between the superior religion of Christianity and indigenous belief systems made up of superstition and barbarism—all adding up to an irreconcilable difference between colonizer and colonized. The Indian past was thus painted red".[9] So with the British construction of their rule in India and the extension of their conquests to India, the British had always tried to determine the extent to which India as a land was fundamentally different and to what extent the Oriental society possessed institutions similar to those of Europe; and how far the Indian people ought to be transformed in Europe's image and how they should be expected to live according to the standards of their own culture. In the process of such an endeavour the British thought they would be able to confirm the intellectual superiority and the righteous authority of the Western civilization and buttress the ideological edifice of imperialism.The British attempt at ordering India's people and their past was an essential part of the larger intellectual endeavour guided by political objectives. The colonial sociology of India was tied to a system of power, where the British necessarily eschewed some of the social categories that would announce India's similarity to Britain and may threaten the colonial order. In the process of such ordering of India's people and society throughout nineteenth century, remarkable internal reviews, reforms and resurgences in Indian society were observed. The rigidity of the social system that had developed around the laws of Karmă was thoroughly interrogated and its commandments were also denied of its undisputed sway. A spirit of service had been grafted on to the fatalistic concepts of Hinduism. The process was slow and gradual, but these innovative developments had made significant inroads into the amoral perceptions of Hinduism. "Yet even as late as 1935 these social and intellectual ferments in India were dismissed by the Western critics as cosmetic changes calculated to infuse fresh vigour into Vedantic Pantheism and to stabilize the extraordinary inertia of the Hindu society".[10] The intellectual fermentation in India is explained by the enlightened observers as peripheral movements, which has resulted from the reflex actions of an arid social system and its insensate consciousness in the face of an extrovert and rational civilization. This was obviously a very insidious viewpoint, which stood as a self-imposed limitation and obfuscated all objective investigations. It provided the general background and constituted the matrix of the imperial sensibility.

During the second half of the nineteenth century, there was no insulation from the external world on the Indian sub-continent. As India was considered and had already been recognized as central to the empire, so the Raj was integrated within the world capitalism. Again imperial perceptions of the Raj in due course had already accommodated skillfully the social, political and economic changes in Indian life and the responsive attitudes of the Indian people to the rational impulses from within. So the identification of the exclusive external impact on the Indian developments could only be complete with due reference to the remarkable internal impulses. The Lindsay Commission in 1931 not only affirmed this but also maintained that although ferment was in process within Hinduism, the Vedanta still retained its control and moulded consciously the fundamental attitudes of the vast majority of the Hindu people. It contended that politics with its contentions filled the air with clamour; patriotic passion swayed the life of many; superficial secularism was rampant; the higher aims of social service were being superimposed on an amoral individualism of Hinduism. Lindsay exclaimed that these changes had been so radical, so vast and so rapid that it appeared apparently as entirely a new country. But these impulses from within were dismissed as the "Outward polish of life".[11] Although the Lindsay Commission disregarded the symptoms of Indian regeneration there were others who viewed the historical proceedings in India more pragmatically. They were depressed for the futility of the Christian endeavours in India. The missionaries who were operating on rapport with the Christian movement in India had already become unable to carry with their missions effectively, which had also been deeply regretted by them. Viewing the whole thing from this vantage point, they presumed that the religious and social institutions of India should be accorded a sympathetic treatment. Stanley Jones, being one of those few liberal missionaries being distressed by the sterile world of Indian Christianity, gave a call for the rational analysis of the Indian society for incorporating the best and finest elements of the Indian traditions into the perspective of the Christian movement.[12] He considered it necessary and prudent in not concentrating on the darker sides of the Indian society which would merely arouse contempt of the West towards the East. He had striven hard along with some others in assembling the basic terms of reference for a firm and lasting 'Indian road' to Christianity. He had contended that over-emphasis on the seamy sides of the Indian behaviour caused much disservice to the Christian movement in India. Further he advocated that the whole exercise had been conceived to inspire a sense of pity and repugnance in the minds of the readers. He also cautioned that consequently these reckless endeavours could be counterproductive and even disastrous. He argued, it was feasible on the part of an eastern traveller in the west being tempted in etching an unfavourable and unpleasant portrayal of the Western world by carefully selecting uncomfortable facts according to his own convenience. Stanley Jones did not of course question the depiction of the image of India as was done by Western observers. He was, however, uncertain about the portrayal being discreet and judicious. The vital failure of the Western scholarly observers in reckoning the changes in the Indian society and viewing it in its integrated totality was also emphasised by him.

Stanley Jones along with others also thought that rational attempts should be made in evaluating the attempts made by the Indians in combating their social evils. He believed that the racial lines were so drawn and structured that it would be realistic to leave India to settle her own house in order and she should not in any way be pressurized to do so under compulsions. Jones pitched his hopes on the expectation that the foundation of the Christian missionary objectives in India could thus be laid deeper in the mind of New India. Strangely enough, whereas the potential similarities between European and non-European responses to Christian ethics were dismissed as irrational and unfounded, the Imperial mind raised the question of the traditional Christian belief in the spiritual equality of white and non-white people. Imperialism implanted a profound antipathy towards the black race. The native converts' ideas of Christianity were made to appear fairly hollow and their attraction to Church was too materialistic. They may be described as nominal Christians, who were definitely worse than the outright heathens and avowed 'scoffers' and 'skeptics'. So the suspicion of the futility of marginal conversion was very much widespread. With the warning of the enthusiasms of evangelical circles at home, both government and missionaries in India were dovetailed in an integrated imperial assault. The missionaries got them intertwined with the power structure of the colonial situation and thus found it difficult to distinguish between Christianity and culture.[13]

European attitude towards the non-European societies were largely conditioned by a significant Euro-centric consciousness. To all intents and purposes Europe had been presented in sharp contrast to the non-European world as the center of the universe. Rest of the world had always been regarded only as a solid mass of inert barbarism. Thus the west pronounced with remarkable equanimity that the Orient constituted an area where no element of change did occur at any point of time in history without the inspiration and intervention from without or outside. So quite naturally the West declared that the East did not have any history excepting some dynastic changes and had absolutely no historical document. The Eastern world was seething with incoherent power, unorganized intelligence and sudden violent irruptions. Sylvain Levy, the President of the Society Asiatique between 1928-1935, with all his expressed humanity and compassion for the fellow Asiatics, counselled patient endeavour on the part of the West as a superior civilization and advised it not to push on to a crisis point owing to inherent jealousy and rancour. T.E. Lawrence thought that as a white expert, he could assume the role of an Oriental prophet-giving shape to the upsurge in new Asia. The Arabs of Duncan Macdonald and Indians of Rudyard Kipling were the childish primitives; while the westernized ones were the obstinate Orientals involved in a great conspiracy against the Western supremacy much before the task of reconstruction was complete. To Chirol and most of the European experts on 'Orientalism' there was no room for rapproachment between the white West and the coloured East, while Curzon, Cromer and Lugard spoke in the same imperial lingua franca and upheld resolutely the undisturbed rule of the West over the East. The establishment of the School of Oriental and African Studies was held by Curzon as the necessary furniture of the empire.[14]

These Euro-centric laws of historical development by its very logic imposed a sacred obligation on the Western civilization for its expansion towards the non-Western people even without any valid legal or social approval and despite their stiff opposition and passive resistance. The West has been credited as the recipient of Greek virtues like philosophy, individualism and democracy. In sharp contrast, particularism and exclusiveness of Judaism on the one hand and the litharge of the fallen Islam on the other had ossified the Middle East. Indian culture had been characterized by 'Oriental ease and response which could be distinguished by self sufficient village communities dominated by the state as the ultimate landlord and absence of any change in a self perpetuating social structure.

The most influential philosopher who offered an integrated social frame for the articulation of imperial perception was G.W.F. Hegel. He had analyzed the independence and dependence of social consciousness, which provided the blueprint of imperial psychology and thus left a permanent imprint on European thought and philosophy. According to Hegel, the self assured, arrogant and domineering self-consciousness existed only in being acknowledged. In this forceful philosophy, life was the natural setting of consciousness and it was necessary for pure self-consciousness. In order that independent self-consciousness be survived and perpetuated, the pure consciousness needs to exist as two opposed shapes of consciousness. The first was represented by an independent consciousness whose essential nature was 'to be for itself' and the second one was represented by a dependent consciousness which lived and toiled for the other. According to Hegel, the former may be called as the lord and the latter as the bondsman. He asserted that subjugation of the bondsman to the lord was a natural order of things and its recognition led to the liberation of the individual. It was a widely held axiom that the action of the lord was represented as pure and essential and that of the bondsman was impure and unessential.[15] This conceptualization of Hegel formed the parameters of imperial consciousness.

The essence of the relationship between the lord and the bondsman was servitude. The supreme test of the success of the lord was the experience of servitude of the bondsman. Hegel emphatically asserted that the disinterested service to the lord for the bondsman would keep his ephemeral desires, a self-destructive phenomenon in check. It would ensure a terrifying fear in the heart of the bondsman. This would cause the beginning of true wisdom and thus the bondman's self realization would be formed and shaped. The essential conditions for the liberation of the bondsman would constitute absolute fear, unhindered service, and formative activity. During the liberation, he was to experience 'absolute fear' of the 'absolute independent self-consciousness'. So this liberation would constitute the bondsman's 'rediscovery of himself by himself 'as he was urged to be aware of the confusion in his own mind resulting from the "dizziness of a perpetually self-engendered disorder" and to submit before the truth as deduced by the lord from a universal "absolute dialectical unrest". Hegel asserted that the whole process of the evolution of self-consciousness would be helped by the punitive constraining and rewarding instruments in the possession of the lord. Hegel's "*Phenomenology of Spirit*" published in 1807 was prescribed as an essential classic for the perusal of gentlemen during their formative years. As a result the dialectics between "Lordship and Bondsman" left an indelible mark on the imperial mind. Without any shred of doubt it authentically confirmed imperialism as a logical and legitimate phase in the evolution of Western Civilization and the salvation of mankind. Now the significant signposts of imperialism constitute domination, dependence, service, loyalty and fear. When imperialism started running amuck in the name of Western civilization in foreign lands overturning the polity and culture of the 'heathen' and impure 'bondsman', the colonial mind of the nineteenth and twentieth centuries was conditioned by these sentiments and sentimentalisms.[16]

With the arrival of Lord William Bentinck as Governor-General in 1828 the British avowedly embarked upon a thorough-going programme of reform. Building upon the vague expectation that somehow British rule ought to bring improvement to India, free traders, utilitarians, and evangelicals created a distinctive ideology of imperial governance shaped by the ideals of Liberalism. From Bentinck's time to that of Lord Dalhousie (1848-56), this reformist sentiment gained a near universal ascendancy among the British in India. The liberal view of Indian society found its fullest expression in James Mill's classic work '*History of British India*', first published in 1818. Mill was a man who prided himself on his philosophic disinterestedness. He had served the East India Company for some seventeen years from 1819 until his death in 1836 and he rose to the post of 'examiner', the highest post in the Company's home government. Because he was informed with the historicist ideals of the Scottish Enlightenment, which laid out a series of stages which could measure the degree of civilization of any society with scientific precision, he set himself the task of ascertaining India as a 'true state' in the scale of civilization. Mill followed Bentham in asserting that the criterion utility was the measure of social progress. Exactly in proportion as utility is the object of every pursuit", he wrote, "may we regard a nation as civilized". He scrutinized India's arts, manufactures, literature, religion and law, and disputing the claims of Sir William Jones, he claimed that the Hindus did not possess and never had possessed 'a high state of civilization'. They were rather a 'rude' people who had made but a few of the earlier steps in the progress to civilization. There existed in India, he wrote a 'hideous state of society' inferior even to that of the European feudal age. Bound down to despotism and to a system of priest-craft, built upon the most enormous and tormenting superstition that ever harassed and degraded any portion of mankind, the Hindus had become "the most enslaved portion of the human race". Moreover, Mill agreed with Jones—Hindu society had been stationary for so long that "in beholding the Hindus of the present day, we are beholding the Hindus of many ages past, and are carried back, as it were into the deepest recesses of antiquity'.[17] So there was keenness among the utilitarians to overthrow the hold of the flimsy faith that had endorsed a sentimental adoration of the immobile despotism of the East. Thus Mill found at the root of the "disgustingly ugly" Indian social institutions—that "barbaric conglomeration"—primitive social formations a vast despotic polity and religious tyranny. Many others confirmed Mill. There was a distinct line of continuity running through Hegel, Macaulay, James and John Stuart Mill, Fitzjames Stephen, John Stratchey, Gladstone, Morley and the more extrovert exponents of imperialism.[18]

Contempt for the Indian society and polity, over emphasis on efficient government, ruthless suppression of native insubordination, cold and callous opposition to native leadership, insistence on law as a regulated force and on the requirement in India of a despotic government with power, authority and will to enforce stern laws with some of the prescriptions of the so-called investigative modalities of the Raj.[19] All these formed the permanent backdrop of imperial endeavours and consistituted the core culture of Imperialism. All those who mattered agreed even as late as 1942 with James Mill and Fitzjames Stephen that the integrated ingredients of administration were despotism, power and authority. Taken together, these constituted the soul of the Raj. In enforcing stern laws, undaunted by ephemeral public opinion, the administrators were recommended a warm heart and a lively imagination unaffected by superficial sentimentalisms. The British Empire established by firm, and strong hands "from Adams Bridge to Peshawar" beyond the shattered walls of Delhi and over the Fort of Lahore, was the embodiment of the peace. It was by the empire builders and confirmed by the historians following the demise of the Raj.

The British Raj had been tremendously influenced and inspired by the vision of the Roman Empire. The Romans virtually left the world a legacy more lasting than bronze or marble. The enduring Roman influence is reflected pervasively in the contemporary language, literature, legal codes, government, architecture, medicine, sports, arts, engineering, etc. Much of it is so deeply embedded that we barely notice our debt to ancient Rome.

For centuries almost every educated soldier knew a little Julius Caesar, including his famous dispatch after the battle of Zela, "Veni, vidi,vici- I came, I saw, I conquered". That ranked as history's greatest military message for about 1900 years—until the fateful day in 1843 when the British General Sir Charles James Napier came up with a Latin dispatch that was even better. Napier had set out with a small force hoping to capture Sindh in modern Pakistan. Back in Delhi his Commanding Officer, Lord Ellenborough, anxiously awaited news—"Does Napier have Sindh?" Finally Napier's message arrived from the front. Ellenborough impatiently tore open the envelope and found a single word "peccavi". Naturally the officers at British headquarters could recognize this as the present perfect tense of the Latin verb Pecco, meaning, *"I sin"*. In other words, "I have Sindh".[20]

It was universally claimed that the Raj was the inheritor of the political and cultural legacy of Rome. The significant characteristics of this Roman legacy were snobbery, ruthlessness and intolerance. These were given the nomenclature of patriotism, loyalty and fortitude under the British Raj. Economic benefits were dressed in idealist garb; mercenary motive was disguised in a moral crusade; and romance and adventure camouflaged political and military aggression. Again the adoration of character instead of brains was closely associated with it. The American films arrived as a substitute to Greek and Roman theatre. Early Christian films complete with gladiators and lions, those of Tarzan and the Apes, the "Westerns" with trigger-happy cowboys chasing the feathered Indian were followed by the urbanized Westerns where cars replaced the horses and the 'cops', the cowboys.[21] It had been wishfully thought by some of the civil servants and politicians that the nationalists would never graduate in the school of administration and the British would be welcomed back once again. There was in it a strange admixture of nostalgia, guilt, adventure and imperial pride. It had also been believed by them that if the inarticulate rural masses were given the opportunity by a genuine electoral choice, the Englishmen would be welcomed back in India.

Although the British claimed that the British mission in India was completely fulfilled, there was an undercurrent of melancholy, despondency about the incompatibility of the two civilizations, the inevitability of political withdrawal and the glorious uncertainty of the permanence of British achievements in India.

Going beyond the ephemeral Raj syndrome, in recognizing the realities of the Raj, India had continued to haunt British sensibility down to the days of Mountbatten even till date, as the-sought-for playing field of the chivalrous knight errants of the empire "that spread its wings wider than Rome".[22] It was power, autocracy, and social Darwinism. It was glamour, snobbery and the basis of imperial economy. It was a certain indicator of imperial might. It was the principal signpost of Britain's sun-lit empire where "boxwallah missionary, clerk, lancer, planter carried maxims or gospels to lighten a dark continent.[23] The Raj was the cult of Christian military heroes. It was the principal instrument to direct the class-consciousness of the labouring men in Britain into the controlled decorum of imperialism and to help the extensive diffusion of its core culture. It was the barometer of British imperial sensibility.

To sum up, the ephemerals of the Raj syndrome had its footprints in the colonialist elitist historiography, which concentrated itself on its ambitions and achievements credited mostly to the British colonial rulers, administrators, policies, institutions and culture. The colonialist histories of the Raj fall roughly into two classes. The first corresponds to the initial mercantilist phase of British power in the sub-continent. It had been phrased in the idiom of coercion. It emphasized the moment of conquest rather than order. Alexander Dow, 'Lieutenant Colonel in the Company's service' testified truly to the inspiration derived from the sword by the pen in this particular genre as he dedicated one of its most representative specimens. '*The History of Hindostan*' to the King of England thus: 'The success of your Majesty's arms has laid open the East to the researches of the curious'.[24] The better-known scholars of this school were Verelst, Bolts, Scrafton Grant, etc. The essential aim of this mercantilist historiography was to educate East India Company. By investing the relation between government and landed property in the pre-colonial period, it wanted to equip the Company with a knowledge that would help it to extract the highest possible amount of revenue and to use it to finance its maritime trade. There was the sincere attempt at reducing the quantum of wisdom and wit to the minimum, so the impact was remarkable and significant. Besides, the idea of the "chosen people" operating on the doctrines of Christianity was superimposed on this. It was assumed that God would back only the Christians. It was asserted that Christianity was synonymous with science. Science was called service and service was the other name of sharp shooting guns. The imperial ideologies emphasized on cruelty as necessary for the "savage wars of peace". The cult of the Raj was a racial congregation and it was hypocritical to think that it could be humanized by 'purdah' parties or the patronizing admission of the rais and the notables of the natives to its charmed circle.[25]

Eric Stokes, debating on imperial sensibility, distinguished the spirit of the Raj from various types of imperialism in the world. In contrast to the imperial experiments in South Africa, Malaya, Egypt and Nigeria, a unique and distinct demeanour is clearly visible in British India. In India, there was an unflinching sense of duty and commitment towards the fallen and downtrodden people. As the proud chronicler of the glories of the British Empire, Stokes emphasized that the evangelical spirit of the Raj did not allow itself to be misled by any concern to buy support or earn cheap popularity. The Raj, Stokes proclaimed, cared not for flattery, odium or abuse. Stephen and Strachey had been, he added, its spokesman; Kipling was its poet and Curzon gave fullest expression to the Imperial idea in India. Stokes imperial eloquence had, however, always remained transparent."[26]

It was not surprising that the prospect of the independence of India would be viewed from Britain as a signal for the retreat of the empire from its traditional fortresses in Africa and Asia. The strains and stresses of the Second World War, the growing influence and hegemony of Indian Nationalism, the declining strength of British elements in the services, the increasing insubordination in the armed forces and the persistent implorations of the international public opinion in favour of the Indian cause had rendered withdrawal from India almost unavoidable. The Raj had passed its prime. Its liquidation and withdrawal was considered very painful.[27]Although the independence of India had become quite apparent, there was the continuity of British imperial arrogance. There was still a marked absence of real will to help in making a free India in the full sense of the term. There was too much exploitation of "partly real and partly unreal" communal differences in India which was partly "made and partly exploited by ourselves...".[28] Attlee's pronouncements and Wavel's attitudes confirmed that the British government was still committed to Viceregal veto, defence portfolio, native states, rights of various minorities and retention of British connection with India in some form. The Cabinet Mission plan held out the prospect of a fragmented India. It was envisioned that the departure of the imperial authority would be followed by a spectacle of a congeries of states with different levels of tensions and affiliations dividing and binding them. A posture of self-righteousness was adopted by the Raj as it prepared itself to leave the shores of India and watched gleefully its freed 'bondsmen' taking rapid steps on the road to violent self-destruction.

Most of the writers of this School were quite candid about their political motivation, as witness the administrative prescriptions, which figured so prominently in every exercise of this kind. They have concentrated more on the coercive element of dominance. This provides maximum objectivity in comparison to the historiography of later generations. They were completely unaffected by the idiom of improvement. So they were unconcerned to promote any affection among the conquerors for the conquered. Thus it maintained a considerable distance from the bulk of the masses. In that perspective the physical features of the land acquired by the sword showed up as clearly as the details of the religion, customs, manners, etc., of the people subjugated by the sword. It was a matter of observing a set of objects.

By the end of the eighteenth century, the colonialist historiography outgrew the mercantilist concerns and acquired within the next two decades a new look conforming to the requirements of the British Capital in the age of industrialization and those of metropolitan politics in the "Age of Improvement". James Mill, the utilitarian philosopher, appropriately pioneered this orientation. His '*History of British India*', published in 1818 earned for him celebrity as "the first historian of India".[29] It was more significant in the sense that it indexed a nineteenth century European prejudice, according to which the pre-colonial India was said to have no history and therefore, "the first historian of India" had to be English. This prejudice occurred in its most systematic form in the philosophy of Mill's German contemporary, Hegel. Mill more arrogantly denounced a substantial part of "India's pre-colonial history as barbaric in his 'History". Even as he argued that India had no history due to stagnation in its social development, Hegel wrote admiringly about "this country so rich in spiritual achievement of truly profound quality".[30] But to James Mill it was all a matter of arrested mental development. "It is allowed on all hands that no historical composition existed in the literature of the Hindus, he observed; "they had not reached that point of intellectual maturity, at which a value of the record of the past for the guidance of the future begins to be understood".[31]

Apparently he wanted to provide background information to the conquerors about this sub-continent. So in the pre-amble of his work, he announced his intention 'to exhibit as accurate a view as possible of the character, the history, the manners, religion, arts, literature and laws of the extraordinary people with whom this intercourse had thus begun, as well as of the physical circumstances, the climate, the soil, and productions, of the country in which they were placed".[32]

Mill's history displayed massive digressions. It served the avowedly didactic purpose announced by Mill at the outset of his work. "The subject forms an entire, and highly interesting portion of the British history", he wrote; "and it is hardly possible that the matter should have been brought together for the first time, without being instructive... If the success corresponded with the wishes of the author, he would throw light upon a state of society, curious and commonly misunderstood; upon the history of society, which in the compass of his work presents itself in almost all its stages and all its shapes; upon the principles of legislation, in which he has so many important experiments to describe; and upon the interest of the country of which, to a great degree, his countrymen have remained in ignorance..".[33] No mercantilist historian had ever written all these. The perspective had already been shifted. It was no longer that of a conqueror but of a legislator. So Mill had set out to give India a government administered according to the principles of utility. He spoke therefore, in the idiom of 'Improvement' rather than of 'Order'. He was very much a child of his age to seek a site for his reforms in the Orient. He advanced his plan for the amelioration of the newly conquered territories of Bengal. Besides, he wanted the demolition of the indigenous culture of the colonized on intellectual grounds so that he could then go on to posit his own system into that vacancy. This demolition was an act of spiritual violence. It amounted to robbing the subject people of their past which was one of the principal means of their self-identification. It prepared the ground for a substitution of bad Hindu history by a good history in the making under the colonial auspices. To this end, the record of the intervening period of about five hundred years was mobilized in such a way as to make of the Islamic component of Indian culture an accomplice of colonialism. But the Muslim, however, superior to the Hindu, was still far below the British in the scale of civilization. Thus the substitution of the Indian culture was completed in two successive movements—the abolition of the historic culture of the Hindus followed by the suppression of that of the Muslims. British Asian territory would have its spiritual complement in a British appropriation of the past of the subject population, allowing all of colonialist historiography to be guided by Mill's assertion: "The subject forms an entire and highly interesting phase of the British history".[34] Mill had insisted throughout his work on the point that India was entirely different from Britain in every respect; in religion phase, manners, civilization and language—indeed in every qualitative detail.

The Raj had, however, interjected liberal western values and helped thereby to promote social reform, combat superstition and generally raise the level of the indigenous culture. The theme of the civilizing mission began to lose its credibility as colonialism had its records assessed by an increasingly critical subject population. To the latter, the benefits of the officially sponsored social reform seemed to have been cancelled out by the aggravation of what was believed to be officially engineered caste and communal conflict designed to keep the natives divided in order to perpetuate foreign rule. This skepticism, combined with a nationalist pride that refused to take Western superiority in culture for granted, forced historiography to shift its emphasis from reform to education as the main component of Britain's spiritual gift to India. Education remained one of the chief determinants of nationalist politics and their genesis was clearly linked with those Indians who had been schooled by Western methods.[35] Thus Mill's idea of reducing Indian history to a portion of the British history was realized thus in the reduction of Indian politics to Western education. This idea of reductionism received much criticism afterwards and as a result the genesis and determinants of politics were no longer sought in education. These were searched for in government. This second idiom was also derived from Mill. It had been surmised that the structure of the imperial government could provide clues to the way Indian politics developed. The atmosphere of the imperial government was to be found in the complex of organizations, activities, discourses, the bureaucracy with all its rules, orders and schedules, all levels of officially sponsored institutions from the central to the local, as well as the laws and executive decisions made by them and the practical measures used to implement these. Taken together they stand for the ensemble called the colonial administration. The mode of historiography, which is primarily concerned to deal with it, is administrative history.

Administrative history had developed as a genre of historiography almost from the beginning of the colonial rule and it had never been anything but an integral part of political history. It was the very nature of the colonial state that the theme of administration should figure prominently in its earliest accounts. As an autocracy, which had originated in conquest and ruled over an alien population almost entirely by the sword for the first fifty years, the early colonial state had no means other than its administrative apparatus to record, measure, and assess its own articulation. Evidently at the initial stage there was no political history that did not read like administrative history and vice versa.

So the Indian history of the period between Plassey and Partition continued to be taught, written and propagated for the most part, as a portion of the British history in accordance with the parameters fixed by James Mill. The British paramountcy over its South Asian Empire had induced its political and intellectual culture thoroughly to absorb knowledge, techniques and attitudes which informed and sustained that paramountcy for two hundred years.

References

1. Alvares, Claude, *Decolonizing History,* Goa, 1991, p.244.
2. Chakraborty, Suhas, *The Raj Syndrome : A Study in Imperial Perceptions,* Delhi, 1989, Preface.
3. *Ibid.*, p.3.
4. Metcalf, Thomas R, *Ideologies of the Raj*, Cambridge, 1995, p.67.
5. Koebner, Richard, *Empire,* New York, 1965, pp.85-104.
6. Thorton, A.P., *The Imperial Power and its Enemies: A study in British Power*, London, 1959, p.72.
7. Cromer, *Earl of, Ancient and Modern Imperialism*, London, 1910, p.75.
8. Metcalf, T.R., 1995, *op.cit*, p.X.
9. Guha, Ranjit, *'Dominance without Hegemony and its Historiography', Subaltern Studies* VI, Delhi, p.211.
10. Chakraborty, Suhas, 1989, *op.cit.*, p.215.
11. Lindsay Commission,*Report of the Commission on Christian Education in India*, London, 1931. Cited in Chakraborty Suhas, *The Raj Syndrome: A Study in Imperial Perceptions*, Delhi, 1989.
12. Jones, Stanley, *The Christ of the Indian Road,* London, 1925.
13. Chakraborty, Suhas, 1989, *op. cit.*, p.216.

14. *Ibid.*, p.302.
15. Hegel, G.F.W., *Phenomenology of Spirit*, Oxford, 1979, pp.104, 138. (Translated by A.V. Miller with an analysis of the text and foreword by J.N. Findlay).
16. Chakraborty, Suhas, 1989, *op. cit*, p.303.
17. Mill, James, *The History of British India* (*Reprint*), Chicago, 1975, pp.226-27, 236-37, 248.
18. Chakraborty, Suhas, 1989, *op. cit.*, p 219.
19. Stokes, Eric, *English Utilitarians and India*, Oxford, 1959, pp.234-322.
20. Reid, T.R., Roman Legacy, *National Geographic*, Vol 192, No 2, Washington, August, 1997, pp.61-62.
21. Cf Richards, Jeffrey, *Visions of Yesterday*, London, 1934 (the author provides a full survey of all the imperial films particularly those of Hollywood).
22. Chakraborty, Suhas, 1989, *op. cit.*, p.231.
23. *Ibid.*, p.231.
24. Dow, Alexander, *The History of Hindostan*, Vol I (3rd Edition), London, 1792, p.i.
25. Chakraborty, Suhas, 1989, *op cit.*, p.220.
26. *Ibid.*, p.220.
27. *Ibid.*, p.221.
28. *Ibid.*, p.222.
29. Bain, Alexander, *James Mill – A Biography*, New York, 1967. p.178.
30. Hegel, G.W.F., *Lectures on the Philosophy of the World History: Introduction: Reasons in History*, Cambridge, 1975, p.136.
31. Mill, James, *The History of British India*, Vol II (4th Edition), London, 1840, p.67.
32. *Ibid.*, p.2.
33. Mill, James, *The History of British India*, Vol I, London, 1840, pp.2-3.
34. *Ibid.*, Vol I, p.2.
35. Seal, Anil, *The Emergence of Indian Nationalism*, Cambridge, 1968, p.16.

5

Orientalist-Colonialist Historiography

(A)

SEVENTEENTH AND EIGHTEENTH CENTURY ORISSA : A STUDY OF THE RAJ SYNDROME

The appropriation of India's past began with the East India Company's accession to Diwani in 1765. In order to collect land revenue and to manage its administration, it was necessary on the part of the Company's officers to know the structure of the landed property and the relation between the state and the landed magnates in the pre-colonial times and its implications for the East India Company as a successor regime. In order to understand that relation, the appropriation of the past was the only alternative. So the officers were required to write the history of the regions. The primary purpose of this endeavour was to help the administration in determining inheritance along the lines of descent within the leading landlord families of a district. These specimens of historical essays contain the stamps of elitist bias in British Indian historiography. This bias was clearly reflected in the British assumption that the local aristocracies were the natural proprietors of the land in India. This assumption was taken up as a fact of Indian history and used as an argument in favour of a Zamindari settlement. Further as the British extended their rule across the lengths and breadths of the Indian sub-continent during the late eighteenth and early nineteenth centuries, they were confronted with the problem of governing this far-flung dependency and justify this governance to themselves. After the rapacious years of conquest following Plassey and the eventual construction of their rule in India, the British drew upon a range of ideas that had for a long time shaped their views of themselves and more generally of the world outside their island home. With the most effective leadership provided by the administrators like Warren Hastings and Lord Cornwallis, philosophers like Edmund Burke and Thomas Munro, the British had begun by 1800 to lay out ordering principles for what was to become the most extensive empire after Rome. In order to justify their rule to themselves and shape a coherent administrative system, the British had to devise a vision at once of India's past and of its future. The British as agents of progress in India had to set India to modernity and simultaneously they were required to work as custodians of an enduring India formed for ever in antiquity. While constructing their 'India', the British rulers had to negotiate throughout the nineteenth century with the disjuncture between an acknowledgement of "similarity" and an insistence upon "difference". For serving the needs of the Raj, varied pasts of India ought to be created. This would help them in creating for themselves a national identity. The varied British histories of India thus produced shaped the way the British constructed the difference they ascribed to India.

Preliminary exercises in colonialist historiography, whether done on a local or global scale, abetted directly in laying the foundations of the Raj. This had been better illustrated in the way Indian past was mobilized by all the contending parties in the debates within the Company's administration during the last three decades of the eighteenth century. The history of the subject population was reconstructed there over and over again as the central question of the relation of property to empire became the subject of controversies between Hastings and Francis in 1770s, between Grant and Shore in 1780s and between Shore and Cornwallis in 1788-92 on the eve of the permanent settlement. The outcome of such attempts at appropriation was to provide legal and administrative support for those measures, which set up British rule in the sub-continent eventually as a rule of property. All the energies and skills of the nineteenth century British scholarship were ascribed to this project.

During the seventy years between Mill's, *History of India* (1812) and Hunter's *Indian Empire* (1881), India's past was thoroughly investigated, recorded and written up by many hands. As a result a vast corpus of historical literature was produced, which came to constitute a new kind of knowledge. This knowledge was scientific and may be called as colonialist knowledge. Its function was to erect India's past as a pedestal on which the triumphs and glories of the colonizers and their instrument, the colonial state, could be displayed to very good advantage. In advancing this knowledge, the victorians set out to order and classify India's past with greater emphasis on 'differences'. The victorians, as children of the enlightenment, had made 'the study of India' a scholarly enterprise, while seeking rational principles that would provide a comprehensive and comprehensible way of fitting everything they saw in the world around them into ordered hierarchies. It was a matter of urgency that this knowledge was created and the categories within which that knowledge was constructed was shaped essentially by the unequal power relations of imperialism. However, Victorian science and its historicism necessarily and consciously fitted India into a hierarchical relationship with Europe and provided the firm footing of legitimacy with which the British sought for their Raj.

There were obviously persisting tensions and conflicts between the claims of similarity and those of differences, which had informed the ideology of the late Victorian Raj in the arena of history, race and gender. They tried to understand India's past and its present in order to devise structures for ordering its society. This appropriation and understanding of India's past was effected by conquests, which carried with it the risk of rebounding upon the conquerors. It could end up by sacralizing the past for the subject people and encouraging them to use it in their effort to define and affirm their own identity. This appropriated past served as the sign of the other not only for the colonizers, but ironically for the colonized as well. The colonized Indians on the other hand, in their turn, re-constructed their past for purposes opposed to that of the Britishers and made it the ground for marking out their differences in cultural and political terms. Thus history was made into a game between the two to be played as the alien colonialist project of appropriation was matched by an indigenous nationalist project of counter-appropriation.

European attempts in general and British attempts in particular at appropriating, understanding and interpreting the country's traditions can be put into at least three distinct categories, which may be called as exoticist, the magisterial and the investigative. The exoticist approach concentrates on the wonderous aspects of India. The focus here is on what is different, what is strange in a country that as Hegel put it, "has existed for millennia in the imagination of the Europeans". The magisterial approach deals with notions of India as an imperial territory from the point of view of its governors. This outlook assimilates a sense of superiority and guardianhood needed to deal with a country that James Mill defined as "that great scene of British action". This, of course, is primarily a British phenomenon, but a great many British observers did not fall into this category and some non-British ones did. The investigative approach is the most catholic of all, and covers various attempts to understand Indian culture and tradition from the outside, without looking only for the strange and without being weighed down by the magisterial burden.

The drift and propensities of the imperial perceptions and sensibilities outlining the Raj Syndrome can very well be etched out throughout the history of the Raj initiated with the beginning of commercial trade by the East India Company. These are perceptible in the appropriated Indian past by the magisterial historians. The task of ruling a foreign country does not go easily with seeing the subjects as equal. It is quite remarkable that the early British administrators in India including controversial Hastings were as respectful of the Indian traditions as in fact they were. The empire under the Company, of course, was in its infancy and it was being expanded rather gradually and tentatively.

There are quite a few good examples of magisterial approach to India fostered by the Raj Syndrome, which are perceptible in the observations of Mill, Maine, Lyall, Vincent Smith, Rudyard Kipling and Katherine Mayo. They not only influenced the bureaucratic activities of the British governors, but also helped the governors in great ways for certain characterization of the country.

The colonialist magisterial approach had its imprints on the British writings on Orissan history during their whole period of subjugation of Orissa. The land and people studied by them and the histories thus appropriated by them pointed to a nexus between the Raj and the empire. William Bruton during his visit to Cuttack and Puri in 1633 on a commercial mission had attempted at studying the life style of the people of Orissa. Although a travelogue, Bruton's account of Cuttack and Puri is a noteworthy work from the historiographical point of view. There were absolutely no imperial requirements in the first half of 17th century behind these enterprises, but studying the commercial motives associated with the interest in collecting information about the people of this land speak certainly about the larger European imperial projects in the creation of differences in the long run.

Discussing the life and behaviour of the people of Cuttack and Puri, Bruton had stated, 'The most of the people have no learning, but do all things by memory: they wear commonly long hair, and are very strict in their time of fasting; but when the ceremony is over they freely commit all kinds of wickedness again. In some places they have their edicts or laws written and in other places unwritten, they know not what belongs to bonds or bills, and they lend without witnesses, or any sealing of writing, even upon their own words, and he that is found to deny his promises, hath the top of his fingers cut off. Their habit is varied and different, some of them go in linen and woollen; some are clothed with beasts skins, or birds feathers; others go naked and cover only their secret parts; their bodies are for the most part black, which is not accidental but naturally arising from the quality of seed they are begotten; most of them are of a large stature; they have many wives, which they purchase and buy of their parents; some they (key) keep to their vassals, to do their drudgery; others which are handsomer for issue sake and pleasure. Here are greater store of beasts than in any other part of the Indies: as oxen, camels, lions, dogs, elephants; they have dogs which are as fierce as lions with which they usually hunt and pursue those wild beasts, as we do our bucks for their delight and pleasure. They ride on goodly horses, booted and spurred so likewise do their women.

"These people are notable ingenious men, let it be what art science so ever and will imitate any workmanship that shall be brought before them: for the most part of them hate idleness and those that do not study in some art or other are counted drones and stand for ciphers and dead men among the best and chiefest sort of people; they have custom that always before dinner, they call their children and young people in their houses together and examine how they have spent their time from the sunrising; if they could not give a good account of it they were not to be admitted to the table; and so everyday; and if they did not the next time improve themselves in some knowledge of laudable things they are most severely punished and chastised.

"These barbarous and idolatrous people, although they be so ignorant in the true worship of God, cannot endure a perjured person, not common swearer, nor a common drunkard, but will punish them very severely by stripes, or else by forfeiture of their commodities, a perjured person, say they, is an arch-enemy to their God and them; and it is so hateful that if it be committed by their father, brother or kindred, they presently condemn him, according to the nature of the offence; for though they love the perjury, by reason of benefit that cometh unto them by it, yet they hate the person, even to death; for say they, he was sometimes perjured in their behalf, may undo what he hath done, and speak the truth when time serves. They instance a story of Solyman (Sulaeman) the great Turk, who loathed and abhorred the traitor that betrayed Rhodes into him, and instead of his daughter whom he expected to be given him in marriage for a reward, he caused him to be flayed and falted and told him in derision that it was not fit for a Christian to marry with a Turk, unless he put off his old skin. Likewise they instance Charles the fourth who rewarded the soldier (that betrayed their Lord and masters Krantius) with counterfeit coins and being desired to deliver them current money answered that counterfeit coin was the proper wage for counterfeit service. Thus a liar, or perjured person amongst the idolatrous people,they will not believe though he had spoken or sworn the truth: for he that hath been once false, is ever to be suspected in the same kind of falsehood: wherefore just and upright dealing is aptly compared to a glass, which being once broken can never be repaired: or to opportunity, which once omitted can never be recovered. And so I conclude the relation, wishing all men to prefer knowledge and honesty before wealth and riches: the one soon fadeth, the other abideth for ever; for amongst all the goods of his life, only wisdom is immortal".

This brief report, which contained a lot of information regarding earlier explorations, travel records, stately palaces, court life of king Mukundadev and the life style of the people of Orissa is a part of post-renaissance European project of establishment of familiarity with things Indian by the merchants, ambassadors and missionaries. Bruton in his narrative of the 8th May 1633 had stated about the preparation for a war against Qutbshahi Sultan of Golconda. This is an interesting historical information. Bruton's description of the Oriya people as backward, illiterate, barbarian and idolatrous, sexual perverts besides being ingenious definitely point to the fact that the account contained some amount of reliability, and a curious admixture of observation and fantasy. Some of the observations contained internal contradictions. Bruton came to Orissa in May and continued to stay here until the middle of November 1633. During his stay for about seven mouths he had traversed a number of towns and places.The description of places such as Harssapoore (identified with Harispur or Harispurgarh situated at extreme south east of Cuttack district at the mouth of the Patua river; Coteke or Malcandy (Cuttack or Mahanadi); Balkhada (identified with Balikuda in Cuttack district); Haraharrapoore (identified with Hariharpur, the old name of modern Jagatsinghpur in the present Jagatsinghpur district); Pipely (identified with a port named Pipli on the Subarnarekha where Portuguese had their factory. It was situated on the opposite side of Shahbandar village. The whole town of Pipli has been washed away by the river); Ballazary (The modern spelling is Balasore); Maden (This seems to be modern Madhab where there is a temple of Jagannath); Amudpoore (identified with Ahmudpur about a mile to the north of Satyabadi Police Station on the Jagannath Road from Cuttack to Puri); City of Jagarnat (City of Jagannath or Puri town); Catigan (identified with modern Chittagong) Satagan (Saptagrama of Bengal near Hugli) are noteworthy from the point of view of the historical geography of the region and the trade routes existing in the early part of 17th century. While describing about his passage through the fourth gate of the palace of the king of Malcandy (Mahanadi), Bruton stated, "Going through this gate, we entered into great broad palace, or street much of the breadth of the street between Charing-cross and white-hall or broader, and no dwelling in it; here we passed the wall of the king's house or palace, till we came to the court gate".[2] The comparison of a street of Cuttack City with that of a street between Charing Cross and White Hall, two important palaces in London city is a real marvel. But that speaks of the Euro-centric observations on things that are totally Indian in shape and structure. There is also another vital piece of information regarding the time keeping machine, which was kept at the eastern end of the palace. Bruton wrote, "At this east end there was also a second gate, where was a guard of an hundred men armed; here stood also men that did keep the time of the day by observations of measures of water, in this manner following; first they take a great pot of water, of the quantity of three gallons and putting therein a little pot of somewhat more than half pint (this lesser pot having a small hole in the bottom of it), the water issuing into it having filled it, then they strike on a great plate of brass, of very fine metal, which stroke, maketh a very great sound; this stroke of a parcel of time they call a goomt* (It may be a ghanta in Oriya); the small pot being full, they call a gree; eight grees make a par, which par is three hours by our account. (Grees may be taken Ghadi in Oriya and par represents Pahara in Oriya). They likewise begin the day at six in the morning; and it is ended with them at six at night".[3] The description of the palace which includes the architectural designs, sculptural representations well decorated gateways derbar hall, the pavement of which was spread with rich carpets; pillows of red velvet and pillows of gold provide vital information for archaeological enquiry. The study is associated with large amount of scientific precision and high degree of objectivity.

The commercial activity of the people and the growth of towns and centres of commercial concern on the banks of the rivers are also found reflected in the work of Bruton. He had described the town of Balkhada as a strong and specious thing, very populous; there are many weavers in it and it yielded much of that country fashion cloth.[4] Again about the city of Cuttack, he stated, "the seventh day of May we went up and down the town of Coteke, it is very populous of people and hath daily a great market in it of all sorts of necessaries which the country affordeth; it is seven miles in compass and hath but two great gates belonging to it; it is three miles between the one gate and the other.[5] While describing about the court of Malcandy in Bengal Bruton had referred to a very fairly rich market place. He stated, "Going from the house of Mersymomeine, we passed over a long stone causeway of some two feet in breadth and at the end thereof we entered at a great gate, and having conducted along further, we came into a buzar or a very fair market place, where was sold a great number of all sorts of fruit, herbs, flesh, fish, fowl, rice and such like needful commodities and necessaries as the country yielded (which is very fertile). Having passed this place we entered in a second gate where was a guard of some fifty armed men and so we came into a place all paved with great stones or it may filter be called, a fair and spacious street, where merchants seated on both sides of the way, were buying and selling all kind of their own and foreign wares and merchandises, that were very rich and costly".[6] On his return journey from Coteke Bruton arrived in Harharrapur (Jagatsinghpur) on 12th day of May, 1633. About this town of Harharrapur, he stated, "This town of Harharrapur is very full of people, and it is in bounds of six or seven miles in compass; there are many merchants in it and great plenty of all things; here is also cloth of all sorts, great store, for there do belong to this town at least three thousand weavers, that are house keepers besides all other that do work, being bound or hired".[7] The descriptions thus made about the people and the commercial activities of the people in some of the towns visited by Bruton definitely point not only to the inquisitiveness of the author about the people and land of an unexplored and little known region in the Orient, but also to the typical British attitude and British sensibility in unearthing the socio-economic conditions of the people, which would help them in the long run in finding a place for themselves in the commercial bargain of the country.

While Bruton on his way to Puri on the Company's business, arrived at a place called Amudpoore which is identified with a place called Ahmudpur[8] near Satyabadi or Sakhigopal. Here he came across a large horde of people and had described, "The sixth day of November, I, William Bruton, travelled eight course, which is thirty two miles English and came to a town named Amudpoor, where I found, met together of men, women and children, more than three thousand, and all of them were travellers and rangers of the country, having no residence but are called Ashmen (because they cast ashes upon themselves) also they are called Fackeires which are religious names given to them for their supposed holiness, but indeed they are very rogue, such as gypsies are here in England, when they see their time and opportunity to put roguery and villainy in practice at this town I made no great stay for I had a good charge about me of the Company's.[9] In the account, there is a digression in which Bruton mentioned the places of Satgaon and Chittagong in Bengal. After this he returned to the town of Puri where he did not find liquor or wine used by the people. All this information is quite interesting. But the equations of the fackeirs of Orissa with the gypsies of London are based on bad logic. The description of fackeirs as rogues and their actions as villainous sounds uncanny. There is a clear-cut attempt at the denigration of the people. "Bruton's statement that, 'he is no wise merchant that ventures too much in one bottom, or that is too credulous to trust or Infidels' speaks about the viability of gradual attempts at securing trading rights and gradual control of the market forces in totality. Again the description of Mohammedans as Infidels, who are not to be trusted at all point to some of the pre-conceived notions of the British about the Muslim people as barbarians and obviously this was an earliest attempt by the British traders in establishing European and Christian superiority over their Asian counterparts.[10]

One of the earliest British factories in India was established at Hariharpur (Jagatsinghpur) in Orissa in 1633 A.D. Subsequently other factories were established at Balasore on river Burabalanga and Pipli on river Subarnarekha. These trade establishments in Orissa helped the British in the furtherance of their trade in Bengal. Long before the appearance of the Britishers as rulers of Orissa, they had a firm foothold over the merchandise of Orissa. So the primary object of Bruton in exploring the social and religious life of the people of Orissa was essentially lying in the creation of avenues and background for the growth of mercantile trade in the south east coast of India. This was however not only maiden but also a path breaking study of the history of Orissa.

Again he had pointed out the scarcity of spices in this part of India. The degree of scarcity had been stated to be similar to that of England. This particular piece of information highlighted in the statement speaks about the meticulous attempts of British at studying and observing the demand and supply sectors of the market for creating a background to launch their imperial campaigns in the long run.

Among the earliest British factories, the factories established at Balasore and Pipli were most important. "These two Orissa harbours formed the basis of our future greatness in Bengal".[11] Within few years factory at Balasore was developed into a thriving centre of maritime trade. In 1670, of several factories in Bengal, Bihar and Orissa Balasore was the seat of their Chief and his council.[12] Balasore, however, continued its pre-eminence as a commercial centre for quite a long time. With the shifting of East India Company's trading concerns to Hugli and Calcutta in the 18th century, Balasore started declining.

Orissa was brought within the orbit of East India Company's imperial sceptre after the Battle of Buxar. On August 12, 1765, Lord Clive received the Diwani and proprietory rights of Bengal, Bihar and Orissa. In the hey days of the Great Mughals the territories of Bengal, Bihar and Orissa were formed into one administrative unit. But the Orissa of this Diwani grant was corresponding only to the district of Midnapore. Immediately after the grant of Diwani, Clive made some attempts at the possession of Orissa proper through negotiations with the Marathas. In 1766, he sent Thomas Motte on a commercial mission to Sambalpur to explore the possibility of diamond trade. At the same time Motte was entrusted with the task of meeting the Maratha Subahdar at Cuttack to initiate political talks on the issue of transfer of proprietary rights of Orissa in favour of East India Company. Accordingly, Motte met Bhawani Pandit, the Subahdar twice.[13]

After his travel to Sambalpur, Motte wrote the travellogue entitled *"A Narrative of a Journey to the Diamond Mines at Sumbhulpoor"*, which was first published in 1786 in the *Asiatic Miscellany* and then again it was printed in the *Asiatic Annual Register of 1799*. In the *District Gazetteer, Sambalpur* published by the then Government of Bengal, Calcutta 1909, Motte's narrative relating to Sambalpur was printed at Pp. 40-52 under the heading *"Sambalpur in 1766"*.

This narrative contained detailed information about the route of communication from the northern end of Orissa to Cuttack and also from Cuttack to Sambalpur in the Mahanadi Valley. As a traveller, Motte had written what appeared to him to be of general interest to the Englishmen who were then keen to know the details of the geography and people of Orissa. As the British were to create a separate space for themselves within the Indian frontiers and in the empire itself these early explorations were imperial adventures blessed by the will of God.

Before undertaking the travel to Sambalpur in Orissa, he had developed apprehensions about the safety of his journey through a barbarian country. He had stated, "His Lordship (Lord Clive) being then a great loss for means of remitting money to England, proposed to me to return with the vakeel to the mines, and to endeavour to open the diamond trade. He offered to make it a joint concern, in which I was to hold a third, he the other two; all the expenses to be borne by the concern. The proposals dazzled me, and I caught at it without reflecting on the difficulties of the march, or on the barbarity of a country in which Mr. Mallock, sent by Mr. Henry Vanisiltart for the same purpose, durst only stay twenty four hours".[14] Henry Vansitart was the Governor of Fort William from 1760-1764. Motte's record was the earliest British record to give any information about Mallock's visit to Sambalpur. In this context this may suffice to say that Orissa provided the base for the future greatness of the British in Bengal and the description of the people of this land as barbarous sounds ludicrous. With the establishment and expansion of the British Empire in India, in the early decades of the eighteenth century, the British would be found to have been utilizing this perception of the people of Orissa and the whole of India in general for intensification of imperial propaganda. They would tenderly nurse the idea that it was the birthright of the just and the noble to conquer the wild people of the earth.

After the battle of Buxar and grant of Diwani, the British became frantic and impatient in the establishment of their suzerainty over Orissa. "His Lordship instructed me to make what enquiries I could into the state of the Mahrattas, supposing that a government connected by such very slight ties might easily be divided and by such division, that the power of a people so formidable in India might be weakened. He directed me also to send the officers of Jannojei's Court, whether he would not cede the Province of Orissa, for an annual tribute, and thereby give a contiguity to the British dominions in India, which would strengthen them greatly".[15] This evidently points to the fact that only by adhering to Machiavellian tactics, they could come out successful in finding a space for themselves in the political bargaining of the sub-continent in the 18th century.

Plassey, Buxar and Diwani provided ample scope for the historians to conclude that history could be made by trickery alone. Of course after the receipt of Diwani they became confident of their tactics. Being nostalgic about the Lockean mercantilist thought, they used the same Machiavellian methods in the furtherance of British commerce in India and also in the establishment of the British dominion in India. It is crystal clear from Motte's statement that the primary intention of Clive in sending Motte's dispatch to Sambalpur was not only to explore the possibility of diamond trade but also to create avenues in entering into political bargains with the Maratha overloads over the fate of Orissa. This points to their eagerness for the expansion of the British dominion in India. "His Lordship instructed me to make what enquiries I could into the state of the Mahrattas, supposing that a Government connected by such very slight ties might be easily divided and by such division, that the power of a people so formidable in India might be weakened. He directed me also to sound the officers of Jannojei's court whether he would not cede the province of Orissa, for an annual tribute, and thereby give a continuity to the British dominion in India, which would strengthen them greatly."[16] British had always nursed the idea that "the birth right of the just and noble" was always to conquer the wild people of the earth. The expansion of Pax Britannica was unfailingly an unavoidable commitment and a hallowed obligation, which had to be advanced. It has always been considered by the English that God had given them the responsibility to inhabitate and reform the barbarous nations all over the world. So the British wanted to take advantage of the lawlessness and administrative disorder of the neighbouring countries for the physical expansion of the British Empire, which was still in its infancy in the early decades of the middle of 18th century. On many occasions throughout the travellogue, Motte had referred to his purpose behind his explorations of Sambalpur. "Between the end of the town Budruc (Bhadrakh) and the river Sollundee is the tomb of Rajaram Hircarra (Rajaram Harkara); this was a servant of the Nabob (Nawab) of Bengal but dismissed by Shurajah Dowlat (Shiraj-Ud-Daula), joined Colonel Clive when landed in Bengal in 1756 and was extremely useful for his extraordinary local knowledge of the country, so long as the English continued in an active state; but the inactivity of the succeeding government, rendering him of no consequence he became dissatisfied and entered into correspondence with the Marathas, for which he was obliged to fly, and died here in the way to Cuttack".[17] This is one fine instance of imperial strategy and imperial arrogance cited by Motte. Motte after reaching Cuttack city met Mr. Charles Alleyn, working as a Postmaster in order to maintain the communication system and then escorted by him he proceeded to the Court of Bhawani Pandit, the Governor of Orissa. "I found at this place Mr. Charles Alleyn, a gentleman employed by the Government of Calcutta as Postmaster, to keep up the communication between Madras and that place. He waited on me to the court of Bowani Pandit, the Governor of Orissa where I was received with more politeness than state. I delivered him the letters from Lord Clive, which desired him in general terms, to pay all attention to what I should say, as I was in his Lordships confidence. I began by opening to him my desire of purchasing diamonds at Sumbhulpoor as the object of my journey thither. He looked at me with a penetrating eye, and said, so trifling a matter could not be all the meaning couched in his Lordships letter, nor all the purpose of a man of my consequence, for the diamond trade of Sumbhulpoor could not be carried on to any considerable amount. His suspicions were that I was employed to form alliances with the mountaineers, through whose territories my road lay. He explained to me the just demand Jannojey, his master, had on the company for the arrears of the tribute of Bengal and Bahar (Bihar). I seized this lucky opening entered at once on the discussion of the point and answered, I understood the revenues of Orissa were made over to Jannojei, in lieu of the tribute of the three provinces, and that the best mode which could be adopted, was to restore it to the company, who should pay a stipulated sum, and send a resident to the Court of Nagpoor as an hostage. I urged that by so doing, a mutual confidence would be formed between that court and the Court of Calcutta, for the advantage of both.

"Janoojei's situation was at that time extremely critical. A bitter inveteracy had arisen between him and Maddo Row (Madhu Rao), the Paishwa (Peshwa), in effect the sovereign of Poona, while he became detested by the Nizam of the Deccan, his old ally, for his treachery at the conclusion of the last campaign. The Paishwa resolved to make him feel the weight of his resentment. Bowanee Pundit (Bhawani Pandit) was too good a statesman not to comprehend the use which might be made of an alliance with the English. He caught the idea with the vivacity of a Maratha, told me the interests of his court and ours were the same; that he would write what he had said to Jannojei, and desired me to write to Lord Clive. Business being finished, he became extremely cheerful, supplied me with guides, and promised me every assistance. I then paid a visit to Laicmunjee Jazie, the Commander of the Citadel, who treated me with great civility".[18] Here many things are evident including the eagerness of the British in order to enter into political bargains with the Marathas for extension of imperial dominion over the state of Orissa. Bhawani Pandit had the apprehensions, Motte might enter into political alliances with the mountainous countries of western Orissa by bribing them for creating political instability, anarchy and confusion in the country. In reality on many occasions, Motte's actions were found to have been projected in the same direction. Bhawani Pandit had been very deeply impressed by the behaviour and dealings of English. May be he had already assessed the vulnerability of the Maratha Oriya defence against English expansion. In his dispatch to Motte, while the latter was staying in the state of Baud, he had described in greater detail about the state of political affairs existing in the Nagpur State. In this dispatch he had made Motte aware of the political instability, divisions among the Maratha ruling families, and among the nobility and also the futility of any bargain with the Maratha overlord for forming alliance with them in order to extend the sphere of their influence. "I halted this day of Boad, the residence of the Rajah, a large fenced village. Here I was overtaken by letters from Bowanee Pundit of Cuttack, acquainting me with the fate of his master and Goree Punt (Gouri Pant), a Maratha of some consequence, on his way from Nagpoor, who related to me all the circumstances. The Marathas are divided into two parties".[19]

There was some touch of sentimentality attached with the explorations thus carried out by the early British invaders of the country. Fears for unknown lands and terrains were very much there along with fascinations and inquisitiveness. There were always the search for similarities and differences between things Indian and things British. A search for markets had always been the overriding priority in the imperial calculations since the establishment of British dominion in India in 1757.

While moving towards Sambalpur at Midnapore, Motte searched for Mr. John Graham, who has been described by him as an old friend and a man superior. Finally at a place called Beerkul (may be Birkul) he located him. Describing the place he stated, "I found him at Beerkul, on the sea side at the foot of the braces. Here I had a sight of the sea, that spectacle of magnificence and terror; that most august object under the heavens. It is viewed by the Europeans banished to this country, with a pleasing regret, for they regard it as the road to the place of their native".[20] Here there was something common between the European landscape and environment of Beerkul, which provided an object of attraction for the Europeans. Throughout the British Raj, it had remained the endeavour of the British to search for the similarities in the things Indian and careful suppression of all those.

Motte had described in his account all the places he had traversed on his way towards Sambalpur. The topography of the places, the people, their food habits, trade, both inland and foreign, the etiquette of the people, the river systems, communication, social structure, religious beliefs and mythology, security, Maratha administration and reaction of the people towards it, gender variations, climate and diseases, etc., have been beautifully projected.

Among the places which he had come across are Midnapoor, Beerkul (Birkul), Jallasore (Jaleswar), Putchumber (Paschimabad), Ballasore (Balasore), Mohur Bunge country (Mayurbhanj), Ommerdnagar (Amarda in Balasore dt.), Multanekubur (Multani near Kanpur, not far from the Rly. station of Amarda Road); Busta (Basta), Gurpudda (Garhpada), Ramchunderpoor (Ramchandrapur), Phoolwar Gaut (Phuladighat), Raj Gaut (Rajghat), Piply (Pipli) Neelgur (Nilgiri); Maun Govindpoor (Man Govindpur), Mauntree (Mantri), Bimdah (Bhimda), Bommin Goutee (Bamanghati in Mayurbhanj dt.); Hurrarpoor (Hariharpur) (Modern Haripur in Mayurbhanj dt); Ectiurpoor (Actiarpur in Balasore); Oonjur (Keonjhar); Shooroo (Soro), Beguneah (Begunia); Budruc (Bhadrakh); Daumnagar (Dhamnagar); Cunnia (Kanika) Jehazpoor (Jajpur); Burwar (Burwan); Altee (Altai); Hurreepore (Haripur); Arrucpoor (Arakhpur); Jipoer (Joypur) Mansuompoor (Mansumpur); Puddamapoor (Padmapur); Cuttac (Cuttack); Lolbaug (Lalbagh, the residence of the Governor of Orissa); Barahbattes (Barbati fort); Ottugur (Athgarh); Ghilobonk (Gailbank); Boad (Baud); Bonkey (Banki); Sumulpoor (Similipur); Chadgeka (Churchika), Tigorea (Tigiria); Dhinkanol (Dhenkanal); Burumba (Baramba); Nia Patna (Nuapatna in Tigiria); Monneabund (Maniabandh in Baramba); Bidissur (Baidyeswar); Simhanath (an island in the middle of river Mahanadi); Cundea Parra (Khandapara); Collo (Kantilo); Cunter Bi (not identified; Chelka (Chilika) Nersinghpur (Narsinghpur); Tolchair (Talcher); Hindole (Hindol); Goorjang (Gorujang); Rodgeong (Rodjang); Dusspulla (Daspalla); Bailparra (Bailpada) Burmule (Barmul); Khussumgur (Kusumgarh); Burmuls Gantee (Barmul ghatti); Puddumtolah (Padamtala situated in the western border of Baud is famous for its elephant hunting. Firozsha Tughlaq visited the place in 1360 AD); Ungool (Angul) Landacole (Rairakhol); Koocheemol (Kuchimul); Coogul (Kugul) [Kuchimul and Kugul may be identified with Kadligarh in the Karandi valley in Rairkhol]; Joojoomsoora (Jujomura); Monisur (Maniser); Sumbhulpoor (Sambalpur). Speaking about the territories, Motte had referred to a number of neighbouring countries. These were Boora Shumbhur (Bodasambar or present Padampur town); Rottunpoor (Ratnapur); Bimbera (Bamra); Lunda Cole (Rairakhol); Coondon (Karund or Kalahandi); Gungpoor (Gangpoor); Soorgooja (Sarguja). On his return journey he had also traversed across some new places such as Whoamah (Huma on the Mahanadi); Jonepoor (Sonepur); Sindole (Sindol); Gurdunnesser (Godhaneswar).[21] Motte had not merely described the places visited by him. He had equally and also meticulously studied various aspects of village life existing in the 18th century. The study of the economic production, security and significance of the place names had also been attempted. The reference to Nilgir hills in regard to place name significance is noteworthy. "I left Balasore the 27th of April and halted under a tree near Ectiurpoor, where I entered Neelgur, formerly dependent on Mohur Bunge. It is bounded on the north by Mohur Bunge (Mayurbhanj); on the east by small talooks and on the south and west by Coonjur. It gives name to that range of hills which extend to the west of Midnapoor. Some Englishmen, fond of anglicizing it and perhaps in love with a lady of that name called them the Nelly-green-hills and which you find them in the directory for sailing to Bengal. This is a better etymology than most geographers give of the names of the places; for my part almost all the names of places in this country are the names of the founders with the addition of Gur or Nagur (Garh or Nagar) for a fort, Abad for a city, and Poor or Gunge (Pur or Ganj) for a village; and as Neel is a common name among the Hindus, I shall venture to pronounce it Neelguru."[22] The study of the land and people had been a part of the larger colonial scholarly enterprise.

Besides the study of the places Motte had also described the river systems and nullah sections, which he had come across during his visit to Sambalpur. This was essential to acquaint the company's officials with the topography of the region, so that the company's officials would find it easier to establish there mercantile relations with the people of the unknown terrains. Among the river systems which came under his mercantile enterprise were Sooburnreeka (Subarnarekha); Boree Belaun (Burhabalang); Cauns Bauns (Kansabansa); Sollundee (Salandi); Toonda Nulla (present name is Kapali); Gaintee (Genguti); Betrunnee (Baitarani); Lussonea (Lasunia a rivulet); Bommonee (Brahmani) Kimmera (Kumbhira or Kimiria or Keulo); Nullah Gulgalla (Sagadia nullah); Hurreepoor (Haripur river); Jipoer (Joypor); Maha Nuddee (Mahanadi); Connur (Kana or One eyed river); Cotjuree (Katjori); Kouakai (Kuakhai); Hebe (Ib); Tail (Tel), etc.[23] The study of the places and the river system had been done very carefully. Mottee had pointed out some peculiarities in naming the rivers in the State of Orissa and Bengal. "Indeed the rivers both in this country and Bengal, change their names so often, as makes it difficult for travellers to ascertain them; and as hircarras (Harkaras or messengers) scorn to be ignorant of any thing, ask one of them the name of the river, he seeing it has no current, and being ignorant of the name of the next village, pronounced it a connur Nuddee or One eyed river, a name common to all such as do not run the twelve months. This the traveller sets down as the proper name, on which account you meet with so many connur rivers in the English surveys". This has helped the preparation of Rennel's Map in 1788. As the British wanted to establish a patron-client relationship between themselves and Indians, so they relied mostly on Indian collaboration in the furtherance of their colonial activities. In the initial years of the foundation of British rule in India after the receipt of Diwani in 1765, the British deemed it necessary in studying the land and people from the point of view of imperial expansion.

Motte had also referred to a number of places having commercial importance. The existence of market towns have also been reported. "Jallasore is a small town on the Shooburnreeka, bounding on the English territories to the southward".[24] The reference to English territories expresses clearly an imperial psychology demonstrating the diplomatic ascendency of the British over the Indian ruling class. Regarding the functioning of different foreign factories in Balasore, Motte had stated, "The French factory is at old Balasore, a small village three miles to the Eastward of the new town. The Dutch have a factory near the English one, between which are two lofty pyramids, erected to the memory of two Dutch ladies. There is also a Portuguese church, and a small number of Portuguese and Armenian inhabitants."[25]

"The country between the Gaintee and this river (Brahmani) is by much the finest part of Orissa. It is inhabited by a great number of weavers, who weave muslins in pieces chiefly for turbans. Manufacturers will always settle in those parts where they are most free from oppression; and for this reason, so many flock hereabouts; ..."[26]. Throughout the work there have been many references about the exploitation and oppression of the people by the Maratha raiders, which had virtually paralysed the economy of the state.

At Mansumpoor (Mansumpur) two weekly markets are being regularly held. "The town of Puddamapoor (Padmapur) on the left bank of the one-eyed river mentioned earlier was a military station under the command of Futtee Khan (Fateh Khan) the Principal Officer in the service of the Nabob (Nawab) of Orissa and may be called the advance guard of the Maratha camp. The area is thoroughly cultivated. It is in consequence of being well protected, a considerable village, inhabited by a number of weavers[27]. Describing the city of Cuttack and the Lalbag palace (residence) and the business of the town Motte stated "Lalbag is the residence of the Governor of the province, a large building laid out in a number of courts in the Morisco taste, but much out of repair; the Governor, when one part is ready to fall, removing to another. From the Principal entrance of this palace, runs the great street, formerly built in a straight line, one and half miles long and still the chief place of business in the town. On the right of it is the English factory, the meanness of which does no credit to so flourishing a company".[28] The existence of the same business street has also been referred to in Bruton's account. The description of the Barabhattee Fort as too small to make a long defence against a European enemy obviously pointed towards the so-called European superiority, invincibility of their war machine, and also their arrogance, which may all be labelled as some of the parameters of British imperial sensibility.

The descriptions of the villages of Banki had a completely different look. "Four miles from the pass of Ghilobonk (Gailbank), I entered the Zameendary of Bonkey (Banki), where the country begins to wear a different aspect with respect to cultivation, the consequence of more numerous inhabitants. The manner in which the small villages are built was also new to me. The houses are placed in a regular street close to each other; and have neither door nor window, except in front. At each end of this street is a fence made of bamboos, knit together like cow cribs in England. This serves to protect the inhabitants and their cattle from bears, wolves and tygers (tigers), which came from mountains every night to these plains in search of prey. The large villages are not built in the same manner, because the Marathas will not permit anything that looks like a fortification in the ground road".[29] This was an attempt at highlighting the autocracy and misadministration of the Marathas.The exposure of the Maratha interference in the traditional countryside settlement pattern seems to be motivated by the imperial justification of the British rule in India. Tigiria had been developed into a prominent commercial centre because of the benevolence of its King Chumput Sing or Chumupati Sinha. He had taken great pains over improving the state of affairs in the state by restoring law and order in it. "When Sheeoo Butta (possibly Siva Bhatta) laid waste the Zameendaries of Dinkanol and Burrumba because they did not pay their rents, Chumput Sing invited the weavers, who fled from thence to settle in his capital, Niapatna (Nuapatna in Tigiria) granted them extraordinary privileges and has since given all possible encouragement to merchants. That place therefore bids to be a flourishing manufacturing town if not nipped in the bud by the rapacity of the Marathas".[30] Here the Marathas had been held responsible for the destruction of the peace and stability of the kingdom and also for the commercial decline of various centres of trade. The town of Monneabund (Maniabandh in Baramba) has been described as formerly being a considerable place of trade but it had been found to have been declined during the time of Motte's visit.

During the period from May 14 to May 16, Motte stayed in Khandapara and Kantilo. Both the places have been described as places of commercial importance, where necessaries were procured for the rest of his journey to Sambalpur. "The Bonkey country reaches only five miles beyond Bidissur (Baidyeswar) when you enter the

Cundeaparra (Khandapara) Chucla Cundea Parra, the residence of the Rajah is three coss S.E. from Collo (Kantilo), where I halted two days to provide my servants with necessaries, as I understood they could not meet with another place where they could be supplied; the rest of my journey being through a country thinly inhabited, mountainous, ill cultivated, and barbarous in every sense of the word.

Collo (Kantilo) is a large village, the most considerable place for trade in this road. The merchants of Berar, and the inland parts of India, bring cotton and other goods hither on bullocks, which return loaded with salt, which is made a Cunter Bi (not yet identified) on the Chelka (Chilka lake in Puri dist.), and in the parts to the southward of that river, which is the only kind of salt in consumption, the rigid Hindus thinking their purity would be doubted, if they eat salt made by an inferior tribe. The trade of Collo is founded on the same principles as the fairs in Europe were, and the increase of the wealth gave rise to merchants on speculation. During the months of January, February, March and April, the traders of the inland parts of Hindosthan form themselves in Caravans for the better security of their property, and bring their goods on bullocks hither, where they are met by the traders from the sea-coast with salt and European commodities. Business is carried on by barter; so that very little money passes between them. They live in huts, with which they are furnished by the factors they employ, who furnish them also during their abode here, with food and necessaries at reasonable rates and for their troubles draw only one per cent. A month before the setting in of the rains they take their departure; and the factors who are by no means opulent remain the only inhabitants of the place in which condition I found it. Nothing could induce the inland merchants who bring their goods five or six hundred miles, to carry them one hundred twenty miles farther to the sea; but this I attribute to the dread they have of the noxious effects of the salt air".[31] Two things are clear from this observation regarding the flourishing trade existing in Kantilo as a centre of commercial activities. Motte had time and again referred to the political instability and chaotic state of administration and exploitation by the Maratha raiders, which had adversely affected the mercantile activity in the coastal region stretching from Midnapore to Cuttack. Despite the political disturbances more or less prevalent in varying degrees throughout the state, commerce and business in Kantilo had completely a free passage. The British were in frantic search for business pockets, which in the long run could be utilized for political bargains in the countryside.

Talcher and Hindol were centres of best quality bamboos, which are used for palanquins. These are mostly produced in the mountain slopes of Gurjang and Rodjang. The bamboos had great demand in the local markets.

Daspalla in Puri district provided a completely different picture of imperial arrogance "Twelve miles from Coolo (Kantilo), I entered Dusspulla Chucla and came to Balipara where the Rājā collects duties on travellers for passing the straits of Burmule (Barmul), which are 14 miles distant; so that if any person proves refractory, he has time to send orders to his people stationed there to prepare for the reception of an enemy. The commanding officer of this place knew not in what manner to treat me, when I showed him the edict of his majesty Shah Alum, then residing at Allahabad, concerning me. I was surprised to observe the respect with which he received it; for the gentle conquerors of the race of Timur are still beloved by tradition, even in parts where they ceased near a century to reign; he also paid attention to Lord Clive's letter, for his fame was then at the highest; but when I showed him the Maratha pass which Bowani Pundit (Bhawani Pandit, the Governor of Orissa) had given me, he laughed at it and said the Marathas has always paid him presents when they passed that way. He assumed the bully, demanded bills on Cuttack for a large sum; but finding by his frequent changing his note, that he was irresolute. I was apprehensive lest if I submitted to his extortions his people should behave treacherously when I was entangled in straits; I therefore assumed a superiority, ordered the sepoys to seize him and attend me through them himself, at the end of which if he behaved well I would make him a present. I served my sepoys out with fresh ammunition in his presence. His people outnumbered mine five to one; but struck with my firmness, although they at first put on a threatening appearance, submitted to let him escort me with twenty men. Indeed these people are far more necessary as guides than formidable as enemies; for a small body might, inspite of such ill armed troops, force its way if it could but find it".[32] Since the beginning of the British rule in India, British imperialism had to confront barbarism, superstitions and tyranny throughout. On many occasions everywhere in the subcontinent the British imperial retribution was inevitably provoked because of the existence of lawlessness in the native states and society. In such circumstances imperial excesses and brutalities were presented as decisive steps in the march of the civilization and thus were mostly excused and condoned.The assertion of Motte's superiority over the commanding officer stationed at Balipada (at the entry point of Burmul pass) reflected the symbol of chivalry, righteousness, courage and sacrifice and also presented a rare scene of individuality, quaintness and wisdom, which could also be considered as the backbone of a Christian recompose and restoration.

Besides the identification of business pockets, Motte's concern had also remained in identifying strategic and vulnerable points in different parts of the state. He located one such point in the Barmul pass or Barmul ghati. "I left Burmule early, and entered the grand pass, which is the key of Orissa. The whole way from this place to Khussumgur (Kusumgarh), may with strict propriety, be called a pass, since it is everywhere defensible; but that part called Burmuls Gantee (Barmul ghati) is more particularly strong. The entrance is 600 yards from the fort of Barmule, and it continues near a mile. It is formed by two very lofty mountains, almost perpendicular, 200 yards from each other, between which the road lies. Through this valley runs a deep rivulet with a very muddy bottom. The stream being at first close under the southern mountain, I was forced to dismount my horse and climb the crags the little way, since the consequence of a false step either of man or horse would probably be either a broken neck or suffocation in the mud of the rivulet. Beyond this, the river glides across the valley from the foot of the northern mountain and forms a beautiful plain 500 yards long and 200 wide, at the end of which the stream is again close under the southern mountain, where the path is better than the former, being ten yards wide but spread with craggy rocks. This valley is therefore a strong pass; and if the straits of Thermopylae were as strong, we must acquit Leonidas and 300 Spartans of temerity."[33]

Communication was a problem with the early English adventurers. The growth of trade and expansion of their dominion depend on a variety of factors such as knowledge of trade routes, political situation, ability of the traders in conversing with local folk, study of the temper and sentimentalisms of the people in local regions, behaviour of the people, constraints of the people, etc. Acquaintance of the imperialists with all these conditions could help them create and develop a framework for their colonial projects. The foundation of the British Empire in India virtually reinforced the British culture with a renewed interest in militarism, royalty, national heroes, cult of personality, racial ideas of superiority and a contrived sense of Christian mission.

The passage through the hilly tracts after the Barmul pass was vulnerable and the risk factors were maximum. But Motte undertook the journey with militant spirit and very cautiously. "If any body of men refuse to make the mountaineers a present, they fell the largest trees, and lay them across the road, so as to obstruct, the passage of horses; and this obliges the travellers to buy their assistance for removing them; so that they pay at last whether, however, you pay them or not, they will plunder any part of your baggage that straggles, if they can master it. I was protected from anything of this kind, by having the commandant of Bailparra in my company; and every hour we travelled together, he became more conversable as we became better acquainted".[34]

In a very peculiar development, it was also found that the British at some points had referred to issues to which the people of Orissa were very sensitive "As nothing refreshes the people of this country so much as a whiff of tobacco which fire is necessary to the preparation of the mountaineers whenever they see a withered tree, put a little fire to the stem of it; which burning slowly near a mouth, affords travellers a supply. This accounts for a circumstance Mr. Marriott mentioned. He said, that on the Neelgur hills were many volcanoes, and that from the top of the factory at Balasore he saw during the months of April, May and June, pillars of smoke issuing from them. The volcanoes I judge to be nothing more than burning trees, as well set on fire by the mountaineers to the above purpose, as such as take fire of themselves; for during these months; the sap being down in some measure, and the wood being more inflammable, if one tree is by the wind rubbed against another, the friction will cause it to take fire. From observing this, mankind were probably taught to kindle a fire, by rubbing two pieces of dry wood against each other; a mode in practice from Kamschatka to the Cape of Good

Hope".[35] The primitive way of making fire and keeping it burning had been in existence in Orissa in those times. Motte had deliberately referred to the existence of the same practice in Africa, obviously to establish the backwardness and primitivism of the people of the hilly tracts of Orissa as was the case in Africa.

As a mercantilist Motte knew very well how to win the friendship of unknown people by exploitation of the fascinations of the people, which has been generated by the foreigners since long towards things that were foreign and modern. While descending from the hilltop, he had described the journey as follows. "I then commenced my descent, which I found more difficult than the road up, though not quite so rugged. But first I dismissed my conductor, with a present of a piece of scarlet broad cloth, a fusee and a pair of spectacles, with which he was highly pleased and vowed an eternal friendship for me".[36] Descending from the hill, he came to a very small village called Khussungur (Kusumgarh). Motte had developed a very peculiar perception about the people of this village and region. First of all he described them as barbarous and then as suspicious and not being dependable at all. "The policy of the Marathas in the government of this country appears very strange to a son of liberty, taught that government was instituted for the protection of every individual, and that the meanest who feels himself oppressed, has a right to complain and ought to be redressed, if such redress is not inconsistent with the common weal; while the people of this country endowed by nature with a stoical indifference which blunts all sensibility and finding in their own hearts a dastardly mean perfidy, which bars all confidence in their neighbours, and forbids an alliance with them who might protect them, submit to everything the individual cannot resist; who in the midst of his misery, impiously pronounces the visitation the will of God".[37]

After leaving Khussumgur he traversed across about 10 miles and finally halted, at Ramgur (Ramgarh) on May 21, which has been described by him as a considerable village on the banks of the river. This region had again been identified by him as another vulnerable point, where there was a danger of the belongings of the travellers and merchants being plundered by the people of the mountains. "May 22 I found my road today much more open, I passed from one valley to another by intervals in the hills, which ceased to be mountains. The villages were also planted more closely for in the distance of fifteen miles, which I travelled today, I passed three. The merchants who travel in these parts apply to the Rajah of the country they are passing through and making him a present, get a guard, who convey them into the territories of the next Rajah. This certainly is more for the interest of Rajahs, than to plunder them, since in such a case, the mountaineers would run away with the greatest part of the booty, while the Marathas, getting intelligence of such a prize, would immediately send a force to claim it, and oblige the government to refund the amount of plunder, aggravated by fame to five times its real value".[38]

Motte had not missed mentioning the simplicity of the people and their customs in entertaining their guests in some parts of the country.The friendly and generous attitude of the Rājā of Boud had deeply impressed him "During the halt, the Rajah of Boad sent me a present of provisions, according to the custom of the country; and at the same time gave me notice, that he proposed doing him the honour of paying me a visit, but insisted I should return it. I answered that as it was impossible in my weak condition to return the compliment, I must beg him to defer the intended favour till I came back. He sent another person privately to examine if I was really ill, lest his honour should be hurt; and being satisfied on that head came to see me. His train consisted of about three hundred men, some armed with bows and arrows, some with swords and shields about twenty with Matchlock pieces, but the great number with spears and hatchets. I received him as he alighted from his palankeen. His dress was a cotton cloth about his loins; and another thrown over his shoulders; a large turban; two pearls and an emerald strung on a gold wire suspended to each ear; and some charms about his neck, enclosed in gold cases, like the baubles of a lady's watch. Our conversation was short, consisting of observations on the consequences of the present drought with respect to the cultivation of the country, curses on his tyrants the Marathas, and professors of regard for each other. At going away, I made him a present of a pair of pistols".[39] Discussions held with the king of Baud regarding the state of economy existing in the state and the reasons of such state due to the tyranny of the Maratha rule, ostensibly point to the necessity of establishment of the British dominion in this part of the Indian sub-continent. His presents of a pair of pistols to the king was a definite attempt at the assertion of British superiority over their Indian counterparts; at the same time it was also aimed at infusing a sense of fear in the Indian minds.

Motte was mostly suspicious of the people of this country. Even if he had not missed describing his own guides and guards as treacherous and not dependable. On his way from Baud to Rairakhol, he had to pass through mountains and forests covered mostly with bushes. In this context he had stated. "The first ten miles was among mountains, not so lofty as those I had already passed, but overgrown with bushes, and the same kind of dwarf trees as before. As I understood there was a better road, I was disgusted at my guide the ambassador, and I had reason soon to think he was treacherous".[40] The villages situated between Kuchimul and Kugul in Rairakhol were found to have been thickly populated. Motte spent the night on May, 27 in Kugul. In the morning on May, 28 problems arose on the question of presents to the village. "In the morning my servants told me the Kelladar (Killadar) of the village was resolved not to let me pass unless I made him a present, and that Surdar Khan, the ambassador who had supped with him the preceding night had instigated him to this attempt at violence; for which purpose he had collected about one hundred men, armed with bows and arrows. Despising so mean a force, and reflecting that to submit to an indignity of that kind, would make my character at Sumbhulpoor less respectable, I marched the sepoys and drew them up in front of the village; telling the Kelladar, I would pay him for any mischief my people did, but that if he opposed my march, I would burn every house to the ground. This menace had the desired effect; he let me pass without the least molestation".[41] Motte's contemplation of Sardar Khan the ambassador's connivance/ conspiracies with the Killadar and his show of strength through the parading of his soldiers and guards before the Killadar and villages and finally his expectation of respectability from the king of Sambalpur were just some aspects of the representations of "imperial ethics", the essential object of which was to shelter an imperialism behind an irrational ideological shield so that it could be placed beyond rational social analysis. This may be explained simply as an imperial offensive necessary mostly for the civilizing mission of Britain, the onward march of masculine and scientific Christianity and the assertion of the superiority of the British imperial pride. Since the establishment of British rule in India 1757, everywhere they had to confront barbarism, superstitions and tyranny or lawlessness, which necessitated imperial retribution.

The lawlessness, tyranny and barbarity of the country of Sambalpur were highlighted by Motte in his further descriptions of the land. "My situation was at this time truly critical: I was entering a place so remarkable for perfidy, that captain Malice durst not stay twenty four hours in it; with a body reduced extremely low by a nervous fever, and no medical assistance at hand. The sepoys and servants on whom I depended for protection against secret treachery, but which in their best state, were insufficient to guard against open violence, instead of marching in good spirits, were obliged to be carried on a hurdle on the heads of two men; for almost all my people were burnt, several of whom died after I entered the town. These circumstances presented to me in all their terrors; but the state I found things in at Sumbhulpoor prevented many of the bad effects".[42] About the town of Sambalpur he stated he had found the town in great confusion, on account of the state of the government ever since the death of the late Rajah".[43] The lawlessness of Sambalpur is further reflected thus. "In a country thus torn by dissentions, I had little prospect of doing any business, but the rains being set in, I could not return by land, nor could I get boats to transport me by water; so that I was obliged to sit down as contented as I could".[44] This lawlessness and tyranny existing in the state government in the country of Sambalpur was highlighted, which the imperial administration took advantage of and could plan for the extension of the British dominion in this part of India. Describing the people of this country Motte stated, "The natives in general are very abstenious, eating only once in twenty four hours, and that in the evening. Their meal is then two pounds of rice; and they keep the water in which it has been boiled drinking the next day; raw water being apt to give them a flux. The men are low in stature, but well made, lazy, treacherous and cruel. But to these ill qualities of the tiger, the Almighty has also, in his mercy added the cowardice of that animal; for had they an insensibility of danger equal to their inclination for mischief, the rest of mankind must unite to hunt them down. They profess themselves Hindus, but practice only that part of the religion which consists of external ceremonies".[45] The call for unity of the mankind for the destruction of the mischiefs, treachery and barbarity of the people of this land was obviously directed towards the imperial interventions which may be characterized more or less predestined and as closely related to the idea of progress. On many occasions Motte's actions were found to have the expressions of imperial arrogance, which led him to take recourse to retributive measures in order to establish his superiority over the natives. "I was a good deal surprised the next day to find that a proclamation was issued, that no person should supply me or my people with any provisions, nor have any conversation with us. This was a whimsical order; to be sure however I put as good a face on it as I could, and acquainted the Dewan by message, that my sepoys would bear anything but starving; that if his subjects refused to take their money for provisions, I could not prevent their taking them by force. This matter was decided like most other critical situations, by a circumstance which had nothing to do with it. Akber wanting a sum of money for other purposes, withdrew the prohibition and sent me a few more diamonds the price of which we settled, and for which I paid him, having sent for the money from Cuttack".[46] The British perception of their superiority of their military is also explicitly clear from Motte's description of his sepoys as properly trained and forming a "respectable body on parade".[47] These assertions unquestionably are based on the imperial logic that the British empire was essentially based on force and it had to be maintained if necessary by brute force.

Motte had contemplated the people of this land as barbarians and treacherous and stupid as well. In order to make his passage free from any hurdles and also to carry the imperial objectives in its right direction, Motte wanted to win the confidence of the people. "Having now no European with me, I wished to leave a place where I was likely to do no business; but the rain prevented me. I found the people of the country tampered with my sepoys and prevailed on one of them to desert. Conscious I was in their power, I thought it best to put a confidence in them. I paid them to the end of July; then mustering all my eloquence, I contrasted to them the horrors of the country we were in, with the charms of that we had left; and told them the only chance of ever seeing that dear country again, rested on their adherence to me; that I should conduct them thither as soon as the season would permit. They were struck with my frankness, unanimously declared a perfect confidence in me, and not a man deserted afterwards".[48]

The treacheries and barbarities of the people of western Orissa is also found to have been mentioned towards the last part of the travellogue. During Motte's conversation with Bowanee Pundit, (Bhawani Pandit) the Governor of Orissa posted in Cuttack came to Cuttack while he during his return journey from Sambalpur to Calcutta. Here he had the opportunity of visiting a Maratha Camp. The description of the Camp had also the imperial tinge in it "Oct 19, I reached Cuttack this day and found that Bowanee Pundit, having taken the field against Sehoo Butt was encamped three miles from the town. He sent to pay his compliments and desired to see me the next day.

I went early to the Maratha camp, which I found very unlike to an eastern one, even inferior to an English camp in India, in point of luxury; the tents were very small and low, save that in which the hall of audience was held; the bazaar contained only necessaries, and the baggage bullocks are very few in number. I found Bowanee Pundit looking at his horses, which were picketed in the open air. This he told me was the first morning duty of a Maratha. We walked to the tent of audience, where we sat together on the musnad. His conversation was lively, no more resembling that of the Mughal I had been accustomed to in Bengal, than the liveliness of a Frenchman does the solemnity of the Spaniard. Perhaps the natives think it necessary to keep up that affected gravity, that they may be better on their guard in the presence of their masters. He congratulated me on the escape I had in passing through such villainous countries, and repeated many stories of the treachery of the Rajahs".[49] Finally in the last paragraph, Motte had again referred to the perfidy of the people of Sambalpur. "I reached Balasore the 28th (October), crossed the Shoobunreeka the 2nd November enjoyed at having once more set afoot on English ground. I now contemplate that after so perilous a journey I had carried no one point I wished; but having resided during the most unwholesome season among a perfidious people, thought myself happy in having escaped with my life. The opening of the diamond trade was prevented by the indolence of the inhabitants and by their wretched dependence on the Marathas".[50] The description of the areas from Balasore onwards in the north as English ground has the clear cut imperial sensibility in it.

Another most important observation made by Motte in regard to the state of the people and population was the depopulation of territories due to the anarchical conditions created as a result of Maratha mis-administration. This fact had been very frequently mentioned. The Mohur Bunge country (Mayurbhanj) which had extended from Neelgir hills to the sea was desolate because of the oppression of the tenants by the Marathas. Soro country was another depopulated country referred to in the work. "It appears by the ruins on the N.E. of the river at Shooroo that it was a considerable town: whereas all the houses are on the S.W. side; and indeed in my journey it will be unnecessary to say that any place I came to was once considerable, since all the places which were not so, are now depopulated by the Manhattans, and such alone remain as on account of their bulk are longer in decaying".[51] The City of Barrack was another important example of such depopulation. "By this bridge I passed into the Tallook of Budruc, where I found deep marks of the Maratha claws on the fine tract of land, formerly well peopled, where a human creature is not now to be seen, except perhaps a solitary herdsman attending a large drove of buffaloes or other horned cattle.

From this part of Orissa come all that people improperly called by the English Ballasore bearers, a circumstance, which contributes in some measures to the de-population of the country. Seven thousand of the stoutest young fellows go into Bengal and are employed as chairmen, leaving their families behind. Now although this people stretch the Levitical law so that a brother not only raises up seed to another after his decease, but even during his absence on service, so that no married woman lies fallow; and although very few of those who go to Bengal settle there, yet as they all return with some money, and with hands softened by the luxury of Calcutta, they rather chuse (choose) to loiter after an herd of cattle, than to apply to the labour of the plough, and a tract of land to supply that herdsman with pasture, would be sufficient to support thirty families, if applied to the purposes of agriculture".[52]

The luxury of Calcutta referred to above obviously point to luxury according to European standards. The fascinations of the Balasore youths towards the Calcutta luxury were due to the western mode of life developed in Calcutta by the British imperialists. In postering such a life style, the British being guided by the imperial psychology, wanted to create a European environment, situation and markets in order to live in a state completely different from Indian situations. The Arakhpur village (Arrucpur) was described as formerly a village, which was destroyed by the Marathas on account of a riot. "The plains continue to the Hurreepoor (Haripur) river, overgrown with long coarse grass, such as is usual in marshes. Crossing this river came to Arrucpoor, which was formerly a village, but being destroyed by the Marathas on account of a riot, a good Hindu beggar, built two sheds for the reception of travellers, to which the inhabitants of the neighbouring villages bring provisions for sale, in proportion to the number of persons who halt there".[53] The countries situated about miles afterwards from Collo (Kantilo) was found sparsely populated. The reasons of citing the examples of de-populated lands was essentially to highlight the anarchical conditions existing in the country sides of Orissa due to the exploitation of Maratha sardars and the general apathy of the Maratha authorities. This necessitated the extension of British dominion to this part of the country, by which civilised administration could be made available to the people.

Motte had been deputed to Orissa by the East India Company to initiate political negotiations with the Maratha authority for the transfer of Orissa to the British. On Motte's presentation of Clive's letters to Bhawani Pandit, the Subahdar of Cuttack, the latter reminded Motte of the just demand of Janoji Bhonsla on the East India Company for the arrears of tribute due from Bengal and Bihar. But Motte's suggestion to Janoji was that he should give up Orissa to the Company on payment of a stipulated sum. It was further added that the Company was prepared to send a British resident to the Court of Nagpur as hostage in case an agreement on terms set by the Company was arrived at between the two. While Motte was returning from Sambalpur he met Bhawani Pandit for the second time and reminded him and further reasserted that the best means of forming a closer connection with Clive would be "to cede to him the Province of Orissa for a stipulated annual sum". To this Bhawani Pandit agreed and assured him to transmit the message to Janoji.[54]

Clive's policy of negotiations in order to get possession of Orissa met only with failures. Clive's successor as Governor-General, Verelst, also continued the same policy for almost three years and finally he came to the conclusion and declared that Janoji "has studiously avoided any declaration of his sentiments".[55]

After the death of Janoji Bhonsla in 1772, the situations in the Nagpur kingdom took a different turn and internal dissensions became very frequent. With the arrival of Warren Hastings as Governor-General in 1774, a bolder policy for the consolidation of the British empire brought fruitful results in favour of the empire. His diplomatic monouvres brought tremendous success and he succeeded in bringing Madhoji Bhonsla, the Rājā of Nagpur, into close alliance with the British during the First Maratha War. As per the terms of alliance the British troops under the command of Col. Pearse were permitted to march through Orissa. Still then Warren Hastings failed to get possession of Orissa from the Marathas.

Warren Hastings departed from India in 1785. Thereafter Madhoji, the weak and timid ruler of Nagpur, came under the influence of the Poona Court. And thereby the obsolete Maratha claim of 'chauth' over Bengal.[56] Lord Cornwallis was not prepared to accept such a claim. But he was aware of the necessity of conciliating Madhoji, because in case of a war in the south the British troops might be sent quickly from Bengal to Madras through Orissa alone. So towards the close of 1787, Lord Cornwallis deputed George Forster, a civil servant on the Madras establishment, to Nagpur in order to mobilise Madhoji for a defensive alliance with the British. After carefully assessing the strength of Nagpur, Forster came to the conclusion that Nagpur should not be considered as a power to be reckoned with. Therefore, Cornwallis asserted that "no advantage would be obtained from a connection with that government and so far from becoming formidable to the Company, it would always be to the interest of the Bhonsla to avoid giving them the slightest offence, as the Province of Cuttack which belonged to him could from its situation be seized and possessed at anytime with the utmost facility by the Company's troops of the Bengal establishment". Accordingly Foster was ordered to return to Calcutta.[57]

Madhoji died on May 9,1788 and was succeeded by Raghuji II. Then the long expected war between the English and Tipu Sultan broke out in December 1789. Under compelling circumstances, Cornwallis deputed Forster once again to Nagpur in March 1790 to enlist the support of the Bhonsla rājā. Raghuji II agreed to render his assistance to the British in their cause and also permitted their troops to march through Orissa. Proper attention was paid and adequate facilities were provided to the British troops under the command of Col Cockrell when they passed from Bengal to Madras through Orissa.[58]

From Cilve to Cornwallis although the Company endeavoured in the peaceful possession of Orissa, it had failed. It was finally left for Lord Wellesley to conquer Orissa during the second Maratha War. The British annexation of Orissa in 1803 was an easy task for two reasons. First the Rājā of Nagpur did not have adequate forces to offer resistance to the invading British army and, in fact, only feeble resistance was offered in the time of occupation. Secondly, the British army had earned a sound knowledge of the topography of Orissa during their march through the territory on two previous occasions under the command of Col. Pearse in 1781 and Col. Cockrell in 1790. The preparation of the Rennell's map of 1788 also helped the movement of British troops in Orissa in making it much easier. In 1803, they took only one month i.e., from September 14, 1803 to October 14, 1803 to occupy the Province.[59] In the imperial psyche, the expansion of British rule in India was always presented as a spectacular march of civilization. The ears of "prostrate population" were always drummed with the notions that British diplomacy and arms desired justice. In imperial literature British rule always meant law and British force always signified the protection of the weak against a barbarous bully.[60] The British negotiations with the Maratha overlords from 1765 to 1803 for the transfer of Orissa and its final occupation in 1803 was a clear demonstration of the noble and national commitment of the British for the diffusion of order amid anarchy and of universal law in the midst of chaos.

The Treaty of Deogaon was concluded on December 17, 1803 by which Raghuji Bhonsla ceded to the British East India Company in perpertual sovereignity the Province of Cuttack, including, the Port and District of Balasore. Soon after the occupation of Cuttack negotiations were initiated with the feudatories of the Bhonsla Rājā and they were asked to accept the overlordship of the East India Company. Some of them agreed to the British terms and treaties were concluded accordingly. Raghuji also agreed to confirm all these treaties signed between the feudatories and the East India Company. The total number of such feudatories or "*Garjats*" which came under the control of the British were sixteen in number and they were generally known as the Tributary Mahals of Orissa. Two other "*Mahals*" were also added subsequently to the number in 1837.

The Orissa of the East India Company comprised the three districts of Balasore, Cuttack and Puri on the sea-coast of eighteen tributary Mahals in the hill regions to the West. The Tributary Mahals, however, were outside the purview of the British laws and regulations. Thus only the three districts in the coastal region were under the direct administration of the British government.

These three districts were ordinarily known as the province of Cuttack or "the Zillah of Cuttack. "Orissa", which was administered by the British authorities from Cuttack roughly corresponded to these 'areas'. As the Presidency of Bengal included the Orissa province, so quite obviously the Government of Bengal formed policies, supervised the administrative affairs and exercised control over the officers in Orissa. There was no separate secretariat establishment of the Government of Bengal till 1843; the Government of Bengal was then supervising the general administration of India. It was only in 1843 that Lord Ellenborough completely separated the administration of Bengal froms.[61] It is not possible to ascertain accurately the population of British Orissa under the East India Company. John Richardson in 1815 made a conjectural estimate, put the number as 1,462,500 which include Mughalbandi population of 11,25,000 and Garjat population of 3,37,500.[62] In 1847 the settlement officers calculated the population of the District of Cuttack as 1,018,979 and that of Balasore and Puri as 500,000 and 473947 respectively. Thus the population of Orissa excluding the tributary Mahals was about 2,000,000.[63] By 1870 the total population of the three districts and of the eighteen tributary Mahals of Orissa was known to be 3,280,547.[64]

The establishment of the British rule in Bengal in 1757, and the legalization of British proprietorship over it through the grant of Dewani rights in 1765 led the information industry of the Raj in developing and fostering an opprobrious perception of India. The administrators, politicians and the specialists such as historians started exposing the heterogeneous realities of the country, its people, its religions, castes, customs, languages and the fantastic variety of its natural surroundings. This remained the most earnest attempt of the civil servants in claiming for the Raj complete moral and unimpaired ascendancy. They were also successful in mobilizing an overwhelming majority of the Indian people to commit themselves to an uninterrupted continuity of the British rule. It was also much vaunted that the so-called problems of self-determination was arranged and manipulated by a clamorous minority unconcerned about the interests of the inarticulate masses. The basic aim and intent of the administrators, writers, historians, intellectuals and missionaries had remained in locating and scrutinizing the unseemly Hindu practices and in demolishing their implicit social hegemony. In this process, there was the definite attempt at confirming the intellectual superiority and righteous authority of the western civilization and in strengthening the base of the ideological edifice of imperialism. The extension of British suzerainty and the conquest of Orissa in 1803 carried with it the vestiges of imperialism and imperial demeanours and glamour of the Raj left its imprints in the pages of Orissan History. The appropriation and treatment of Orissa's past and history by the British historians remained a part of British imperial/colonial exercise of writing it up as a portion of the "British history". "Of course it is duly recognized that South Asian history of the period between Plassey and Partition continues to be taught, written and otherwise propagated there for the most part as a 'portion of the British history' in accordance with the agenda formulated by James Mill".[65] The vast amount of literature produced during the entire period of British colonialism in Bengal, Orissa and India include not only historical literature, but also administrative reports and correspondences, official orders, statutory official records of 19th and 20th century, the survey reports prepared by the British tourists, geographers, archaeologists, surveyors, etc. All these writings provide information about the knowledge, techniques and attitudes of the British Raj, which informed and sustained the Raj for two hundred years.

(B)

EARLY HISTORIANS : FIRST HALF OF NINETEENTH CENTURY

In the latter half of the eighteenth century the British began to put together their Raj for consolidation. In the process they had to devise and develop a vision at once of India's past and of its future. This vision or perception was necessary not only to shape a coherent administrative system but also to justify their rule to themselves. With the able leadership and powerful ideologies provided by powerful personalities like Warren Hastings, Lord Cornwallis, Edmund Burke and Thomas Munro, the British would begin by 1800 to develop the vision and lay out the principles for the empire that was to become the most extensive and vast since that of Rome. In the early years of their rule in India, the British thought it esssential to develop a perception about India, so that their role in India could be determined. Intellectual exercises of the protagonists of the Raj while developing a perception of India had never been informed with any single and coherent set of ideas. However behind the British vision of India, there had always been an enduring tension between two ideals, one of similarity and the other of difference, which in turn shaped differing strategies of governance of the Raj. "At sometimes and for some purposes, the British conceived of the Indians as people like themselves or as people who could be transformed into something resembling a facsimile of themselves; while at other times they emphasized what they believed to be enduring qualities of Indian difference. Sometimes, indeed, they simultaneously accommodated both the views in their thinking, making it periiously difficult to discern an larger system at all".[66] In generating, fostering and furthering such visions of the Raj, the British had choosen different platforms, where the imperial chanson de geste could be relentlessly chanted. The process of writing down the antiquity of India's past, which started during the last two decades of 18th century was considered as the most important package in developing its own visions of the Raj in India and in providing India a suitable place in the whole of the British empire. The whole exercise was an attempt at studying and analyzing the anatomy of the Raj, so that the vision could be properly structured.

The oriental scholars of Warren Hastings time began the task of unearthing the antiquity of India's past. "It was during Hastings time that the Englishmen from being 'alien forebooters longing to return home shouldering their bag of riches', changed gradually into administrators responsible for the well being of the people.[67] Warren Hastings had been depicted as having designs on strengthening the British hold on India through the study of the laws and languages of the natives. Hastings did neither find the need nor saw the desirability of importing English laws and customs and burdening the people of

India with them. He specially enjoined that "in all suits regarding inheritance, marriage, caste and other religious usages and institutions, the laws of the Koran with respect to Mohammedans and those of the chaster with respect to gentoos shall be invariably adhered to; on all such occasions the Moulvies or Brahmins shall respectively attend to expound the law, and they shall sign the report and assist in passing the decree".

Warren Hastings encouraged Nathaniel Halhed to compile *"A Code of Gentoo Laws"* (1776). It was merely an extension of the same policy. When he found that the Moulavies and Pundits sitting in Court took advantage of their[67]exclusive knowledge and very often misled the English judge for monetary considerations, he realized the need for English judges to know the laws of the land at first hand.

So Hastings decided to get the Indian laws studied and ancient texts compiled and translated. But unfortunately this led later historians to conclude that his "encouragement of Oriental studies had a practical side" and that "in British India Warren Hastings was encouraging the study of Sanskrit for purely utilitarian reasons". These historians did not simply bother to consider that Hastings, though Governor General of India, had to please the court of Directors thousands of miles away, their nominees, the members of the supreme council, which had a fair share of Hastings enemies. The court of directors consisted of businessmen and their only interest lay in making their profits swell. Hastings knew his limitations as well. While he recommended the publication of Wilkins translation of the *Bhagavad-Gita* by the Court of Directors, at the same time he wrote to Nathaniel Smith the Chairman of the East India Company in 1784 by stating that "every accumulation of knowledge and especially such as is obtained by social communications with people over whom we exercise a dominion founded on the right of conquest is useful to the state... it attracts and conciliates distant affections; it lessens the weight of the chain by which the natives are held in subjection, and it imprints on the hearts of our own countrymen the sense and obligations of benevolence".[68] This letter testifies not only to Hastings awareness of the pragmatic value of the promotion of Oriental studies, but also his love of such studies for their own sake. Here Hastings represented the new approach to colonialism. These contemporary scholars who took up Indian studies were products of the age of enlightenment in Europe and especially in England.[68] The preliminary exercises in colonialist historiography abetted directly in laying the foundations of the Raj. During the last three decades of the eighteenth century beginning with the governor-generalship of Warren Hastings, all of the contending parties within the company's administration involved themselves in the mobilization of India's past. The intricacies of proprietorship and the relationship of property to empire remained the basic issue while reconstructing the history of the subject population. This particular problem led to the growth of controversies between Hastings and Fransis in the 1770s, between Grant and Shore in 1780s, between Shore and Cornwallis in 1788-92 on the eve of the permanent settlement. As the British rule in the sub continent was set up eventually as a rule of property, so the general outcome of such attempts at appropriation of India's past was to provide legal and administrative support for those measures. With the passage of time and growth of the British colonial state, there started a more mature and sophisticated discourse on historiography in order to reinforce its apparatus of ideological control and develop the vision of the empire. The history of India was made to accommodate not just the existence of the Raj, but also a course of historical development that made the imposition of British rule its necessary culmination. The Victorians investigated and recorded India's past in accordance with the scientific system of "knowing". They wrote upon India's past in a vast corpus, which worked by many hands during the seventy years between Mill's *"History of British India* (1812) and Hunter's *"Indian Empire"* (1881). All these constituted an entirely new kind of knowledge. "A colonialist knowledge, its function was to erect that past as a pedestal on which the triumphs and glories of the colonizers and their instrument, the colonial state, could be displayed to great advantage. Indian History assimilated thereby to the history of Great Britain would henceforth be used as a comprehensive measure of difference between the peoples of these two countries".[69] The Victorian science like its historicism necessarily and consciously fitted India into a hierarchical relationship with Europe and provided the firm footing of legitimacy which the British sought for their Raj. The appropriation of the past by conquest led to rebounding upon the conquerors. It ended in sacralizing the past for the subject people and encouraged them to use it in their consistent effort to redefine and affirm their own identity. The appropriated past thus served as the sign not only for the colonizers but ironically for the colonized as well. The colonized Indians in their turn had reconstructed their past for purposes opposed to those of their rulers and made it the ground for making out their differences in cultural and political terms. Thus, history became a game for two to play as the alien colonialist project of appropriation was clearly matched by an indigenous nationalist project of counter appropriation.

Because of the unending and indecisive battle in which the two had been locked, the process of recovering its rich and lengthy history was inevitably long drawn out. However, the antiquity of India's past continued to be brought to light by the Oriental scholars since Warren Hastings time. Such men as Jones, Halhed and Colebrooke undertook the path-breaking studies of the Sanskrit language in the 1780s and 1790s. These were followed by exciting new discoveries in the first decade of the nineteenth century. Among the important findings were the decipherment of the Brahmi script, which revealed the existence of the Mauryan dynasty and Ashokan era during 3rd Century B.C., the discovery of the Gandhara Art in the northwest which culturally tied India with Greece, and the translation of Fahien's account of his tour in the fifth century A.D. which[69] together with the discovery of the Ajanta caves in 1819 provided ample evidences to reach at the historical depth to the Gupta empire and the Buddhist experience in India. Although much remained unknown along with the existence of the Harappan civilisation, by the middle of the nineteenth century the broad parameters and major outlines of India's history had been thoroughly established. The British had now come in direct confrontation with the fabulously rich Indian history and antiquity. So, they could not simply dismiss India as a land of changeless villages and feudal principalities. In order to make India subservient to the needs of the Raj, its extended past had at once to be explained. The British tried to assert their own superiority, as James and J.S.Mill had done by referring to the values such as individualism and liberty deeply embedded in European culture. The palpability of the British superiority was asserted by citing evidences from their technological prowess. Technology was taken as an appropriate measure for judging the worth of cultures. This could be seen as marking out differing levels of achievement between Britain and India. In the course of explaining India's history, there was the sole purpose of assessing systematically the similarities and differences of the Indians and the British. In this process, there were discourses about the common origin of the Indians and the British through the Aryan racial theory. But this suffered troubling difficulties. A number of questions were raised on this matter. When the Indians and the British shared common origins, then how could the Indian be treated inferior to the British? Besides, in this situation, how could the British rule over the Indians be justified? Further debates on the issue led to the finding of the answers in the evolutionary theory. There were assertions that, "while the European Branch of the Aryan peoples triumphed over those of other races, those who went to India," as the amateur ethnologist and civil servant George Campbell wrote "lost their purity of race" by intermingling with the aboriginal races, and by the innate decay of enervation by the climate". [70] This theory of Aryan decline in India was of course fully dependent upon the characterization given to India's non-Aryan peoples. But in reality India's Aryan institutions remained as powerful at the end of India's historical development as at its beginning. The modern Hindoos were in fact taken as a whole a mixed race like the Europeans with much of the same varieties of features that are found in Europe. For the racial theorists the Turanians or the Dravidians who stood opposed in everyway to the Aryans by isolating themselves in the jungles and hills of the south had preserved their nationality pure and unmixed. The rise of Buddhism reflected the opposition of these depressed classes against the Aryans. The Buddhist era provided the perfect milieu to mark out India's greatness. Buddhism provided a rationalistic faith in opposition. Superstition and priestly despotism of Hinduism, has been vehemently disparaged by the victorians. The British who had defined Indians as racially inferior had created a religion and an art, which represented the apex of India's cultural development. The Gandhara School of Buddhist art, which had incorporated western classical forms, pointed to the superiority of European art forms. The discovery of Bactrian coins, the superiority of the Gandhara sculpture over that of Mathura and Central India, and finally the brief invasion of Alexander the Great in 326 B.C., which has been described as the climactic moment of ancient India's history, provided ample opportunity to scholars like Alexander Cunningham and Vincent Smith to conclude that the finest Indian works were produced with inspiration derived from Greece.

It was with the decay of Buddhism and training of the Greek influence following the fall of the Bactrian Kingdoms, the Aryans drifted themselves mixed [70] with the indigenous people and reasserted their dominance. They adopted the absurd fables and monstrous superstitions of the Turanians, who had till then remained opposed to the Aryans in every way. As a result the purer religion of India was degraded into the monstrous system of idolatry. Although the contemporary Hinduism stood on the pedestal of ritual orthodoxy and usage, still then the 'genius' of the Aryan race remained outside its influence. Both Fergusson and Maine insisted that the influence of the Aryan "intellect" remained powerfully impressed on every institution of the country. Nevertheless, the racial history of India made it a fundamentally different place from Britain.

India's downward trajectory was also clearly visible in art and architecture. The later buildings were described not only as degraded but also barbarous and vulgar. India's architecture lacked universally valid aesthetics shaped by certain principles of balance and proportion. This would suffice to state that "the lessons of science and of history were the same, temples that housed the deities of a "degraded" faith were not surprisingly constructed according to false principles, while the use of a false architectural design testified to the existence of a degraded civilization.[71] The creative spirit of Indian art that had flourished in the era of India's archaic beginning was more or less stifled by Turanian influence. As a result the nobler, lovelier forms of flowers and trees inherent in the Aryan love and worship of nature were discarded and replaced by a meaningless elaboration of forms. So neither India's art nor the larger culture in which it was embedded could be allowed to challenge Britains and Europe's predominance.[71] British perceptions in this historiography were that the spiral of India's decline could be halted only by an intervention either from without or outside. The set of invaders who conquered India during various periods of its history included the Greeks, the Scythians, Arabs and the Mughals. But none of the invaders could keep themselves aloof from India's peoples and its institutions and in due course of time they got themselves absorbed in indigenous population. As a result of this their physique degenerated, their individuality vanished, their energy sapped and their dominion passed from their hands into those of more vigorous successors. The

Marathas, who had emerged from within India were known for their individuality of character and tenacity of purpose. The British thought that they inherited these characteristics from their Scythian ancestors. Although India declined from its ancient Aryan glory, yet as viewed by the late Victorians, all elements of its culture did not degrade simultaneously. India kept alive its crafts, as its villages, cherished values of a shared past. Fergusson argued that India's architecture was a living art practised on the principles, which caused its wonderful development in Europe in the twelfth and thirteenth centuries. James Morris opined that India's art works were founded on the truest and most natural principles. In general, however, art and architecture had always been expressed as "barbarism of a debased land." The British colonial historians and protagonists while writing down the pages of Indian history had always tried to ignore the contradictions within the ideologies of the race and language. The similarities demanded by the Aryan theory had somehow been accommodated. But the differences were accentuated. All these were essential for them to ensure a space in India for the Raj. It is against this background in which India's past had been treated by British colonialists that the history of Orissa needs to be studied. It is to see whether the broad parameters of British historiography fits well into the structures of Orissan history and culture. The way the political and dynastic history of Orissa and intrinsic cultural traits had been studied and articulated by the Victorians and late Victorians needs to be analyzed here. As a product of the age of enlightenment in Europe and especially in England, Andrew Stirling when he arrived in Orissa began immediately the task of unearthing Orissan past. He had an official assignment with the British imperial administration. With his continuous stay in India he gradually evinced some interest in historical researches which was necessary to course in view of the larger Victorian project of seeking rational principles to fit everything they saw in the world around them into ordered hierarchies. Beginning with the mercantilist historiography of Alexander Dow, Verelst, Bolts, Scrafton, Grant, etc. in the effort to educate Indians in liberal views during the five decades following the Battle of Plassey of 1757 to the colonialist historiography of Mill's generations, there had always been consistent efforts both in the regional and national level the ulterior motive to justify the British rule in India. It would be really unjust to club Andrew Stirling either among the Mercantilist or among the colonialist or magisterial historians. Andrew Stirling had pioneered the study of the history of Orissa and appropriation of its long past. He was confronted with serious problems in regard to factual presentation and interpretation. He was never critical of the political and administrative history of Orissa due to certain limitations. His limitations were not because of his imperialist approach of the line of Mill and Smith, but that he was a primer in the methods of professional historical research and that when he began writing the history of Orissa, the sources were scant. Indeed Stirling was critical of Mill's approach towards India's history and pointed out that Mill's observation on Hindu history does not hold good with regard to Orissa. Mills observations go like this: "whilst we receive accounts the most precise and confident regarding the times of remote antiquity, not a name of a prince in after ages is presented in Hindu records. A great prince named Vikramaditya is said to have extended widely his conquests and dominion and to have reigned at Magadha, 396 years after Chandrabija. From that time even fiction is silent. We have no more of the Hindus and their transactions till the era of Mohammadan conquest; when the Persians alone become our instructors".[72] The writings called classical indeed take no further than the period indicated in the above passage. Andrew Stirling had tremendous confidence that Orissa would provide sufficient literary texts to be accounted for as historical source materials. But he had little access to archaeological sources and his accounts were mostly traditional. Before going deeply into Orissan history and historiography at the very outset Stirling concluded that Orissa did not have sufficient source materials for writing down the history of Orissa. Approaching the sources on Orissan history, Andrew Stirling wrote, "The earlier histories of the country are of the legendary or fabulous class, copied from the purāṇās but embellished or disfigured by a plentiful admixture of local traditions. Their later annals assume an air of authenticity about the date of the family called Kesari Vaṁśa, 473 A.D. (This date is not accepted by sober history) prior to which the accounts are so replete with falsehoods, contradictions, inconsistency and anachronism as to be equally unintelligible and unworthy of notice. The memory of a few great names and events only has been preserved up to the fourth and fifth centuries of the Christian era and to adapt these to their favourite system of chronology the Brahmins who will never admit want of information on any subject, have been obliged to give an expansion to the reigns of their traditionary rājās, in some cases of five or six[72] hundred years and in all far beyond the natural or possible turn of human life. As however it will not be uninteresting to those curious in researches into Hindu antiquity to learn the traditions of the natives of this district in the earlier ages. I shall begin my sketch of the contents of their annals from the remotest period to which they profess to go back".[73] Stirlings comments on the Brahmins speak about his ignorance about a form of Vedic literature called as Śruti literature. Śruti is the most popular kind of oral literature prevalent during ancient times, when information and knowledge about events and chronologies of history are carried from one generation to the other through remembrance. The Brahmins being the repertoire of knowledge throughout the course of Indian history down to modern times is never new to Indian history. So Stirling's comments may better be termed as unwarranted and superfluous. Stirling had the feeling that despite all interpolations, the Hindus of Orissa have left documentary evidences as proof of their historical past. These documents provide very interesting information and make the reading interesting also. Stirling had used all the literary source materials available to him from all corners. He had also tried to classify the sources and attempted at critically assessing them and utilize them for writing down the pages of Orissan history. "The sources from which my information has been chiefly derived are, a work in Sanskrit called Vaṁśāvalī, belonging to a learned Brahmin of Puri, said to have been originally composed by some of his ancestors, three or four centuries back and continued down in the family to the present date. The chapter of the Madāla Pañjī or records preserved in the Temple of Jagannath called 'Raj Charitra' or 'Annals of Kings' in the Uria language, which records are stated to have been commenced upon more than six centuries back and to have been since regularly kept up. Another Vaṁśāvalī or genealogy written in Sanskrit on leaves of the palmyra tree, procured from a Brahmin living in the family of the Rājā Puttia Sarenggarh, one of the branches of the royal house of Orissa. Less certain and trustworthy guides than the above are to be met within numerous Genealogies, or Bansabali Pothis, as they are vulgarly termed, possessed by nearly every Pañjia or Almanac maker in the province. They in general abound with errors and inconsistencies, but occasionally a few facts or illustrations may be gleaned from them"[74]. The description of Bansabali Pothis (Geneologies) or family records as vulgar sounds really unconvincing and funny. There is the clearest imperial tinge in it. Stirling's preconceived notion of lack of historical sense among the Oriyas might have led him to draw such conclusions. Andrew Stirling thus mainly depended on "Madāla Pañjī" for his account of Orissan history. The historical trustworthiness of this Pañjī had remained a debatable question among the historians of Orissa over a long period of time. In view of the doubtful credibility of the account the historical limitations of Stirling's work can pretty well be surmised.

Stirling who had been elected as a member of the Asiatic Society of Bengal in 1822 communicated and presented a copy of his work *"Account Geographical, Statistical and Historical of Orissa Proper or Cuttack"* in the first meeting of the Society held on 8th March,1823. Stirling's Account of Orissa is the first comprehensive study of the state; he described its physical features; giving details of the soil, products rivers and towns and also dwelt on the population, the castes and customs, political institutions and the land tenure system. His account of the history and antiquities of Orissa is of great interest to us. As far as the political history of Orissa is concerned, Stirling had dealt with the Gajapati rule in Orissa at length with a lot of elaborations from the *Madāla Pañjī*. He had also discussed to some extent the Maratha administration in Orissa till the British occupation of Orissa in 1803. Utilising the evidences from *Madāla Pañjī* he had tried to draw the history of Orissa from Kali age. Stirling was very much interested to draw a complete chronology of Orissa. So he attempted at filling the gaps if occurred at any point with genealogies traced from local traditions with, personalities borrowed from purāṇās or from local traditions. In the absence of historical data, Stirling had to draw on myths and legends; the heroes of the *Mahabharata* all the heroes of Stirling's history and we have kings reigning for two, three, five and seven centuries. In this way he drew up a chronology beginning from Kali Yuga down to the fall of Vikramāditya in which he placed thirteen kings who are made to reign for the monstrous term of 3173 years. This conclusion of Stirling sounds ridiculous and superfluous. In the pre-Christian centuries preceding the reign of

Rājā Bhoja during the period from 180 B.C. to 53 B.C., Stirling referred to some Yavana invasion of Orissa. "In the reign of Hans or Hangsha Deo, the Yavanas again invade the country in great force from Cashmir and many bloody battles ensue. Respecting these Yavanas, who are so often mentioned in the legendary portion of Orissan history I should observe that the word in all the original Uria accounts is written Jaban and the Indians whom I have employed to translate both these and Sanskrit Vaṁśāvalīs, always render it Mogul who they really were, if they ever entered the country at all, may be plausibly guessed in some instances from their being said to come from Babul Des and Cashmir, by which the Hindus understand generally Persia, Afghanistan and part of Tartary. Nothing however can exceed the looseness and confusion of my authorities, in speaking of the countries and nations beyond their own immediate frontier. They often bring theYavana* from Delhi, by which appelation they seem to point to some great monarchy or monarchies lying to the northward and westward, of which they have preserved an indistinct notion, rather than to the particular city so named. Dr. Buchanan has remarked a similar degree of confusion on this same point in the historical recollections of the Brahmins of the southern countries of India. He observes (Vol.III page 113 chapter XV) "who were these Yavanas? The word properly signifies an European but as the Hindus speak with great confusion concerning the northern and western nations, it is often confounded with the Mlechhas and Turks, Arabs or Tartars and all these terms are frequently applied to the Mussalman"[75]. Stirling's open reverence of the Yavanas and his acceptance of Buchanan's equanimity of the Yavanas with the Europeans, speaks little of his botherance about the sentimentality of the Oriyas. In this observation, the Europeans alongwith the West Asians are projected as superior to the Indians. The imperial tinge is very much explicit in this explanation.

Stirling had referred to the invasion of Orissa by a Yavana named Rakta Vahu immediately after 318 A.D. and during the time of Subhan Deo. In this connection some wonderful and incomprehensible happenings had been reported. The king of Puri escaped from the town taking away the image of Puri in order to save the honour of the God being ravaged by the Yavan. "The Yavanas unable to understand how he had escaped then began to institute enquiries on the subject, when some of the low people of the coast informed them of the way in which their approach had been discovered. Enraged with the ocean for disclosing his secret, *The 10th Chapter of the Account classes 'Yuvanas' as one of the degraded races of Kshyatriyās or Hindus.[75] Rakta Bahu drew out his armies to chastise its waters. The sea on observing such formidable preparations, retreated for nearly a cos - the infatuated Yavanas rushed on... when the tide suddenly returning with tremendous noise and fury; swallowed up a great portion of army and inundated the whole country to a frightful extent. The flood reached inland as far as the Baronai Pahar of Khurda taking with it immense quantities of sand. It was at this time that the Chilka lake was formed by the eruption of the waters of the ocean".[76] These fictious descriptions reflect Stirling's account being the admixture of legends with history with no attempt at a critical assessment of the legends from the historiographical point of view. In connection with the above-said Yavana invasion, he surmised that the tradition he had described might have some connection with fierce religious disputes which raged between the worshippers of Brahma and Buddha about the period in which the invasion of foreigners and the flight of Jagannath are placed and which as is well known terminated in the expulsion of the latter from the continent of India".[77] These derivations have never been supported at any point of time either in Orissan history or Indian history by any other corroborative evidences. Stirling's assertion about the entire occurrence is nothing more than the work of imagination and the necessity of much learning and ingenuity required for unraveling the truth, which he did not possess, pointed definitely towards the fact that genuinely he was a true and sober historian as well.

Stirling's account of Orissan history had always remained a curious mixture of history, legends and traditions that certainly make interesting. He had discussed in greater detail the religion, antiquities temples and civil architecture of Orissa with all their minute details. He had the strong belief that Utkal desa had always remained a holy place. He stated that the temple of Jagannath is the symbol of harmonious relationship amongst all sects here.

It is always difficult to deduce any value judgements in his account excepting his analysis and ideas about the religious practices of Oriyas. While tracing the history of Orissa proper he made out certain conclusive dates for latter-day scholars to raise serious questions and ponder over authentic answers for a sober history of Orissa. Some of the important dates, which were fixed by him, are as follows. "Towards the close of his reign Rājā Jayati Kesari began building of Bhubaneswar".[78] Rājā Nrupa Kesari, a martial and ambitious prince, who was always fighting with his neighbours, is said to have planned a city on the site of the modern Cuttack about 989 AD.[79] "The reign of Markat Kesari was distinguished for the construction of stone rivetment or embankment faced with that material to protect the new capital from inundation in AD 1000".[80] The categorical reference by Stirling about the foundation of modern Cuttack in 989 AD have raised severe debates among the historians of modern Orissa in current times. This debate was culminated when some people in the frenzy of celebrating the millenium of the foundation of Cuttack city had taken for granted at its face value the date fixed by Andrew Stirling. Thus the Millenium celebration was organised in 1989 to which the President of India was brought as the Chief Guest. In fact Stirling had misconceived this reference in the "Raj Charita" of Madāla Pañjī" as 989 AD which otherwise on the exact reference of Madāla Pañjī should have been 989 Srahi. This 989 Srahi cannot conclusively be taken as 989 AD. The evidences furnished by *Madāla Pañjī,* Nagari Copper plate dated Saka year 1151 or 1229 AD and the archaeological discoveries undertaken by the Archaeological Survey of India in 1990s conclusively prove that the Cuttack city or Abhinava Baranasi Kataka was founded on the south bank of Mahanadi sometime during 1211 AD and 1229 AD. So the possibility of its having been founded by Nrupa Kesari should have been outrightly rejected. In a similar fashion there is nothing to show that the stone rivetment of the Kathjori was constructed early in the Kesari period. This rivetment which runs in a horse shoe pattern starting on the left bank of the Kathjori from near Khannagar and stretching westward up to Chahatghat of the Mahanadi and after that extending on the right bank of Mahanadi as far as Jobra ghat suggests that it was constructed at the bifurcation of the Kathjori from the Mahanadi and this bifurcation at the time of construction of this rivetment was not far away from Chahatghat. Since the time of the construction of this rivetment the Kathjori appears to have receded as far as the rock of Naraj. "Even as late as 1790 Kathjori was flowing off the Mahanadi at a place south of Dhavaleswar and Mr Lekei who crossed the river that year states that about two miles from Cuttack to the west at the foot of a Hindu temple the Cutjora separating itself from Mahanaddy flows to the southern side of the town".[81] All these facts taken into consideration cannot lead to the conclusion that this great engineering work may not be as old as the time of the Kuśān rule and it was possibly constructed sometimes after the foundation of Abhinava Baranasi Kataka by Anaṅgabhīmadeva III and at the time of its construction, the Kathjori was issuing from Mahanadi at Chahataghat.[82] But the editors of the two volumes of "*Cuttack: one thousand years*" published by Cuttack City Millenium Celebration Committee at the "Universe", Cuttack, despite being eminent historians in their own merit had to take a balanced view about this. They asserted that "there is divergence of opinions about the exact date of the foundation of the city. Yet a balanced consideration of the local traditions as well as the views of Stirling who based his conclusion on the Rājacharita of the Madāla Pañjī has led to the general acceptance of the date as 989 A.D.[83] Stirling had always been conscious and careful about the ethics meant for professional historians. Whenever and wherever Stirling failed to derive any conclusion out of the facts he had taken for consideration, he never concealed his inability. In one such example it is stated, "it appears unacceptable too why the sum of the revenues should be stated in gold when we know that the cowries always formed the principal currency of the district" he humbly admits his failure saying "as I am unable to furnish any satisfactory elucidation on these points, I must leave the statements as it stands, content with having presented a faithful translation".[84]

Stirling took an impartial stand while explaining the battles between the Gajapati rulers of Orissa and the Muslims of the south and as the facts of history went in favour of the rulers of Orissa, he acknowledged the boldness, valiance and enterprise of the Hindu Kings of Orissa against the Muslims who had been fierce against the Hindus throughout the medieval age. While describing the downfall or decline of Orissa during 16th Century he stated that the weakness, timidity and sexual indulgences of the kings and princes of Orissa are alluded to have been the major causes of decline. Describing about the rule of Mukund Harichandan the last Hindu rājā of Orissa, he stated, "All the native accounts concur in describing their last independent rājā as a man of courage and abilities. He has been honoured with a notice in the work of Jesuit Tieffenthaler, who extends our knowledge of his character by informing us that the last king of Orissans was called Mukund who was very polite to strangers and, had four hundred women. The early part of his reign was employed chiefly in constructing monuments of public utility or superstition as temples, tanks and brāhmanical śāsans".[85] In connection with Mughal arrangements for the management of the new Suba of Orissa by Mansingh, Stirling had referred to certain political theories related to the sovereignty of the countries. The general has always acknowledged the title of sovereignty, voice and feeling of the country, to vest in the Rājās of Khurda, though disputed formerly by the other branches of the royal house that have now sunk into entire insignificance. The former received by far the largest and most valuable portion of the country, in Mansingh's allotment and cession of Puri alone was a sufficient acknowledgement of these superior claims. Down to the present moment the Rājās of Khurda are the sole fountain of honour in this district and all deeds whatever drawn out in the Uria language bear the date of the Aṅk or accession of the reigning prince of that house, and one prefaced with a recital of his titles which run precisely in the style adopted many centuries ago by the great Rājā Anaṅg Bhima Deo".[86] These observations of Stirling very clearly display his liberal view of Indian history and historicist ideals of the Scottish enlightenment.

Coming back to the problems of decline of Orissa, Stirling's reiteration was that "the southern part of Orissa proper must have suffered much from the constant wars, insurrections and internal commotions, that prevailed during the early times of the Musselman government. The Mughals seem to have been actuated by a peculiar rancour and ill-will towards Jagannath and lost no opportunity of annoying and disturbing the Hindus in the performance of their devotions at the temple to say nothing of other fruitful sources of jealousy and animosity. This interference alone was sufficient to produce many bloody encounters between the two nations, in which the success was often doubtful. On the whole, however, the native princes suffered the most severely and gradually sank before the superior energy and civilization of the Mughals".[87] The Muslims were surely "Oriental despots" and they had a brilliant beginning. Despite conquest and rapine, the Mughal rulers discovered generous abilities and tastes, which made their courts centres not only of warfare but also of artistic patronage. They had been adhered to a rigorous monotheism that was no vain superstition, but a true religion and hence was deserving of respect. All these made the Mughals a developed and superior civilization. The situation, which made the discomfiture of the Mughals empire inevitable, was also found to have existed during the 16th century Orissa. Deducing conclusions from Stirling's account, this may well be stated that the anarchy that resulted during the sixteenth century, the Oriyas were left a leaderless multitude swaying to and fro with political storm, and clinging to any power, natural or supernatural that seemed likely to protect them. Concisely the Oriyas were scattered without a leader or protector, while the political system under which they had long lived was disappearing in complete disorganization.

Stirling's opinion on the Maratha administration was as follows. "The administration of the Marathas in Cuttack was, as in every other part of their foreign conquests, fatal to the welfare of the people and prosperity of the country, and exhibits a picture of misrule, anarchy, weakness, rapacity and violence combined, which makes one wonder how society can have been kept together under so calamitous a tyranny. All the head offices of the district as those of the Subahdar, Dewan, and the kiladarship of Fort Barabatti were openly bought and sold at Nagpore. It frequently happened that appointments were given to two or three persons at the same time and still often the individuals in charge refused to retire under various pretexts. The different claimants assembling their followers would fight most obstinate battles and lay waste the country with their dissensions before the right to succeed was settled. Pressed by the urgent irregular demands of the Court of Nagpore for remittances, and by the necessity of reimbursing themselves for the expenses incurred in obtaining office, the most ruinous shifts and expedients were perpetually resorted to, wring a higher revenue from the lands while their resources declined in proportion to the tyranny exercised over the cultivators. Not—withstanding that large military bodies were posted all over the district, the Marathas were quite unable to retain the Khandaits and their paiks in any sort of order".[88] This state of affairs was essentially due to the anarchical conditions prevailing in India after the decline of the Mughals. Of course each wave of conquerors, Greeks, Scythian,

Arab, Mughals that entered the country by land became more or less absorbed in indigenous population, their physique degenerated their individuality vanished, their energy was sapped, and dominion passed from their hands into those of more vigorous successors. "Even those warriors who seemed to emerge from within India, like the Marathas, could claim their individuality of character and tenacity of purpose only as part of an inheritance which had come to them from supposed Scythian ancestors".[89] The attempt of deducing conclusions about the origin of the Marathas from Scythian ancestors was a definite attempt by the British to connect the Marathas with Greek lineages and this was an expression of the synodromic behaviour of the Raj. Speaking well of his British mind in relation to this rule in India, he was obsessed with the liberal line of thinking and was sarcastically at pains to tolerate such a tyrannical rule. This was explicitly clear when he wrote, "As it would be impossible to render interesting to the general reader, the never-varying details of oppression, mismanagement and suffering displayed by the Maratha annals, I shall content myself in my account of this fourth stage of Orissan history with a brief enumeration of the successive subadars who obtained authority, as far as any can be made out amidst the perpetual conflicts for power which disturbed the peace of the country and with noticing a few events of general importance which mark that period".[90] On the whole Stirling's account of Orissa under the Muslim rule was more accurate. Especially the account of the Mughal period, which was based on *Ferishta's history* and the *Ain-i-Akbari* was highly objective and accurate. Similarly the account on the Marathas was based on solid truth.

Stirling's liberal thinking had its reflections on his explanation of the pilgrim tax. He believed that the realization of opulence of Indian temples and institutions of worship led the Muslims who initially resorted to the plunder of the temples in India, to change their attitude and impose pilgrim tax instead, which would bring them more revenue than plunder and destruction of these temples. In connection with bitter conflicts and severe contests between the kings of Puri and the Mughals, Stirling had referred to the imposition of pilgrim tax, which brought an end to the warfare. "This religious warfare was at last set at rest by the institution of the tax on pilgrims, which if we may credit the author of the work translated by Gladwin, under the title of *'History of Bengal'*, yielded to the Mughal government a revenue of nine lacs. Under such circumstances religious antipathies, however, strong on the part of the ruling power must have yielded gradually to the considerations of self-interest".[91] The consideration of self-interest is a clear indication of effeminacy and corruption inherent in eastern dynasties. In due course of time, the Muslims were subjected to such practices and, despite a brilliant beginning, the Muslim states of India sank into inevitable decay. Andrew Stirling's description of the car festival speaks of his myopic and shortsighted attitude towards the Hindu faith, which fits well into the structure of the imperial programmes of Britain. He had frequently described the image of Lord Jagannath as a monstrous 'idol' and as being hideous.[92] He did not even really care to know the significance of the ritual "Pahandi Bijay" of Sri Jagannath and described it as a cruel joke.[93] The description of the idols was highly derogatory and rude. "These celebrated idols are nothing more than wooden busts about six feet in height fashioned in to a rude resemblance of the human head resting on a sort of pedestal. They are painted white, yellow and black respectively with frightfully grim and distorted countenances and are decorated with a headdress of different coloured cloths shaped something like a helmet. The two brothers have arms projecting horizontally forward from the ears. The sister is entirely devoid of even that approximation to the human form".[94] He was highly critical of the whole car festival itself. "The joy and shouts of the crowd in their first movement, the cracking sound of the wheels as these ponderous machines roll along, the clatter of hundreds of harsh sounding instruments, and the general appearance of so immense a moving mass of human beings produce, it must be acknowledged an impressive, astounding and somewhat picturesque effect, whilst the novelty of the scene lasts, though the contemplation of it cannot fail of exciting the strongest sensations of pain and disgust in the mind of every Christian spectator".[95]

Stirling's description of the car festival indicates how cynical and misanthropic were the early British administrators and scholars in their attitude towards the religion and culture of India. He was never optimistic about the perpetuality and continuance of the festival to a later date in its present form. "Even the Gods own proper servants will not labour zealously and effectually without the interposition of authority and I imagine the ceremony would soon cease to be conducted on its present scale and footing, if the institution were left entirely to its fate and to its own resources by the officers of the British Government".[96] This observation and assessment was quite an immature one. The conclusion drawn by Stirling about the future of the car festival was proved wrong considering the fact that the car festival continued to be celebrated even today at Puri with the same magnitude and enthusiasm as it was two centuries back during the time of the historian.

Stirling's account of the *antiquities of Orissa* is quite interesting. He was the first writer after Abul-Fazl to have noticed and described the temple of Konark and he pointed out the errors in the latter's account. "Abul Fazl's quaint, but lively and picturesque, description of the temple of the Sun, is of course familiar to those who have perused the *Ain-i-Akbari* with attention. Although however it affords a good general idea of the character of the building, it is strangely inaccurate in respect to measurements no less than in the descriptions of the emblems and ornaments which embellish it".[97] Stirling had criticized the Hindu knowledge of architecture by stating that, "If the style of Black Pagoda betrays in the rude and clumsy expients apparent in its construction a primitive state of some of the arts, and a deficiency of architectural skill, at the period of its erection, one cannot but wonder at the ease with which the architects seem to have wielded and manages the cumbersome masses of iron and stone, used for the work, in an age when so little aids was to be derived from any mechanical inventions, and it must be allowed that there is an air of elegance combined with massiveness in the whole structure which entitles it to no small share of administration. There is much, however, about this remarkable building, which it is difficult either to describe or to comprehend".[98] About the sculptures of Konark he remarked, "Generally speaking the style and execution of larger figures are rude and coarse, while the smaller ones display often much beauty and grace, but it should be observed that the whole have suffered materially from the corrosion or decomposition of the stone of which building is chiefly composed viz., the coarse red granite of the province which is singularly liable to decay from exposure to the weather. The skill and labour of the best artists, seem to have been reserved for the finely polished slabs of chlorite, which line and decorate the outer faces of the door ways. The whole of the sculpture on those figures, comprising men and animals, foliage and arabesque patterns, is executed with a degree of taste, propriety and freedom, which would stand a comparison with some of our best specimens of Goethic architectural ornament. The workmanship remains too as perfect, as if it had just come from under the chisel of the sculptor, owing to the extreme hardness and durability of the stone".[99]

In these descriptions, one would observe both sides of approach to history. On the one side the general parameters of Raj syndrome, more especially the British perception of downward trajectory of Indian culture is evident. On the other there is also the touch of sober history and impartial treatment of culture and history from the point of view of sober historians.

While giving concluding remarks about the civil architecture, which includes the bridge architecture Stirling had adopted a clean-cut "Euro centric" approach. "...it is quite obvious from a consideration of their bridges style and architectural ornaments, that they are of pure Hindu origin, and belong to an age ignorant of the use of the arch. A short description of the Atharehnaleh bridge at Puri, will serve to illustrate sufficiently this part of the subject. It was built of a ferruginous coloured stone, probably the iron clay early in the fourteenth century by Rājā Kabir Narsinh Deo, the successor of Langora Narsinh Deo, who completed the Black Pagoda. The Hindus being ignorant of how to turn an arch substituted in lieu of it the method often adverted to above of laying horizontal tiers of stones on the piers, the one projecting slightly beyond the other in the manner of inverted stairs until they approach near enough at top to sustain a key stone or cross beam; a feature so remarkable in Hindu architecture, that it seems strange it should not have been hitherto particularly notice in any description of the antiquities of the country".[100]

In all these discussions Stirling was conscious of his British origin and the nature of colonial administration notwithstanding, exposed the superiority of the British over their Indian subjects. This was manifested not only on administration but also on art and architecture. Stirling was also the first to notice the caves and inscriptions of Khandagiri and Udaygiri which later revealed king Kharavela, history. Stirling could not decipher the inscription in the caves but he guessed correctly that "the character has some connection with the ancient Prakrit and that it resembled the inscriptions of Firuzshah at Delhi and a portion of the Allahabad pillar. According to centenary review, Stirling's remark though based on conjecture than sound evidence, come really much nearer the truth than he at that time would know".[101] Stirling had copied and published the inscriptions and contented also that many of the letters of the inscription resembled Greek characters. But this similarity drawn by him was purely accidental and actually the alphabet was related to the Sanskrit family.

Stirling had his own limitations as regards the sources available to him and his approach towards these. His association with the British imperialist administration in India had conditioned his attitude, which had restricted him in producing a sober history of Orissa. Still his contribution to the history of Orissa was significant. Moreover his was the pioneering work in the writing of the history of Orissa. Basing on local traditions, which considered the Gajapatis of Orissa as one of the four principal dynasties or races that ruled the country, Stirling had knowingly or unknowingly admitted the unified character of Indian civilisation even at the age of battles and empires. This alone does not suffice to club him closely among the hardline British imperialist historians on India, as far as the historiography of Orissa is concerned. Stirling's *"An Account, Statistics, Geographical and Historical of Orissa Proper or Cuttack"* gives the impression of a copy of the *Madāla Pañjī*. Stirling's efforts on writing history as a part time activity had rather popularised the *Madāla Pañjī* than producing a complete history of Orissa based on sufficient value judgments from the historiographical point of view. Modern Historiography of Orissa owes a lot to James Princep for the construction of Ancient Orissa. Although Princep had worked in close association with Mill in collecting the legends, Sanskrit texts, law texts for the purpose of constructing Indian history. Mill set himself the task of ascertaining India's true state in the scale of civilization. For Mill following Bentham, the criterion of utility was the measure of social progress. He stated, "Exactly in proportion as utility is the object of every pursuit, may we regard a nation as civilised". He scrutinized India's arts, manufacturers, literature, religion, and laws, and concluded while vigorously disputing William Jones claims that the Hindus did not possess and, never had possessed, a high state of civilisation. They were rather a rude people who had made but a few of the steps in the progress to civilisation. There existed in India, he wrote, a hideous state of society inferior even to that of the European feudal age. Bound down to despotism and to a system of priest-craft built upon the most enormous and tormenting superstition that ever harassed and degraded any portion of mankind, the Hindus had become most enslaved portion of the human race'. Mill had agreed with Jones that Hindu society had been stationary, for so long that 'in beholding the Hindus of many ages past and are carried back, as it were, into the deepest recesses of antiquity".[102] As far as visions of Princep is concerned in relation to Mill, the former worked throughout objectively in reproducing the history of India in its true, logical and scientific form. His endeavour in deciphering ancient Indian inscriptions was really remarkable. James Princep identified the character of the inscription on the Khandagiri rocks in Orissa, which had been published by Andrew Stirling. He had disagreed with Stirling's contention that many of the letters of the inscription resembled Greek characters, holding that this similarity was purely accidental and that the alphabet was related to the Sanskrit family. Princep's skill and ingenuity in deciphering ancient Indian inscriptions more especially the Ashokan inscriptions on May 11, 1837 virtually gave a new direction to the rediscovery of Indian history. After ascertaining the Aśokan rule in Indian history, basing his judgments on Aśokan inscriptions, another important dynasty was made known by Princep when he deciphered the Hāthigumphā inscription, which Stirling had communicated to the Asiatic Society of Bengal in 1823. Princep derived that the inscription was of importance and he requested his colleague, Lieutenant Markham Kitoe who was then in Cuttack to take the first opportunity of copying the inscription. The task was a difficult one, still then Kittoe visited the caves of Khandagiri from March to December, 1837 and examined the inscription and worked hard to transcribe it.[103] Once Princep received the copy of the Hāthigumphā and Udayagiri inscriptions, he set to decipher them and once again he lets us peer over his shoulders while he worked. "In my search for some of the catch words which had proved of such avail in explaining the purport of the inscriptions at Bhilsa and Sainhadri, I would neither meet with the daman of the former, nor the dayadhamma of the latter,—but in their stead I remarked a very common if not constant termination in a word of two syllables preceded in most instances by the genitive affix—'sa' and in the only case as of exception by an equally regular genitive 'sirino' from the noun 'siri' (Sanskrit root gen) a worshipper of the Sun. It was not until after many futile attempts with the pundit to find a better that we were led to the supposition that the words *lonam* or *lenam* must be the Pali equivalent for the Sanskrit participal noun *lunam* cut or excavated in this the vowel is changed from 'U' to O and the 'N' from dental to the Prakrit cerebral; but in sound it must be confessed that there is little difference, while in sense the term satisfied precisely the circumstances of Udaygiri caves, which are generally small holes cut with the chisel from the solid rock—a stone of loose consistency easily marked with the rudest tools. The catch word once attained, the reading of this new string of inscriptions was an easy matter".[104]

In the article carrying the decipherment of the inscription Princep regretted that the lack of time did not allow him to do the inscription full justice. However, he deciphered the name 'Kharavela' but he could not gather details about the career, the personality and the achievement of the great prince, which the later historians like K.P. Jayswal, R.D. Banerjee and others did. Princep, however, realized the value of the discovery and called the inscription "the most curious that has yet been disclosed to us". Despite the hasty and incomplete work, Princep started a process, which brought to light one of the most important and fascinating characters of Indian history—king Kharavela of Kalinga.

Among the most indefatigable of Princep's associates was Lieutenant Markham Kittoe. He investigated the ruins in Orissa and discovered an important series of inscription on a rock at Dhauli in Puri (then Cuttack) district. The inscriptions discovered by him proved to be identical with those received from Girnar in Gujarat, being a series of inscriptions of King Aśoka. "Some remains of its ancient greatness were evident as late as the year 1838, when Lieutenant Kittoe during a tour in the country, acknowledged that it (Orissa) possessed more temples, sacred spots and relics, than any other, province in Hindustan".[105]

During the Ghumsar disturbance in 1836-37, the Government of Bengal deputed him in November 1836 and in course of his journey with the sepoys he had the occasion of visiting Jajpur, Chhatia, Choudwar, Cuttack, Rautrapur and Baidyeswar. During the course of his journey to these places, he collected a large number of material remains, executed the drawings of all the temples and antiquities found on his route. He collected the map of Dhauli and prepared a short account of the caves and temples in Khandagiri and Udaygiri. He had also reported the discovery of a large number of inscriptions in Cuttack and got the facsimile of them transcribed. In November 1837 Kitoe visited Naraj from Cuttack and wrote a letter to the Secretary, Coal Committee, about the possibility of coal reserves in the region. Kittoe's second and third tour of Orissa was undertaken in February 1838 and 17th April, 1838 respectively. In his notes on the ruins and remains from various places in Orissa, he had given brief notes on the history of the concerned place. As the historical accounts were mostly related to the construction of the monuments and relics, so there was no scope for painting the history red. Still then he could not free himself from giving some unwarranted remarks about the Oriya people and their traditions. These of course were due to the call of the Raj.

Kittoe's observation of the use of coal by the people of Orissa goes like this. "Newarj" is about seven miles in a direct line (due west) from Cuttack; it is at this spot that the Mahānadī throwing off its branch called Kutjooree, finally quits the hilly country and the great valley hence to Burmool. The natives look on this curious rock as the work of "Siva" under the denomination of Siddheswar to whom a temple (of great antiquity) is dedicated and situated at the top of the rock, the lower storey of it, as well as the enclosure or terraces are hewn out of the solid laterite rock in which there are (besides) several caves, formerly inhabited by rishis (ascetics). The black rock is exported to Pooree for the purpose of making the "tillak" or frontal mark of the Hindus, the red, yellow, pink & C & C are used to paint the houses in the vicinity".[106]

In his third tour of Orissa for the exploration of coal and search for antiquities, he came over to a place called Khargparsad (Khadagprasad) on 19th March, 1838 near Talcher. There on 20th March he referred to a magical show staged by him. "The following day I again visited the coal beds, and lighted a large fire, to the amusement of the natives who had never seen stones ignited".[107] This was a deliberate attempt at exposing weaknesses and ignorance of the

Oriyas, which could be exploited for the economic benefit of the British. The backwardness of the people had also been highlighted on a number of occasions. The personality had also been challenged.

After describing the legends of Kalapahar regarding destruction, he stated "The superstition and timidity of the people of these provinces exceeds anything I have ever witnessed in any part of our presidency from Ludhiana downwards".[108]

While describing about the temples in Baidyeswar in Banki sub-division of Cuttack district, "I observed several idols executed in a very superior style in chlorite, among them was a figure of Buddha erect, with the different Budhas in the sitting posture encircling him similar to that dugup at Sarnath by Lieutenant Cunningham; it was besmeared with sindoor and ghee, the same as the other idols. I endeavoured to persuade a Brahmin, that he was guilty of heresy in thus worshipping BUDH; he assured me that it was not BUDH, but Mahadeva. So much for the knowledge of the people of Orissa, for I have remarked the same wherever I have been".[109]

While exploring ruins and pillars at Jajipur (Jajpur), he might have come across some Brahmins, who had probably troubled him. That led him to generalise in regard to the Brahmanas of Jajpur in the sense that, "The Brahmanas are more troublesome here than in any place I have ever visited, they complained loudly of their loss, since the high road through Akuapadda (Akhuapada) had been established, which deterred pilgrims from visiting their Kshetra*"[110] Some of the unwanted and unwarranted remarks of Kittoe's about the labour class of Orissa was highly pinching. During his return journey from Khurda to Khandagiri he had made some such remarks; "I returned immediately to Khurda (as it was past sunset) and reached that place at 8 p.m. I left again at 5 a.m. for Khandagiri and coming to the insolence and perverseness of the bearers who wanted to take me inspite of every remonstrance to Bhubaneswar, I did not get there till 1 p.m. I had only ten miles to travel, yet as late as 11 a.m. (six hours), they only took me eight miles, when they set me down and went away to cook their meals. I was then obliged to lock up my palkee and taking my drawing materials and pittarahs on coolies, I walked the rest of the way in the heat of the sun: the bearers brought the palkee up a few hours afterwards. In the meantime having got some milk and few plantains to refresh me, I set to work to draw all that was most worthy of notice; I commenced work at 1 p.m. and continued till long after dark, using a torch: I regret that I lost so much time owing to the conduct of the bearers and that I could not remain another day".[111]

Despite these shortcomings in his work, Kittoe had been very much professional in his work. Throughout his explorations in different parts of Orissa, he had been sincere and committed in his approach to archaeology. Being a keen student of Archaeology, while working on the archaeological treasures of the state and doing explorations, not only did he just report the discoveries, but also simultaneously he tried to get them catalogued in the right way. In the process he tried to prepare sketch maps of the sculptures, paintings and architectural buildings, along with the sketch history of the regions. The history thus drawn by Kittoe was in many ways similar to that of Stirling. The accounts were mostly legendary and thus the chronologies and dates were invariably defective. As a serious archaeologist whenever he came across vandalisms being done to monuments of archaeological importance, he pointed out to them and criticised even if a European officer might have effected the work. The first place visited by Kittoe in Jajpur was the mosque in the outskirts of the town. "At a short distance from the mosque is a dargah or shrine of a Mussalman saint who destroyed a famous temple and converted the terrace on which it stood into an open mosque and burial place for himself and family. Beneath the terrace are three idols of enormous dimensions and exquisite sculpture representing Indrānī, Varāha (Varahi) and the Kālī (Chamunda), the latter figure is the most worthy of notice though a more hideous object could not well be imagined, it resembles (as it were) a living skeleton of an old fury. Mr. Stirling gives a good account of these fine specimens of ancient Hindu sculpture; it is much to be regretted that these idols have so suffered from masons chisel, in late years employed by a European officer to detach relics. A part of the mundmāla of Kālī and a hand of Indrānī have been thus lost. It is also a great pity that these curiosities are not removed to the Museum in Calcutta (which could easily be done in rainy season) and thereby placed out of the reach of such would be antiquarian relic hunters".[112]

About the Fort (Barabatee) at Cuttack, Kittoe stated, "We remained at Cuttack several days, the Fort (Barahbattee) being the first object that attracted my notice. I shall first describe it, or rather what is left of it, for it is fast disappearing, the stones being taken for various public works; the greatest drain has been for the light house at false point and for the macadamaixing the cantonment roads".[113] Near the inner gateway of the Fort there were inscriptions inscribed on stone slabs. About one of the inscriptions it is stated by Kittoe that, "over the archway was another inscription which is the possession of the Executive Engineer".[114] When P. Acharya, the Chief Editor of the *Orissa Historical Research Journal*, searched for the slab in 1949, which contained the inscription, he found no trace of it in the office of the Executive Engineer, Cuttack. This is a clear case of how archaeological evidences were destroyed and how strings of history were cut because of the vandalism of the few. "The candelabra mentioned by Mr. Stirling has been removed to a garden in Chowlegunge, it is a chiragdan about 15 feet height and of Mogunee or chlorite, being an octagonal pillar 1&1/2 feet at its base and about 10 inches at its summit on which is a vase the shape of a lotus, but intended to hold a "*tulsee*" plant, it is not one shaft, but a number of layers about 10 inches deep, each having four brackets projecting out of four of the sides of the octagon and every other layer having its brackets on different faces so as to allow of one blank every way between each bracket; it is of modern workmanship and belonged to a temple built by the Marathas which was pulled down many years ago and was used for illuminations at the Dewallee festival; there is another very like it, before a temple, in the cantonment by the river side, also built by the Mahrattas".[115] Archaeological methods never allow the shifting or the transfer of any archaeological object or remains from its original context, as it could destroy objectivity.

Vandalisms caused to the Konarka temple was explicitly clear in various of his statements. "The Kurdaraja has demolished all three entrances and is removing stones to Poree; the masons pick out the figures and throw them down to take their chance of being broken to pieces (which most of them are) such they leave on the spot those that escape uninjured are taken away. The elegant doorway called the Nawgriha, a drawing of which is to be found in the 15th volume of the *Asiatic Researches*, has been completely destroyed. I remarked three or four niches in the different doorways in which slabs of cholorite with inscriptions had existed; they were removed about 1815 or later by a European officer, but what has become of them I cannot ascertain; it is probable that they were sent to Europe. It would be worth while to institute some inquiry after these valuable records of antiquity which might throw some light on the origin of this wonderful specimen of human ingenuity and labour and would also add to the knowledge already obtained from such records regarding the early history of Kalinga".[116] Kittoe was seriously concerned over the vandalism thus caused to the great monuments not only by the natives but also by the Europeans. This definitely speaks about his sobriety as a professional archaeologist. He was really serious and committed to give Orissan history a new direction by searching for inscriptions everywhere he had visited. His explorations for the antiquities of Orissa were really marvellous.

In connection with the style and techniques adopted by the Indian architects in building massive architectural specimens Kittoe's observations were minute, specialised and perfect. While Kittoe was visiting the Temple of Grameswar near Ratrapur on 8th December, 1836 he paid a visit to one Śiva Temple situated on an island lying about a mile away from the village. He observed the temple in order to understand the style and technique of the building and critically evalued it. "At quarter of a mile above the village (The village of Khandhurpur) is an island separated from the rocks on the main land by a broad and exceedingly deep channel of the river flowing between. On this island (which well-wooded) are the remains of a very ancient temple dedicated to MAHADEO by the name of Panchameśwar also "Manjithākur" or the "Steersman Lord". The style of the temple is that of those in the Carnatic (if I mistake not) and like a few of more ancient temples of Bhubaneswar it has evidently never been completed, the stones are laid without mortar and are fixed with iron claraps which have aided in no small degree to destroy the edifice. It is much to be regretted that the Indian architects of olden times had recourse of such an endurable method of fastening their masonry, many of the most elegant buildings at Agra, Delhi and elsewhere have been destroyed by this ill-judged practice, the iron after the lapse of a few years expand from corrosion and splits off large masses of the masonry.

The Taj has suffered greatly from this cause which was discovered even before the work was half finished; copper and brass fastenings were then substituted, these have saved the dome from injury; brass clamps have however been used in other public works of antiquity in India, for several have been found in the masonry of the Fort of Cuttack during its demoiition for the use of false point light house.

It appears that it was formerly the practice to build the temples with the material rough wrought and to sculpture them afterwards; this temple is one of the many instances of such a custom".[117] Kittoe's analysis carries with it scientific truth while Stirling challenged the Hindu knowledge of architecture and criticised the architectural skill of the Hindu architects without referring to any defect in any of the monuments described by him. Kittoe was object specific in his work and he exposed one of the basic weakness of the Indian architecture. That really speaks of his inquisitiveness to learn more about the Oriya system of knowledge by going deeper into the whole system. Kittoe's explorations were not restricted to the discovery of ancient and medieval sculptures, paintings, idols, inscriptions, coins, etc., at the same time while on the road from one place to another his inquisitive eye did not miss even very significant and small objects like insects and fishes, etc. He had tried to collect the objects and analyse them. While describing the village of Atteiri near Khurda, he referred to a particular insect. "Close to the village Atteiri is a small tank hewn out of the laterite rock in which I found a kind of fresh water sponge adhering to the stones, it was perfectly white and had a very delicate and beautiful appearance, I brought away a piece but in the course of few hours, the insect dying, it became putrid and decomposed, so that I was obliged to throw it away".[118] In the Talcher region Kittoe came across different kinds of fish, which virtually amazed him "A great variety of small fish were brought, among which I observed some species quite new to me, of a couple of which I took drawings".[119]

In connection with his visit to Ratrapur, he referred to the white ants. "I would infer that the huts of former times were just the same as those now constructed, namely of a timber frame work to support what is known in Europe by the name of "Wattle and dab" which from the swarms of white ants that (I may say) infest these regions, cannot be very durable, some however are more substantial, being built with mud and unhewn stones".[120] On 15th March, 1538, Kittoe visited the famous hill of Kapilasa in present day Denkanal district. It has already been evening when he got down from the hill "It was quite dark before we reached the foot of the hill, we were met by several paiks who had been sent to light us home to our tent, they had torches made of slips of SISSOO wood, tied into long narrow bundles, which once lighted burn to the last morsel, emitting a very strong light with a powerful and delicious aromatic smell, they are in common use throughout the Girijat (Garhjat or hill states).[121] The information thus collected is quite interesting. Another important knowledge, which was accrued by him, was about the method of tilling of the land, which was completely new to him. On 16th March, 1838, Kittoe reached a village called Atturva (Tarva), a large village situated on the bank of the river Brahminee (Brahmani): I here observed a method of tilling the land quite novel to me, the fields are dug with long and heavy crow bars, each clod as it is turned up is bruised with the bar and thus prepared for the seek without using a plough; indeed the stiff nature of the soil, would not admit of its being ploughed in the dry seasons. This practice I found to prevail throughout the valley of the Brahminee, which tract is very fertile".[122] This is an important point, which always attracts the notice of an ethnographer and an ethnoarchaeologist.

Briefly Kittoe's activities in Orissa included the following: Lieutenant Kittoe prepared the facsimile of the principal inscription in the old Lat character of Aswasthama near Dhauli and short notes on the caves and temples discovered thereby himself. Besides he had drawn a map of the place. He reported the discovery of large numbers of inscriptions at Cuttack. The most important among them was one, which occupied 270 square feet of area. It was carefully covered with plaster to save it from the spoiling hands of collecting antiquarians. This inscription was inscribed on the two sides of the jambs of the Lingaraj Temple. Kottoe was not successful in getting them copied. Kittoe had executed beautifully all the temples and antiquities that came on his route. He prepared the facsimile copy of the Hāthigumphā inscription inscribed on the Khandagiri and Udaygiri rocks in Bhubaneswar. He had also prepared the sketch of a section of hill called "Newraj" (Naraj) in Cuttack district. Besides M. Kittoe had collected 6 arrows used by the paiks in the Kattak (Cuttack) hills; a kund arrow from Boad (Baud) and sikh spear. The sketch of Subhastambha and Garuda image from Jajpur; sculptures from the Temple of Grameswar near Rautarapur in Athgarh in Cuttack district; temple of Durga at Baidyeswar near Ramnath were life-like and all these really display marvel. Although Kittoe belonged to the school of historiagraphy run by Mill and its influence over his work was faintly visible, but actually his work was free from any sort of bias, fear or favour, thus paved the way for the production of a sober history of Orissa. He was highly talented. He had multifaceted activities to his credit. He was a valiant military officer, a sincere archaeologist, a sober historian, a thorough-bred ethnographer and ethno-archaeologist, an epigraphist par excellence, a true biologist, a serious painter and an ardent cartographer. His contributions to Orissan history and modern historiography were enormous.

Very close to the time and work of Markham Kittoe, was the tour diary of J.R.Ousley. Major J.R.Ousley was the agent in the various districts which had formed the south west frontier agency in Bengal during the years 1840s. He toured this part of Orissa during the period. The tour account provided by him affords authoritative and first hand information relating to the political, economic and social condition of the people and the land. Therefore, it forms an important source for the construction of the modern history of the country. Ousley toured the country and collected information relating to the land and people of the country with the pre-conceived notion that the British people were a superior people and the British civilisation was a superior civilisation. It was to enact moral ascendancy of the British over their Indian counterparts and to pave the way for the Indians to taste the fruits of modernity and modern civilisation. It has also been held by him that the British rule in India is the logical culmination of the long run tyranny of the Mughal and Maratha governments. The tour diary was written purely in the diary style. He toured the regions such as Singbhum, Keonjhar, Bonei, Cheria Pant, Bamra, Sambalpur, Saurungarh, Chanderpur, Singra, or Bargarh, Champa (in the Chhatisgarh district of Nagpur), Chechowli, Kurba (now Korba in M.P), Dhangaon, Oopuroa, Sirguja. The descriptions were stereotyped, which included the political status of the countries, the population, subsistence economy, exploitation of the people by the kings and the zamindars misrule and lawlessness, etc. Ousley's diary provides a very good account of the contemporary history of the countries and regions visited by him. Ousely's mission behind the tour of the country was to assess the political and economic conditions prevailing in the countries lying in the south west frontier agency in Bengal, so that avenues could be created for the expansion of the British empire. He wanted to foster and further the ideology like Mill and his school of philosophers including Lord Curzon that the British empire implied the disappearance of misery, oppression, anarchy, superstition and bigotry. It connoted the extension of peace, justice, prosperity, humanity and freedom of thought and expression. Ousley thought it essential to bring the country under the direct administration of the British government, so that law could be extended to the people living in the remotest corner of the earth and thus the conflicting interests of the people and their immediate exploiters could be co-ordinated. Throughout the diary there was the description of the common folk living in a country known for its scarcity amidst plenty, oppression, brigandage, misrule, anarchy, water truce, dirt and diseases. Law was indispensable for any ordered society and it was spelled out as common knowledge that "strength of the pack is the wolf and the strength of wolf is the pack".[123] Wherever he went on his tour he pointed out the anarchical conditions prevailing in the regions. He visited Singhbhum on 18th November 1840 and stated "The amlah of the minor rājā of Singhbhum having mismanaged the country and appearances of disturbances between Rājā's people and the Zamindars of Rourkela, Kera and Bondgaon having been reported. Ousley directly proceeded to Porahat the young rājā's capital.

The estate of Singhbhum had been reduced from the first rank to a mere name by the separation of Saraikela and Khursawan many years ago and by the British assumption of the direct management and sovereignty of Kol peers in 1837. Still the extent of the country was very considerable though in a miserable state of depopulation apparently the work of years, for all shades of desertion appeared in the fields and more or less covered with jungles. Owing to the misbehaviour of those in charge of the young rājā Arjun Singh, a minor of 10 or 12 years of age, Ousley had procured the sanction of the government to placing the whole estate in charge of the political assistant, Singhbhum adopting all the forms of wards management in regulation provinces. Many years must elapse before the ravages occasioned the agricultural pursuits by misrule would be restored... The jungle abounded in natural resources such as lac, khowa and hurra but the bad faith of those surrounding the rājā had till then prevented merchants speculating freely.

The blessings of British rule were becoming more apparent daily, the plundering habits of the inhabitants were checked and the happiness in living in security appreciated. A finer field for the missionary never existed. The British occupation of the country had introduced a crowd of Oriya Brahmins who would not have shown themselves before and who were then endeavouring to make a mongrel kind of Hindu out of them. Ousley had applied to His Lordship the Bishop of Calcutta for assistance in that way on Lient Tickells mentioning it to him that the opportunity was fast passing away when they might be induced in a body to come over to a true religion. He had not till then the honour of a reply. The subject was however of the highest importance, far exceeding what could be done even with the expenses so cheerfully afforded to convert the population of some small and distant island in the Pacific ocean. Here among persons who were unchecked by caste, having no recognised religion whatever, eating and drinking indiscriminately what was offered from the English table, could be laid the foundation for the general conversion of the whole of India. In themselves a bolder and finer race than most of the people of the country, they would undoubtedly be the means of extending the knowledge that they would now receive. A school had been sanctioned (letter from Secretary to Government dated. 6.1.1832) but no schoolmaster had undertaken the task. Major Wilkinson's arrangement and conciliatory methods of ruling them as enforced by Lient Tickell had impressed them with favourable opinion of the English in everyway".[124] Ousley's study of congeniality of atmosphere for the general conversion of the people to Christianity was one of the most important methods of establishing British control over Indian culture and thereby furthering the achievements of the Rājā. This process of conversion and christianization of Indian culture became syndromic with the planning of the Raj and this continued unabated since then. This unending process which has been going on since then had resulted in generating communal tensions during various periods of Indian history. British colonialists, while developing methods in order to justify their rule in India has sponsored the propagation of Christianity and mobilisation of the people for conversion to Christianity by Jesuit missionaries in various ways. The justification was lying in the fact that they tried to identify the western civilisation as the Christian civilisation. But the 1850s and 1860s

Christianity was for most Englishmen increasingly a mark of their own distinction from and superiority to their Indian subjects. Of course, the British government abandoned the much hoped—for conversion of India, immediately after the Mutiny of 1857 and repudiated any desire to impose their convictions of any of our subjects and enjoined abstinence from interference with the customs or beliefs of the Indian people. Still then the Jesuit missionaries continued their activities in their private level without any government sponsorship. Their areas were shifted to the peripheries, mostly to tribal regions. Even after fifty years of India's independence in the name of civilising the Indians living in the dark terrains and utter backwardness the missionaries had been persistent in conversion of the people which has been generating not only anger among radicals of Indian community but also bloody clashes between the Christians and hardcore Hindus. However, Ousley's role in this process of civilising and christianising the Indian subjects was momentous. After touring Singhbhum Ousley went to Keonjhar which formed one of the tributary mahals under the jurisdiction of the Commissioner of Cuttack. The country was mismanaged, the inhabitants were everywhere discontented; there was a universal complaint of the extortion of Ramghur Light Infantry that was employed to take away money to the post office establishments. These men pressed the people as beggaries, took all money without making any payment and committed extortions enormously. On this Ousley caused the removal of guards from Gora Palsa in the Mayurbhanj Rājā's estate to Jotepur and then had it drawn altogether the post office functionaries, making other arrangements for paying their retainers. These complaints were not confined to Keonjhar alone, but along the whole route to Sambalpur. Every kind of complaint was received from the Runners against the Mutsuddies or Mohorirs at the various states extorting money from them all. The complaints stated that owing to the total absence of people passing along the road, they were plundered with impunity and being unable to get redress were quite at the mercy of the Moharirs who not only took cash but procured trifles of dress such as caps at a value of one or two annas.[125] About the Bonei Ousley pointed out the same problem. He stated that a small portion of the country was under cultivation although the country was well adapted to it. The Rājā Indra Deo a Rajpur was an elderly man and had several sons. He had appeared to be in a degraded state of ignorance and depravity. The Rājā experienced great difficulty in keeping his people in order, he complained of neighbours, the Rājās of Gangpur and Bamra being unable to check the inroads of plundering Thakurs under them who visited his villages carrying off cattle and committing murders constantly. Here Ousley suggested that much could be done if taken directly under British management. He had also referred to other income sources for the Government from the country. The forest produce were hurra, dhowra, resin and wild silk. The wood could be applied to[125] every purpose of architectural requisites. Ousley reported that gold dust was available in plenty in the sands of Brahmani and the gold available in the market at the price of Rs.15 per tola was also of excellent quality. In the state of Cheria Pant, situated about 12 miles east of Bonie (Bonei) near the Kalpani dawk station, the condition of the place was more or less the same. The Rājā was unable to live respectably. He was not serious about procuring improvement of the people. No reports of offences or crimes now made, but it was believed that many offences were overlooked for payment of a sufficient bribe. The complaint against the post office people were as general as elsewhere.

Bamra was described as a much more extensive country than Bonie (Bonei) and it was even more open to improvement but the country was lying waste. The Rājā Tribhuban Deo, a Rajpur, a fine youngman, could not keep his people in order. So he presented petitions to the government requesting them to assist him. He was informed that direct superintendence by the Government would be established. To this he did not object as he could not manage the affairs without money. He reiterated that the Zamindars did not obey his orders, plundered in all directions and opposed force to force when the Rājā endeavoured to coerce. Ousley observed that the effects of misrule were more apparent than in Bonie or Keonjhar. "A country that had been for many miles a sheet of cultivation laid waste in every direction only within 5 or 6 years. The prudence was chiefly rice but the soil was fit for anything, there were extensive forests, fine rivers, and every requisite for an agricultural population. Numerous inhabitants migrated into distant parts.[126] Sambalpur was to be reached by crossing the little river Bhundua. The country was much better managed than the rest of the districts. The Rājā Narayan Singh who was invested with Rājāship only six years ago although respected as (a man) a man of most benevolent and humane disposition was a mere cipher. The richness of the soil and industry of the people far surpassed those of the adjacent districts. The Agent had taken notice of the complaints of all kinds and justice had been attained in many instances, where none would otherwise have been expected. Still the most shocking murders and plundering had taken place within two or three years, chiefly owing to the refractory dispositions of several of the chief Zamindars, who could not consider to bring themselves to consider this Rājā as their rightful lord, but who would never presume to oppose the orders of the British Government.[127] Such optimism on the part of the British to enlist the support of Zamindars upper class people for the British administration was really tremendous and surprising. Regarding the extortion of money from the common people, Ousley had carefully identified the areas and mentioned about them. He mentioned; there are numerous occasions for extorting money, classed under the following heads:

(i) Mālguzārī was realised in 3 equal kiśts e.g. in the months of Aswin, Kartic and Chait.

(ii) Akbari was given in thekāh to a farmer and also realised in 3 equal kiśts and in cash.

(iii) Sayer was also given in thekāh to a farmer and taken all the year round.

(iv) Grains of all sorts was realised in kind from all villages once in a year.

(v) Besides the foregoing dues, the following fees were levied occasionally kamarkushi (War levy), wedding expenses (in the family of the Zamindar), Kanchheda (ear boring), levy on the death of the Rani or relations, Diwani of 5% on any express occasion.

The search for the pockets of appropriation was obviously meant for creating avenues for the appropriation of the revenue by the East India Company. The Sayer's duties were light, but so many different jāgīrdārs had assumed the authority of stopping merchants that it very much checked trade. One shameful duty was levied on all widows of the trading and manufacturing classes. The sale of widows was compulsory among them. On the demise of any man of these classes, his widow was appraised, if young and good looking a higher demand was made for her from the person who desired to have her. Then the money was paid to the Rājā's people and the woman forced to go to her new owner. This had long since been abolished, but occasionally the jāgīrdārs enforced it. Another most oppressive tax was the Murdhun or appropriation of properties of these classes on their death whether they had relations or not. This practice had also been long abolished but abuses still continued. All other exactions, such as feeding all the sapāhīs, sent on duty (by the Rājā) by the people of the country, enforcing labour without payment, etc., were as bad as in any native government of India. This generalisation in regard to the existence of bonded labour everywhere in the country was unwarranted and was not based on evidences. It is of course true to say that bonded labour did exist in the country for quite a long period in history down to the twentieth century, but in comparison to the Roman slavery, this stands nowhere. While computing the revenues of Sambalpur, Ousley was not prepared to accept the verbal statement of the Rājā who asserted that Rs.50,000 was the gross jamā (collection) of the state. He stated that, this was hardly creditable, if exactions above noticed were averaged for a certain number of years and added to present revenue, two or two and a half lakhs of rupees could with safety be taken".[128] While describing about the flora and fauna of the country, he referred to a type of fish found in the Mahānadī, which is quite surprising of course. "Fish to be had in greatest profusion in the Mahānadī of various descriptions. Among others the sword fish or saw fish called there the Harkash was about a yard long, one food of which consisted of saw. It was a sea fish but found its way up as far as Sambalpur".[129] The information was amazing and scintillating. He had also mentioned that Alligators were numerous in Sambalpur, but hardly they hurt the people. Thus accidents did not occur very often. Another important Garhjat state visited by Ousley was Saurungarh which was then just being separated from Sambalpur. It has been stated that the country had evidently once been in excellent order. North and east of the town of Saurunngarh is 14 miles to Chanderpur was a place once covered with a cultivation now fast running into a jungle. The town was a struggling dirty village and of squatted, unhappy looking inhabitants. The Rājā's house was a miserable place surrounded by a stagnant nulla; about three miles was the tomb of

Elliot employed about 70 or 80 years ago on a diplomatic mission to the darbar of the Bhonsla Rājā of Nagpur and who died here'.[130]

Ousley had collected information about Captain Fergusson's visit to this part of Orissa about twenty years ago and he had pointed out the fear psychosis he was able to instil into the mind of the common people, which resulted partly in the desertion of the villages by them while marching from Dhangaon to Turga, he had referred to this by stating that "Falkisson saheb (Cap.Fergusson) had passed these places some twenty years ago with compass, perambulator and some instruments and it had so alarmed the people that they had not yet got over it".[131] On being told that Cap. Fergusson had also crossed Kurba, Churyi, etc., where desertion of the population had not taken place and that Ousley had also passed through other places where he was given comfort and supplies and people came to see him. The Dewan pointed to his forehead and accused his own unhappy karam or fate. The Dewan in the opinion of Ousley was the most repulsive and unfortunate man and he caused the latter a great deal of trouble.

Ousley was highly pragmatic and optimistic about the future of the British Raj in India. He thought that the time had already arrived when the specialisation in crop production needed to be encouraged and the production of cash crops including the higher value food grains needed to be stimulated. And that would require the extension of the market for agricultural crops. That could be possible only with the growth of effective road and railway communication system. This was obviously a part of a larger utilitarian programme of reform and development in India during the early 19th century. Ousley had gone through various parts in Western Orissa in order to observe and report on the practicability of constructing a line of road for the dawks from Nagpur via Pareshnath hill to Calcutta. He had described the climate of Sambalpur as extremely bad. Because of the insalubrities of the air and the metallic taste of the water everyone was attacked by fever and all the inhabitants had a yellow unhealthy appearance. The same had earlier been reported by T. Motte during his visit of Sambalpur in 1766.

Despite his imperial leanings Ousley's work was an important work as far as the contemporary history of the region was considered. He had provided some vital information in regard to the archaeological potential of the countries visited by him.[131] The description of a Killa (fort) at Bonei and information about the existence of a number of deserted temples of carved stone, remarkably well cut at Manpur on the Mohan river are very significant archaeological information recorded by him. In totality, Ousley's account forms an important source of history concerning the country. It is during this period that Fergusson visited Orissa on an archaeological mission. In 1837 he visited Khandagiri and Udaygiri, Bhubaneswar, Puri and Konark and described very briefly about the architecture and sculptures found in the places. The chronologies derived by him were full of mistakes. The date of the highly adorned Konark temple had been fixed by him as prior to the building of the Jagannath Temple. He did not believe in the date of the temples mentioned in the Madāla Pañjī, which ushered serious debate between him and R.L. Mitra in 1870s. Although Mitras's arguments on various controversial topics were completely refuted by Fergusson, he had to submit to the logic and historical analysis provided by R.L. Mitra, in regard to the date of the construction of Konark Temple. Fergusson had always been highly critical of Indian scholarship. The British scholarship on India's past was invariably angered at the Indian claims to equality expressed in the Ilbert Bill controversy. Babu Rajendralal Mitra, though not a member of the Indian Civil Service, was a distinguished Indian scholar. During 1870s he had with the support of the Indian government undertaken the first detailed archaeological survey of Orissa. Such pretensions threatened those like James Fergusson who in such works as the *"History of India and Eastern Architecture (1876)* had long claimed the right authoritatively to define the nature of India's past. Hence Fergusson set out to put the upstart Mitra in his proper place. He did so not simply by a scholarly critique of Mitra's evidence and interpretations, but by disparaging his ability, as an Indian, to undertake such a study at all. The British, he argued, by their policies had weakened the influences of caste and religion, which had given stability to Indian society. In its place "we have tried to substitute an education which they (the Indian people) cannot assimilate and which in consequence remains, in all instances, a useless and empty platitude. For Fergusson, Mitra was a typical specimen of that educated class whom the Ilbert Bill sought to empower as governors of the country. The real interest of his scholarly work, therefore Fergusson continued, in those days of discussions of Ilbert Bills, lay in the evidence it supplied as to whether the natives of India are to be treated as equals to Europeans in all respects. The answer was decisively negative. Fergusson's attitude very clearly demonstrated his perceptions of European superiority. The early history of Orissa during the first half of the nineteenth century was replete with the British vision that Indians differ widely in terms of civilisation and so they needed to be brought under complete dominance of the British. That was necessary to fulfil the civilising mission of the British in India.

(C)

HUNTER'S ORISSA : PERSPECTIVES OF THE RAJ

The process of the conquest and subjugation of Orissa which had to pass through three different and distinct phases was completed when Narayan Singh died in 1849 without leaving behind him a natural heir. Lord Dalhousie immediately applied the Doctrine of Lapse and Sambalpur was amalgamated into the Central Provinces of the British empire. Dr. J.Cadenhead took charge of the district as the principal political assistant and became the first British administrator of Sambalpur. Earlier the Ganjam and the Koraput districts in South Orissa, lying between the Rushikyulya and Vaṁsadhara rivers conquered in 1766, had been attached to the Madras Presidency. After the occupation of the districts of Cuttack, Puri and Balasore, in 1803, it had formed a part of Bengal Presidency. So, by 1850, not only the process of conquest and political subjugation of Orissa was complete, but also the Orissan kingdom underwent a political vivisection. The linguistic and cultural homogeneity of the Oriya speaking people and their identity as a distinct racial and cultural group was thrown to the wind without any compunction. Throughout the pages of Orissa history, the Oriyas are always known for their solidarity and distinct identity. Although the British after the occupation of Orissa did not disturb the religious susceptibilities of the inhabitants of Orissa, still they failed to assess the character of the Oriya people and their martial qualities. The Oriyas resisted the British subjugation right from the beginning. The resistance of the Oriyas had always remained distinctive and singular. While elsewhere in India and in most places the resistance to the British came from the ruling sovereigns and their armies, in Orissa such resistance typically came from the common masses of the people. The British had failed to ascertain the past history of Orissa or the martial qualities of the people from the remotest times till the downfall of the last Hindu kingdom. So their policies in Orissa were never systematic or coherent. There had been consistent effort on the part of the British to force the Oriyas to discern and acknowledge their cultural, social, religious and economic inferiority and trace their restrictive frontiers of life. The information industry of the imperial scholarship was sustained to provide the basis of this supplicant and subordinate relationship. As per the evolutionary theory, once conscious of their status as ordained by the law of creation, the lesser breeds should voluntarily opt for a prolonged period of apprenticeship.

As Edward W. Said conceptualized, the idea of orientalism fashioned an academic tradition.[132] Of course that age's social relations condition the social mentality of the age. Orientalism became a positive doctrine and created closely knit idioms. India figured predominantly in the whole process. Orientalism was characterised as racist, imperialist and ethnocentric. It consisted of a "mobile army of metaphors, metonyms and anthromorphisms".[133] In short it is a sum of human relations which have been enhanced, transposed and embellished poetically and rhetorically. After constant and long use, it seems obligatory to a people. Thus truths gave way to illusions which saturated imperial perceptions. When Curzon declared that "East is a university in which scholars never take a degree", he meant among other things, Edward W. Said put it that East in general and India in particular required European presence for ever and that the relationship between the two was destined to be static and not reciprocal. The white man's burden was thus placed theoretically on force and it was to be held by force alone. It was a sentiment, an attitude, a policy and a reality. As a consequence the whiteman of the west was never to meet the East on terms of equality.

The first decade of the second half of nineteenth century witnessed a serious check to the expansion of imperialism and experiments with liberalism in the form of Sepoy Mutiny in 1857. For the British the searing trauma of this was but the first of a series of checks to the expectation of a slow but steady march of progress whose end point would be the triumph of liberal principles throughout the world. The uprising undoubtedly raised troubling questions about how far the 'blessings of the British rule' and those upon whom they were conferred appreciated liberal reforms with it. Despite the crisis of the Raj precipitated in the Indian revolt itself and subsequent crisis of liberalism in Britain, the British Raj in India advanced and furthered in a more vigorous form the conception of the empire as being more firmly grounded the notions of India's difference. And conservatism was revitalized which gave the empire a central place in Britain's vision of itself. The British rule by the mid century had already become increasingly secure. The reforming impulse had already waned. So colonial search for knowledge took on a new shape. After the Mutiny, anxious to rule India without disrupting its established social institutions and driven by an ever more compelling commitment to scientific understanding the British set out to reduce to a comprehensible order what they saw as the baffling variety of India's myriad peoples. But the 1860s the 'ideas of difference' defined an India that had become a "laboratory of mankind" or "living museum" where ancient customs habits and practices endured up to the present.[134]

So the years following 1857 Revolt witnessed the emergence of new trends in historiography: the study of the people, caste, varṇa, occupational categories through ethnographic methods, the development of photographs preparation of survey maps, study of the gypsies and wandering vagabonds, identification of criminal tribes, division of India's people into Hindu and Muslim, attempt to comprehend contemporary Hinduism, preparation of Gazetteers and moreover the ordering of India's past and its present through systematic archaeological explorations, systematic recording and description of material remains, preservation of monuments. By 1900, in ethnography, history, archaeology and architecture, the British, so they thought could order and master India's past and its present. So they had fashioned for India a past linked to a vision of empire, which led the Viceroy Lord Lytton to tell the Imperial Assemblage in 1877, 'Providence' had called upon the British to replace and improve the constantly recurrent anarchy of its strife-torn predecessors. In the period under review, Orissan history and Orissan historiography had undergone tremendous transformation with monumental works by W.W. Hunter, John Beames, G. Toynbee and many others. It could get a new shape and provided with a new direction.

Sir W.W. Hunter, a thorough-bred magisterial historiographer of India, had tremendous faith in the utilitarian doctrines. He considered the British rule in India as an interaction between Occidentalism and Orientalism which led him to study Indian institutions and society in order to categorise and stratify them. The exponents utilitarians such as James Mill and William Jones were of the opinion that Hindu society had been stationary since ages past. It is as if the Hindus of the present were in the deepest recesses of antiquity. To free India from stagnation and set it on the road to progress, James Mill proposed a remedy which was at once, as he saw it, simple and obvious. A code of laws was vehemently required. That would release individual energy by protecting the products of its efforts. "Light taxes and good laws' he insisted, in good Benthamite fashion, nothing more is wanting for national and individual prosperity all over the globe. In fact, of course the simplicity was deceptive, for Mill's scheme, with its creation of individual property rights, enforced by scientific codes of law, involved a wholesome revolution in Indian society. Nor did it matter to him that India's Government remained unrepresentative. For both James Mill and Bentham, happiness not liberty was the end of government and happiness was promoted solely through the protection of the individual in his person and property. Once their property is secured, the Indians could find their own industry the means for their elevation. James Mill considered that the ancient regimes of the Hindu had failed to understand they could procure the bare necessities of individuals in their relations with state and thus social justice. So the scale of civilisation could not rise higher. The British historiography throughout was edificatory in character. W.W. Hunter, an ardent protagonist of Pax-Britannica, was one of the important priests of the historiography, the sole aim of which was the justification and glorification of British rule in India. A diehard imperialist in the personality of Vincent Smith, who after his return from Indian Civil Service in the year 1900 had joined Dublin as a teacher, became the first product of this school of historiography founded by W.W.Hunter.

Being an administrative historian, history was necessarily the gist of his experience. The result of the ideas to use the technique of contrast was to render history into biographical form dealing with military campaigns and political exploits. In the *"Rulers of India"* series published in 28 short books, he had the aim and idea that these biographical pieces would throw light on the connected view of the history of India and reveal the laws that governed the development and progress of the country through history.

W.W. Hunter who had been a hardcore liberal throughout was never skeptical about India's past and its culture. He had, of course, tremendous love and respect for the Indians and their past culture. He had also developed the vision that the historical progress of the nations and their people depend on the extension of liberalism and that if the English would ignore this historical lesson nemesis would overtake them. In the *"History of British India"* (1899-1900), all these historical theories had been maintained. The Orientalists before Hunter were of the perception that Sanskrit language was a member of their Aryan family of languages. It had been conceived that there were affinities in certain keywords and forms of grammar between Sanskrit and most European languages. On the basis of these similarities some orientalists including William Jones speculated that the people who spoke these languages must have shared a common origin. For the Rede Lecture at the University of Cambridge in 1875, after his return from seven years as Law Member of the Viceroys Council in India, Henry Maine, set out to explain "The effects of observation of India, on Modern European Thought". India shared with Europe, he said, as Sanskrit scholarship since the time of William Jones had revealed, a 'Whole World' of Aryan institutions, customs laws and beliefs, India was thus part of that 'very family of mankind to which we belong'. Yet he went on, "those Aryan institutions had been arrested in India at an early stage of development. The country was as a result, a 'barbarism' but it remained one which contains a great part of our civilisation, with its elements as yet in separate and not yet unfolded". India was implicated with Britain somewhat paradoxically in a common origin, and yet was fundamentally different. In much the same way, the British were in Maine's view, at once agents of progress, charged with settling India on the road to modernity and at the same time custodians of an enduring India forever in antiquity. Thus, India was projected as Europe's past or rather its varied pasts. In India Europe could find alive in the present day, its entire history. "India was at once a land of Teutonic village republics, it was the old heathen world of classical antiquity; it was a set of medieval feudal kingdoms' in the coastal cities something like a likeness of our own civilisation could even be discerned; and India was, of course, also an 'oriental land forged by despotism'.[135] In the later nineteenth century all of these various conceptions of India existed side by side with little sense of congruity. Each of these concepts, in its own context represented, the real India and each of them served the needs of the Raj. In Hunter's writings, these ideas were properly projected and communicated. Hunter wrote his "*Annals of Rural Bengal* (1868), which offered new dimensions to the writing of history. The traditional practice of writing history in the form of biography was abandoned and an attempt was made to study and depict the life of the people. While answering the question of non-development of the concept of nationalism among the Aryans in India he stated that the social system marred with the institution of caste rigidity might be accounted for the same. His conclusion was that the Brahmanical classes threw all manual labourer on the lowest caste and itself became so weak as to permit more vigorous people to invade and dominate India.

Sir William Wilson Hunter wrote the history and culture of Orissa in his rather lengthy two volumes of '*Orissa*'[136] published in the year 1872. He did not face the problems suffered by Andrew Stirling while writing the thesis on 'Orissa'. Primary source materials in the form of inscriptions, material remains, architectural and sculptural specimens, and a large number of literary documents properly analysed were available in plenty. Besides, statistical accounts were numerous. Thus Hunter's scope for writing the history of Orissa whether in sober or imperial form was much wider. Inspite of the availability of many historical source materials, Hunter's approach was mostly traditional. His account of Orissa suffered from the same shortcomings and pitfalls as Stirling's account, particularly as regards the utilisation of the source materials. Like Stirling, Hunter depended on Madāla Pañjī and other similar legendary accounts for his account. Hunter's writing "*Orissa*" depended mainly on "*History of Puri*" and "*Purushottama Chandrika*" written by Braj Kishore Ghosh and Bhavani Charan Bandopadhyaya who had collected their information from *Madāla Pañjī*". He had also referred to Elphinstone's "*History of India*" published in 1839 particularly in relation to Ganga rule in Orissa, where an attempt was made to attribute a Bengali identity to

Ganga rulers.[137] It needs to be emphasized here that where both Braj Kishore Ghosh and Bhavani Charan Bandopadhyaya were not inclined to accept this hypothesis of Elphinstone, Hunter had deliberately choosen this reference in his book. This largely explains the weak senses Hunter expressed in classifying and selecting his sources and developing his own conclusions.

Despite all the limitations and pitfalls, Hunter's work provided a complete and comprehensive political and religious history of Orissa, which in its own merit was a glorious example of Victorian and late Victorian scholarly enterprise of England.

Right from the very beginning of his work '*Orissa*' W.W. Hunter had the unflinching belief and conviction that, inspite of all "breathing and warm" socio-cultural life revealed from the history of Orissa, it could not contribute significantly to the progress of civilisation. "Here has been a fine revolution if we had but the trick to know it. Orissa exhibits a profusion of such primitive races not in a fossil state but warm and breathing, living apart in their own communities, and a world of suggestive types and links that have elsewhere disappeared. The aboriginal peoples of India have, as it were, been hidden away in hill caves until the great ethical movements subsided beneath which they would otherwise have been submerged. Yet the people here fought no great battle for human liberty, nor have they succeeded even in the more primary task of subduing the forces of nature to the control of man. To them, the world stands indebted for not a single discovery which augments the comforts or mitigates the calamities of life. Even in literature, the peculiar query of Indian race, they have won no auspicious triumph. They have written no famous epic, they have struck out no separate school of Philosophy, they have elaborated no system of law".[138] He was very earnest and eager emphasising the fact that the dictionary compilers had used the words 'Utkala' and 'Odra' in the most derogatory and shameful manner. The purpose was to present a very wrong picture of the Oriyas before the Europeans.

In a similar vein, Hunter presented quite a few historical fallacies and misinterpretations, which not only distorted the facts of Orissan history but also raised questions over the objectivity of his work. He had attempted at attributing a Bengali identity to the Ganga rulers, who had remained the most valorous, valiant, volatile and powerful in the whole of the history of Orissa. The main sources depended upon by W.W. Hunter were '*History of Puri*' by Brajakishore Ghosh and '*Purushottam Chandrika*' by Bhavani Charan Bandopadhyay. These two writers as had already been outlined before had not accepted the veracity of Elphinstone's arguments over this question of identity of the Gangas. Hunter had derived corroborative sources from Elphinstone's "*History of India*".[139] He was accused of siding with the Bengali elite in the latter's campaign against the independent existence of the Oriya language. Hunter stated "The origin of the new dynasty, the Ganga dynasty, remains a matter of dispute. The local legends point out to the southern coast as the starting point to the race but evidence is not wanting to connect them with Bengal and their family name, the Gangetic line, appears to support this view".[140] In explaining 'Gangetic Line' the statements which had been provided in the footnote goes like this.

"The palm leaf record accounts that they came from the south (*Purushottama Chandrika* P.35). The native analyst whose manuscript work (*Rājā Charita*) Stirling used, follows on the same side and Stirling adopts this view (*Asiatic Researches* XV.P 267). On the other hand Mountstuart Elphinstone states that they were a dynasty of the Gangetic Valley and even indicates that their original kingdom as lying round Tamluk and Midnapur (*History of India* 243, Mr Cowell's edition): He supports his position by the authority of H.H.Wilson (Preface to *Mackenzie Papers* (XXXVII). For an elaborate, see *Lassin's Indische Alterhumskunde* Vol IV, 17-24 also PP 5,14, and 968 passim. Here as elsewhere I confine myself to stating the conclusion at which I have arrived after considering the entire evidence".[141] Hunter's attitude towards Orissa was explicitly clear from this statement. But it could not explain what led him to describe the Gangas as Bengalis when he himself had stated that both the regions of Medinipur and Tamluk belonged to Orissa.[142]

His plans for the denigration of Orissa and destruction of identity of the Oriyas as a people and Orissa as a nation are also explicit in his analysis of the Konark Temple. "The most exquisite memorial of Sun worship in India or I believe, in any country, is the Temple of Konarka upon the Orissa shore, built according to the most trustworthy records between 1237 and 1282 A.D. Shortly after the triumph of the graceful Vishmarite creed, it concentrates in itself the accumulated beauties of the four architectural centuries among the Hindus. Notwithstanding the indecent sculptures which disgrace its exterior wall, it forms the climax of the Bengal art".[143]

Rajendra Lal Mitra had capitalised on this statement of Hunter. This provided ample opportunity to the later scholars from Bengal in highlighting this point in their concerted effort against the independent existence of the Oriya Language and Province. This movement duly took a furious and vigorous turn in course of its history. Mitra had quoted this particular paragraph in full in his "*Antiquities of Orissa*".[144] Bankim Chandra Chattopadhyaya, Nagendranath Basu and a few other Bengali scholars took advantage of this position and by mixing up some interesting legends with that tried their best in furthering the programmes. Hunter and R.L.Mitra, Bankim Chandra Chattopadhya in one of his essay entitled "*The Sources of Bengal history*" incorporated in the "*Manimala*" a text book for secondary school stated, "The Ganga dynasty of Bengal one day established their state in Orissa. On one side they had built the Temples of Puri and Konark; in another side they had defeated and humiliated the warring Pathans since three hundred years. *O' Bengalis,* you are oblivious of yourself. Do you think, anybody else shall come forward to remind you of your glorious past ! The Oriya soldiers on whom Hunter lavished so much praise in his work were (none but) your Bengalis settled in Orissa".[145]

This arrogance of Bankim Chandra was essentially due to the impact of Hunter's writing. Hunter had so deeply influenced the Bengali historians of the time that they did not simply bother about the objectivity of history. (On many occasions, while proceeding with their plans of denigrating the Oriyas, the Bengali historians exposed their ignorance of Orissa history). Nagendranath Basu and a few other Bengali historians had made the situation more complicated when on the basis of the inscription of Bhatta Bhava Deve inscribed on the walls of Ananta Vasudeva Temple in Bhubaneswar, they tried to prove that the temple under question was the handiwork of Bhatta Bhava Deve, a Bengali. This attempt was later falsified. Paramananda Acharya argues that had W.W. Hunter not attempted to prove that Ganga rulers were Bengalis and Konarka was a Bengali monument, Rajendra Lal Mitra could not have traced how the Bhatta Bhava Deve inscription reached Bhubaneswar from Bengal and Nagendranath Vasu and Manmohan Ganguly would not have tried to prove that the monuments of Bhubaneswar were Bengali monuments. Even Nagendranath Vasu in order to publicise his view point had gone to the extent of writing down a book entitled "Bhavabhumi Barta."[146] None of these scholars had ever cared to refer to the archaeological sources for checking the authenticity of their claims. Following the footsteps of Hunter, Bijoy Chandra Majumdar made concerted attempts during 1916 to 1925 to attribute a Bengali identities to one of the famous dynasties of Orissan history. B.C. Majumdar had gone through the Murarjama copper-plate, published in the *Bihar Orissa Historical Research Journal* in the year 1916 and wrote an essay developing his ideas based on the information of the copper-plate. The plate was issued by Somavaṁśī King Jajati. There was reference to two sets of officers having titles "Datta" and "Ghosh". Surmising the titles as Bengali ones, Majumdar concluded that the said king who had issued the plate was of Bengali origin when he had taken the word 'Vaṁśa' as "Vāṅga" so there was nothing more essential to be corroborated to prove that the kings were Bengalis in origin. He wrote his thesis on the Bengali origin of the Somavaṁśis' in his book '*Orissa in the making*' published by Calcutta University in 1925. He had gone to the extent of saying that as the Somavaṅśīs were the makers of Orissa, so the Bengalis may rightly be called as the makers of Orissa. Majumdar's thesis received positive noddings from historians in the personality of D.R. Bhandarkar when he stated that Somavaṁśī rulers were synonymous with the Kesarī dynasty of Madāla Pañjī and like the Ganga dynasty the Kesarīs came to be identified as Bengalis also. All these distortions of Orissan history were the results of Hunter's erroneous judgments in ancient Orissan history.

Depending on traditional source, Hunter had failed on many occasions to identify the kings and places properly. While drawing the descent of the Bhanja rulers of Mayurbhanj, he commented that, "The present rulers of Mayurbhanj trace their descent to the Jaipur kings one of whose off shoots is said to have founded the principality 2000 years ago".[147] But nowhere had Hunter attempted at giving the identification of this place, Jaipur.

In a similar fashion Hunter considered religious forces as leitmotif behind the progress of Orissan history. That way Hunter drew such a picture of Orissan history, from the clutches of which history writing in India could not be freed for quite a long time. This situation occurred because of his complete dependence on Madāla Pañjī, the credibility of which was never doubted by him. "For the history of religion in India is the history of the people. The ethnical revolutions which brought in new ruling races, ceased in very ancient times and during the last 1500 years, the rise and fall of Orissan dynasties have been connected not with the tribal movements but with the religious reformations. Each new line of kings represents a new era of worship and spiritual belief. Its elevation to power takes place amidst the birth throes of a fresh popular creed, its decay is contemporaneous with the decline of the national religion and its fall is consummated amid the extension of old rites and coming of the new".[148] Hunter admitted categorically that he had been led to give stress on the religious side of Orissa from the firm belief that it forms the key to the right understanding of the people of Orissa. Throughout all northern India, not less than on the remote Orissa shore, dynastic revolutions and religious reformations have for centuries gone hand in hand. Buddhism and Hinduism, the Mohemmadans and the Sikhs represent a conflict of creeds not less than a struggle of races.[149]

Religion had always remained the backbone of Orissan civilisation. Hunter asserted that the cult of Jagannath had congregated all the principal cults or religious sects of Hinduism, which in due course formed the national religion of Orissa. This cult had not only been entwined with the socio-cultural set-up of the country but it had always been associated with the daily activity of the people and the political upheavels and vicissitudes of the different kingdoms of Orissa. In order to expose the cult of Jagannath in a brilliant demeanour, Hunter described that the Jagannath worship embodied every kind of compromise between the religions of the aboriginal people and the Vedic rites of the civilised Aryans. Because of the cosmopolitanism, the Lord Jagannath continued to be worshipped by all classes people down to the present day.

"Besides the perpetual appeal to the popular instinct the worshipping of Jagannath aims at Catholicism which embraces every form of Indian belief and every Indian conception of the deity. Nothing is too high and nothing is too low to find admission into his temple. The fetishism and bloody rites of the aboriginal races, the mild flower worship of the Vedas and every compromise between the two along with the lofty spiritualities of the great Indian reformers have found here refuge. The rigid monotheism of Ramanuja in the 12th century, the monastic system of Ramananda in the 15th century, the mystic quietism of Chaitanya at the beginning of the sixteenth century and the luxurious love worship of Vallabhacharya towards its close mingle within the walls of Jagannath at this present day. He is Viṣṇu, under whatever form and by whatever title men call upon his name. But not content with this representing Viṣṇu in all his manifestations the priests have superseded the members of the Hindu Trinity in their various shapes, and the disciple of every Indian sect can find his beloved rites and some form of his chosen deity with the sacred precincts".[150]

Thus the history of ancient and medieval Hindu Orissa was inextricably linked with the history of Jagannath cult. Continuing to speak about the championship of worship of Lord Jagannath and its relationship with the daily life of the people, Hunter stated "this great yearning after Jagannath is to some extent the outcome of the centuries of Championship in suffering between the people and their god. In every district of Orisssa, Jagannath has borne his share. In every flight of the people before an invading power, he has been their comrade. The priests indeed put the claims of their God upon higher ground. In the first boundless space, they say, dwelt the Great God, whom men call Narayan, or Parameśwar or Jagannath. But without venturing beyond this world's history, the first indistinct dawn of Orissa tradition discloses Puri as the refuge of an exiled creed. In the uncertain dawn of Indian tradition, the highly spiritual doctrines of Buddha obtained shelter here and the GOLDEN TOOTH of the founder remained for centuries at Puri, then the Jerusalem of the Buddhists, as it has for centuries been for the Hindus".[151] Consulting local literatures, traditions and legends Hunter delineated the cult of Jagannath worship in Orissa as a part of the social life of the people.

Hunter was so much fascinated by the influence which the Jagannath cult carried over to the life of the people of Orissa and their nation that he decided to go into the detailed history of the cult and the Car festival. In this he could free himself from his imperial yearnings. He stated; "Here there is a great phenomenon in the inner history of a nation over which those who would study the workings of the religious instinct in man's heart will do well to pause. In order to understand what Jagannath now is to the Hindus, it is necessary to learn what he has for ages been. I propose therefore to examine stage by stage that complex growth of enchaining superstitions and of yearnings after truth, which nourished by pilgrim bones of centuries and watered by the tears of millions of disciples, now spreads itself out in full grown luxuriance upon the Puri sands".[152]

The history which has been recollected by him presented a fair amount of truth. Besides the religious side of the Jagannath cult, one thing which caught his attention was the monastic opulence of the temple. Being a civil servant in the British Indian administration, quite obviously he took a keen interest on the civil and revenue administration of the Jagannath Temple. In this case he made certain generalisations like, "In every country monastic licentiousness has followed hard upon monastic wealth. Orissa has been no exception to the rule; and since the day we took charge of the country, a cry has gone up against priestly luxury and vice. The enlightened part of the community has now arrayed itself against the systematic abuse of religious endowments exhibited in almost every monastery. It is not the poor or the discontented who are loudest in their complaints, but men of education, position and of a sufficient degree of orthodoxy to represent public opinion among the respectable Hindus. The local governments of Orissa had more than once to interfere and to resume endowments which were so grossly abused. In 1810, six years after the British accession, misappropriation had reached such a height as to require a legislative remedy" (Regulation XIX to 1810, repeated by Act XX of 1863).[153] Such generalisation which was more akin to historical truth would have prompted any modern administration to do away with such practices. Since British interest throughout nineteenth century remained accumulation or appropriation of revenue, Hunter said "the British practically decided that all disbursements hitherto made for charitable uses should be continued on the scale which the orthodox Maratha government had established among these costly bequests the superintendence of the Temple of Jagannath was the Chief".[154] At the same time the British officers were to make no arrangements that would hamper the government in any subsequent reform of temple abuses. On the other hand the British government decided to suspend the oppressive and ignominious pilgrim tax. Hunter stated, "the first effect of our occupation was to temporarily suspend the tax on pilgrims as we found the system under which the Marathas had levied it to be grossly oppressive".[155] If the Moslem historians were accurate in their returns, the tax thus levied by the company was barely one fifteenth of what the people had formerly paid. Nevertheless, it formed the substantial part of the total revenue from Orissa. Hunter concluded that the money made from this was to a certain extent the price of the British sanction of idolatry. Hunter was of the conviction that the measure would provide a good name to the British government. Truly the administration confirmed to the continuance of the changed tax. "The good faith of English government was scrupulously maintained indeed so scrupulously as to give offence to many Christian men both in India and England".[156] Hunter was extremely obsessed with and interested in the opulence of the temple. It brought so much of revenue to the administration that he made elaborate preparations for computing the income of the temple as known from different sources. That virtually led him to make many historical generalisations from the evidences available to him. As such very often we come across statements like "an accurate" estimate of the present income of the Jagannath or the value of these offerings can never be known and so on. In fact he did not accept any statement that did not come akin to truth. Hunter was inclined to believe that the religions or monastic institutions anywhere in the world confirmed and stuck to an almost uniform set of principles and Jagannath Temple was no exception to it. He added that "a religious society so ancient and so wealthy naturally gathers round it a vast body of retainers. It is probable that not less than 20,000 men, women and children live directly or indirectly by the services of Lord Jagannath".[157]

This brilliant exposition of the socio-cultural and religious life of the Orissan people and the evaluation of it in the broader Indian context provide Hunter a distinct individuality in the Orissan historiography. One of the most important markers of India's enduring difference was located by British elite was its disease and dirt. The notion of India as a land of disease was inextricably bound up with the parallel notion of India as a sensual society lacking proper self control. The British perceived "the tropics, that is gendered feminine, were a kind of place subject at once to indolence and passion, where disease and sexuality alike flourished. Indeed the two complemented each other".[158] The British were obsessively and ineffectually concerned with Indian sanitation. By the mid-nineteenth century cholera had become a symbol for much that the west feared about a society so different from its own. In fact this was simply because the major nineteenth century cholera epidemics beginning with that of 1817-21, has spread across the globe from India, where the disease had its homeland in the miasmatic paradise of the lower Gangetic basin. It was visibly Indian so it was considered threatening by the British. Furthermore both cholera and small pox were intimately bound up with Hindu superstitions. At the village level, Hinduism gave rise to disease Goddesses and even human avatars', who represented and warded off the disease for their devotees. In the British view the existence of such goddesses, 'disgusting examples of Hindu fatalism' stood in stark contrast with European rationality and the presumed scientific control of disease.

The British were equally disturbed with the link between pilgrimage, both Hindu and Muslim, and the spread of disease. This belief was well founded, for pilgrimage brought large bodies of people together in close proximity, but in the British imagination these gatherings assumed terrifying proportions. Hunter's imagination in regard to the Car festival of Puri, pointed to the same apprehensions. The Jagannath Temple at Puri with its Car festival in which devotees were said to be crushed under the wheels, represented for evangelical Englishmen the ultimate horror of Hinduism. "Probably no spot on earth", as one missionary wrote in 1828, "represents within so small a compass, such completed scene of misery, cruelty and vice, as are presented to view round the Temple of Juggernant".[159] At the same time its concentrated masses of worshippers made this city a central point for the spread of epidemic cholera. Hence it was not surprising that "in western eyes, Puri epitomized all that was obscene, degrading and epidemiological dangerous about Hindu India. Frequently indeed moral and medical condemnation was mixed together. In a report of 1868 Dr. David Smith, the Bengal Sanitary Commissioner contrasted the pilgrims view of Puri as a holy city where they would be freed of their worldly sins, with the sanitarians view of it as anything but 'heaven on earth', containing in its many tanks 'the waters of death and not of immortality'. 'The image of the god'. Smith wrote, terrible in its innate hideousness was yet more terrible in its connection with all the surrounding circumstances of disease and filth".[160]

The link between Indian religion and disease was further reasserted at an International Sanitary Conference held at Constantinople in 1866. The Europeans here sought to cordon off India and pointed an accusing finger of both Hindi pilgrimages and the Muslim pilgrimage to Mecca. Such pilgrimages, they declared to be the most powerful of all the causes which conduce to the development and propagation of cholera epidemics what lay behind such intense anxiety was nothing less than fear of Europe's vulnerability. "The squalid pilgrim array of Jagannath". Hunter wrote apprehensively, in his *History of Orissa* (1872), "with its rags and hair and skin freighted with vermin and impregnated with infection, may any year slay thousands of the most talented and beautiful of our age in Vienna, London or Washington".[161] The self immolation of pilgrims by throwing themselves under the wheels of the Car during the Car festival, which had been seriously criticised by Stirling, had however received a sober treatment from Hunter. He stated, "The official returns now place this beyond doubt. Indeed nothing could be more opposed to the spirit of Viṣṇu worship than self immolation. Accidental death within the temple render the whole place unclean. The ritual suddenly stops and the polluted offerings are hurried away from the sight of the offended God. According to Chaitanya, the apostle of Jagannath, the destruction of the least of the God's creatures was a sin against the creator. Self-immolation he would have regarded with horror. The copious religious literature of his sect frequently described the car festival but makes no mention of the self-sacrifice nor does it contain any passage that could be twisted into a sanction for it.[162] Abul Fazl the keen Moslem observer, was equally silent, although from the context it was certain that had he heard of the practice he would have mentioned it.

So far from encouraging self-immolation the gentle doctrines of Jagannath tended to check the once universal custom of window burning. Even before the Government put a stop to it out officials observed its comparative infrequency at Puri. "It is expressly discountenanced in the writings of the Viṣṇuvite reformers and is stigmatized by a celebrated disciple as the fruitless union of beauty with a corpse".[163] The British throughout the Victorian and Late Victorian era were engaged in the Sati debate in order to inform legislation for reform of Indian morals.The discussion of the condition of Indian women always involved an outrageous expression of horror and the consequent need for the British to save the Indians. As the Indian men so the British conceived did not properly order their households much as the country's previous rulers had failed to provide proper governance for the society as a whole, the British determined that they themselves should act as the protectors of India's women. In so doing they could not only, as they saw it, rescue these unfortunate creatures, they could also make manifest their own masculine character and proclaim their moral superiority over the Indian male. Few of their activities in India gave the British greater satisfaction than this vision of themselves as the reformers of Indian morality which left as its legacy in a range of enactments from the abolition of Sati in 1829, through the Hindu Widow Remarriage Act of 1856, to the Age of Consent Act of 1891 and beyond. The British officials while informing their campaign against widow burning, sought to challenge the same from within Indian tradition and so make themselves the masters of that tradition. At the same time, the observation of Hunter in regard to Sati and the very negation of British assertion, of its presence within India's tradition virtually posed a complex problem in order to arrive at a definite conclusion on their perception of Orissan people and its society.

Hunter's position on the morals of the Oriyas was however confusing. In regard to some of the obscene sculptures and practices, he vehemently criticised the stand of the priests and the sanction of traditions associated with Lord Jagannath. "It would be well for Jagannath if these old calumnies were the only charges which his priests had to answer. Lascivious sculpture disfigure his walls, indecent ceremonies disgrace his ritual, and dancing girls with rolling eyes put the modest female worshippers to the blush. The priests give a spiritual significence to these most questionable features of modern Viṣṇuvism and a devout Hindu no doubt looks on them with different eyes from ours. To the pure all things are pure".[164] In these observations, Hunter wanted to characterise the religion and religious practices of Puri as one of unashamed sensuality and shallow emotionalism.

As far as Hunter's perceptions in regard to the political history of Orissa was concerned, the magisterial Pax-Britannica philosophy found its imprint more clear and explicit. Though the explanation as regards the revenue from the Jagannath Temple and British laws governing the monastic wealth of the temple and the pilgrim tax may not lead to any superficial conclusion as regards his outlook on religious life in India and, the British administrator's role in administering the temple institutions still the generalisations he made thereof, come somewhat nearer to truth.

Hunter developed the notion that Orissa was basically uninhabitable, and uncivilised well until the Aryan colonisation of the country and the country was civilised only through obscure revolutions by which this strip of Indian court had passed from an uninhabited jungle to a province. "No curious mosses nor antique forms of life from its coast have found their way into the amber of the Vedic hymns. The great epic itself, with its bright nucleus in Hindustan, and its broad comet like tail curving downwards in the streams of light to the furthest point of the peninsula, sheds not a momentary flicker over Orissa. In modern times, seen at even less remote distance than that from which English writers on India have viewed the province, its history seems to be little more than an interminable list of kings and of confused dynastic changes. With these changes however, I shall but sparingly trouble the reader. But their effect upon the people, and the revolutions they have wrought in human existence and human beliefs; the struggles by which a race, burried in its primitive jungles, has from time to time painfully cast its skin and assumed new forms of life; above all, the stages by which diverse ethnical elements have grown together into the composite rural communities of the present day".[165] Hunter continued to assert this point about Orissan history time and again and sentences like "little is known regarding this kingdom before 6th century B.C., probably making to the fact of its being uninhabitable",[166] it ceases to be a matter of surprise that the only features of ancient Orissa still distinctly discernible from this distance are that enveloping jungle and the frequent shifting and rising of the land. The earliest legends speak of kings hunting over the sites of the buried cities, and stumbling against the pinnacles of forgotton shrines. The first Aryan settlers from the north found Orissa buried under forests and tall grasses", and that "even after Muslims now affected their settlements, the country was so little adopted for military movements on a large scale that its governors frequently asserted their independence and defined their viceregal troops. The Mohammedan conquerors gladly got rid of the scarcely accessible province as a bribe to the Marathas. Even at the present day it had not been deemed wise to subject the mountainous inland jungles to regular British control and the mouths of the Mahanadi still crop through a region of unbroken forest thirty miles broad to the sea"[167] are very common in his description of Orissa. Hunter's conclusion regarding the Mohammedan possession of Orissa by bribing the Marathas was not correct. It is an established conclusion that a Hindu dynasty which was supplanted by the Mohemmadans in 1568 A.D. did not have any connection with the Maratha authority. After describing the uncivilised character of the people of Orissa at the dawn of history, Hunter went on to identify though not directly the obscure revolutions that civilised this jungle, and uncivilised country throughout history thereafter. Of these obscure revolutions he identified Buddhism as the first while the last in the process was the British control of Orissa. In fact he identified religion as the first civilising factor of Orissa during different periods of history and British control over Orissa came in last. Speaking of the role of Buddhism as the most revolutionary civilising factor of Orissan history, Hunter said that the Buddhist hermits of Orissa seemed at first to have held a position analogous to that of the missionaries who first taught Christianity to the wild tribes of Prussia. Like them they started from the centre of their faith after it had attained stately proportions and had subdued the more civilised parts of the continent to its influences. Like them also they seem to have carried a love of the beautiful in God's works as well as in their conceptions of His being, which led them to fix their abodes in the most exquisite retreats of nature".

The coming of Buddhism in the sixth century B.C. provided an occasion to the depressed classes such as Turanians or Dravidians who had preserved their nationality pure and unmixed by isolating themselves in the jungles and hills of the south, to rise up in opposition to the Aryan and Brahmanical domination. At the same time too, the era of Buddhist predominance pre-eminently the two centuries before and after the coming of Christ, provided a new and attractive way of marking out India's ancient greatness. Untainted by the associations of Hinduism with superstition and priestly despotism, which contributed so much to its disparagement at the hands of the Victorians, Buddhism had at its core a 'great teacher who converted by persuasion to a rationalistic faith. Buddhist art too as revealed in such monuments as Sanchi, approached a European aesthetic which celebrated simplicity of design and a truthful representation of nature. Impressed by the values associated with this classical era, the British had to overlook the obvious paradox that those same people whom they defined as racially inferior had created a religion and an art which represented the apex of India's cultural achievement.

The process of the Buddhist revolution culminated in the rule of Aśoka, which presented the picture of an ancient kingdom governed by a code which elevated the moral duties of man into legal obligation. This patriarchal and orderly state of Buddhist Orissa thereafter dissolved into a despostic era. Continuing with his set of arguments, Hunter asserted that the movement of Aryan colonists down the Valley of the Ganges and skirting around Bengal to Orissa and through this tract to Madras coast brought about conflict of supremacy between Buddhism and Brahmanism as a result of swinging the picture of great political confusion in Orissa before the beginning of the Christian era. As a matter of fact the Buddhist texts of Ceylon, the Brahmanical archives of Jagannath alike declared that five centuries before Christ were centuries of northern invasion and of great confusion in Orissa. Successive waves of colonists from the north allowed the country no rest. Buddhism and Brahmanism in turn claimed the supremacy among the Aryan settlers, but those settlers as a body steadily increased in numbers and in power and imposed their language and their religion upon the people".[168] Hunter viewed that Buddhism played a vital role in civilising the Oriyas and their nation. He accepted the European perception by stating that "the popular notion in Europe is that this religion forms a cataclysm in the history of India, a violent and total upheaval which subverted the social relations and raised the military races and the low castes by the degradation of the Brahmans".[169] Hunter made his opinion on this revolutionary Buddhist religion by describing it as typical a religion of the Sanskrit speaking races as the Brahmanism which went before it and the Hinduism which succeeded it. The earliest form of the Brahmanical faith is the religion of a comparatively smaller race fighting its way among the tribes greatly inferior in civilisation and in spiritual conceptions. The next form is Buddhism which joins the spirituality or the first stage to an intense humanity. The third stage is that of hybrid spiritual conceptions, outward superstitions and inward unbelief which seems to have germinated almost simultaneously in India and Europe upon the breaking up of the ancient forms of aryan faith".[170] Contrary to the revolutionary character of this faith, Hunter found the caste system of the Aryan civilisation as a stumbling-block to the progress of the civilisation, which had been accepted as the starting point for the English to legislate in India not for a single nature, divided by artificial destructions of caste but for the diversity of races belonging to widely separated branches of the human family, requiring a very different treatment and representing distant stages of progress and civilisation.

Hunter considered the social conflict between the Aryans and more over among different castes as the hard reality of Orissan society. So he projected the idea that the Aryan colonisation of India can be accepted as a turbulent revolution of Indian history "while the true character of low castes has thus been established, the Brahmanas are still accepted as an ethnical entity. The priestly settlement by the Orissan Śaivite kings in the 6th century however forms one of many historical evidences which lend me doubt this postulate of Indian liberation. Taken alongwith similar phenomena in different parts of the country, it unfolds the Aryan colonisation of India in a new and rational light. It discloses no trace of that universal and absolute conquest by which the primitive Aryan settlers in northern Hindustan are assumed to have subdued the whole continent to their sway. On the contrary it dissipates the mist which has toned down their multiform migrations into homogenous advance and exhibits the natural compromises by which a small but gifted people affected their entrance among vastly more numerous races sometimes indeed by force of arms but generally by an amalgamation which the variety of later ages has more or less disguised".[171] Continuing his tirade against the caste based orthodox social system of the Aryans that stood in the way of British administration in India to introduce proper legislation to suit their imperialist ends, Hunter described the Brahmans as flexible as the rest of mankind changing with altered beliefs and necessities of the Indian world and amenable to social, perhaps ethnical, compromises and destitute of those august prescriptive rights which so long stood in the way of legislation and reform. The institutions of Hindus were so powerful that even the fury of the barbarian Muslim conquerors of the sixteenth century could not destroy the graceful Hindu architectural creation of the tenth century of Konark. The bigotry of Islam got defeated itself before the force of the Hindu institutions. The most powerful of the Orissan empires, the Gangas of the medieval age, exploited this tendency of the society and took upon the task of revolutionising the religion of Orissa and consequently the natural passion launched itself not on the palaces or monarches but on the temple of the Gods. In India architectural talent reached its meridian with the graver gothic taste of Europe betrayed the first symptoms of decline and finally disintegrated itself in Sun worship religion of the Vaiṣṇavite type, identified with the Vaiṣṇavite dynasty and destroyed after running a brief but beautiful course to give place to the warmer form of Viṣṇuvism represented by Jagannath. Jagannath, Hunter said, continued to hold sway rather permanently and his priests but skilfully working upon the Indian passion for pilgrimage have for six centuries made Orissa the Terra Saneta of the Hindus[172] and Jagannath formed the ultimate in the religious syncretism in Orissa.

But in religious reformations in India, Hunter did not find any form of permanency. In each reformation a process of materialising started soon so that in the course of a few generations the original conceptions lose sight of and the necessity of new reformation returns.

One would safely conclude that the first phase of revolution that civilised Orissa, according to Hunter, was religion and religious movements during different periods of rule under different dynasties. It was initially Buddhism and later Vaiṣṇavism which engulfed and served the imperial interests of different rulers and religion was the national passion and sonum bonum of the Orissa culture.

As Hunter descended upon describing the British rule in Orissa, we entered into the second phase of the revolution that civilised the Oriyas and their culture. This revolution was internly and intimately associated with the British rule in Orissa. In this also British imperial outlook on their approach to Indian history and civilisation became explicit. Hunter's analysis of Orissan history carried the imprints of his utilitarian outlook. Hunter began with the notion that "the growth of intermediate rights in the ownership of land forms the most conspicuous phenomenon in the history of Orissa under its foreign conquerors. For centuries under the Mohammedans and Marathas, the unhappy province knew no government but that of the sword, yet the very roughness of public administration allowed private rights to spring up unperceived and to harden into permanent charges upon the soil-charges which its local princes would never have tolerated. Thus from long anarchy and misery, a fair growth of rights has blossomed forth and the magnificence which the Hindu princes of Orissa concentrated upon themselves, is now distributed in the form of moderate prosperity among a long descending chain of proprietors each with its own set of rights in the land".[173] Commensurate with this line of thinking Hunter argued that three centuries of raids, hollow treaties and mutual wrongs elapsed before anything like subjugation of Orissa by the Muslim took place. Long after the Afghans had trodden the conspicuous Hindu dynasties of India into dust, Orissa asserted its independence and remained the stronghold of the ancient national faith. It was not till its princes had proved false to their trust and legend themselves with the Mussalmans against the patriot cause that they fell. Even the conquest of Orissa was reserved as one of the supreme triumphs of Akbar at a time when the imperial power had reached its culmination. The Mohammedan period in Orissan history is one full of raids and invasions. The history of Orissa stood forth as a type of Mohammedans system of conquest and it was not until the interests of the prince were made identical with the interests of the empire that it became a constituent part of the Mughal empire. Two hundred and fifty years of confused fighting had gone for nothing. In retrospect, Hunter came out candidly with the assertion that "I consign the dreamy hostilities that have made up Indian history".[174] The Mughals lost Orissa only when they had ceased to be worthy of holding it. Wretched as the state of Orissa had been under the Mughals, a half century of deeper misery remained for it under the Marahattas. The memory of these fifty years haunted the whole population like a nightmare long after it passed, under the British rule". Substantiating his judgements and conclusions, Hunter said, "I have most carefully examined the records of these periods but I can detect absolutely no trace of anything like an administration".[176] Another most detesting and heinous feature of this period was the most revolting form of slavery. Contrary to the gloomy features of the administration provided to the Oriyas by the Afghans, Mughals and Marahattas, the British rule in Orissa brought about marked change in the most revolutionary way not only in the political but also in the administrative history of Orissa.

In consonance with the vision developed by the British historians towards their rule in India, Hunter summarised the same as regards the administration of Orissan territory. "Conflict with external enemies became a thing of the past. Invasions and military occupation faded from the memory of the people, a single local rising is the only warlike event I had to narrate, and the province which during the former centuries had formed the traditional asylum of the revolt had lapsed into the most peaceful part of the British empire".[177]

Hunter's description of the British rule in Orissa was replete with statements justifying the British rule in the province. Hunter stated that, "True to our national character we settled in Orissa as merchants long before we made our appearance as rulers. Our earliest factory in Bengal lay within its boundaries but even this factory does not represent the first connection of Orissa with a European power". Establishment of maritime colonies and settlements during the Elizabethan era in England and thereafter during 17th century had become almost the national obsession for the average Englishmen. The early adventurers were all fearless men who set out unarmed to the land of the violent human savages in order to quell a dispute. They encountered physical danger, pitted themselves alone against fate and operated in the distant land. It was claimed that they were only trying to help a black man to lead a happier life or to increase the sum of England's geographical knowledge. There had always been the national euphoria that the territory of the British commerce should encompassed the whole mass of human habitation to an average English man, Cecil Rhodes Maxim "Philanthropy plus five percent", offered deigratia an enticing prospect and he simply fell for the half crazy flamboyance of this enigmatic imperial goliath: "I walked between earth and sky and when I looked down I said—the English shall rule this earth".[179] L.S.Amery described these men as Elizabethan. The suggestion behind the appellation was that they combined patriotism and vision with the love for power, wealth and a reasonable lack of scruple with regard to the methods adopted.[180]

The British eagerness in the creation of avenues for the establishment of factories and growth of commercial mercantilism in

Orissa was so rapid that it found itself being expressed in the dealings of the British doctors treating Indian higher class patients. One such example was referred to by Hunter, "Two years afterwards (in 1636), an English surgeon (named W. Gabriel Boughton of the ship "Hopewell") had the good fortune to cure a daughter of the Emperor whose clothes had caught fire, and in 1640 he successfully treated one of the ladies of the Bengal Viceroy's Zanana. When asked to name his own reward, the patriotic doctor said he wished nothing for himself, but begged that his countrymen might be allowed a maritime settlement in Bengal. The public spirited surgeon died before he could even receive the thanks of his masters, but not before the imperial commissions had been made out granting the English a land factory at Hugli and a maritime settlement at Balasore. These two Orissa harbours—Pippli, founded in 1635 and Balasore, founded in 1642—formed the basis of the future greatness in Orissa.[181]

As regards the situations that led the Mughal emperor to grant settlement permission to the British in Orissa went like this in Hunter's work "The very advantages of the Dutch and Portuguese settlements proved their ruin. They found themselves in the incessant struggles and revolutions which afflicted Bengal long before they were strong enough to take part with safety in so great a game. The Delhi emperor viewed with well ground suspicion that the establishment of an imperium in imperio in the Gangetic Valley. After harassing the settlers with exactions and ignorminies of various sorts, he decided that no European ship should enter any of the Bengal rivers, and when our patriotic surgeon extorted from him a great maritime settlement for the English, he fixed it outside, on the Orissa coast. There we obscurely grew strong, remote from the great events in Mughal history, and generally able to hold our own amid the troubles which in a smaller scale afflicted that province". Even then peaceful Orissa was possible only within the range of the English cannon and thousands of weaving families flocked to Balasore and squatted around the British factory. Moreover the Marathas had made themselves hated by every class of the people, the petty princes trampled for their lands, the peasantry during two generations had lived in a chronic state of flight into the jungle and even the priests of Lord Jagannath had learnt to detest their Maratha co-religionists for their endless extortions. "Half a century of misrule and license had left to the Maratha, little trace of what unflinching courage which a generation before had decided the fate of a hundred battles. Above all the Marathas trampled out every vistage of civil rule beneath their horses hoofs and this surpreme hour of British rule seems to have aroused".[183] Though the Maratha misrule paved the way for the British subjugation of Orissa, Hunter considered the British as worthy enough to rule with law in the country. "If we won the great province of Orissa with little loss to ourselves it is because we deserved to do so. Had our troops started a month earlier, or month later, the four hundred little bearers for the sick would have had much heavier work. A few weeks before, the state of the floods would have rendered the country impossible by our artillery, and the malaria would have killed off our men like an infected flock of sheep. A few weeks later, the dry flat rice fields would have afforded exactly the sort of fighting ground which the Maratha cavalry loved. Their horse would have devoured our little body of infantry, trampling in upon it from every point of compass; harassing it on the march, at its meals, by night and by day, during every minute of the twenty four hours we chose exactly the time which a collector of an Orissan district, after years of acquaintance with the country, would have recommended for the advance of a column of infantry against masses of cavalry. Our free-handed outlay of money for provisions and carriages—our carefully collected information as to the route—our pacific proclamations to the people—our politic benevolence to Jagannath and his priests above all our ceaseless movement in the face of the Maratha soldiery, who were as much foreigners as ourselves and more hateful to the natives—in short, every incident of the campaign merited success and obtained. it".[184] The description of the occupation of Orissa carried with it the ultimate victory of civilisation over barbarism, of modernity over primitivism, of arithmatic over shopkeepers accounts. Besides there were attempts to divide the Indian people into separate nationalities. The description of the Marathas as foreigners like the British, was an attempt at pointing in the same direction. However after the occupation the British administration attempted at giving order to the rule in Orissa and introducing the rule of law in the country to which the Oriyas were not accustomed. Though a series of difficulties beset the British administration every day, the British administrators governed the province on a totally distinct plan.

One of the most important aspects of Indian society, which drew Hunter's attention, was the existence of one of the worst forms of slavery. Both in his attempt at understanding Indian people and also the people of Orissa, he tried to fit elements of feudal mode of economy into the economy of Orissa. Even if he had gone to the extent of concluding that the form of slavery had remained universal throughout the Asian continent. At some points of his analysis we find him being too rash. He stated, "I find that I must dwell for a moment on one of its most revolting details, in order that the reader may rightly understand the difficulties which beset our first attempts at Government in Orissa. In India, and indeed throughout Asia, slavery forms the last refuge of an utterly crushed and despiring people. To the honour of the Hindus be it spoken, that anything like the barbarities of our western plantations had never been known in Hindustan. The slave in the east may be oppressed, but a Hindu master never beats him; the jungle yields an unfailing refuge to the miserable and as long as he remains in service he is sure of his daily bread. In another volume indeed I have pointed out how such serfdom may merely represent the last resource of labour, when placed by over population completely at the mercy of the capital. In Orissa it formed the sole refuge of a people who despaired of earning a subsistence for themselves. During famines, mothers had been accustomed to sell their children for a few pence, and every great household in Bengal, English as well as the native, had domestics of this class. In Malabar alone they numbered 16,574 in 1800 and to this day each of the chief Orissa castes had nominally certain servile families attached to it. Local tradition derives them from the intercourse of castes between whom no *jus connubii* exists and from the old practices of the father-in-law presenting to the bridegroom a bevy of young housemaids along with the bride. Each caste has thus its own illegitimate or servile branch, except indeed the Brahmans who are otherwise supplied".[185] By such observation and analysis Hunter tried to prove that slavery as a system was prevalent as a social practice among all the communities and castes of Orissa. This generalisation about the widespread character of the system was definitely far from historical truth. Although he wanted to exclude the Brahmins, Hunter concluded by stating that the Brahmins were also procuring the slaves from different sources which he did not specify. However, he stated that the history of Orissa is resplendent in the existence of the system of slavery from time immemorial. "This ancient and not unkindly form of serfdom existed from time immemorial in Orissa. But the miseries of Marathas misrule developed a new and altogether different phase of slavery. The peasantry in despair of wringing their daily bread from the soil, either sold themselves across the seas or were driven to the coast like dumb creatures and shipped on board by their marauding governors. The Ganjam records disclose miserable gangs of them who had been landed for sale in Southern India and rescued by the compassion of English officials. While nothing seemed more natural to the Indian mind than the practice of very poor people accepting domestic servitude for life in their native place, nothing could be more revolting to it than a sea-going trade in human flesh. One of our officers has declared transportation across the sea to be as much dreaded in, Orissa as death (*Macpherson's report on Kondhs* Part VII Para 87). Puri road stead was the principal place of their exportation, and many a frail craft with its shrieking freight was driven on shore on the Madras Coast. Wretched footsore parties, reached in southern India by our officers were passed northwards from one British factory to another till they arrived at the Orissa, frontier—leaving a residue of sick and dying in the English hospitals en route. At length the evil reached such a height that the Madras Government had to level a thunder bolt in the shape of proclamation (dated 27th July, 1789) against a practice so detrimental to the country and injurious to the rights of humanity. But neither this nor a similar proclamation issued the year before by the Governor-General in Calcutta and which offered a reward of £5 for each person delivered from slavery could stop the inhuman detestable traffic. In 1794 the slave trade from Bengal had reached as far as St. Helena and the Court of Directors found itself forced to take up the question. Proclamations, rewards, and penalties remained alike in effectual so long as the Marathas held the sea coast of Orissa. From the day we entered the province this abomination also ceased. The memory of it has utterly passed away; but for the original papers which I here cite in support of my statements, its existence at any time would now be denied".[186] The British who had been so compassionate towards this class of people did not bother to go into the origin of the system, which was essentially lying in the lack of a proper and coherent distribution system. The condition of the natives of south and south western Orissa comprising Koraput and Kalahandi district had remained very miserable since time immemorial. The reasons may be found in the continuity of regular droughts and lack of distribution system in the State. After the British occupation of Orissa, they wanted to streamline the administration, police and judicial system which was essential for the assessment and appropriation of revenue whereas they hardly bothered about the expansion of agriculture and introduction of a proper distribution system which could have been done by investing a very insignificant portion of surplus revenue. That virtually led to the great famine of 1866 which exposed the exploitation and misrule of the British in Orissa, about which they had boasted against the Marathas.

However, Hunter's anaylsis of the system of operating in Orissa from the earliest times to the Maratha period carried with it a sober and rational treatment from the historiographical point of view.

Summing up Hunter's conceptions on Orissa History down to the British rule, one can find a distinct imperial attitude, where justification of their rule on the backdrop of limitations of indigenous rule in Orissa, till the advent of the British was imminent. In order to achieve this objective, Hunter started with the notion that Orissa remained a primitive and uncivilised country and the province was civilised through obscure revolutions. He identified these revolutions in two sectors. First, religious upheaval during different periods of her history where the imperial rules exploited the religious passion of the people to thrive on power. Secondly, the advent of the British exposed and stalled the misdeeds and misrule of the Afghan, Mughal and Maratha rulers. The British, Hunter claimed, emerged in Orissa under the popular backing where the introduction of the rule of law was imperative and it was only the British who achieved this. In this indirect, British justification for their rule over India came rather candidly in Hunter's explanations.

Though Hunter took an imperialist view point on the history of Orissa, he made a humble analysis of the source materials of Orissan history and made a presentation of the facts mainly on society and culture which very well fulfil to some extent the requirements of sober history. He did not have any hesitation in comparing the Orissa architecture with those of the best of European history and described the art and architecture of Orissa with all their greatness. Even as a foreigner having an imperial bent in his outlook, he did not hesitate to humbly submit his failures in reading through local source materials. In one case he said, "These curious relics will soon I hope, be treated by a scholar who brings to the subject greater knowledge and technical accuracy than I have been able to devote to it".[187] His sincerity and ingenuity for historical research and inquisitiveness to give a proper shape to Orissan history was so strong that he expressed not only his satisfaction but also his indebted to R.L.Mitra. Hunter referred to Rajendra Lal Mitra, whose famous work "*Antiquities of Orissa*" was going to be published by that time. In anticipation of this work he thought it unnecessary to give his own measurements and other art notes made on the spot. He was indebted to him/Mitra for the photographs of Bhubaneswar. Hunter did not simply take the sources he used for granted. For in accepting Madāla Pañjī the temple chronicle of Jagannath Temple, Hunter said, the records of the struggles did yield nothing of interest to a historian and the native annalists have enveloped the whole with mist of exaggeration and falsehood. At this point, Hunter made his opinion on history rather clear. "A narrative of confused and miscellaneous fighting is not history".[188] This particular statement carried lots of meaning in regard to sober historiography. Similarly Hunter was highly sceptical about the authenticity and veracity of Muslim records. Among the Muslims, the literary instinct, unlike that of the Hindus involved in religious poetry and drama, found a clear outlet in history. In India as soon as a province underwent a permanent and direct association with the Mohammedans its history emerged from the wonderland of temple archives and sacred songs, and became only a question of time in searching out fragmentary allusions to it in the Mohammedan manuscripts "But unhappily these new materials do not form straight paths covering to common conclusions but a labyrinth of crossroads intersecting each other at the most perplexing angles and which after willing on the traveller in the hope of new discoveries often stop short in the midst of trackless jungles whenever two sources of materials exist, Indian history finds itself reduced to an unsatisfactory reconciliation of conflicting evidence. No sooner does it dare to be critical than it becomes inconclusive and passes beyond the open and sunny domain of the annalist into the dim regions of antiquarian research".[189] At this point Hunter brought out the tasks of historian and wanted to draw parameters required for objective history writing. "So long as the past of a country involves at every step an intricate disquisition the free pace and far reaching glance of history one alike dangerous and impossible. It is only when the antiquarian has finished his part of the work that the historian can safely begin and the rash artist which goes sketching in an unmapped country runs an excellent chance of closing his career in a bewildering forest of quagmire. If I have accepted this peril', Hunter said, "the credit is due to those kind scholars who with greater opportunity for such labours than myself have guided me across leagues of unexpected ground and to the patient devotion of the men who in time past have given their lives to Indian research".[190] Similarly in case of Orissan history Hunter felt that it would not be fair to hide the conflict of opinions, which did exist in the scholarly debate. Endless antiquarian discussions were intolerable in a historical work but such a work could even be more disfigured by dishonest concealment. Hunter had very rightly cultivated this thinking in his indological research and had laboured to give all technical details and the process of reaching conclusions in every case. He, however, reached the heights of academic honesty when he said that "We British complained that the Hindus do not appreciate our English institutions or accept our beliefs. Do we rightly understand theirs?". Hunter's articulation of Orissan history displayed a curious mixture of magisterial approach fostered by the Raj syndrome and scientific history.

(D)

JOHN BEAMES' VISION OF ORISSA

John Beames, the clodhopping collector as he was popularly called, belonged to the two last members of Haileyburian elites to be trained under the Company's dominion. He was a member of the privileged Indian Civil Service, which gave him an assured position and the right to be himself. Then, in the districts, the District Collector was the supreme. As the District Collector, his works were extremely varied; there were plenty of it but most of it were interesting. He had the respect of the people among whom he lived. His pay never seemed quite enough for the education of eight or nine children in England, but he had the prospect of an annuity on retirement or pension for his wife, if he died during his service career. John Beames, thus belonged to a very privileged service, in which the Haileyburians kept the crucial senior positions until well into the 1870s. Because of his outspokenness Beames had to face a lot of trials and tribulations throughout his ICS career. Inspite of all his shortcomings and limitations, he rose to the position of Commissioner over a number of districts and for a short time held a seat on the Bengal Board of Revenue.

The young man to be weighed in balance, John Beames reached India from Haileybury's last class. His standing fourth among the thirty two was not a bad achievement, because he excelled everyone else in Persian, and received prizes for Sanskrit and classics. Had he been as strong in mathematics as in languages, Beames would certainly have headed his class. When he reached Calcutta for further language study he realised that he had joined a veritable English aristocracy in India. Nearly every Haileyburian he met was related to or had some patronage connection with some of the high officials of the Government of India. Hence, Beames immediately found his way into the "best society", a matter of considerable significance throughout his career.

Reverend Thomas Beames, the father of John Beames was the perfect type of muscular Christian, an incessant talker, and omnivorous reader, a vigorous sportsman, hot tempered but easily pacified, very outspoken, straightforward and honourable. All these character traits were well inherited by John Beames. John Beames found the Haileybury entrance examination very easy. What impressed him most about the school itself was that India hardly ever became the subject of conversation "except by the few who really worked nor did we as a rule care or know or seek to know anything about it".[191] Later Beames criticised this non-chalance in preparation for the actual experience of Oriental language and culture, or of civil administration. Beames left the impression that the Haileyburian milieu stereotyped India, because it promised the beastly hot climate; on the other, they assumed that the niggers there required tutelage and civilisation if not trusteeship. Because the English could easily grasp the essentials, of Indian administration, they did not bother much about India before they set first in Calcutta. Max Mueller, who had helped prepare ICS candidates, largely held James Mill and his history responsible for inculcating this image, erroneous about India reprehensible for English educational institution.

Given such influences, it was not surprising that John Beames, while approaching his retirement and faced by the prospects of eventual Indianisation of Indian Civil Service, saw his English upbringing, inheritance and education in a different life altogether. While John Beames was in Punjab, the momentous clash of ideologies in British India took place in 1882-83 over the Ilbert Bill. At stake in this piece of legislation, which sought to empower Indians acting as Magistrates in the countryside to try European British subjects, were contending views of the nature of the Raj that cut to the pore of the British justification for their presence in India. In the course of this controversy, which grew ever more embittered until its final ambiguous resolution, the British were forced as never before to choose between the fundamental principles of imperial governance. The supporters of the Bill insisted that the Indians and the Britons must, when similarly qualified, be accorded equal treatment. On the one side were ideals dear to the hearts of the liberals: equality before the law and the transformative power of education on the other side stood the Bill's opponents who insisted on the essential difference of race, and argued for a legal system that would accommodate that difference. One was a vision of eventual '*sameness*', the other of enduring difference. Between these views of an empire, founded on equity and one avowedly grounded in force the alternatives were starkly posed. Writing as the Commissioner of Burdwan district against the Ilbert Bill (1882), he shuddered at the anomalous situation raised by admitting a young native gentleman, particularly a Bengali to his covenanted Civil Service and to the bench of the High Court. He nevertheless, maintained the camaraderie of the Haileyburians in Indian administration. Of this scheme comprised of "Victorian sons". Beames stated "the Haileyburian men in most cases turned out well in India and our having two years together governs a camaraderie which the competition had not".[192] While in Punjab he wrote of standing shoulder to shoulder with men of respect due to an official superior was "compared by the spirit of espirit de corps which made us all support each other and by feeling that official rank was a mere temporary accident and that we are all really English gentlemen socially equal"[193] Side by side, there were the ideals of despotic rule in regard to the administrators' role in relation to people, which was found to have been reflected in the works of Beames. The British codifying procedure was never wholly compelling. The enlightened Britishers still continued to believe that India was a land suited for despotism. In part a nostalgia nourished by early nineteenth century Romanticism, this dissident ideal flourished principally among officials in newly conquered territories, before the courts had been established. These were called as non-regulation provinces. It reached its ultimate flowering in the Punjab during the years following the conquest of it in 1849, when the province was ruled by the brothers John Beames and Henry Lawrence. For the officers of this Punjab school, the ideal as John Beames described it, was that of 'personal government', in which the Magistrate would decide cases either sitting on horse back in the village gateway, or under a tree outside the village walls, and write his decisions on his knee ... and be off to repeat the process in the next village. Not all officers, as the dissident Beames reported, like being turned into "homeless vagrant governing machines" and in any case regulation and the rule of law could not for ever be kept at bay even in the Punjab".[194] Still throughout the later nineteenth century, self assurance fostered by the Punjab ideal permitted officers in the province a wider range of discretionary authority than was customary elsewhere in India. These discretionary powers allowed to the Punjab officer virtually marked out a path that was to lead in 1919 to the infamous Amritsar Massacre.

When confronted at Champaran in Bengal by an explosive indigo planter, Beames could write, 'it was not as some of my detractors alleged, from mere lust of power that I insisted on being master of my district and having my own in all things, but because the district was a sacred trust delivered to me by the government and I was bound to be faithful to that charge...."[195] That official doctrine W.S.Setonkerr declared in 1864 had been inherited from Haileybury.[196]

During his career in India, Beames ran into troubles and was dragged into controversies many a time because of his assumed doctrine of bureaucratic egalitarianism for all Europeans. The memoirs demonstrated that, Beames resented Richard Temple's ego building at his own expense. He was highly critical of his superiors and of the jobbery so characteristic within the service and particularly many of the military civilians. As it was normal in government service he had frequent transfers and postings. But undaunted, Beames used his powers as a Magistrate-Collector to apply the new codes of law developed earlier. It had been held that the British were determined always to mark out the Raj as a moral, civilised and civilising regime. For this purpose, they viewed that a rule of law conceived of as the use of standardised impartial procedures for the settlement of disputes was essential. Although it was impossible on their part to give to India their own English law, they could give India codes of legal procedure, even if the English law could be fashioned and its substance could be introduced. In this process, they could fulfil to their satisfaction their avowed civilising mission. "The establishment of a system of law which regulates the most important parts of the daily life of the people constitutes in itself a moral conquest more striking, more durable and far more solid, than the physical.[196] W.S.Setonkerr's speech at Calcutta in 1864 at a dinner for Haileyburians. (see *Memories of old Haileybury College*, 1894, pp. 90-95).

"Conquest rendered it possible. It exercises an influence over the minds of the people in many ways comparable to that of a new religion ... Our law is in fact the sum and substance of what we had to teach them. It is so to speak, a compulsory gospel which admits of more decency and disobedience".[197] In Champaran, where he was appointed because of his success in Purnea, had to confront determined indigo planters that led to further trouble with the government. When government ascertained that Beames had supported the royats (cultivators) in the local resistance movement against the planters, he was temporarily suspended from government service and later was reinstated and was posted at Balasore. Beames had to experience the disgrace and vindictiveness of the government because of his criticism of John Lawrence's frontier policy with respect to Nepal. John Lawrence as Viceroy was not interested in the advice of young civilians on such points anymore than what he was earlier in Punjab,

Beames had spent happy years of his civil service career while he was serving in Balasore during 1869-1873 and in Cuttack during 1873-77. Eventually he officiated as Commissioner at Cuttack at a salary of about three thousand pound sterling. Beames had always been highly critical of the sincerity of the British government in regard to its liberal policies and reformist commitments. Beames imagined that the British Raj had never been visible during its initial formation. He stated it was like one of those large coral islands in the Pacific built up by millions of tiny insects age after age. Men admire the beauty of the land and profit by its fertility, but who thinks of the insects who built it up?"

Sharp, intelligent, clever and straight forward, Beames was mentally set for confrontation and was prepared to fight exploitative zamindars, abusive planters and pompous officials. But never was his approach to liberal reforms doctrinaire or crusading. For example, when he witnessed innumerable abuses in the Cuttack Collectorate, he tackled them one by one and vented his criticism appropriately. Whereas George Campbell while on furlough in 1852, published three books in order to influence the parliamentary review of Indian affairs, John Beames reserved his tilting at windmills to official provincial India. That virtually led Mason in aptly characterising Beames as a "nose the ground reformer".[200]

At Purnea, he organised family relief and initiated strong sanitation measures and also tried to enforce sanitation habits among the people. At Champaran, Beames asserted his authority as the Collector and organised relief programme by the mutual co-operation of the government officials and planters. When a severe famine struck Cuttack in 1874, only eight years after the terrible famine of 1866, Beames faced the personification of all he disliked in the British Indian administration. "The obstacle was not the plantocracy but Richard Temple, sent by Lord Northbrook to manage the relief. Temple, however, mismanaged it to the extent that George Campbell resigned as the Lieutenant Governor of Bengal and Temple replaced him. Temple—and not only Beames implied this—excelled in self promotion. Beames described the mode of operation thus: "In his usual theatrical way he rode at the rate of fifty or sixty miles a day through the districts, farming as he said, an opinion of the conditions of the people and the state of the crops". Beames wondered how he could possibly form any form of opinion at such a gallop. But at night he would sit down and write 'a vain glorious minute', upon which the government then acted contrary to the advices of local officials and at a great waste of money and grains".[201]

At Balasore, Beames protested against the fines imposed on peasants, irrespective of their producing salt or not, but living near areas of salt production. The government had monopoly over the salt production. Consequently, they were allowed to produce and process salt for their own use, but not for sale. Also in Balasore, Beames exposed the zamindars who charged tikkus (cesses of all kinds) from the ryots, who under the permanent settlement were left quite unprotected. Zamindars and their agents took advantage of the situation by levying taxes citing varied pretexts. Beames unsupported by the government of which Temple was then a Finance Member (1868-74) stopped large number extortions without further legislations.

In his observation on Ilbert Bill, Beames evinced remarkable analytical powers. Neither his promotion in service nor his publications as a philologist gave him sufficient confidence to expose his thinking on the fundamental issues raised by Ilbert Bill (1882). Fortunately, Barun Dey illuminated those silent years by his study of Beames 'paternalism' and its defensive reaction to Indian nationalism".[202] The controversy over the Ilbert Bill led directly to the appointment of a Commission to study the demand, based on English promises for fifty years, for the Indianisation of the Civil Service. Unfortunately Beames betrayed the same degree of contempt towards the Bengalis and Oriyas, as he did for his superiors in the Secretariat. So the explicit concern of Beames for the social welfare of the peasants had to be discounted. The behaviour of Beames displayed the facts that he wanted, to be 'lord and master' over all sectors of society in his districts where he served. More fundamentally as Beames himself revealed in 1883, he could not bring himself to recognise individual Indians who had advanced into the ICS as his academic and cultural equals. In fact, he preferred to see the Bengali 'competition-wallah' in the ICS as a dangerous revolutionary. Necessarily, he was to be kept in his place lest he would subvert the very power base of the English rule India. Comprehensively, he feared the rise of the Bengali elites with his 'extravagant pretensions, and excessive self conceit' and its desire for political power. He and many of his peers believed strongly that the Bengali could never be entrusted with the rule of India. In 1883, he summed up his visions for opposing the Ilbert Bill by stating, "... the measure is not called for by any administrative convenience (in having Europeans judged by Europeans) that it is not desired by the natives as a body that it is intensely distasteful and humiliating to all Europeans and that it will tend seriously to impair the prestige of British rule in India. In fact, under a very simple and insignificant form, it conceals the elements of a revolution which may ere long prove the ruin of the empire".[203]

This scholarly attainments of John Beames in India was extraordinarily significant. When one thinks of the scholarly dimensions of Beames' achievements, it was unfair that Lyall should reign as the man of letters and Beames remained as the clodhopping collector. In his linguistic ability Beames was compared favourably with Robert Needhm Cust, who had complete mastery over eight Asian and eight European languages. Beames had won a medal in Persian and a prize in Sanskrit at Haileybury. He picked up Bengali, Punjabi, Hindi and Urdu in India. He had knowledge of classical languages and knew German, French and Italian. And his facility in English far exceeded that of the average Briton.[204]

Beames had found gratification in Oriental Studies, particularly in philology. Fortunately, Beames' grandson and C.E.Buckland in their *Dictionary of Indian Biography* had provided a complete history of his philological writings. First came his '*Outlines of Indian Philology*' in 1867. Then followed his edition of Henry M. Elliots's '*Supplementary Glossary of Indian Terms*' in 1869. During the happiest years of his collectorship (1872-79), he produced his magnum opus '*Comparative Grammar of the Modern Aryan Languages of India*' in three volumes. Beames himself wrote that this work was 'favourably reviewed in English and German papers and adopted as a text book in many universities. It won me considerable reputation and fame'.[205]

Inspite of the dislikings against John Beames, because he did not prove himself to be a 'specimen of the Punjab official', Cust took notice of the philological works of Beames as early as 1878. In his '*The Languages of the East Indies*' Cust wrote of the great grammarian, who came in the wake of the army of linguistic skirmishers, who dealt with a single language like the missionaries Carry and Marshman. This recognition of Beames as first of this class of grammarians was confirmed as early as 1960. Suniti Kumar Chatterjee declared Beames to be the 'founder of a science, a pioneer who laid down the great principles of comparative linguistics of the Aryan languages'. In fact, Barun De suggested that Beames may have inspired the work of George A. Grierson, who in his *'Linguistic Survey of India'* acclaimed Beames as one of the first authorities in the field. Barun De, despite all his reservations had placed Beames among the most brilliant scholars in the ICS who endeavoured to learn all the dialects and languages of the district to which they were posted. As late as 1891, Beames wrote a grammar for the Bengali language which in 1922 was still being used as a text book for the ICS probationers.

It was only the linguistic expertise and academic pursuits with which John Beames virtually saved the independent existence of Oriya language vis-a-vis the onslaught of the Bengalis who started a concerted campaign under the leadership of Babu Rajendralal Mitra against the Oriya language. John Beames vehemently opposed their arguments. In one session of the Asiatic Society of Bengal, 1870, he strongly refuted arguments of Babu Rajendralal Mitra and Kanti Chandra Bhattacharya on Oriya language. In that session he read a paper entitled, "*On the Relations of Oriya to the Other Modern Aryan Languages*", wherein Beames argued that despite being spoken by a few people in terms of linguistics and grammar, Oriya was a fully independent language. Further, if Oriya was to be suppressed because it was spoken only by a few millions of people, it might also be argued that Dutch, Danish or Portuguese could be obliterated also. Basque should also be stamped out and the same argument would apply to Romanic or modern Greek and would justify the Russians in trying to eradicate Polish or Austrians annihilating Czechs.[207] John Beames' straightforward arguments in favour of the Oriya language foiled the attempt of some Bengali elites in their anti-Oriya language movement. Thus Oriya was once again established as the official language. The wrong impressions created about Oriya being a sub-language of the Bengali language, because of some phonetic similarity, was removed. Giving geographical account of Orissa, Beames had said that "Oriya was spoken by over 50 lakhs of people and this was also the mother tongue of the hilly people of this State".[208] Beames considered Bengali as a relatively younger language. During his tenure in Orissa, he patronised with great zeal the Oriya language and literature and brought to light many Oriya palm leaf manuscripts. It was his generous support and encouragement that provided opportunity for the rise of 'Vyasa Kavi' Fakir Mohan Senapati, the father of Oriya novels. In his '*Atmajivan Charita* (Autobiography)' Fakir Mohan Senapati had acknowledged the greatness of John Beames in high sounding words. He wrote, 'In civilian circles and educated Indian society the then Balasore District Collector Mr John Beames was famed to be an extraordinary learned man with proficiency in eleven languages. He was engaged in his '*Comparative Grammar of Indian Languages*' and whilst writing this twenty lingual opus, required a scholar versed in three languages Bengali, Oriya and Sanskrit. My benefactor Halm Saheb took me to meet him. He asked me a few grammatical questions, incorporated them in his grammar. I suddenly became known among the Europeans as a scholar: In a treeless region even the tiny castor oil plant is regarded as a tree. Beames told me to come to see him at least once a week. Sometimes, when I was a day or two late he would ask, the moment he saw me, "What explanation have you to offer for this delay in coming to see me?" Our talks were invariably linguistic though ranging over such topics as Sanskrit couplets, Bengali prose, the Oriya '*Rasakallola*' and *"Snake and witches charms"*.[209] Fakir Mohan's association with John Beames virtually stalled the Bengali conspiracy of destroying Oriya identity. Beames contributed enormously for the development of female education in Orissa and enrichment of Oriya language. During a controversy between the Bengalis and Oriyas, Fakir Mohan had stated Bengali officers and senior clerks feared me because I enjoyed European favour. Virtually all the senior officers and better paid office staff in Balasore were then Bengali. Beames strongly supported me in the promotion of female education in Balasore and in the presentation and enrichment of the Oriya language. Whenever I landed in a scrape it was invariably Beames who rescued me. Indeed that magnanimous man was the taproot of all my worldly success. I shall remember his sacred name to the last moment of my life".[210] Fakir Mohan was so much impressed by his scholarship and interest in Oriya language that he dedicated his book '*Kalakanda Ramayana*' to John Beames.

John Beames, however, was never significantly prolific in the field of historical writing. Some of his historical works appeared in the *Journal of Asiatic Society of Bengal*, the *Indian Antiquary* and the *Indian Observer*, which had distinct value in their own standards.

He wrote the manual of the district of Balasore. But this could not be published because Richard Temple doubted the credibility of the accounts and pointed some errors within it. Beames made the presentation on the morning after he had mimicked Richard Temple on the occasion of the latter's visit to Cuttack. Having just been mocked by one whom Temple considered a '*par venue*', the great man refused, understandably, to give the Balasore manual the official approval. Beames never touched the manual again. His major historical work "*Notes on the History of Orissa Under the Mohammedan, Maratha and English Rule*',[211] which reads like a chronicle met with the same fate. This was initially written in the form of notes and as chapter two of the manual of the district of Balasore. The work when completed was laid before Sir Richard Temple, then the Lieutenant Governor of Bengal, but for certain reasons Beames wanted to keep it secret the work could not be printed. In 1872 the Secretary of the Asiatic Society of Bengal Mr Blochman sought his permission to print the work but Beames did not comply with his request. Later, when he was entrusted with the charge of Burdwan sub-division, the necessity of certain research work prompted him to publish the work ultimately. John Beames had two other major articles to his credit, namely, "*The Altai Hills in Cuttack*",[212] and '*More Buddhist Remains from Orissa*'.[213] Besides, his '*memoirs*' contained a lot of historical information and judgements along with aesthetic observations of some of the archeological monuments of the places he saw as a civil servant. These stray writings of Beames exposed the historical sense, attitude, and expertise, which could be expected only from the professionals. These works revealed that Beames had noticed and analysed the archeological monuments of Orissa as an expert art critic.

His reports to the House of Commons on Orissa as part of his official duty as Collector and Commissioner also contained significant historical references and his attitudes and conceptions imbibed thereon. John Beames served the first four years of his ICS career in Orissa (1869-73) at Balasore, during which he wrote "*The Manual of the District of Balasore*". The manual contained detailed information about the history, geography, land tenures, caste, industries and all sorts of things, thus making the work fullfledged in every respect. "*Notes on the History of Orissa Under Mughal, Maratha and English Rule*" was written initially as a part of this manual.

Quite obviously, he had dealt with the life and culture of Balasore, notes on the people, their language, and life style, fighting between the Afghans and Mughals at this place, British trade, revenue administration and other things. Indeed the people of Balasore were provided a special and distinct status in his writing. For quite a long time, the Bengali elites were demanding Balasore as a part of Bengal and to consider that the language of the Oriyas was derived from the Bengali language. John Beames had vehemently opposed this argument of the Bengalis. Beames reiterated that "they are not an offshoot of the Bangali is proved by the fact that their language was already formed as now we have it, at a period when Bengali had not yet attained a separate existence and when the deltaic portions of Bengal was still uninhabited, so that, in fact, they could not have sprung from the Bengalis simply because there were then no Bengalis to spring from".[214]

John Beames had also referred to some political, historical and geographical factors, in order to prove the separate identity of the Oriya language. "Numerous as are the allusions in early Oriya history to the north western and western parts of India and frequent as were their expeditions to the south, it is remarkable that there is no-where in all their annals more than obscure occasional mention of Bengal and then even as a far—off inaccessible place. The similarity between the languages is not by any means so great as some Bengali writers have sought to make out and what similarity there is due to the fact that they are both dialects of the eastern or Madadhi form of Prakrit".[215]

"Notes on the History of Orissa During Mughal, Maratha and British Rule" presented a true and complete picture of Beames Magisterial readings of British perception in India. He believed in the British historiographical conception that only intervention from without could halt the spiral of decline and progress of India's civilisation. "ex Occidente Imperium', as Risley put it, "the genius of the empire in India has come to her from the West".[216] This was the determining factor both of India's ethnology and history. It had been frequently held by the British that India's Muslim conquerors were made to share with the Aryans the task of revitalizing a decadent society. These nations had its imprints right from the beginning of

Beames' thesis. In order to justify his arguments, even he had referred to Stirling's work which was silent about Balasore. Beames stated, "Stirling's account of Orissa has been long in print, and is so well known that it would be superfluous to repeat what is there said about the various dynasties of Orissa. It will have struck many readers of that work that often as the towns and the regions of the Cuttack and Pooree districts are mentioned in the historical portion, Balasore is hardly spoken of. One would not of course expect to find it mentioned under the name of Balasore, because Balasore as a town is the creation of the English and quite a modern place, but no other towns, villages or parganas in this part of the province are ever mentioned. Till the arrival of the Mussalmans, no event in Oriya history took place there, nor is there any evidence of its having been scantily peopled, if at all.

It will not, therefore, take long to put together the scattered notices that exist during the Hindu and Mohammadan periods. From the people themselves not much can be got, the best informed of them cannot with few exceptions, go back further than the sanads granted to their ancestors by the provincial governors under Aurangzeb or at farthest Shah Jehan and the majority do not as a rule know who their own great grandfathers were and do not care".[217] The arguments thus put forward by Beames displayed clearly his imperial visions and side by side his ignorance about the methods of modern scientific historical investigations. The conclusions were too rash and exhibited his Popperian style. So, Beames concluded that Balasore was completely a newly built modern town for there was no village or Parganah in this name at that time. Discussing about the fighting between the Mughals and the Afghans at Balasore, Beames said that indeed Jaleswar was the battleground of these imperialists and they were engaging themselves in battle whenever they liked and according to their convenience. On Afghans he said, "The Afghans of Orissa were for many years in a characteristically Afghan state of riot and quarrelling and Balasore, lying it does between Cuttack and the Bengal frontier, was often the battlefield between the rulers of the two provinces. None of the battles, were however, very decisive, nor John Beames had tried to establish the role of the British traders in building up the modern city of Balasore. To substantiate his arguments Beames had said that the British were the first to establish settlements at Balasore. Though the Dutch people initially tried to settle there, their settlement was not in a convenient position. Beames argued that the British were the first to settle there, because the Dutch coming to Balasore first would certainly not have choosen such an inconvenient place for their settlement. Considering all these, John Beames very safely concluded that the English were the first to reach Balasore and establish this place completely as a modern town and a trading centre. In view of the dimensions of historical research carried on during the last one hundred years and more resulted in the unearthing of innumerable source materials relating to the history of coastal tract of Orissa and because of the discovery of large number of monuments, coins, forts and other material remains of archaeological interest, this would not only suffice to refute the conclusions of Beames, but it could also lead to the conclusion that Balasore had remained throughout the pages of Orissan history a flourishing town, but also a centre of constant human activity. However, Beames had been very specific in stating that the English established themselves as traders in Balasore which was more important in the sense that as an European his interest was focussed more on trade and revenue.

As a British administrator in India he had his larger interest to justify the British imperialism in India and more so the attitude of their superiority. Like Bruton, Motte, Stirling, Hunter and many others of his predecessors, Beames mentioned about the lawlessness and tyranny of the Maratha administration. "The last Maratha Faujdar of Balasore was Mayura Pandit commonly called Moro Pant who lived on the site where the Jagannath Temple in Balasore now stands. He appears to have been a rapacious tyrant, and there are several allusions to him in Captain Morgan's early letters. When defeated by the English he retired to Cuttack plundering the riots as he went...".[219] He had also described the Afghans being characteristically rioting and quarrelsome. He discussed about the low prices existing in the country and regarding the failure of the people to take advantage of the situation, he pointed out that the extortions of the people by the Marathas were the reasons for the same. He wanted to justify that the conquest of Orissa by the British was essential for the benefit of the masses. He was of the conception that the situation prevailing in Orissa was congenial for the conquest. Beames outlined the state of affairs in Orissa in the like manner. "A seer of rice was sold for 15 gandas or about 70 sears to the rupee (it was 65 seers in 1805 and now in favourable seasons sells at 30 or 32). Opium cost a pan of cowries per masha, salt 14 karas per seer. The advantages of low prices were, however, much counter-balanced by the capricious exactions of the rulers. Although they seem to have had the sense not to drive away the trade by oppressing foreigners, yet upon the natives of the province, itself they had no mercy. It was dangerous to be rich, or at least to display any amount of wealth, lest the attention of the Marathas should be called to the fact, and plunder and extortion follow as a matter of course. It is not surprising therefore that when the English appeared on the scene, the Marathas were left to fight their own battles, quite unsupported by the people. Indeed they seem to have been so conscious of their unpopularity as never to have attempted to enlist the sympathies of the Oriyas on their behalf. Had they done so, the turbulent Rājās of the hills and the sea coast might have given us a great deal of trouble and enabled the Marathas, to hold out for sometime".[220] Discussing about the shortage of rice at Cuttack during the famine years, Beames said that the Marathas were atrocious tyrants. This state of affairs came to an end only after the advent of the British. Once forced, the ryots became antocratic, they became so that they did not even bother to care the laws framed by the British. That was because they were accustomed not to give anything without pressure. As such they were not interested to comply with the British liberal laws. About the Amils in charge of the collection of revenue, especially in places such as Soro, Bhadrak and Dolagram, Beames not only doubted their honesty and integrity, but also developed utter contempt towards them. Even Beames had gone to the extent of deducing conclusions from the dishonesty and irresponsibility of handful of Amils by stating in a very generalised way that the Oriyas were experts in finding clues for not doing their own jobs and responsibilities. He stated, "The Amils were in league against us, as they had for a long time taken advantage of their position to hold the lion's share of the profitable export trade to Madras, and did not wish to sell in Cuttack. The commissarial officers were shamefully inert and incompetent, and notwithstanding all the above drawbacks could if they would only exert themselves collect a much larger supply than they fit. Colonel Harcourt appears to have taken some effective steps to remedy this state of things, for no further rice was required from Balasore during the rest of 1804 or in 1805.

"Rājā Tirupati Raj was at this time sent from Cuttack to Balasore to act as Amil or Collector of the Revenue and was put under Captain Morgan's orders; and Amils were appointed at Soroh, Bhadrak and Dolgram, who also were directed to send in their accounts to that officer. They all appear to have been thoroughly untrustworthy; making use of every conceivable pretext to avoid doing what was required of them and carrying that exasperating policy of passive resistance at which the Oriyas are such adepts to the highest pitch. The correspondence teems with complaints against them. They would not collect, the revenue punctually, they never knew anything that they were asked about, they could not be found when wanted, denied having received this or that order, sent their accounts imperfectly drawn up, long after time, and sometimes not at all, and on the whole behaved as badly as any set of men in their position well could. This indeed appears to have been the general tone of everyone in the province. Well aware of our ignorance of the country they all with one accord abstained from helping us in any way, no open resistance was ventured upon, but all stolidly sat aloof—papers were hidden, information withheld, boats, bullocks and carts sent out of the way, the Zamindars who were ordered to (proceed) to Cuttack to settle for their estates did not go, and on searching for them at their homes could not be found, were reported as absent, on a journey no one knew where. But if from ignorance the English officers committed any mistake, then life suddenly returned to the dull inert mass and complaints were loud and incessant".[221] So throughout his discussions Beames expressed his agony and dissatisfaction over the general behaviour of the people. That was obviously an attempt at establishing the superiority of the Britons.

Writing about the Road cess which was the most hotly debated question of the time and which Beames himself successfully implemented in Balasore district*, he said that "the weak points of the scheme were numerous. No one really knew the Zamindars could expect them to send in correct returns. Many of them were careless and indolent, mere puppets in the hands of the unscrupulous followers. Many more were crafty, dissembling money grabbers. No reliance could be placed on their statements. The threat of criminal prosecution was mere brutum fulmen because in order to secure a conviction it was necessary to prove first that their returns were false and secondly, that they were intentionally and wilfully misleading. We had no data whatsoever for proving the first point for there had never been any official check or control over the management by Zamindars of their estates and as to the second it was easy for the Zamindars to bring half of the country side to bear witness that he was easy giving and careless and had never kept any accounts in his life and had not the slightest idea as to what were his profits so that the return submitted was mere guess work and not intended to be misleading. Then again so great is the dependence of the ryots on the Zamindar that to give the latter the right of collecting the cess would open a wide door to all sorts of exactions".[222] In some of his articles published in the "*Indian Observer*", Beames had set forth all these considerations, as he himself stated, in the form of an imaginary history of what took place on the estate of a typical Zamindar, who had been created by him on the occasion. In several of his articles Beames had entered fully into the actual condition of the ryot and the relations between him and the Zamindar. Sir George Campbell, as it afterwards turned out, knew that Beames was the writer of the articles and it created some stir at that time in the government circles. Although he disapproved many of the policies of the government, still then Beames carried out the orders issued at various periods more actively and efficiently.

"From 1805 to 1815 when there was no British Resident Collector at Balasore, the place was kept under the administrative jurisdiction of Puri Collector. Because of this, Puri Collector had virtually no control over the Zamindars at Balasore. Due to this laxity in control for a long time, the people of this district did not bother to obey the rules. It is perhaps to this relaxation of control for many years in Balasore that we may attribute the special characteristics of the inhabitants of the district which led them to carry on their affairs without any reference whatsoever to the law or to the officials of the government. They never took the trouble to enquire about what the law was on any particular question and wanted to settle it in anyway that might seem best to them. To the same cause may be ascribed the excessive prevalence of the practice of levying illegal cess, the existence of many kinds of singular and pernicious customs and the general muddle of conflicting interests observable in connection with landed property".[223]

John Beames assumed the charge of the Commissioner of Orissa Division, which included the three districts of Balasore, Cuttack and Puri, on the 12th August, 1873. Narrating his critical experiences, Beames wrote that "Ever since the terrible Orissa famine in 1866, the work of the large and heavily worked Cuttack Collectorate had fallen into confusion and immense arrears of business had accumulated which successive collectors had toiled in vain to clear off".[224] So Beames found everything in confusion. Being highly sceptical about the capability of the Oriyas and being a thoroughbred imperialist he had tremendous confidence in the efficiency of the English Civil servants and he wanted to expose and highlight the errors of the Oriya ministerial staff, by which he could establish the superiority of the Europeans. He had stated, "the immense accumulation of arrears of work was due not merely to the disorder caused by the famine, nor to the unmethodical habits of the two last collectors. It was due in a great degree to the slowness and dishonestly of the native ministerial staff. It would be impossible without going into technical details, which would not be intelligible to those who have not served in the Indian Civil Service, to explain the exact way in which these men act and had acted in this case. The heads of various departments were old men deeply rooted in old fashioned ways and grooves, each of them had an army of dependents and filled all vacant posts with his relations. They all with one accord strenuously resisted improvements and changes of all sorts and where they were unable to prevent their introduction, laboured hard and successfully to render them inoperative when introduced. A strong hand, an inflexible will, and rigid method and punctuality were required to restore order to this large and important district. As soon, therefore, as I had set my own work as Commissioner in order and had allowed Stevens time to clear off his arrears, I had my official inspection of the Cuttack Collectorate. I made it as close and searching as I knew how, with the result that I discovered countless abuses, a total want of system, and an organised confederacy among the native officials to resist all change or improvement. In order to break the nexus of the opposition I resolved on drastic measures, dismissed the heads of all the departments or compelled them to retire on pension, filling their places with younger men of more advanced views, some of whom I brought from my old district of Balasore...".[225] Similarly John Beames has his contempt towards the Garjat (Princely) rājās of Orissa: "with many of these Rājās; threats and admonitions were useless, because they had not the wits to understand what was expected of them. They were wild, jungly, uncivilised creatures, mere savages in fact. Others were more intelligent and educated. Much good was done by the Superintendent's tours. He went round every year and inspected the Rājā's court and offices, blaming or praising as the case might be indicating improvements and so on. By this means a rough sort of administration, quite as civilised as the people were fitted for, was maintained, and the mistake was avoided of trying to govern in the principles of the highest cultivation a primitive people living in the forests, many of whom wore no clothing but the leaves of trees and lived on roots and such games as they could shoot with their rude bows and arrows".[226]

Beames was, of course, the first administrative historiographer of the country. His analysis of the problems of Indian administration, and his general theorisation of his experiences in Indian administration was really noteworthy. He was highly critical of the implementation of laws in India. Beames had said, "One can only do one's best while in a place and leave the future to one's successor, who as likely as not will take an entirely different view and upset all the arrangements one has made.

"This, in fact, is one of the great problems of Indian administration though it is one which people in England and especially in Parliament know nothing about though they talk so loud and lay down the law so very confidently. It cannot be too often repeated that the difficulty lies not in the laws and rules that are promulgated, but in getting them carried out. It is not always easy, I admit, to make a law, which exactly meets the requirements of all the complicated systems of land revenue, and other matters which occur. But the greatest care is taken in making a law. Facts are collected with the most scrupulous and conscientious care, opinions are obtained from all those who know the subject (and from many who do not). The draft bill is widely circulated for criticism and criticism carefully weighed, the bill is then brought before the council, many eloquent and clever speeches are made, it is referred to a special committee who cut and carve, add and strike out, argue for hours over every point and submit it as revised to Council again, where it is again speechified over and voted section by section. When it is finally passed the Governors,

Secretaries, Councillors and Boards at headquarters sit down and fold their hands and say the affair is settled".[227]

Beames then discussed about the real problem, when the law was to be enforced all over the country. The Act after being printed would be sent to all the Collectors and other officers of whom Beames had said, 'some of these are stupid, some are indolent and careless, some have been opposed to the measure all along and do not mean it to be a success. Then there is the vast mass of the native population who are affected by it. The native lawyers are as sharp as needless and very soon tear the heart out of it. This section may be made to work in one way, that section in another, while most of them can be interpreted in more ways than one. The rural masses of course, neither know nor understand a word of it. So then cases are instituted in the courts, and appealed and appealed till they reach the High Court. That august tribunal always considers itself the legally constituted interpreter of all laws, and proceeds to put an interpretation of its own on section after section. These interpretations are embodied in the decisions of the court and these decisions are printed and published as 'rulings'. So that before long there are two laws the actual statute as passed by the legislative body and the mass of rulings thereon as pronounced by the judicial body. The lawyers are very proud of this; they call the former 'substantive law' and the latter 'adjective law' and very much prefer the latter, as their own creation. Now in as much as in arriving at their decision the judges carefully avoid taking into consideration the circumstances which led to the making of the law and examine not what the legislature meant to lay down, but what the words of the Act really import, it not infrequently happens that their decisions turn out to be very opposite of what the law was intended to mean. Then a new law has to be passed to rectify the error. Divested of technical language, such an amending act is simply a confession of a blunder. It says, virtually, 'whereas in a former act we rule that two and two make four, but from the wording of the Act it appears as if we had rules that two and two make five, now we hearby alter that wording and substitute the two following words which make it plain that henceforth two and two shall make four and not five'. It has happened within my experience that the High Court has sat upon the 'Amended Act' and observed that 'the law as now amended implies that two and two make six".[228] This observation and analysis made by Beames on the legislative procedures and the judicial shackles very aptly was significant in the sense that the procedure was totally faulty which destroys the real meaning of the law. The constraints of the administrators were too many. The whole procedure destroyed the meaning, the fist and the logic of the situation. It verily exposed the weaknesses and destructive elements lie in the parliamentary procedures and the taboos emerging from the theory of separation of powers and their balancing. The whole set of analysis leads to the conclusion that Beames was not only the foremost of the administrative historiographers of the country, but also one of the greatest political theorists of the country.

As regards the implementation of the laws so passed, Beames had reiterated that, "...however carefully both the legislative and judicial bodies work at establishing the law, there remains always a great deal of weakness and uncertainty in carrying it out in the country.

The vast extent of the country, the very various views, temperaments and mental acumen, of the persons charged with administering it naturally lead to its efficiency being very different in different parts of the country, and being more or less impaired in all. More especially is every law of importance hindered in its working by frequent changes of district officers. The secretariat mind favours frequent changes. It considers that if a man stays long enough in a district he gets into a groove. This means that if a man stays long enough in a district to acquire a real insight into the condition and wants of the people, he is able to see the vanity of the fine theoritical cobwebs which the Secretariat mind is so fond of spinning, and can administer inconvenient pricks to their windbags and prove by his extensive local knowledge their emptiness. So, they like to have men new to the district who swallow all their nostrums".[229]

The main purpose of John Beames going for dissension of the legislative procedure seems to have been catching upon the British procedural law which they professed to be the mainstay of civil administration. But Beames was critical of the systems prevailing, which made the implementation farflung and difficult. However carefully both legislative and judicial bodies worked at establishing the law, there remained always a great deal of weakness and uncertainty in carrying it out in the country.

One of the most important aspects of British imperialism in India was force and its coercive impact on the subjects. The agents of imperialism always coerced subject peoples in varying degrees and this depressed the latter's sense of well-being and freedom. Coercion, however, was an ubiquitous phenomenon, originated either randomly or in the intimacy of personal relationships, and often directed against traditional or established institutions by those who themselves feel unconsciously constrained by their norms. The officers demonstrated their forcefulness to those they suspected of wishing to break down those norms. It was manifest in many ways from the threat to life and limb to the withdrawal of love or other highly regarded values. The history of British imperialism in India was blotted by the coercion on society and people in many ways. The indiscriminate firing of General Reginald Dyer upon a crowd of some 5000 Indians, who had gathered peacefully in an open area in Amritsar, called the Jallianawala Bagh, to listen to nationalists speak about independence on 13th April, 1931, was just a page from the history of British Imperial coercion.

John Beames, however, believed in the rationality of imperial coercion as one of the methods of subjugation of Indian subject population when he was working as Collector of Cuttack during 1875-77, Beames had referred to the submissiveness of the native Rājās. He had stated, "The system in force in 1877 when I took charge was as follows. The Rājās were allowed the general administration of their territories, but any of their subjects who felt himself aggrieved by any act of his Rājā might appeal to the Commissioner, who asked for an explanation from the Rājā, and finally decided what ought to be done and communicated his decision to the Rājā. If the Rājā had refused to obey, no one exactly knew what would have happened. But it was tacitly understood that he would not refuse and as a matter of fact, he knew better than to do so. This is what is called 'moral influence'. When backed by bayonets it is a great power".[230] Nothing could be more illustrative than that which pronounced clearly his belief on the efficacy of coercion over the Indian subjects.

Beames was quite optimistic about the progressive effect of the British Indian administration in Orissa. Beames has said, "As the early years of our rule in Orissa were fertile in changes, and worked a complete revolution in the position of the classes connected with the land, it would have been interesting to trace the progress of our laws and rules and their effect upon the province. I am, however, precluded from doing this by the fact that from 1806 to 1828 there was no...[231]*

All these clearly vouchsafe to the magisterial superiority John Beames had displayed in his writings which was obvious among the ICS personnel from the Haileyburian School to which he belonged. This sense of British superiority was evident in his historical readings. Speaking about the British conquest of Orissa, Beames said in his memoirs, "when the English conquered Orissa in 1803 with two regiments of native troops from Madras, the Marathas fled westwards through the hill country back to their own land. Our knowledge of the geography of Orissa was at that time so slight that Colonel Harcourt, who commanded the little force did not venture to follow them. This did not much matter as they were caught by Sir Arthur Wellesly at Assaye, where they arrived in time to share in the crushing defeat of their nation. In the course, however, of his enquiries Colonel Harcourt and the Chief Commissioner Mr. Melvill, learnt of the existence of a number of independent and semi-independent chieftains, each ruling a small tract of territory in those wild hills. Not understanding the status of those men and assuming them to be far more powerful than they really were, Harcourt and Melvill executed on behalf of the British government treaties of alliance with each of them by virtue of which, they were to be confirmed in their possessions on payment of a peshkash, or a small annual tribute. One cannot read without a smile in these treaties a solemn promise in the part of each of these microscopic potentates not to wage war against the government—as though a gnat should promise not to fight an elephant. In later times, when we knew all about these people, it was seen what a mistake we had made in treating them as independent potentates. A careful study of the records and documents subsequently discovered, proved beyond a doubt that those hill chiefs had been from the earliest times feudal vassals of the kings of Orissa, under whom they had held their land chiefly on the tenure of military service. This, they themselves frankly admit. They say we knew this all along, and everyone in Orissa knew it, but if colonel Harcourt was good enough to grant us the position of independent rulers it was not our business to undeceive them. Inspite of their treaties they willingly consented to be treated as Vassals, provided their '*Peshkash*' or tribute were not increased. They were then placed under the general management of the Commissioner of Orissa who was ordered, as Superintendent to control them, guide them elevate them and so forth".[232] This clearly demonstrated the general British perception of extension of the frontiers of civilisation. The conquest of Orissa was a logical necessity for the British. The justification behind the imperial expansion was that the British empire implied the disappearance of misery, oppression, anarchy, superstitions and bigotry. It connoted the extension of peace, justice, prosperity, humanity and freedom of thought and expression.

John Beames tried successfully to establish the British civilisation over their Indian counterparts. Simultaneously, he considered the British as superior to the other Europeans. The British interest in India had always remained in trade and commerce. Orissa before the advent of the British was a case of lawlessness anarchy, exploitation and atrocities. It was only the British who civilised the people here and elevated the status of the Oriyas in the Indian context. In the initial phase of their administration a lot of changes were effected in Orissa. Particularly the British administration succeeded in bringing about revolution in socio-economic relations among different classes of people associated with the land revenue administration. He also exposed various forms of exactions by the existing landed gentries of the common people. He was the first administrative historian of India, who developed the study of administrative historiography in the most brilliant manner. He had referred to subaltern consciousness for the first time in modern Indian historiography. Moreover, the British administration brought order in the life of the people and enforced the rule of law.

Despite all his magisterial leanings, John Beames was an extraordinary and brilliant oriental scholar. It was evident from his brilliant archaeological notes on different monuments in Orissa, particularly found in and around Cuttack. The notices he had made of these monuments, particularly the Buddhist remains of Orissa were spectacular. He had analysed very neatly these monuments and made critical evaluation. All these presented as an art critic, although he had not that sort of expertise as an archaeologist. Further, as an administrator, having served as Magistrate and Commissioner at Balasore and Cuttack, he had made magnificent analysis of towns and developed the cities in that spirit. He also spoke on all the big or small monuments that came across his way in Cuttack and Balasore. Among the important archaeological edifices which were noticed and studied by him were the massive rivetment built by the Marathas round the Cuttack city to protect it from frequent floods, the Lal Bagh building, where the Commissioner's residence stood, which he called as "Faulkner's glory". Beames wanted to build a market by the side of the Lal Bagh palace. In order to build that he thought of two things. First, he wanted to renovate the ancient dilapidated buildings. Secondly, he thought of building new structures using the stones from ruined buildings. Finally, he opted for the second alternative. He had stated, "Meanwhile I was busy with improvements in the town of Cuttack. The old market, a strange, ill-arranged mass of low, dark, stone vaults had fallen into the hands of a close corporation of Koyals as they were called. The word means "weighers" and their function, under the native governments, had been to weigh all grain brought to market. No sales could take place unless these men, who levied a small fee for the service and paid a fee to the native ruler for the appointment, weighed the grain. They acquired power by degrees, as in India such middlemen always do and presumed to regulate the market rates and prices and in many ways interfere with business tyrannize over the traders, demand heavy payments on various pretexts and in many ways oppress and defraud the people. When I proposed to rebuild their market they objected and produced an ancient document granting them the proprietary right to the building. It was impossible to say whether this document was genuine or not (probably not), but when I consulted the law officers, I was advised that there was no legal means of contesting it, as though the carelessness of the former collectors, the Koyals had been allowed to remain in possession long enough to establish a prescriptive right to the buildings, as well as to the exclusive exercise of their functions. This market was built against the outsider of the great wall surrounding the part in which the Lal Bagh—the Commissioner's residence stood. Attached to this ancient wall, and dating from the sixteenth century or earlier, there were several other half ruined ancient buildings, empty and disused; strange, tall, gloomy structures of dark red stone. I first thought of making use of these for an opposition market, but they were found to be too ruinous to be put into repair and inconveniently shaped and situated. So I had to search elsewhere and at length at the eastern end of the town—the old market was at the western end - I found a large neglected patch of ground grown over with jungle which was said to have been the site of the Maratha Governor's Law Courts. It was the property of the government, so I could do what I liked with it. On clearing the jungle and digging up the soil the workmen came upon six or seven beautifully carved capitals of pillars and by degrees unearthed the drums of the pillars themselves, together with numerous finely carved fragments of sand stone and great quantities of laterite blocks, which had evidently been used for building. With these materials I set to work and designed a handsome market, which was built on this site. It was of laterite, a lofty hall with chambers for water housing grain, and in front a long wide portico supported by the pillars above mentioned which were duly pierced together. A little on one side we found a deep ancient tank lined with laterite and adorned with carvings of gods, goddesses, men and animals. All these we restored, cleaned out the tank, rebuilt the ghats or steps and made a very handsome place of it. I put up an inscription over the front of the market house and opened it as a public market free from all interference of the Koyals. In India one never remains long enough in any place to see the fruits of one's work. I do not know whether the new market was successful or not. It began well and doing well as long as I remained in Cuttack".[233]

From the analysis given above the following deductions could be made.

(1) Beame's Sincerity in creating a market place operating under the government management and free from the interference of the so-called middlemen was definitely to allow the merchandise and commerce a free passage. This was in consonance and conformity with the national character of average Britons.

(2) Beames' analysis of proprietory rights of the government over the public buildings was a definite assertion of moral right of the British to control the public properties and to use them as per their own whims.The assertion of rights over properties had remained a definite imperial gesture throughout the British economic history of India.

(3) By utilising the unearthed carved pillars, drums of pillars, carved fragments of sand stone and large quantities of laterite blocks for building the new market building without recording

their contexts and doing sampling of them and analysing them for archaeological research, he destroyed some of the important evidences of history and archaeology. That spoke about his ignorance in archaeological research methodology.

(4) By stating that "In India one never remains long enough in any place to see the fruits of one's work", he expressed his displeasure over the government system of transfer and also he caricatured the Indian beliefs and did not simply bother to understand the reality of the situation in terms of time and space.

Beames' description of "Udaygiri hills" and its archaeological and historical potential was quite interesting. During his tenure at Cuttack he visited the place, which he described as a very curious place. He called the Udaygiri hills as the 'Sunrise mountains: He wrote that it was an isolated rocky place of no great height with a mosque on the summit, small, modern and ugly. On seeing some images in a ravine nearby Beames along with Faulkner came upon a deep well of the kind called 'Baoli', a large circular hole line with stone masonry. Of his explorations here, Beames wrote, "In one side of this wall is an arch way and a broad flight of stone steps leading down from another archway at the top. At the bottom of the steps is a platform of stone in the middle of which is the mouth of the well. It is full of water and apparently very deep. On the sides of the wall going down the steps were rudely carved numerous names, apparently of pilgrims, main archaic character, the so-called Kutila, which has not been used since about the ninth or tenth century. The inscription must thus be more than a thousand years old... Beyond the well was a pathway flagged with stone and on either side for the most past overturned and lying under the bushes were great quantities of statues of Buddha of stone. These were of all sizes from a few inches to four feet high. We counted some hundreds of them. At the end of the pathway, which was more than half a mile long and ascended gradually, we came upon a beautiful gateway of stone, the lintel and the side posts of which were covered by delicately carved groups of figures illustrating events in the various Jātakas or former birth of Buddha. Looking through this gateway we were startled to see, deep in the gloom of dense, overhanging trees, a colossal seated Buddha in the usual attitude of meditation. The image was buried up to the east in débris and soil but the huge upper half stood up so high that a tall man standing on the palm of its right hand only just could touch its shoulder.

The whole place had evidently in ancient times been a Buddhist monastery and place of pilgrimage. Here as everywhere in Orissa, the nose of all images had been broken off. It was the custom of the Mohammedans thus to disfigure all the statues of gods and others they found in any part of India. The local legend says that at the sound of the battle drums of Kalapahar all the noses of the Gods in Orissa fell off."[234] Beames was so much moved by the architectural beauty and aesthetic appeal of these monuments that he decided to preserve some of these carvings and thus shifted the colossal Buddha image to Chauliaganj.

During the nine years he spent in Orissa, John Beames visited, sketched and wrote articles about the ancient temples, forts and statues of Orissa. He also described Orissa as an old world province, the home of the most bigoted, Brahmin-ridden Hindus in all India.[235]

In 1875 John Beames conducted extensive explorations in the "Altai Hills of Cuttack' and described the place as a perfect mine of archaeology.[236] Beames was led to explore these hills after going through an article written by Baba Chandrasekhar Banerjee, then Deputy Magistrate of Jajpur sub-division, which was published in the Society's journal. He made scholarly analysis of the name 'altai' based on the legends available. He also described the origin of the 'Takht-i-Suleman mosque' on the hill drawing references from many sources. He also made a sketch of the temple present on the hill. This was the only antiquity in the hill to present interesting results. Beames described the images of the Buddha on the hills as all exactly alike but as fine pieces of sculpture.[237] He had provided the detailed topography of the mosque and analysed the inscription written on it and presented the idea that 'the hill on which this mosque stands is called by the Hindus "Borodihi", or great site and was according to local tradition the seat of the palace of some great king whose identity and period had remained undetermined by the authorities.[238]In this article Beames also described in greater detail his explorations carried out in Udayagiri from where he had brought the colossal Buddha image. He had studied the inscription found at Udaygiri with a fair amount of accuracy, and he had described the gateway of Udayagiri as a glorious specimen of Orissan architecture. He studied the architectural and iconographic representations on the gateway in greater detail saying, "the band is divided into tablets each of which contains a beautifully carved group of male and female figures engaged in what I may venture to call flirtation of an active kind. The beauty of these carvings is very striking though they are much worn and covered with lichen, some indeed were so defaced that I could not make them out".[239]

John Beames, who served in Orissa as a Collector and Commissioner at Balasore and Cuttack respectively during his nine-year stint in Orissa had thus combined in history a magisterial sentiment and Oriental scholarship. Even though he belonged to the Haileyburian school, particularly trained to rule in India and where the expression of British superiority was a natural choice, Beames had displayed many departures. He had differed widely from many of his British colleagues and his official superiors in Indian administration on different occasions, for which he had faced many strictures and punishments. By upholding and fostering the interest of subalterns, he came in clash with the British authorities many a time. In Orissa he had showed his real soft corner for the Oriya language, culture and history. Nonetheless, the study of archaeological monuments was his real interest in which he engaged himself very often. This Oriental scholarship only immortalised Beames as a historian of Orissa despsite all his magisterial inclinations. Beames was so much sentimentally attached to the land, people and culture of Orissa that he got disappointed when he was transferred to Chittagong. He had said, "I was bitterly disappointed at leaving Orissa, to which "I had grown very much attached".[240]

Throughout his Indian career, the outspoken Johm Beames stood by the people against tyranny. Ironically, he shared the prejudices of his peers and did not recognise Indian ICS officers as his academic and cultural equals: He strongly distrusted the Bengali intelligentsia. His outspokenness which held him down in his career was his chief strength as a writer and tremendously enhanced the value of his estimates of men and affairs of his time. Beames wrote without being either pompous or timid. The history and people of Orissa owed a lot to him for his contribution in preserving their separate identity.

(E)

THE POLITICO-ADMINISTRATIVE HISTORIOGRAPHY OF ORISSA

Administrative history of Orissa had developed as a genre of historiography almost from the beginning of the colonial rule. It has remained an integral part of political history throughout. It was in the very nature of colonial state that the theme of administration should figure prominently in its early accounts. The British rule was an autocracy, which had originated in conquest and ruled over an alien population almost entirely by the sword for the first fifty years. So the early colonial state had no means other than its administrative apparatus by which to record, measure and assess its own articulation. It was imposed externally on India's population and had not arisen out of a churning of the indigenous society itself. Thus it was completely divorced from the political life of its subjects. It was a phase of self-absorption. The political stimulus was addressed singularly to its own administration. This denotes the sum of all transactions amongst the developing organs of the state. As a result, at this initial stage all the political history read like administrative history and vice versa. Further, regarding the basic origin of administrative history, it would be appropriate to state that the genesis and determinants of politics were sought for in the Government and administration. "It is our hypothesis that the structure of the imperial government can provide a clue to the way Indian politics developed."[241] In order to be conversant with the politics of colonialism one had to involve oneself in discourses on the administration of the Company's territories. This was apparently clear in William Bolt's *Considerations on Indian Affairs* (London, 1772), Harry Verelsts' "*View of the Rise, Progress and present State of the English Government in Bengal*" London 1772), James Grant's "*An Inquiry into the Nature of Zamindary Tenures in the Landed Property of Bengal*". And these had focused on the administration of land revenue, and the relation between the state and the landed magnates in pre-colonial times and its implications for the East India Company as a successor regime. The first colonizers were initially engaged in the tribute gathering and mercantilist project of primitive accumulation. Politics and administration was coalesced with each other in the historical works of those first colonizers. There was no difference between the two. During the first half of the eighteenth century, the colonialist dominance was matured into a vehicle of metropolitan, industrial and financial interests. Inspite of some variations in the magnitude of constituent elements of the capitalist forces, the whole economic system did not change radically to create differences between politics and administration. So the colonialist state had remained a "dominance without hegemony".[242] The administrations had to be firmly stapled to politics. So it was not thought necessary for historiography to develop any modal distinction between the two in its own discourses. Thus, the notion of a gap between administrative and political history had little to support it either in the fact of historiography or in any intelligent political theory of colonialism.

In the new Cambridge approach, politics was a matter of imperialist stimulus and native response. The stimulus was coming from the government in two ways. In the first place, it trained the subjects in the use of the institutions of colonial government, rewarding the learners by material and spiritual resources (ranging from jobs and canal water to knighthoods and liberal values), and generated among them a competition for the available prizes and a shared sense of collaboration with the Raj. Secondly, the stimulus worked by encouraging the natives to replicate the institutions of government by setting up institutions of their own and develop in that process a matching non-official arena where all, in its turn, would be modelled on the institutional procedure, reward system and patron-client nexus of the primary official arena. "The sum of the relations, activities and discourses generated by the governmental stimulus in these two ways is what constitutes politics according to the current version of Cambridge historiography".[243] This historiography, in which political and administrative history had been married in a sort of 'Sanatan Hindu Wedlock', taught us about colonialism both as a political system and as a persistent intellectual influence in the post-colonial era. Its aim was to write up Indian history after Mill, as a 'Portion of British History'. The historical writings of this nature invariably was bound up with Indian collaboration. This collaboration, which had been endowed with liberal bourgeois attitudes, had transformed the relation between the rulers and the ruled into a patron-client relationship.

Among the vast panorama of politico-administrative historical writings of Orissa produced during the nineteenth century, Walter Ewer's *"Correspondence of the Settlement of Khoordah in Pooree"* (1818) and G. Toynbee's *"A Sketch of the History of Orissa* (From 1803-1828)', (1873) were important works to be taken up for study.

In order to understand the causes of the widespread disturbances of 1817, the British Government decided to set up a Commission on September 16,1817 for enquiry into the general state of affairs which prevailed in Orissa and particularly in the territories where the disturbances had occured. The Commission constituted of two officers, Major General G. Martindell and Walter Ewer. Ewer singularly prepared the report and submitted it to the Government on May 13,1818, in which he had discussed in greater detail all the aspects of the Early British administration in Orissa.[244]

Ewer had discussed in considerable detail the factors responsible for the rebellion at Khurda. He had found out that its inhabitants had lived in ease and contentment under the government of native princes. He stated, "....they had lived happily and unmolested under that Government and were not anxious enough for change to run any risk in accomplishing it. The half formed design was in consequence immediately relinquished and the Rājā continued as before the most obedient and submissive of our subjects".[245] There was the regular assessment of land revenue and the rate of tax was light. The ryots or the cultivators of soil had the privilege of approach and appeal to the ruler at all times against the misconduct and misbehaviour of inferior officers of the Government. All these afforded them an effectual security. Khurda was brought under the direct control of the British government in 1805. Major Fletcher was entrusted with the task of its management. He had started the land settlement of the estate which was afterwards completed and revised by the first Tehsildar, Golam Kadir. Ewer had stated,"...by which the capabilities of the district the actual quantity of land in cultivation, the nature and value of the produce, and the amount of population were ascertained with tolerable accuracy, and this is the only document of the kind existing in the collector's office. The assessment of Major Fletcher and the first Tehsildar, amounting to Rs.1,06,000 or on average about 7 & 1/2 annas per bigha appears to have been moderate enough although higher than that which the ryots had been accustomed to pay. The plan of settlement, however, as I shall have occasion more particularly to show hereafter, unavoidably upset in a great degree the former system and institutions of the country and was less favourable to the ryots than before. The 'Surburakars', before mere ministerial agents of the Government, became now a sort of farmers of the revenue, and all practical restraint being removed from them, it must be supposed that they would sometimes be guilty of abuses, in fact, the oppressive exactions of the Surburakars have been urged as one cause of the ruin of Khoordah. In place of the mild, revered and the efficient authority of the Rajah was now substituted that of the Judge and Collector in Cuttack, to whom an ignorant inhabitant of Khoordah would seldom dream of appealing and the unfeeling, tyrannical and oppressive sway of a Mussalman police Darogah".[246] Naturally the common people suffered greatly under the British administration from the beginning.

The subsequent events had added much to the initial sufferings of the people. An increase of about Rs.10,000/- was made to the Jumma. In 1809-10 Khurda was let out in farm for 10 years to a Bengali speculator named Shamanand Raee (Shamanand Ray) and Ewer was convinced that the rapid deterioration of Khurda territories began from that year. He narrated, "From that inauspicious era all concur in dating the commencement of the rapid deterioration of this unfortunate country. Such was the rapacity of the unprincipled speculator, that he is said to have nominally doubled the Mosfusail Jumma. It was of course impossible to collect anything like this amount, but his extortions were such as to have left a lasting impression of horror on the minds of the people of Khoordah at the very name of Mostajir. His conduct speedily met with proper punishment. Many of the Ryots fled the districts and unable ...upon his removal most of the ryots returned to their homes and Khoordah might again have begun to hold up its head, when a fresh course lighted upon it in the appointment of Mirza Mendy to the situation of Police Darogah who had just been driver from Pooree by the clamorous and tumultous representations of a large part of its inhabitants, who declared that if they could not be relieved from his tyranny by application to the local authorities, they would proceed to Calcutta to petition council. I am skeptical as to the amount extorted by this man from the people of Khoordah and his costly style of living might be explained by reference to the value of his numerous estates, and extent of his commercial concerns, without supposing him to have realized a fortune in so poor and exhausted a country. But as an evidence of the merciless system of exaction laid down by him ...".[247] In this observation of Ewer, a curious mixture of balanced judgment and imperial demeanour was clearly expressed. On the one hand he had referred to the exactions of the people by the agents of the government and on the otherside he had made it clear that the people of Orient should not be taken into confidence.

The Government subsequently increased the "Jama" of this estate without proper enquiry and in 1815-16, the "Jama" was much above the original assessment of Major Fletcher. Ewer did not hesitate to point out that the oppressive weight of taxation on the cultivators in 1815-16 was twice the "Jama" of 1804-5: Such a ruinous land revenue policy combined with misadministration in other departments had created a state of desperate misery for the people of Khurda which culminated in the outbreak of 1817.

Then Ewer proceeded to analyse the factors which had led to the discontent of the people in general in other parts of Orissa. In the southern parts of the district the discontentment was due to the extension of the salt monopoly. Ewer had stated, "The extension of the Salt monopoly in 1814 to the southern division of the district must of course have increased the misery of the unhappy people by trenching materially upon their consumption of an article of almost indispensable necessity, with the free use of which they had till then been indulged, and by depriving many of the ryots of the petty, but profitable traffic which they had before driven in purchasing salt at very low rate at the places of manufacture, which they carried into the countries of their Gurjhat neighbours, where they received an ample and lucrative remuneration."[248]

Ewer had found out that the basic errors of the land revenue policy were responsible for the general discontent of the people. The people always spoke of the constant transfer of landed property by public and private sale with strong feelings of disgust. It was calculated that more than two third of the original proprietors were displaced from their estates during the first fourteen years of British administration. It had led to undue extortion from the cultivators by the new proprietors. Ewer had declared that he did not remember a single instance of complaint on the part of the ryot in the estate of an original proprietor against his Zamindar. But, from ryots and 'Mukaddams' of the estates which were held in farm or belonged to the foreigners (denoting Muslim, Bengali and other non-Oriya Zamindars who came in the wake of British administration), the complaints were numerous and distressing. The cultivators complained that their Zamindars frequently increased the land rents and even it was doubled at times. On the other hand the Government had increased the 'jama' of their estates continually without any reference to their resources. Thus, Ewer asserted, the ultimate responsibility came to the shoulders of the Government. This extortion of the people by the agents of the government had led to the desertion of villages by the people. Ewer had stated, "It is now well known and generally admitted that previous to the insurrection, Khoordah was becoming strikingly and visibly depopulated. At least from 5000 to 6000 houses of ryots were deserted. The miserable remnant after disposing of their little all, their clothes, furniture, bullocks, cooking utensils, and sometimes even their wives and children, existed of course in the state of the desperate misery and irritation which well prepared them to rush blindly into the project of bettering their condition proposed to them by a leader of high and commanding influence. It is indeed only by a reference to the state of the people that we can understand the boldness and rashness which prompted them to be the first to rise against the might and majesty of the British Government".[249] The emphasis on the superiority of the British arms explained the imperial arrogance of Ewer.

In connection with the discontent of the people, Ewer had raised the question of the failure of the British laws and regulations which were introduced in Orissa. It was a matter of grave concern that not a single regulation had been translated into Oriya, the language of the people of Orissa. They were translated only into Persian and Bengali. This was obviously due to the persistent efforts of the British in subverting the Oriya identity. To add to this inconvenience the Government had followed a policy of systematic exclusion of the natives of Orissa from all offices in their administrative machinery. Not only were they thrown into the background, but also they had been subjected to the exactions and injustice of the Bengali '*amlas*', who monopolized all subordinate offices of the administration at that time.

Ewer's discussion on the entire issue of the exclusion of the Oriyas was guided by the belief that the Oriyas were backward, ignorant and uncivilised people. The entire analysis bears the imprints of detours of the 'Raj Syndrome'. Regarding the lack of total confidence on the part of the Oriyas towards the usefulness of the British laws, Ewer had stated, "...I could not but be struck also with the utter hopeless ignorance of the British system, principles, and character of our laws and regulations, and of the regular modes of proceeding in our courts, evinced by the Oriah the total want of confidence either in power or inclination or both of the civil authorities to enter into their cases and redress their wrongs, and their evident dread and mistrust of the "Adwalut". I am persuaded that many of the natives think that the Maratha Government, with its entire absence of system was better adopted to the state of society in which they exist than the British government with its enlightened humane and refined one. They seem unconscious of any particular benefits which have resulted to them from the operation of the British law and regulations, whilst it is very apparent that they have increased the assessment, required payment of revenue in silver instead of cowries, augmented the price of salt to six times its former rate, and dispossessed upwards of two thirds of the original native proprietors from their estates. The people of the interior seemed also to have thought all applications to the court vain and fruitless of late years, unless besides the legal, authorized, overwhelming expense of stamp paper, fees and they could further produce a considerable sum to purchase the favour or at least the forbearance of the sudder Amlah".[250]

About the ignorance, stupidity, inherent inferiority of the Oriyas, Ewer had stated, "In the first place the state of the intellectual acquirement against the Oriahs is far below that of any other people in India. Their ignorance and stupidity are indeed almost proverbial and they do not hesitate to acknowledge their own inferiority in intellect and comprehension to their more highly gifted neighbours. Those European officers to whom the management of the district was first entrusted when it passed from the Marathas to the Company's government, seem to have contemplated with wonder and dismay the excessive ignorance and incivilisation of the people amongst whom they were introducing a new system of laws. Mr. Ker observes in one of his letters on record: 'Such is the gross ignorance of the land holders in Cuttack that the best amongst them are decidedly inferior in point of intellect and information to the lowest order of the same class in Bengal', and in another he describes the people of Khoordah as 'sunk in the most abject state of human degradation and intellectual and corporeal imbecility'. I can safely offer from my own observation that this character of the Ooriah understanding is not an overcharged one, and that it still applies with equal force to the great mass of the population as when Mr. Ker wrote. "It is evident that this low state of mental intelligence and endowment must ever present most formidable obstacles to the success of any scheme of good Government that could be devised".[251]

Ewer had developed so much of contempt and hatred towards the Oriyas that he tried to put forward his arguments in favour of the exclusion of the Oriyas from public offices. He had stated, "An almost systematic exclusion also of the genuine Hindoo natives of Orissa from every situation about the courts in the Police, in the Revenue and salt departments, had prevailed from the very beginning. After a whole race having been thus long prescribed and thrown into the background, it may well be supposed that at the distance of 14 years the utmost difficulty is now experienced in procuring men tolerably qualified for any of the higher and more important posts and the Acting and Joint magistrates have as yet been unable to select any of those brought up in the district for the situations to which they certainly possess the best claim...."[252]

Being motivated by the call of the Raj, Ewer tried to demonstrate the racial superiority of the Europeans and wanted to highlight the obvious differences between the Europeans and Indians. He had remarked, "... I think to degrade the people in their own estimation over a primary cause of deterioration of moral character to make them feel actually the disadvantages of the condition of a conquered nation, when all not only offices of emolument but even every respectable mode of giving a livelihood is taken from the educated classes and worse still it has widened in Cuttack the vast immeasurable gulf whichever yawns between the European authority and the native subject whilst the ear and the confidence of the former being possessed apparently by a set of foreign agents and advisors who came into the country possessing nothing but shortly rose on the ruin of the natives of the district to opulence and enjoyment of immense property to undesirable impression has produced that the British Government view with peculiar favour its subjects from other provinces, and that the local authorities would always support their views and promote their interests whatever the consequences to the suffering population of Cuttack.

The exclusion of the native Ooriahs from all offices of trust and respectability has also tended in a degree to check and confine the diffusion of a knowledge of our system. The information derived by the better educated and instructed classes employed in "Sudder" and families and connections and to those in whose society they resided, and must in time have produced their effect. At present all are alike ignorant and uniformed regarding the British laws, regulations and systems of government".[253] In this observation, the British complacency regarding their superior knowledge, laws, rules and regulation having a liberal touch was clearly vouchsafed.

The ignorance and backwardness of the Oriyas had also been cited in other instances. Regarding the reasons behind the imperfect collection of revenue Ewer had observed, "Material causes of want of punctuality and ultimate failure in the discharge of their engagements may be found in the extreme rudeness, ignorance and incivilisation of the genuine Ooriah proprietors, the entire removal of all those checks to wasteful and thoughtless expenditure of funds on the part of those engaging to pay the public revenue, which are supposed to have existed under the Maratha government... thereby having lost in a great degree the tact and experience requisite for the management of their concerns... from a knowledge of the practices and characters of the amalahs in this district, that many of the ignorant, infatuated Ooriah Zamindars have been at different times fooled and cheated out of their estates..."[254]

Ewer was of the opinion that there was no industrial development in Orissa, because of the ignorance and backwardness of the people. It led him to deduce a rash conclusion without considering the industrially potential Orissa existing in cloth production, salt industry and ship building industry, which were quite prosperous in those days. He had stated, "Every ryot or householder may be allowed on an average a family of four souls, besides himself, who are mostly dependent on him for their subsistence, particularly in a rude and uncivilised province where manufacturing industry is either wholly unknown or very confined."[255]

In order to advance arguments in favour of imposition of control over the Oriyas and to justify the action of government in regard to the British decision of enhancing the price of salt, Ewer who had always been critical of the Maratha system of Government had tried to find out the best advantages that could be accrued from their government. That was one way of finding corroborative parallels of the British system of extortion in the Maratha exploitation of the native people. He had remarked, "The system of management of our predecessors with all its glaring and notorious vices and imperfections, had its advantages, as being in many respects well suited to the rude and ignorant condition of the people at large. Under the English rule, I believe, the ryots to have been subject to burdens and impositions before unknown to them".[256]

As regards the feudal army prevalent in the Garhjat states (feudatory states) and their system of management, Ewer was highly critical. He had assigned the same characteristics which were given to the people of the coastal areas. He stated, "As far as I can discover, these rude and uncivilised chieftain, under all governments were allowed the unrestricted management of the internal affairs of the country.... The nature of the country occupied by the Gurjhats and the invariably greater livelihood and ferocity of character of the inhabitants of the hills and jungles, probably determined the selection from amongst them of the feudal military of Orissa and the particular system of management adopted with regard to them, whilst the more timid, passive, obedient and industrious inhabitants of the open and fertile country were required to pay a regular revenue to the state either in money or in kind. Some differences in appearance and disposition is still observable between the common ryots of the Mogulbundee and those of Rajmarch, but the paiks of the latter exhibited strikingly every feature of the most rude, savage, ferocious and uncivilized character and can scarcely be allowed to rank as members of civilised society".[257] The intention of Ewer in such c haracterisation of people was to justify British rule in the sub-continent and its civilising mission.

The imperial rulers and administrators in subjugating the unruly people had always used coercion as an instrument. In order to bring the rebellious Paiks of Khurda under the complete subjection of the British rule, Ewer had stated that coercion was the only alternative "I should hope that in many of the smaller gurhs (forts) the very name of paik has become extinct and lost. But I am well aware that in others the lawless and predatory habits of that peculiar class, if not their name, still continue, and the most vigorous exertions of the police must be long necessary before they can be effectually quelled".[258] Further in order to provide the empire an effectual security from the onslaught of the barbarian Paiks, Ewer reiterated that force was essential. Exemplary punishments had to be inflicted to seal the chances of future rebellion on their part. Ewer had said, "The consequences of the Cuttack rebellion, however temporarily inconvenient, will I trust terminate finally in general good to the country. As far as the question of the Paiks is concerned, I think that when the late ferment and ebullition in Khoorda and its vicinity, as well as in some of the small Killahs have completely subsided, the bond which held their communities together, feeling of common respect for and submission to the chief of former authority and importance will trance, will found in many cases snapped as under. Some Khundaits and Dulbehras were killed during the insurrection; others have been compelled to fly the district and many thrown into jail on charges of rebellion, which is to be hoped they will never leave alive. By the removal of these chiefs, necessarily discontented and dissatisfied with the company's government, one very important step is certainly made towards securing the future in offensive conduct of their followers".[259]

Ewer had suggested several measures for the improvement of the land revenue administration in Orissa. He wanted that the system of biennial and triennial settlements should cease as speedily as possible. The land holders should be allowed to enjoy for a long period of years the full profits of their industry and outlay of capital in their estates. At least they should obtain the certainty of a respite for sonie time to come from increased demand on lands actually in cultivation. It did not appear to him that permanent settlement was indispensable for such an end. He believed that only a limitation of the existing amount of taxation for a number of years would cure one of the worst maladies from which Orissa was suffering. He had recommended that a settlement of land revenue should be made for a number of years and warned the authorities that any promise or allusion to a permanent settlement should be cautiously avoided. In this connection, Ewer pointed out that though some Muslim and Bengali Zamindars were eager for a permanent settlement, no Zamindar of Orissa complained about the matter in his long list of grievances against the British administration. He had concluded that for the peculiar circumstances of Orissa and its sufferings it had the extraordinary claims to the grant of a permanent settlement as early as possible.

To sum up, Ewer's report had revealed the shortcomings of the British administration in Orissa during the early years, analysed its causes and suggested some changes in the policy for the amelioration of the condition of the people. While dealing with the causes of the rebellion he had made many unwarranted remarks about the people of Orissa, by describing them as rude, barbarous and uncivilised, which clearly demonstrated his imperial sensibility. He wanted to establish the superiority of the Christians and Europeans over the Indians and their civilisation. He had asserted like a hardcore imperial protagonist, the necessity of British rule in India. The civilising mission of the British government in India had to be advanced. While providing suggestions for the improvement of the condition of the people of Orissa, he was certainly influenced by utilitarian principles. Thus Ewer displayed both imperial and utilitarian sentiment in his report.

After Ewer, the most celebrated administrative historian of Orissa was George Toynbee. He was a class by himself. Toynbee's *"A Sketch of the History of Orissa"*, was the first comprehensive history of the Province, which had dealt with the early years of British rule in Orissa. This work was a part of the larger scholarly enterprise launched by the Victorian scholars of enlightenment. The work dealt with the political and administrative history of Orissa during the period from 1803 to 1828. Englishman's justification in India and English commitment of conquering India and holding it for colonial aims had remained the basic intention of Toynbee in writing his history. From the very first paragraph of the book, his imperial leanings and sensibility was clearly visible.

Toynbee had begun the work by stating, "The subjugation of maritime Province of Cuttack formed a part of that glorious campaign under Sir Arthur Wellesley which culminated in the complete overthrow of Maratha power at the battles of Assai and Argaun. So splendid was the fame of the greater events that history has of necessity passed over this minor and subsidiary expedition almost in silenoe. Mere mention is all that has been accorded to it. Although however it may possess no special importance in the eyes of the general reader, its every detail is full of interest to those who have passed several years in the Province of Orissa and have to appreciate and sympathise with the people".[260] Explicitly the impact of imperial arrogance and liberal values was clearly visible throughout his work.

Describing the capitulation of Cuttack on October 10, 1803 Toynbee had referred to the hostile nature of the people and the British commitment to protect their civil liberty. Just before analysing the progress of the troops for storming the Fort of Barabati at Cuttack he had cited Stirling's description of the fort and thereafter he had made his own account on the present condition of the fort. He had expressed his anguish over the vandalisms caused to the fort by the Public Works Department and the lack of aesthetic sense on their part. Toynbee had said, "There is little in the present appearance of the fort which answers to the above description (Stirling's account). The Public Works Department have converted this fine building into an unsightly series of earthen mounds and the ground within the moat into a wilderness of stone pits. The stones composing the walls of the moat which surrounds the fort are now being used to build a hospital. Some of the fort stone was, I believe used for the light house at False point and for other public building; the dust of the rest is shaken off our feet against us on the station roads. The 'great arched, gateway of the eastern face', as Stirling calls it and fine old mosque, called after Fatteh Khan Rahman are almost the only objects of antiquarian interest which remain intact. The fate of many interesting ruins in the province has unhappily been similar".[261] This has proved Toynbee's historical sense and his love for objects of archaeological importance.

Toynbee had given credit to the organised planning of the conquest of Orissa by the British force for their ultimate success. Further he had described in considerable detail the conquest of the Province of Orissa, Pindari Rebellion and the Khurda Rebellion of 1817. In part II of the book, he related the principal events connected with civil and revenue administration with much more clarity and a fair amount of accuracy. In this regard true to his training and aptitude in historical scholarship, he had enumerated the revenue policies of the native rulers, the Marathas and the Mughals and simultaneously he had pointed out the importance of Mokadams or intermediaries engaged in the land revenue work. He had outlined the details of the difficulties faced by the British authorities in procuring information about the customs and usages of the country.

The British were earnest in amassing as much wealth as possible from land revenue. That led them to introduce a number of harsh measures including the sale of proprietorship. Toynbee had stated, "...Instead of taking the Uriya proprietors as they were, our early Revenue Officers having already made them into Bengal Zamindars determined to try and make them what they thought, they ought to be in the matter of the punctual payment of their revenue. This policy made our demands seem harsh and unjust in their eyes and rendered them unwilling as well as unable to fulfill their engagements. They could not reconcile with our otherwise just and lenient rule, our unbending determination to realize to the uttermost cowrie the revenue for which they had engaged and our stern refusal to listen to pleas of remission and sets off which under the Marathas they had been accustomed to make with uniform success.

This hostility of the proprietors brought collections to a deadlock and matters to a crisis. In 1806 many estates fell into arrear for heavy balances. The Collector applied to the Revenue Board for authority to bring them to sale under the Bengal regulations. To this proposition in its entirety the Board wisely demurred. They adopted the expedient of ordering the estates to be advertised for public sale, in the hope that the proprietors would in their alarm at the prospect of losing them, pay up the balances due without further delay. To give force to the threat, seventeen estates, with a jama of over Rs.30,000 were brought to the hammer and sold by way of making a public example. It had, however, little or no effect; next year the balances increased to an enormous extent and as the threat of sale had proved of no avail, it was determined to try the reality. This was the beginning of that fatal policy by which the old Uriya proprietors were ruined and their places filled by absentee Bengali millionaires and the amla of the courts".[262] These had demonstrated the determination of the

British to coerce the Oriya people and extort them for their economic interests.

Then Toynbee discussed various settlements put into force by the British government during the period from 1808-09 to 1827-28. He had also mentioned about various other forms of taxes like Pilgrim tax, house tax and octroi or transit duties collected from the people from the period of Marathas and onwards. His calculation of the number of pilgrims who had visited Puri in 1807-08 and the amount of taxes collected from them was an important information for studying the history of tourism in Orissa. He had stated, "In 1807-08 the total number of pilgrims to Pooree was 83,685. Of these 56,763 entered Puri town from the north and 26,922 from the south; 72,051 were exempted from the payment of any tax as Kangals (Paupers), and 11,634 paid taxe amounting to Rs.40,500 (sicca). From 1807-08 to 1813-14, the collections averaged Rs.68,350 (sicca) yearly. In 1813-14 they were Rs.1,23,118 (sicca) and 1814-15 Rs.2,08,519 (sicca). The Collector writing in 1814, says that with proper supervision the annual collections should never be less than five lakhs of sicca rupees. But from the figures given above, this climate would appear to be much too sanguine".[263]

In the concluding portions of part II, Toynbee had assessed the levels of improvement the Oriyas had attained within a span of only thirty years of British rule. He had stated, "when we first acquired it in 1803 there was hardly a single native of Orissa in Government employ...until 1805 that the commissioners directed that in all written communications should be written in Uriya as well as in Persian. This order necessitated the employment of Uriya Mohurirs who though skilful enough with their iron pen and bundle of palm leaves were almost helpless when required to write on paper with an ordinary pen. They are said to have been slow in acquiring any facility in the (to them new method of writing, ignorant of business in general, and especially of the English system of revenue accounts as indeed they well might be). XXX (there is no coherence in this sentence) All the best ministerial appointments were consequently in the hands of Bengali amla, who attracted by the high pay that had to be offered to procure the requisite standard of efficiency, left their homes in Bengal and bringing their family with them, settled in the province and became naturalized Uriyas; their descendants hold at the present day the chief offices in the various courts of revenue, criminal and civil law. They had ample opportunities of making money independent of their pay and they did not hesitate to take advantage of them. Bribery, corruption speculation and forgery were rife in all the courts and public offices, and notably in the Judges... In 1821 the Magistrate writes as follows:- Scarcely a single real Uriya receives a salary of more than Rs. 10 per mensem, but several are naturalized Bengalis or Mussulmans I always give a preference to Uriyas, but at this moment, I scarcely know a single Uriya possessing qualifications to fit him for being a common Mohurir". He however adds, which is more improvement on the previous state of affairs—'The people do not at present suffer from any severe oppression from the amla".[264] Corruption was rampant in those days. The analysis of Toynbee clearly demonstrated that the Government was not sincere in curbing that, which resulted in the sufferings of the people. This would be appropriate to state that the corruption in the present day India is a legacy of the British rule. Toynbee had referred to a statement of Mr.Ricketts, who, writing of the amla in 1828, said, "No care, attention, shrewdness or circumspection can provide efficient checks to their innate and incorrigible roguery". In the present day though we have provided tolerable safe guards against any flagrant cases of corruption, we know that bribery is still almost invariably resorted to; and so long as the people generally consent to offer bribes, we are powerless to prevent the amla from taking them".[265]

Part III of the book dealt with the Police—Crime, Jails; communication system; public buildings; trade, prices wages, etc., in greater detail. As regards crime and police, Toynbee made some interesting observations as regards the effect of the changes made by the English. Instead of bringing good to the people, it became one of the most repressive institutions. Toynbee stated, "Crime consequently increased, and the tyrannies of the new police became unbearable. Not a quarrel could happen in any family but the police made capital out of it. Regulation VII of 1811 therefore limited their interference to the maintenance of the public tranquility and to the adoption of prescribed measures for bringing to justice persons accused of the commission of those species of crimes which are most injurious to the peace and happiness of society. They were prohibited from taking up cases of a private nature such as adultery, calumny, abusive language and petty assaults.... Utter inefficiency of the police in putting a stop to petty thefts and burglaries, which became about that time alarmingly prevalent.

Of the village chowkidars the Magistrate says in 1813, "It is notorious that the generality of the watchmen are themselves the thieves on most occasions. This arises from their not being sufficiently paid for their trouble by the land holder, whose interest it is to protect the property of their tenants. The Zamindars themselves had the reputation especially in Jajipur and Bhadrak, of being hereditary receivers of stolen goods, if indeed they did not take a still more active part in crime against property.... the Magistrate attributes the prevalence of petty thefts and burglaries to the extreme poverty and wretchedness of the lower classes their loose notions of honesty and the ease and impunity with which such offences could be penetrated".[266]

At the end of Part III are added appendices No. I, II, III enlisting the regulations issued during the period, the list of officers who served in Orissa from 1803 to 1828, the price list of various commodities existing during the period 1811 and 1817. Besides a good number of official correspondences, sanads, sale deeds were attached at the end of the volume.

In its totality, Toynbee's *A Sketch of the History of Orissa (from 1803-1828)* displayed an objective history of the period without any bias from the historiographical point of view. It duly qualified itself to be put into the bracket, "the administrative history". It was the first of its kind in the historiography of Orissa. It was definitely written with the sole purpose of acting as a torch bearer to the administrators of Orissa. It might have been used as an instrument of imperial propaganda. It carried with it the syndromes of the Raj.

Both Ewer and Toynbee provided a new dimension to the study of Orissan history by writing the contemporary history of the time. In their attempt to understand the land revenue system, and customs and usages associated with it, Ewer and Toynbee tried unsuccessfully to touch the subalterns and their role in the economic system of the country. But their obsession with the collection of land revenue, led them to go for different permutations and combinations with landed magnates. With that the subaltern domain was surgically removed from the discourse and the historiography remained essentially elitist. Both the writings dealt with a political and intellectual culture which had absorbed the knowledge, techniques and attitudes of British colonizers.

References

1. Acharya, P (ED) *'Bruton's Account of Cuttack and Puri* (compiled) *The O.H.R.J* Vol X (No 3) Bhubaneswar 1961, pp.49-50.
2. *Ibid.*, p.34.
3. *Ibid.*, p.35-36.
4. *Ibid.*, p.52.
5. *Ibid.*, p.42.
6. *Ibid.*, p.34.
7. *Ibid.*, p.44.
8. *Ibid.*, p.45.
9. *Ibid.*, p.45.
10. *Ibid.*, p.32.
11. Hunter W.W., *Orissa* Vol II, London 1872, p.32.
12. Fawcett, Charles *The English Factories in India*, Vol II, p.325.
13. *The Asiatic Miscellaney*, Vol II, Calcutta 1786, p.29.
14. Motte, Thomas *"A Narrative of a Journey to the Diamond Mines at Sambalpur,"* in *The O.H.R.J* Vol II (No 3), Bhubaneswar 1952, p.1.
15. *Ibid.*, p.2.
16. *Ibid.*, p.2.
17. *Ibid.*, p.10.
18. *Ibid.*, p.18.
19. *Ibid.*, p.29.
20. *Ibid.*, p.2.
21. *Ibid.*, pp.2-49.
22. *Ibid.*, p.6-7.
23. *Ibid.*, pp.2-49.
24. *Ibid.*, p.2.
25. *Ibid.*, p.5.
26. *Ibid.*, p.12.
27. *Ibid.*, pp.15-16.
28. *Ibid.*, p.17.

29. *Ibid.*, p.29.
30. *Ibid.*, p.21.
31. *Ibid.*, pp.22-23.
32. *Ibid.*, pp.23-24.
33. *Ibid.*, p.25.
34. *Ibid.*, p.25-26.
35. *Ibid.*, p.26.
36. *Ibid.*, p.27.
37. *Ibid.*, pp.27-28.
38. *Ibid.*, pp.28-29.
39. *Ibid.*, p.30.
40. *Ibid.*, p.30.
41. *Ibid.*, p.31.
42. *Ibid.*, p.32.
43. *Ibid.*, p.33.
44. *Ibid.*, p.37.
45. *Ibid.*, p.40.
46. *Ibid.*, p.42.
47. *Ibid.*, p.42.
48. *Ibid.*, p.45.
49. *Ibid.*, p.48.
50. *Ibid.*, p.49.
51. *Ibid.*, p.8.
52. *Ibid.*, p.9.
53. *Ibid.*, p.14-15.
54. Patra, K.M, "*Orissa Under the East India Company,* New Delhi, 1971, p.xiii (Introduction) cited from *The Asiatic Miscellaney* Vol. II, p.29.
55. Patra, K.M., *Orissa Under East India Company*, New Delhi, 1971. p.31-32.
56. *Ibid.*, p.89.
57. *Ibid.*, pp.104-05.
58. *Ibid.*,p.XV cited from *Calendar of Persian Correspondences,* Vol: LX, No 247 and 290.
59. *Ibid.*, p.xv.
60. Chakraborty, Suhas, *The Raj Syndrome: A Study in Imperial Perception,* Delhi 1989, p.10.

122. *Ibid.*, pp.21-22.
123. Kipling, Rudyard, KIM, London, 1967 (ed) p.79.
124. Basu, K.K., *"Tour Diary of J R Ousley"* in *The Orissa Historical Research Journal*, Vol V (3 & 4), Bhubaneswar, 1957, pp.166-67.
125. *Ibid.*, p.167.
126. *Ibid.*, p.169.
127. *Ibid.*, p.170.
128. *Ibid.*, p.171.
129. *Ibid.*, p.171.
130. *Ibid.*, p.173.
131. *Ibid.*
132. Said, Edward W., *Orientalism*, London, 1985.
133. *Ibid.*, p.203.
134. Metcalf, T.R., Ideologies of the Raj, Cambridge, 1995, p.66.
135. *Ibid.*, p.66.
136. Hunter, W.W., *Orissa*, Vol I & II, London, 1872.
137. *Ibid.*, p.9.
138. *Ibid.*, pp.1-5.
139. Acharya, P, *Odissara Pratnatatva O' Anyanya Prabandha (Oriya)*, Bhubaneswar, 1969, p.364.
140. Hunter, W.W., *op. cit.*, p.278.
141. *Ibid.*, pp.278-79.
142. *Ibid.*, pp.383-84.
143. *Ibid.*, p.288.
144. Mitra, Rajendra Lal, *Antiquities of Orissa,* Vol II, Calcutta, 1880, p.170.
145. Acharya, P., *op. cit.*, pp.367-678.
146. *Ibid.*, p.372.
147. Hunter, W.W., *op.cit.*, p.112.
148. *Ibid.*, p.5.
149. *Ibid.*, p.6.
150. Hunter, Stirling, Beames and Sahu, *A History of Orissa*, (ed) Vol I by N.K. Sahu, Calcutta, 1956, p.78.
151. *Ibid.*, p.5.
152. *Ibid.*, p.8.
153. *Ibid.*, p.27.

154. *Ibid.*, p.30.
155. *Ibid.*, pp.30-31.
156. *Ibid.*, p.52.
157. *Ibid.*, p.33.
158. Metcalf, T.R., *op.cit.*, p.173.
159. *Ibid.*, p.174.
160. Arnold, David, *"Cholera and colonialism in British India" in Past and Present*, No 113,. n.p, p.132.
161. Hunter, W.W., *Orissa*, Vol I, 1872, pp.166-67.
162. Hunter, W.W., Stirling, Beames and Sahu, *op.cit.*, p.38.
163. *Ibid.*, p.38.
164. *Ibid.*, p.38-39.
165. *Ibid.*, p.48.
166. *Ibid.*, p.50.
167. *Ibid.*, pp.51-52.
168. *Ibid.*, p.69.
169. *Ibid.*, p.69.
170. *Ibid.*, p.96.
171. *Ibid.*, p.99.
172. *Ibid.*, p.133.
173. *Ibid.*, p.154.
174. *Ibid.*, p.171.
175. *Ibid.*, p.175.
176. *Ibid.*, p.176.
177. *Ibid.*, p.178.
178. *Ibid.*
179. Morris, James, *Heavens Command: An Imperial Progress*, London, 1973, pp.522-526.
180. Metcalf, T.R., *op.cit.*, p.235.
181. Hunter, W.W., et al, *op.cit.*, p.179.
182. *Ibid.*, p.180.
183. *Ibid.*, p.189.
184. *Ibid.*, pp.192-93.
185. *Ibid.*, pp.193-94.
186. *Ibid.*, pp.194-95.
187. *Ibid.*, p.91.
188. *Ibid.*, p.147.

189. *Ibid.*, p.155.
190. *Ibid.*, p.156.
191. Penner, Peter, (ed), John Beames, *Memoirs of a Bengal Civilian*, New Delhi, 1984, p.vi.
192. *Ibid.*, p.75.
193. *Ibid.*, p.125.
194. *Ibid.*, pp.101-03.
195. *Ibid.*, p.173.
196. W.S. Setonkarr's speech at Calcutta in 1864 at a dinner for Haileyburians. See Memories of Old Haileybury College, 1894, pp.90-95.
197. Stephen, J.F., "Legislation Under Lord Mayo" in *W.W. Hunter, Life of Lord Mayo*, Vol 2, London, 1875, pp.168-69.
198. Beames, John, *op. cit.*, pp.179-86.
199. *Ibid.*, p.252
200. Mason, Phillip, *The Founders* (J.C.P, 1963, ed. First published in 1953), p.15 cited in Peter Penner edited *"Memoirs of Bengal Civilian: John Beames"* P.XV, New Delhi,1984.
201. Beames, John, *op. cit.*, pp.231-32.
202. De, Barun, "Brajendranath De and John Beames—a study in reactions of patriotism and paternalism in ICS at the time of Illbert Bill" in *Bengal Past and Present,* 81, (Jan-June 1962).
203. *Ibid.*, pp.4, 19, 25-27, see paragraph 31 of Appendix.
204. Beames, John, *op. cit.*, p.81, 100, 305.
205. *Ibid.*, pp.215-16.
206. De, Barun, *op. cit.*, p.28.
207. John Beames quoted in Bansidhar Mohanty, *Oriya Bhasa Andolan,* Cuttack, p.39, 1985.
208. *Ibid.*, p.40.
209. Senapati, Fakir Mohan, *Atmajivan Charita*, translated by John Boulton, 1917, reproduced by Orissa Sahitya Akademi, Bhubaneswar, 1985, pp.25-26.
210. *Ibid.*, p.26.
211. Beames, John, *"Notes on the History of Orissa Under Mohemmadan, Maratha and British Rule"* in *Journal of Asiatic Society of Bengal*, Vol 52, 1883 pp.231-257, reproduced in Hunter, Stirling, Beames and Sahu, *"A History of Orissa"* Vol II (edited by N.K. Sahu), 1956, Calcutta.

212. Beames, John,"The Altai Hills of Cuttack" in *Journal of Asiatic Society of Bengal,* 1875, Calcutta, pp.19-23.
213. Beames, John, "More Buddhist Remains from Orissa, in *Journal of Asiatic Society of Bengal*, 1872, Calcutta.
214. Beames, John, "The history of Orissa under Mohemmadan, Maratha and British rule" in *A History of Orissa*, Vol II, edited by N.K. Sahu, 1956, Calcutta, p.392.
215. *Ibid.*, pp.292-93.
216. Risley, Herbert, *The People of India*, London, 1915 (reprinted; Delhi, 1969), pp.53-61.
217. Beames, John, *"The History of Orissa Under Mohemmadan, Maratha and British Rule"*, *op. cit*, pp.293-94.
218. *Ibid.*, pp.297-98.
219. *Ibid.*, p.309.
220. *Ibid.*, p.310.
221. *Ibid.*, pp.317-18.
222. Beames, John, *Memoirs of a Bengal Civilian,* 1896 (reprint, 1984), pp.204-05.
223. *Ibid.*, p.257.
224. *Ibid.*, p.217.
225. *Ibid.*, pp.219-20.
226. *Ibid.*, p.264.
227. *Ibid.*, p.243.
228. *Ibid.*, pp.243-44.
229. *Ibid.*, pp.244-45.
230. *Ibid.*, p.261.
231. Beames, John, *The History of Orissa Under Mohemmadan, Maratha and British Rule, op.cit.*, p.230.
232. Beames, John, *Memoirs of a Bengal Civilian*, *op.cit.*, pp.259-60.
233. *Ibid.*, pp.232-34.
234. *Ibid.*, pp.255-56.
235. *Ibid.*, p.257.
236. Beames, John, "Altai hills of Cuttack" in *Journal of Asiatic Society of Bengal*, Calcutta, 1875.,p.19.
237. *Ibid.*, p.21.
238. *Ibid.*, p.21.
239. *Ibid.*, p.23.
240. Beames, *Memoirs of a Bengal Civilian*, *op. cit.*, p.174.

241. Seal, Anil, "Imperialism and Nationalism in India" in J. Gallaghar, G. Johnson and Anil Seal, *Locality, Province and Nation*, Cambridge, 1973, p.6, cited in Ranjit Guha, "Dominance without Hegemony and its Historiography" in Ranjit Guha (ed) *Subaltern Studies*, VI, Delhi, n.d, p.292.
242. Guha, Ranjit, "Dominance without hegemony and its historiography" in Ranjit Guha (ed), *Subaltern Studies*, VI, Delhi, p.294.
243. *Ibid.*,p.295.
244. Ewer, Walter, "Correspondence of the Settlement of Khoordah in Pooree", Calcutta, 1818, in *The Orissa Historical Research Journal,* Vol III (4), IV (1&2), IV (3&4), Bhubaneswar, 1955.
245. *Ibid.*, p.iii.
246. *Ibid.*, p.xii.
247. *Ibid.*, p.xiii..
248. *Ibid.*, p.xiii.
249. *Ibid.*, p.xiv.
250. *Ibid.*, pp.xvi & xvii.
251. *Ibid.*, p.xvii.
252. *Ibid.*, pp.xvii & xviii.
253. *Ibid.*, p.xviii
254. *Ibid.*, pp.xxvii & xxviii.
255. *Ibid.*, p.lii.
256. *Ibid.*, p.lix.
257. *Ibid.*, pp.llii & lliii.
258. *Ibid.*, p.llvii.
259. *Ibid.*, pp.llviiiI & llix.
260. Toynbee, G, "A Sketch of the History of Orissa (from 1803 to 1828)" Calcutta, 1873, reproduced in the *Orissa Historical Research Journal*, Vol IX (1&2) (3&4), Vol X (1&2), Bhubaneswar, 1960, 1961.
261. *Ibid.*, p.4.
262. *Ibid.*, p.41.
263. *Ibid.*, p.59.
264. *Ibid.*, pp.66-67.
265. *Ibid.*, p.67.
266. *Ibid.*, p.71-72.

6

Nationalist Historians

Nationalists' historiography in India emerged as a reaction against the British policies defended by the colonialist historians of India like James Mill and Vincent Smith, and, as a result of the national awakening against British paramountcy it crystallized in the form of a struggle for freedom under Mahatma Gandhi. The historians of this category in their anxiety to defend their heritage often became subjective, but it was only a natural impulse when European scholars were doing no better. Even when positive evidences were available, some of the western scholars were bent upon denigrating Indian achievements by suggesting that Indians must have borrowed heavily from the Greeks or Assyrians or Persians or Babylonians. Even the origin of some of the regional dynasties of India such as the Pallavas was traced to some foreign country like Persia. Besides western scholars, at least a few, stressed the weaker elements in Indian culture ignoring its brighter aspects. Naturally the Indian scholars who had entered into this arena with a vengeance to settle all accounts paid the contestants in their own coin. In doing this exercise, the nationalist historians, barring a very limited few, expressed meticulous concern for accuracy on the exhaustive collection of all available facts and an almost obsessive avoidance of systematic evaluation and generalization. Many of these nationalist orientalists displayed a genuine affection and enthusiasm for their own subjects.

What was more offensive to Indian scholars was the attempt of the Christian missionaries (some of whom took historical composition) to make much of the social abuses and religious superstitions in Hinduism. The second aspect of the historical writing, apart from the refutation of western charges, is the attempt of the Indians to prove that they were mature enough to deserve political concessions and even full freedom.

The relative merit and demerit of the nationalist historiography in India can be summed up as follows:

(1) By presenting an encouraging picture of the past it filled the people with great self-confidence that was needed for boosting the national consciousness.

(2) This ideology produced splendid research works and certain points regarding the prevalence of limited monarchy, republics and local self-government, and international law in ancient India came to be accepted by nearly all scholars, inspite of the dissenting note of Vincent Smith that it was not safe to rely on the admonitions of early sages about the ideal king.

(3) The positive outcome of this ideology (and that of imperialists also) is that the political unity of India was accepted as a reality.

(4) On the other hand, it hardly touched (conscious intellectuals) interested in the masses of peasants and workers who were being drawn into the nationalist struggle after 1920s.

(5) Such an ideology gave a sense of value to Indians.

(6) In its craze for proving the superiority of our ancient institutions over those of the ancient west it hardly tried to examine them in the light of the evolution of tribes as known from anthropology.

(7) Going to prove the superiority of Indians the nationalist historians went on to support the Indian colonisation in South East Asia, a concept which is implicitly antagonistic to nationalist ideology.

As regards the nationalist historiography of Orissa, the historians of this genre in Orissa not only subscribed to some or all these characteristics we find in the context of nationalist Indian historiography but also took a regional nationalist stand, This was particularly in view of the socio-political situation of Orissa before it became a separate province in 1936. Naturally, therefore, they had to present a similar picture of Orissa's past glory as was done of Indian's past by the nationalist historians. The historians of Orissa of this category like Pyarimohan Acharya, Jagabandhu Singh, Pandit Nilakantha Dash, Pandit Krupasindhu Mishra and Birupakshya Kar were not professional historians and had no training whatsoever in historical research. They were all active participants in the movement for the formation of Orissa as a separate province, and, obviously, the character of history writing found in their works was more guided by regional patriotism, a stand which is considered absurd after independence. They were somewhat justified in taking such a stand as the Oriyas were then frantically trying to unite the different aspects of the history of Orissa and some of them wrote a somewhat complete account of Orissan history. Despite all the limitations of their work, they certainly pioneered historical research in Orissa before independence.

I. PYARIMOHAN ACHARYA (1851-1881)

Pyarimohan Acharya was one of those front-ranking Oriyas who dedicated themselves for the development of the modern Oriya language during the 19th century. He wrote the *History of Orissa* (in Oriya) when the Oriya speaking people had to fight for the survival of the Oriya language. Pyarimohan Acharya was born on August 5, 1851[1] in the Kuanpala village under Mahanga Police Station of Cuttack district. His father was an eminent lawyer of those days. With no facilities for English education available and Oriya text books being extremely scarce, Pyarimohan completed his primary school education in a *'Pāthaśālā'* in his village. At the age of twelve, he came to Cuttack and completed his high school education from Ravenshaw Collegiate school, then known as Cuttack Zilla School. From this time his creative talents were recognized. He mostly indulged himself in intellectual debates on different aspects of Orissan history and culture through the magazine *'Utkal Putra'.* In 1869 he joined Cuttack Collage for the F.A. degree. At Cuttack college he came in contact with the poet laureate Madhusudan Rao. This friendship proved a boon for Pyarimohan and both of them wrote a number of articles and translated many English books into Oriya. Greatly influenced by the Principal of Cuttack College, Professor Haranath Bhattacharya, a Brahmo-Samajist, Pyarimohan, along with Madhusudan joined the

Brahmo Samaj and involved himself in the propagation of the principles of Brahmo-Samaj in Orissa.

During the early part of the nineteenth century, the Christian missionaries opened up English schools in Orissa. In 1822, the missionaries established the first western style school "Cuttack English Mission School" at Cuttack and handed over the management of the school to the British resident administrator at Cuttack. These Christian missionaries also set up the first Oriya printing press in the form of the Cuttack mission press at Cuttack in the year 1838. From this press was printed the first Oriya magazine *"Jñānāruṇa"* in 1849, and in 1856, *'Probodha Candrika'* was published under the editorship of one Englishman named Charles Lassley. During this period Amos Sutton also contributed phenomenally for the development of Oriya language even though such efforts were implicitly serving the purpose of the propagation of Christianity in Orissa. At the same time the Christian missionaries also tendered their role in establishing modern education and imparting western type sophistication and modernism into the Orissan society. The British revenue administration, the resistance movements and the deadly famine of 1866 opened up a new vision in the thought process of the Oriyas, and consequently a period for establishing the Oriya identity began.

Pyarimohan was one of the products of this intellectual awakening. Himself a Christian and born to an educated father who was then an established lawyer, Pyarimohan had a good English education and a grooming in the elitist social environment to provide the necessary intellectual outfit required for the intellectual reawakening of Orissa. Being an Oriya intellectual, he had the interest of the Oriyas in mind. Tuned to the necessity of the time, Pyarimohan had edited and published the fortnightly magazine *'Uṭkala Putra'* young Pyarimohan fearlessly wrote about the British exploitation of the people and the social stigma of the time. This not only exposed his intellectual ability but also perturbed the powerful British government for which he had to leave his college studies for one particular article 'Darakhasta Jutian' published in *'Uṭkala Putra'*. The article bore the spirit of the new Oriya sentiment. This did not put a stop to Pyarimohan's courageous efforts but gave him further fillip to carry on with his intellectual exercise. In 1875, Pyarimohan joined a privately run school at Cuttack as a teacher. This school had the distinction of having persons like the revolutionary Bipin Chandra Pal as its headmaster. Pyarimohan could not continue with this school for long but used to look after the management of the school. Then he joined Damapada Palace as the private tutor. Later when Fakirmohan Senapati resigned as Manager of the palace, Pyarimohan Acharya replaced him. Whatever money he got from this assignment he spent for the management of a school named 'Katak Academy' which after his death was renamed as 'Pyarimohan Academy' .

During the Oriya language movement in the seventies of the 19th century Pyarimohan Acharya strongly raised the voice in favour of the Oriya language. He had dreamt of the formation of the states in our country on the basis of the languages spoken. He strongly advocated that Sambalpur and Ganjam were parts of Orissa and, if these areas were included, the territory of Orissa would be double that of Bengal. This vividly explains Pyarimohan's Oriya nationalism. The unceasing efforts he made through *'Uṭkala Putra'* for uniting the Oriya-speaking tracts will forever immortalise him in the memory of the Oriyas. Pyarimohan breathed his last at a very young age of thirty after a brief illness.

Pyarimohan's *'Orissan History'* (in Oriya) was written at a time when Oriya language was suffering from an identity crisis and Oriya-speaking people had to fight it out with the Bengali elite in order to establish their own independent and separate existence. This was the period when the Oriya people fought vigorously for the protection of their language, culture and unification and amalgamation of all Oriya-speaking tracts. In this movement, Orissa felt the necessity of a comprehensive and complete history of her own. Pyarimohan filled this void excellently in 1875 though his book was printed after the British approval in 1879.[2] It was an occasion that gave him the chance to write the history of Orissa. In 1875 the Joint Inspector of Schools in-charge of Orissa gave an advertisement for writing the history of Orissa in Oriya language which was proposed to be introduced as a text book in different Orissan schools if approved by the Joint Inspector. Pyarimohan undertook this task and submitted a copy of the manuscript which eventually got permission after one year and was finally published in the year 1879. He received the 300 rupees award and the book was introduced in schools as a text book.

In this pursuit for presenting a comprehensive history of Orissa, Pyarimohan Acharya showed a high degree of perseverance. He followed largely the works of Hunter, Stirling, Rajendra Lal Mitra, the reprot of G. Toynbee, the Indian accounts of Elphinstone, Bloughman and Marshman, the Muslim accounts on India in general, various Asiatic Society journals, many literary texts in Sanskrit, Bengali and Oriya and many new and old documents from the Commissioner's office.[3] He also took the help of Rangalal Bandopadhyaya in scanning through the copper-plates concerning the history of Orissa. In dealing with those source materials he took extreme care and caution to present the history as far as it would help in enlightening the nationalistic spirit of the people of Orissa much in consonance with the spirit of the times. Of the scant source materials he had at his disposal, Pyarimohan very diligently tried to maintain the historical sequence for presenting a complete history of the province. In order to satisfy this end, he accepted the interpretations of some copper-plates and the *'Mandāla Pañjī'* by Hunter, Stirling and Rajendra Lal Mitra which were erroneous[4] but nevertheless served the purposes of the text book. He was equally careful about the historical flaws of their works. As regards *'Mandāla Pañjī'* he did not accept the entire *'Pañjī'* as historical truth.[5]

In *'Orissan History'* (in Oriya) Pyarimohan nearly dealt with everything on Orissa province. It was not merely a political account of Orissa but he dealt with her geography, people, religion, culture, education, trade, etc., up to the British period. Since during that time Oriya speaking tracts of Ganjam and Sambalpur remained outside the jurisdiction of Orissa division, Pyarimohan humbly admitted his lapses for not including the geography and history of these regions in his book.[6] This non-inclusion might well have been due to the fact that the book was to be used as a text book after being approved by the British authorities. Since the book was meant for use as a text book in schools, Pyarimohan had to keep his descriptions short. Nevertheless, he kept the essential and vital facts of Orissan history while presenting his narrative.

As a compiler of historical facts Pyarimohan excelled all his contemporaries. Considering the time and the absence of adequate historical source materials, his book exemplifies the value of his perseverance and efforts. In some of his interpretations we find a high degree of erudition. Making observations on the Greek conquests of India he concluded that, since evidences of Greek influence on art, culture were not traceable in Orissa, a Greek conquest of Orissa could not simply be believed.[7] He gave similarly an erudite interpretation of the word 'Yavana'[8] and threw new light on the origin of God Jagannatha.[9]

The Oriyas of his time were much concerned about maintaining a separate identity of theirs. This influenced Pyarimohan so much that he believed the internal factions and infighting to be the main causes of Orissa's disunity and decline. He observed that the Ganga and Gajapati rule in Orissa were the periods of triumph when Orissa's military glory reached her zenith. These rulers were so benevolent that they even treated well their feudatories who acted as a strong force for the emperors and defended the empires at the times of external invasion.[10] Like some other historians, Pyarimohan was critical of the Marhatta rule in Orissa. But he attributed to the British the progress of Orissa which was halted during the Marhatta rule.[11] This might well have been due to the fact that the book was meant for students in schools after the due approval of the British government. Being a Christian he believed that the modernization of the west was possible due to rapid progress in all walks of life and wanted to introduce sophistication into the socio-cultural life of Orissa. Pyarimohan presented his historical ideas in a clear manner in his book and concluded that Orissan history presented a picture of continuous development.[12] He observed that, though there was imperial rule, the people were largely benefitted.[13] Everything was only put to a halt during the Marhatta rule and one had to wait till the British administration in Orissa when the revival process began.

Whatever flaws we find in the book as regards historical interpretation was due to the inadequacy of source materials. But this book which was incidentally the first history book on Orissa created a sensation in the academic circles. Kalipada Banerjee scathingly criticised the book and even wrote to the Cuttack District Collector to ban the use of the book as a text book which was done.[14] The allegations made by Banerjee were successfully challenged and refuted by Pyarimohan Acharya who stood by his convictions.

Pyarimohan's *'Orissan History'* (in Oriya) presented a highly useful and documented history of Orissa. His language in the book was polished so much so that a literary value can be attached to it. Though many of his conclusions are not historically sound, his work was an inspiration to the leaders of the Oriya language movement and a source of information for general readers of Oriya books.

II. JAGABANDHU SINGH (1876-1948)

Jagabandhu Singh, a leading freedom fighter was born on 15 February 1876 in Bhubanpur village near Nimapara in Puri district. Completing his primary education in a village primary school, he studied for his entrance examination in Puri Zilla School and thereafter completed F.A. from Ravenshaw College at Cuttack.

After the successful completion of LL.B. degree, Jagabandhu Singh joined the Chamber of Utkal Gaurab Madhusudan Das, the veteran lawyer of the time, as his junior. The sense of patriotism he learnt from Madhusudan enlivened his spirit throughout.

He came to Puri to practise law and devoted his heart and soul to this profession and established himself as a prominent pleader within a very short time. During this time he associated himself actively with the Utkal Sammilani and played a prominent role in the movement for the formation of Orissa as a separate province. Through his personal efforts, the 5th, 9th and 16th annual conferences of the Utkal Sammilani were held at Puri. He also presided over the Utkal Sammilani at its Singhbhum session. For many years he served as the Vice-Chairman of the Zilla Parishad and was a great champion of the co-operative movement in the state.

His association with Pandit Gopalbandhu Dash is a memorable event in the Oriya movement. He served as a member of the Bihar – Orissa Legislative Assembly from 1924-26 and successfully placed the problems of the people of Orissa before the assembly. After the formation of Orissa province he was elected to the provincial assembly from Puri as a Congress candidate in the year 1937.

Jagabandhu Singh's contribution to the history and literature of Orissa was phenomenal. His *'Prachina Uṭkala'* was the result of his untiring efforts to unearth the history of Orissa which was till then a monopoly of the European writers. He was a member of the 'Historical Investigations' Committee formed in the year 1947. He had also many other literary works to his credit. The great nationalist and crusader for the Oriyas died on 17 May 1948.

Jagabandhu Singh, showed exemplary perseverance in collecting historical information to present a complete work on Orissan history. His *Prachina Uṭkala*,[15] which portrayed the greatness of ancient Uṭkala, first appeared in book form in the year 1929. It was serially published in the form of articles in the Oriya monthly *'Mukur'* since 1919. This work shows his high degree of patriotism and love for the country. That the book has not lost favour among the Oriya readers for over half a century since its publication, explains its potentiality as a good piece of literary and historical work.

The book, *'Prachina Uṭkala'* containing twenty chapters, is generally considered to be a nationalist work. Several works on Orissan history existed when Jagabandhu Singh entrusted himself upon this daunting task. These were mainly Hunter's *'Orissa'*, Stirling's *Accounts on Orissa*, Pyarimohan Acharya's *Orissan History* (in Oriya), Nagendranath Mitra's *Puri Tirtha,* Manmohan Ganguly's *'Orissa and her Remains'* and Rajendra Lal Mitra's *'Antiquities of Orissa'.* Jagabandhu Singh read all these books but was not at all satisfied because none of these works presented a true picture of the different aspects of the history of Orissa from an Oriya's point of view.

In this endeavour Jagabandhu Singh was greatly encouraged by Fakir Mohan Senapati, the father of Oriya novels, Pandit Nilamani Vidyaratna and poet laureate Radhanatha Ray amongst others. The first publication of the book came out from Puri Press.

Jagabandhu Singh's endeavor to write the history of Orissa was strengthened more or less by the movement that was going on in Orissa in an organized manner since 1903 under the leadership of Madhusudan Das for unifying the Oriya-speaking tracts. Ever since the formation of Uṭkal Sammilani in 1903, a sort of intellectual revival was conceived in Orissa when scholars of all hues attempted to trace the glorious culture of Orissa, its indigenous nature, and contributions to the mainstream of India civilisation. Jagabandhu Singh's *'Prachina Uṭkala'* is considered a work of that order and a work which guided the leaders of the movement for Oriya nationalism.

During his time the archaeological evidences being very scant, Jagabandhu Singh depended mostly on literary works. He studied extensively the *Mahābhārata*, the *Rāmāyaṇa*, the *Harīvaṁśa* and the sources of the *Purāṇas* to establish the antiquity of Uṭkala.[16] To write his *Prachina Utkala*, Jagabandhu Singh relied mainly on relatively less authentic works like *Madāla Pañjī*, Basudeva Ratha's *Gaṅgā Vaṁśanucharitam*, Chintamani Padhiari's *Madāla* and Padmanabha Mishra's *Gaṅgeya vaṁśāvalī*.[17] Since all these texts were complied at a very late time, the political accounts given in these texts are found to be highly unreliable. As a result, much of the conclusions arrived at by Jagabandhu Singh naturally got refuted when inscriptional evidences were discovered later and many also do not stand worthy of any further historical enquiry. Still the trend of historical research he set, remained a guideline for the historians of successive generations.[18] In the thematic treatment of his subject, Jagabandhu Singh took a more positive approach. He tried to look upon Orissa's history from an Oriya's point of view and thus concentrated on unearthing new source materials for the history of Orissa. Instead of merely taking the earlier British and Bengali historians on Orissa to task, he successfully refuted their historical misconceptions by forwarding strong arguments. He has equally admired the efforts of the British administrator-historian Hunter who, despite all his limitations, brought to light many archaeological and unknown literary evidences on Orissan history. Jagabandhu Singh writes "because of Hunter's efforts, we came to know about these books today. There might have been some errors in his writings. Still Uṭkal is indebted before him. The foreign scholars are making a lot of efforts to fix the chronology of Orissan history but it is certainly a matter of regret that we Oriyas are not giving much attention to this."[19]

Introducing his "*Prāchina Uṭkala*" Jagabandhu Singh had clearly set out his objectives and purposes for writing the history of Orissa. He writes that the during various periods of her history, the "wings of our glorious past had been clipped"[20] This deliberate act has very badly affected our traditional pride.[21] The Oriyas over the ages have tolerated this serious anti-Oriya act.[22] The plight of the Oriyas living in different states like Bengal. Madhya Pradesh and Andhra Pradesh was miserable. He argued that the Oriyas couldn't develop unless they were united and came under one single administration. In the past the people of Orissa excelled in all the areas of human endeavour as they belonged to a single kingdom.

Modern Uṭkal meaning Orissa which is divided cannot develop unless and until it is united.[23]

The formation of Uṭkal Sammilani by Madhusudan Das had helped in creating some sense of nationalism among the people of Orissa. Just before this Orissa had nearly come under attack from the Bengali elite who also made an attempt to introduce Bengali language in Orissa. Since sufficient text books were not available in Oriya language, Bengali text books were taught in the Oriya vernacular schools. Jagabandhu Singh writes that Sri Bichhandra Charan Pattanaik and Gouri Shanker Ray saved Orissa from this Bengali onslaught. In the process of this Bengali attack on Oriya language, the Oriyas of Medinipur region lost their identities. No wonder that many of them lost their Oriya affinities, and the independent existence of the Oriya language during this time was under sever threat. This prompted the Oriya intellectuals to retrieve Orissa's lost glory and "*Prāchina Uṭkala*" was a humble attempt in this regard.[24]

Till that time Orissa did not have a comprehensive and elaborately connected history of her own even though there were plenty of source materials in the form of inscriptions, copper-plates, ancient texts and legends. After Orissa came under the British rule, many English and Bengali scholars wrote on different aspects of Orissan history both in English and Bengali. But these authors lacked objectivity and were not careful of interpreting the source materials in an independent manner. Jagabandhu Singh had not merely engaged himself in finding faults with these writers but had taken a more positive outlook to trace out the originality of Orissan culture. He was humble enough to admit "I cannot proudly claim my writings in the book to be absolute truth."[25]

Jagabandhu Singh was critical of some scholars particularly Bengalis for adopting a parochial approach towards Orissan history.[26] These scholars, Jagabandhu Singh says, had pre-conceived their own greatness and superiority, and sitting upon this egoistic position, they had attempted the writing of the history of Orissa. For them the architectural heritage of Orissa was not original. Being overwhelmed by parochial instincts, they hadn't felt shy to even claim the historical monuments of Orissa as works of Bengali artists. They even described the history and culture of Orissa in a highly degraded manner. Their overall intention in such attempts was to prove that Orissa really did not have any greatness to her credit. Jagabandhu Singh says that these are nothing but attempts to sow the seeds of Oriya discontentment.

Here the ire of Jagabandhu Singh was directed against the Bengali scholars who spearheaded the Bengali hatred towards the Oriyas. He says that they tried to project a very low profile of Orissa and her culture and thus presented the history of Orissa in a very degraded manner. Such a stand was taken to project Orissa as a part of Bengal. Presenting the history of Orissa in such a way, they have certainly failed in their tasks as historians. Jagabandhu Singh believed that these Bengalis could make such attempts only because Orissa did not have a complete and comprehensively written history of her own. Had there been such a documentary history, these Bengali scholars could not have tried to paint Orissa's past in this manner.

Thus speaking of his purpose of writing the history of Orissa, Jagabandhu Singh identifies the tasks of a historian. He was especially caustic in his remarks against some of the Bengali Scholars.[27] He says that the tasks of the historian cannot be directed against any particular society or particular historian or writer.[28] The historian should always try to give sufficient attention towards reading the historical truth.[29] What is necessary is pure objective discussion and impartial enquiry of historical materials.[30] If the source materials are carelessly used much injustice will be done towards any nation, society and culture.[31] Unnecessary criticism or exaggerated praises lavished on any one is against the process of natural justice. Just to glorify one's own nation or society or culture, one should not denigrate the cultures of others.[32]

At this point of discussion, Jagabandhu Singh takes a rather nationalistic stand.[33] He says that every state in India has a distinct role to play in the progress of Indian civilisation.[34] Only when these states develop the country would automatically develop.[35] There is every need for preserving ancient monuments and presenting the proper history of every state.[36] That is necessary for the progress of Indian civilisation as a whole.[37] As such the primary task of every Indian historian should be to write the history of India with this idea in mind.[38] But unfortunately some historians have not given any attention to this noble idea.[39] They had not felt any thing bad to describe the great monuments at Puri, Konark and Bhubaneswar and Kathajori dam as not the works of Oriya artisans. By writing this way, the historians have only belittled their own importance. Stating this as childish words, Jagabandhu Singh says that these cannot undermine the greatness of Orissa's past glory.[40] In this brilliant exposition of Jagabandhu Singh's idea of history writing particularly in reference to Indian history and provincial history, he considered India as a united entity.[41] This is more or less in tune with the nationalist historians who with their sole intention of objecting the imperialist notions towards Indian culture and civilisation considered India as one complete entity.[42] This is also in tune with the national movement for India's independence.[43] Accordingly, the British writers have come in for severe criticism by Jagabandhu Singh for not objectively looking into the country's past and not properly interpreting Orissan history.

After identifying the tasks before the historian, Jagabandhu Singh explains in greater details the necessity and purpose of writing history. According to him "we cannot totally rule out the uses of history. Ancient history is the torchbearer for a nation's progress. It is the nation's most valuable treasure and basis for the nation's progress. Jagabandhu Singh believed that the ancient boosted our strength for future progress."[44]

Singh says that all the foreign writers and a few Bengalis who wrote Orissan history before him gave not only an erroneous picture of the history of Orissa but also, being very jealous, made a myopic presentation of it.[45] Their myopic attitude was quite well-known so much so that they have narrow mindedly analysed the very name of the province that is Uṭkal. None of the history writers before him have tried to be objective in their criticism as was done by Jagabandhu singh.[46] He has thus taken the western and Bengali historians on Orissa to task, the British historians for their imperialist attitude and the Bengali historians for their anti-Oriya stand.

The book '*Prăchina Uṭkal*' is equally considered a treasure house of Oriya literature, for it has dealt with many Oriya laureates of ancient and medieval period. Singh has also fixed the dates of the writings he unearthed from different manuscripts on the basis of available corroborations from other relatively reliable source materials. This book was indeed a potential accession to the history of Oriya literature. He was a pioneer in this field, for he showed the way for the collection and editing of manuscripts. He has devoted nearly 150 pages for the study of these literary works.

Jagabandhu Singh has strongly refuted the arguments of some scholars on the Bengali origin of poet Jayadeva and his famous work *"Gīta Govinda"*. Inspite of the scant evidences available to him, Jagabandhu Singh strongly refuted the antiquity of "Radhavinod Temple" on the banks river "Ajaya", the Jaydeva episode in Sanskrit *"Bhatamala"* of Chandradatta and the arguments on Jayadeva's birth place in Keshaba Mishra's *"Alaṅkāra Śekhara"*.[47] All his arguments were borrowed by the later generation historians who identified Jayadeva with Sadhu Pradhana Jayadeva of Kenduli inscription.[48] Jagabandhu Singh presented his *"Prăchina Uṭkala"* as documentary proof on Jayadeva's Oriya identity.

Besides, Singh has devoted much of the book in delineating the greatness of Orissa's past. He studied the politcal history of Orissa under the heading "Reference to Valorous Past". In this he thrived upon explaining the ancient and medieval periods of Orissa's past as a sheer display of extraordinary valour. He also devoted many pages to analyzing Orissa's maritime exploits in Borneo, Malaya, Ceylon and Burma during different periods. He has also described in greater detail about Orissa's industry, economic conditions, social life, art, architecture, culture, trade, commerce, industry and religion, Shri Jagannath Temple and cult, etc. All these have made the *"Prăchina Uṭkala"* an almost complete work on Orissan history and culture. Jagabandhu Singh presented all the above aspects of Orissan history with substantial and cogent arguments and established the cultural identity of the Oriyas. What has always been the point of attraction on Orissa for different sets of historians is the art and architecture where the scholars are always engaged in finding out the external influence as per their individual preference and necessities. Like all other historians, Singh also considered architectural artisanship as the main identity of any nation's cultural excellence. The greatness of any country's national character is determined by its level of excellence.[49] In explaining the architecture of Orissa, Shri Singh has not blindly accepted the British historians conception regarding any Graeco-Roman influence on Orissan architecture. On the other hand, he has admired M.M. Ganguly for presenting a correct picture of the architectural remains of Orissa wherein Ganguly has described Orissan architecture as of a type by itself.

In his explanation of architecture we also find another important conception, which is hardly perceived in case of any of his contemporaries. Jagabandhu Singh strongly opposed the evolutionary hypothesis[50] resorted to by the European scholars in their study of construction activities in ancient Orissa. He believed that the "European scholar's evolutionary hypothesis can hardly be applied in the Orissan context. The existence of thatched houses side by side of the huge temples cannot be considered as objects for application of the evolutionary hypothesis. The reason is to be found in the religious attitude of the people of Orissa. It is natural that people would choose the easily available material for constructing the houses. In Orissa also we find many temples constructed with bricks. But we found very few buildings worthy of human use. Barring a few houses most of the houses are built of bamboos, wood and earth. Lack of money is not the main reason for this. Their financial status was extremely good. They could have used bricks and stones in constructing houses if they had wanted. But they have not given attention to that aspect at all. The religious-minded Hindus believed that the temples should be constructed of the best materials available. As such religiously guided, they were constructing the permanent structures (temples) using durable materials and spending their money in such works they considered extremely holy".[51]

This religious attitude of the Oriyas greatly contributed to the development of many fine architectural remains. Moreover, Singh considers architecture as the symbol of national intellect. This intellect is manifested in the fineness, the beauty and the excellence of the nation's architectural remains.[52] He was candid enough to say that the great specimen of architectural beauty found in Bhubaneswar and Konark speak well of the greatness of Orissa. In another place Jagabandhu Singh reiterates his argument saying that the Oriyas had the strong religious belief that the Gods are only worthy of staying in stone-built houses. The kings also had to stay in stone-built houses. People considered constructing temples for Gods as an extremely pious activity, and one cannot denigrate a culture for not constructing stone buildings for common use while doing it for temples.[53]

Arguing this way, Jagabandhu Singh strongly opposed the application of evolutionary hypothesis to analyzing the Orissan architecture but says that the presence of thatched and earthen houses along with such beautiful stone structures cannot be considered as due to Orissa's poor character but due to the religious sentiments of the people.

The political history of Orissa, Jagabandhu Singh says, is "the tale of valourous military exploits. When Orissa's military strength waned, they submitted themselves to the invaders. The Orissans were a fighting people right from the beginning of her history. In both religion and war, the Orissans showed a high sense of catholicity and valour."[54] In fact Singh discussed in details the valourous activities of the Orissans of the ancient days and determined the cause for the loss of valour during the present age.[55] "Why Orissa has been subjected to such a plight at present?" was his question for which he provided an answer. The fighting spirit was vital for the state formation during the early days and the Oriyas had shown this valour until well past the medieval rule. But for the defeatist attitude that cropped up among the Oriyas thereby leading to the fall of Orissa it was the result of internal bickering. Mukunda Deva being confused with his two options lying before him i.e., whether to fight the external forces or internal foes finally submitted himself before the enemies.[56]

Jagabandhu Singh believed that "people had always had a role in holding the nation together. So long as the people fought the enemies side by side with the king, the Orissans kept their independence intact. The decline in their strength was, in other words, due to the increase in the distances between the rulers and the ruled. The subjects are like the sons of the ruler. The ruler cannot always ignore the public in any of his decisions. The result of disregarding public opinion is ominous. Whoever does this, naturally does considerable harm to the nation. The real state policy should be to consider seriously the grievances of the people. In case of necessity, this opinion must be duly considered. The ruler who rules arbitrarily causes harm to the state.

In this both the ruler and the ruled will suffer. It is most dangerous if the ruler curbs the independence of the people". This explains to what extent Jagabandhu Singh considers the role of the people vital for the formation and consolidation of the state system. He observed that Orissa got finally defeated because the rulers considered their own self-interest very vital instead of looking into the interest of the people.

Jagabandhu Singh concluded that Orissa should learn from the past happenings. He considered history as vital for setting the future right. The study of history while cautioning the nation for the past mistakes, creates new hopes for the future. History is vital for setting the future right. The study of history while cautioning the nation for the past mistakes, creates new hopes for the future. History is necessary, for it creates the materials for building future history.

III. PANDIT NILAKANTHA DASH (1884-1967)

Pandit Nilakantha Dash was a living witness to the radical changes that occurred in almost every sector of human life and intellect in Orissa during the first six decades of the present century. This great statesman and scholar-politician was born on 5 August 1884[57] in a respectable Brahmin family of Sriramachandrapur village under Satayabadi Police station of Puri district. He had a brilliant academic career which had won him many laurels. Completing his childhood education in a village *Pāṭhaśālā,* he came to Puri Zillah school for his schooling where he was awarded a scholarship of Rs.15 per month. After completing school education at Puri, he joined Ravenshaw College for his F.A. degree. He was awarded Mayo scholarship for passing out F.A. degree with distinction. From here Pandit Nilakantha also successfully completed his B.A. Degree. During his studentship at Ravenshaw College Pandit Nilakantha came in touch with Pandit Gopabandhu Dash, a great freedom fighter and one of the architects of modern Orissa. After taking his B.A. degree, Nilakantha returned to Sriramachandrapur to join the nationalist institution at Satyavadi Vana Vidyalaya. Pandit Nilakantha then went to Calcutta University to study M.A. in philosophy and after obtaining the Masters Degree came back to Satyavadi to take charge of the school as headmaster.

He, along with his mentor, Pandit Gopabandhu and a few other committed fellow teachers and social workers succeeded in raising the standard of this school as a nationalist institution. Mainly through their efforts, Satyabadi became a centre of nationalist awakening and an institution championing the cause of the Oriya people. In September 1920, Pandit Nilakantha joined Calcutta

University as Professor of the newly created department of Oriya language and literature. But he could not continue there for long. In 1921 he resigned his Professorship to join the non-cooperation movement, which started that year under the leadership of Mahatma Gandhi. In February 1923, he was arrested on charge of intimidation against the British government and was sentenced to four months imprisonment. During his jail term, Pandit Nilakantha translated Kalidasa's "*Raghuvaṁśa*" into Oriya. In November that year, he was elected to the Central Legislative Assembly. In the election of 1926 he won the support of 'Orissa Congress through Pandit Gopabandhu Dash and was elected again to the Central Legislative Assembly despite strong opposition from a faction of the Congress party. After the death of Pandit Gopabandhu Dash in the year 1928 the mantle of leading Orissa Congress fell on Pandit Nilakantha who actively participated in our freedom struggle and had undergone several jail terms. He played a leading part in organizing the annual session of the Indian National Congress at Puri in the year 1932 which however could not be held.

In 1938, Pandit Nilakantha set up the Naba Bharat Press and started a daily called *'Naba Bharat'* under his editorship. During the 20s and early 30s, as a legislator he played a vital role in the movement for amalgamation of the Oriya speaking tracts. Under his efforts the Utkal University was set up in the year 1943. After the country's independence he was elected to the Orissa Legislative Assembly till 1961. He had never lost in any election to the Orissa Legislative Assembly, no matter whichever party gave him the tickets. He was elected speaker of the Orissa Legislative Assembly in 1957 and remained in that position till 1961. In 1962 he retired from active politics in the year 1962 and spent the remaining part of his life in different philanthropic works. Pandit Nilakantha Dash passed away on 6 November 1967. He was cremated with full state honours in the bakul groves of Satyavadi where his other colleagues from Satyavadi like Gopabandhu Dash, Godavarish Mishra and Krupasindhu Mishra were already laid to rest earlier.

The beginning of the swadeshi movement and the gradual consolidation of the freedom struggle in the first decade of the present century brought in its wake a movement to open educational institutions to teach nationalist ideals. This concept of national schools had its finest fulfillment in the Visva Bharati established by Gurudev Rabindra Nath Tagore at Santiniketan. In Orissa Pandit Gopabandhu Dash and his dedicated associates accomplished the task. In an enthusiasm to open a national school with nationalist ideals Pandit Gopabandhu along with Pandit Nilakantha and a few others drew up a plan in 1903/4 which got finally materialized in the year 1909. On the day of Kumar Prunima the Satyavadi School was founded in the groves of the bakul trees.

Satyavadi was a *'Vana Vidyalay'* where in the most beautiful natural surroundings a great experiment in education began. Through the ideals of the founder Pandit Gopabandhu Dash, a sense of human brotherhood was developed and the human qualities in man was allowed to grow. The school was Pandit Gopabandhu's brainchild but it was Pandit Nilakantha who translated Gopabandhu's ideas into action and instilled actual life into the institution. The school had a select band of highly educated, committed and dedicated teachers like Pandit Nilakantha Dash, Pandit Krupasindhu Mishra, Acharaya Harihar Dash, Pandit Godavarish Mishra who imparted the highest quality of education and ethical values to the students. Satyavadi was much more than just a school. It was a complete society in itself, a living community, vital and developing. But official recognition was yet to be given to Satyavadi. The ideals on which it was founded were looked with askance by the British authorities. The government of Bihar and Orissa and the University of Calcutta kept blaming each other and did not give the necessary affiliations. Satyavadi was suspected of being a terrorist hide-out in the government circles and the authorities were reluctant to sanction its unorthodox teaching methods with wide extracurricular activities. Nevertheless the school attracted countrywide attention and many great nationalists visited the school and admired its curriculum. The teachers of the school were creative writers as well as educationists and two influential journals *'Satyavadi'* and *'Samaj'*, then a weekly were published from Satyavadi. The year 1917 appears to have been the best year for Satyavadi. In April that year, Sir Edward Gait, the Lt. Governor of Orissa and Bihar, came to visit the school. He was particularly impressed with the holding of the classes in the bakul groves and the selfless attitude of the teachers. The celebrated educationist, Sir Ashutosh Mukerjee, also praised the school in glowing terms after a visit to the school.

Pandit Nilakantha Dash was closely asociated with Mahatma Gandhi, Dr. Rajendra Prasad, Netaji Subash Chandra Bose and many other great leaders to whom India owes much for her independence. He was an intellectual and teacher whose study and independence of judgment remained undiminished till the end of his life. He left his marks in public life as one of the three architects of modern Orissa— the other two obviously being Gopabandhu Dash whom Nilakantha regarded as his preceptor and Madhusudan Das who declared Nilakantha as his heir. Living as they did in the period of transition from traditional orthodoxy to reformist nationalism, from subjugation to the Brahmin absolutes and the British authorities to a creative and independent flexibility free from arbitrariness, the teachers of Satyavadi worked for a separate state for the Oriyas and for the independence of the country.

Pandit Nilakantha started life as a teacher at Satyavadi Vana Vidyalay which was essentially dedicated to the cause of social reform and to train the students to play a meaningful role in the national movement. That way Satyavadi School started a full-fledged mission for the cause of the national movement. It also championed the cause of Oriya language and the people.

Having spent much of his time in active politics, Pandit Nilakantha still succeeded in establishing a standard of good writing that has deeply influenced later generations of writers. In his efforts to put the spoken language on an equal footing with the classical tongue, Pandit Nilakantha used his literary skill and mastery over the Oriya language.

An erudite scholar, a teacher and a freedom fighter, his interest revolved round a wide range of subjects: literature, politics, history, etc. True to his self, he excelled in all these fields. He left his imprints as a poet laureate. In politics, he left his marks as a founder of modern Orissa. Though not professionally a historian, his interest in history was mainly derived from his teaching and his role in the national movement. This was known right from 1914 and 1915 when he studied and referred to students the great historical works of his time like Vincent Smith's '*History of India*', Hunter's '*Orissa*', M.M. Ganguly's '*Orissa and Her Remains*', R.L. Mitra's '*Antiquities of Orissa*' and Radha Kumud Mukerjee's '*History of Indian Shipping and Maritime Activity* ', etc. He wrote quite a few erudite essays on the history and culture of the Indian people and on the history of Orissa. Of these '*Arya Jivan*' is one of his longest essays which vividly explains the socio-cultural history of the Aryans. It is also considered one of the finest historical compositions.

Pandit Nilakantha was equally a great orator and delivered many speeches on Orissan history and culture. One of this is a remarkable speech he delivered on the history of Kalinga at Andhra University in the Year 1927. The lecture was published in the *Journal of Andhra Historical Research Society.*The article made a brilliant sketch of the history of Orissa warranting serious historiogrpahical study.[58] He had two other articles on Orissan culture, viz. 'Visva *Sanskrutiku Odissara Dana*'[59] and '*Bharatiya Sanskrutiku Odissara Dana*'[60] both being written in Oriya.

Pandit Nilakantha's attitude towards history can be studied on the basis of his role in India's freedom struggle and the movement for the formation of a separate province for the Oriyas. He played a vital role in the Satyavadi School, which trained the students to participate in the national movement. Scholars of this school were actuated by nationalistic aspirations and always had a vision of a free and independent India. Coupled with this, the Oriya movement in which Satyavadi School played an anchor role incited the spirit of Oriya nationalism among the people. Pandit Nilakantha as the front ranking leader of this movement did not spare any effort to take nationalistic view of Orissan history and culture.

His conception of history and historical research is clearly discussed in two of his writings. These were the erudite essay '*Arya Jivan*'[61] and his lecture at the Andhra University on Orissa history which was reproduced in the *Journal of the Andhra Historical Research Society*.[62]

During this time the nationalist historians of India only concentrated in counteracting the imperialist interpretation of Indian history by the European scholars. Their main aim was to glorify anything of the ancient Indian history, culture and society and counter the stand of the imperialist historians who justified the British rule in India. In doing this, nearly all the nationalist historians, knowingly or unknowingly glorified the Indian colonisation of the Far East.

Pandit Nilakantha also did the same like the other nationalists historians. He took pride in the fact that imperial Kalinga had vast trade and territories both inland and across the ocean and had its colonies on the coasts of Burma and the East Indian islands. He says that "not only our pensive and pale memory moreover hovers over the glorious centuries in the history of imperial Kalinga. This would certainly brighten up prospects for a future equally great and noble if we care to command the manhood we have been heir to our past."[63] This is indicative of Pandit Nilakantha's opinion on the uses of history that history is progressive and the important use of history lies in the fact that it provides the necessary impetus to the progress of human civilisation. Such a conception as regards the veritable uses of history could only be expected of an intellectual and writer like Pandit Nilakantha. This was more so because he was first a freedom fighter and politician and next a teacher and historian. Still he exemplified the veritable characteristics of a professional historian when he went on to explain the characteristics of historical research in India. He observed that our glorious past still mostly remains in the dark[64] particularly because the history of India meant for so long the history of imperial Magadha. Other empires and the history of different kingdoms of the south are gradually getting developed into small and scattered fragments.[65] This explains to what extent Pandit Nilakantha was concerned about the neglect meted out to the studies in regional history. He considered every region to be a part of the Indian mainstream as he described the Indian nationhood as a commonwealth of Indian races.[66]

As regards the history of Orissa, Pandit Nilakantha lamented that no systematic or ciritical history had ever been attempted. He took the book '*Orissa in the Making*' by Bijoy Chandra Majumdar to task for providing preposterous ideas based on misconceptions and bias. Still he gives credit to Majumdar for making an attmept to present a connected history of Orissa. He, however, commented that lack of interest for intensive research on Kalinga history indirectly helped historians like B.C. Majumdar in making out grounds for biased historical writings and to hand them down as historical facts.[67]

He took nationalistic pride while describing the greatness of Orissan culture. In his description, Pandit Nilakantha mainly focussed his arguments on the Kalingan attempt for colonisation beyond the seas. He wrote "Its boundary being far flung Kalinga was famous from the earliest times for its colonial activities and overseas trade. But towards the 3rd and 4th centuries B.C. Kalinga was conquered thrice by the emperors of Magadha but it did not mean permanent annexation of Kalinga by the kingdom of Magadha. At a time, Kharavela commanded extensive domains for Kalinga and had seaborne trade with Persia. Probably he had colonies in Burma and further Indian and established trade relations beyond the eastern seas."[68] In later centuries the spirit of cosmopolitan faith and religious toleration of Orissan culture in its full flourish made the Oriyas colonise Ossa or Pegu and give the stamp of art and culture to other states in that land of legend across the ocean.[69] For this he critically examined the different historical contentions about the boundaries of Kalinga. He took a more regional approach to counteract B.C. Majumdar's arguments that Kalinga's capital was situated near Samapa and not Tosali while accusing Majumdar for making offhand statements.[70]

Pandit Nilakantha himslef suffered from the same mistake. He did not give any arguments in favour of his conclusions either. The same problem crops up the on identification of Trikalinga. About the colonisation of Sri Lanka by Kalinga, Pandit Nilakantha has taken the views found in the *'Cambridge History of India'* for granted. He criticised B.C. Majumdar's observations of Kalingan colonisation of Ceylon and Burma. This is a weakness from which many nationalist historians suffered. They relied on every argument given in favour of India's overseas civilisation in general. Not many of the conclusions derived by Majumdar in this regard and accepted by Pandit Nilakantha Dash can be proved archaeologically or otherwise.

Pandit Nilakantha described Indian art, religion and culture as cosmopolitan in character.[71] He believed that it was only the cosmopolitan character of Indian civilisation that held the commonwealth of Indian races together.[72] The prime example of this characteristic civilisation is traced in the Puri Sri Jagannath Temple. Here the Hindus rid themselves of casteist feelings and created a holy atmosphere where caste and untouchability are altogether discarded in practice. Thus they have an example to the whole humanity how the culture of soul and nothing else is the basis of true and natural religion of man.[73] He was so convinced about the role of religions in state formation and decay that he attributed the political fall of Kalinga during different periods of history to religious orthodoxy.

Pandit Nilakantha was more explicit in his essay *'Arya Jivan'*[74] initially published in the pages of the monthly, *'Satyavadi'*, during the year 1914-15 and considered as one of the finest essays written on Vedic culture. This essay presented his sense of universal consciousness in the fact that he entiled this essay *'Arya Jivan'* instead of *'Hindu Jivan'*. This he did because he felt the work *'Arya'* has a wider connotation that Hindu. In this essay he summarily concluded that Indian civilisation had no indigenous origin[75] and throughout their history the Indians had projected a national idealism. The originality of Indian civilisation is enlivened in the Indian villages but the western influence is only destroying the great character of our civilisation. Again the ideals of Aryan life were at one time followed in all the western countries. Pandit Nilakantha has also discussed at length the spiritual character and greatness of Aryan life in India. In an anexure to the essay[76] he has elaborated upon the effect of the absence of nationalism on any civilisation. This explains his sincerity in quest for historical research. In this he has explained that while the Greek hero Alexander defeated the Aryan forces in Punjab through sheer skill and diplomacy, the Aryans did not follow this tactics against them. Further that the foreigners have always tried to influence and have brought radical changes in the Aryan idealism and way of life.[77] Despite that Indian civlisation has survived all kinds of onslaught and maintained its originality. When the Rajputs were subjugated by thes Moghuls, Pandit Nilakantha felt that the Aryan culture would have lost its individuality but for the reformers like Ramananda, Kabir, Nanak and Chaitanya. They preached Vedantic philosophy and this created a sort of national liberalism. They gathered devotees from all segments of society and religion and helped the Aryan culture to thrive and strengthen. When the Aryans here were blindly following the European sophisticated life style, reformers like Dayanada Saraswati and Raja Rama Mohan Ray helped Aryan culture to survive the western onslaught.[78]

In this article also Nilakantha vehemently criticised the European view of Aryan life in India. He says, whatever we have so far learnt about the Aryan life were from the mouths of the Europeans, because we have not been able to make any serious attempt to study the glorius aspects of our civilisation. The Europeans have certainly seriously laboured to unearth the characteristics of Aryan life but still they cannot sincerely experience or be able to explain the true Aryan self, for the way of life in the East and west are diametrically opposite to each other. While one is based on evolution through religious dutifulness, the other is concerned about the consciouness of human rights. As such there is nothing surprising in the fact that the Europeans would be misguided while unearthing the real character of a civilisation diametrically opposite of what they are. Here Pandit Nilakantha Dash was more careful about the objectivity in historical research which he believed could help in explaining the history of a civilisation as it really was in all its aspects.

To sum up, it may be concluded that Pandit Nilakantha Dash evinced keen interest in history and its usefulness as a motive force to the progress of mankind. He was a nationalist when he talked about the history of Orissa's overseas trade but looked far beyond the mere Indian nation while speaking about the greatness of Indian civilisation.

IV. PANDIT KRUPASINDHU MISHRA (1887-1926)*

Pandit Krupasindhu Mishra, a teacher of the Satyavadi Vana Vidyalaya was born on 27 June 1887 in village Bira Harekrushnapur situated barely 10 kilometres from Puri. But he was adopted by a family in Birapratappur right from his childhood. He was the nephew of Pandit Nilakantha Dash and was just three years junior to him by age. He belonged to a lower middle class family and spent most of his student days in the house of Pandit Nilakantha Dash in village Sriramchandrapur. All through his career he did extremely well as a student and was awarded scholarships. Since his student days he was closely associated with Pandit Gopabandhu Dash, Pandit Nilakantha Dash and Pandit Godavarish Mishra. Completing his post graduation from Calcutta University he straightway came to Satyabadi Vana Vidyalaya and joined it as a teacher. Though he had the highest educational qualification, he never intended for a service in the government of the British and instead, preferred to serve the Satyabadi school, a nationalist institution, engaged in creating independent-minded young men endowed with national consciousness.

---

* Details about Pandit Krupasindhu Mishra's biography here have been given on the basis of the book Sangrami Guru *(Pancha Sakha)* by Prof. Dr. Bikram Dash, 1988, Cuttack.

Studying books and conducting research in different historical themes were his favorite past time. He played a significant role in teaching the illiterate, so much so that his wife, who was illiterate, was taught by him. She later played a significant role in the documentation of the all historical works. Krupasindhu was a dedicated teacher of Satyavadi School. Later when such schools were planned in different parts of the state, Pandit Krupasindhu went to Bahadagoda upper primary school as its headmaster.

During the Non-Cooperation Movement in 1921 Satayavadi School was turned into a national school with the aim to produce dedicated nationalists for the freedom struggle. Krupsindhu Mishra was the headmaster of this school at that time and inspired many students to join the freedom struggle. He successfully managed the school despite all adversities and was its headmaster till the closure of the school.

As was said earlier, Pandit Krupasindhu engaged himself in historical research on Orissa. Ever since his student days, he sincerely tried to unearth the glorius aspects of Orissa's history and culture. He completed a book on *"Barabati Fort"* (in Oriya) during his student days. And this established him as a serious researcher on Orissan history. Though he tried all his best to complete the *"Uṭkal Itihāsa"* or History of Utkala even when he was on his death bed the work could not see the light of the day during his life time. It could only be published after his death. The last thirty pages of the book were added by his mentor Pandit Gopabandhu Dash. He was engaged in writing the history of the English trade in India and prepared some notes but his premature death left this project incomplete. He breathed his last at an early age of 40 on 12 February 1926. A brilliant scholar himself, Krupasindhu contributed significantly to the knowledge of the history of Orissa, not merely as a part of his duty as a teacher but more as a nationalist who wanted to present a glorious account of Orissa's history and culture. As such, he came out with two major historical works which may not be considered as serious research works on Orissan history proper, but as glorified accounts of Orissa's past. Two of his works, "*Bārābatī Fort*"[79] (in Oriya) and "*History of Uṭkala*"[80] (Oriya), respectively published in 1914 and 1929 are devoted to this purpose. He also wrote a textbook on "*History of England*"[81] in a very simple style which was popular among the students and remained as a text book for a long time.

The main purpose of Pandit Krupasindhu Mishra was to present an account of the history of Orissa that would remind the Oriyas of their past history and culture. It would be pertinent to mention that his time was the period of the Oriya Movement and the Gandhian Era of the freedom struggle. As such, all his contemporaries from Satyavadi school dedicated themselves to the cause of the Oriya Movement and the freedom struggle and they tried to prove the independent nature of Orissan culture. Accordingly, it can be said that Krupasindhu Mishra's writings on the history of Orissa was essentially in tune with the spirit of his time.

Krupasindhu presented a complete and connected account of the history of "Orissa". Much in tune with this objective, his book "*Uṭkal Itihāsa*" touched upon the entire period of the history of Orissa right from the dawn of Orissa's regional culture and civilisation,. In his book running into barely two hundred pages, Krupasindhu synthesized the entire history of Orissa from his own nationalist perspective. Here the use of superlatives and dramatisation to glorify historical events reigned supreme over the sober treatment of historical source material in presenting different topics. In "*Uṭkal Itihāsa*" we certainly have a complete work of the history of Orissa dealing with almost all aspects of Orissa's political history, society, culture, religion and art. But as far as the compilation of historical facts are concerned the book simply dealt with all those in general terms, with a method that subscribed to the norms of an amateur nationalist historiography. The book "*Bārābatī Durgā*" is not a departure from this line of approach. Here also he presented brilliantly the greatness of Orissa's past as this great historical fort remained a mute witness to the vicissitudes of time. The book analysed all the available source materials on the subjects, namely, the inscriptions, the Muslim accounts of the Sultanate and Moghul period, the British accounts, the Jagannath Temple chronicle '*Madāla Pañjī*' and local legend. The Bārābatī Fort has been brilliantly portrayed by him as the living witness to the rise and fall of Hindu rule in Orissa.

For presenting the history of Orissa and the Bārābatī Fort, the nerve centre of Orissa's glorious military past, Pandit Krupasindhu relied heavily upon the '*Madāla Pañjī*' and the '*Biswakośa*'. Though it is clearly perceived that Krupasindhu interpreted and used the source materials as per his own requirements he did not blindly accept the source materials as complete and final. For he says that the writer of '*Biswakośa*' was ignorant about many rulers of the Gaṅgā dynasty and blindly relied on the writings of Stirling's account on Orissa.[82] He also did not accept the dates given by '*Biswakośa*' and Stirling about the construction of the Barabati Fort. Similarly on the *Madāla Paṅjī*, Pandit Krupasindhu writes that though *Madāla Paṅjī* was started to record events concerning God Jagannath's rituals and the facts about the Temple, it contains some stories about the main events of Orissan history. Had this been written more carefully by experienced writers, *Madāla Paṅjī* would have remained as the main source material for the history of Orissa. He observed that, despite all errors, it is certainly an important source for the historians of Orissa of his days.[83]

But Krupasindhu believed that historians who have worked on Orissa have mostly based their source materials on their visits to different places and in a majority of cases have mixed up their personal taste with the historical facts so as to only belittle Orissa's great cultural tradition. He did not even spare his emotions by speaking out that "this tendency among these writers was because of the fact that they could not merely tolerate the greatness of the Oriyas."[84] "Though opinions are bound to differ on the basis of personal interpretation and outlook, unrestrained writing has only taken the facts of Orissan history far from the point of truth. Calling for detailed research to unearth the historical truth, he says that, while differences of opinion are recognizable, unrestrained historical writing cannot be accepted in anyway."[85] He concluded that examples are galore as regards such kinds of careless historical writings on Orissa.

Such selective and purposeful use of source materials, though natural with nationalist historiography is not found in Pandit Krupasindhu's work. He heavily dwelt upon the temple chronicle *Madāla Paṅjī* whose historicity has not been fully accepted by him.

For Krupasindhu "Orissa is the land with all the extraordinary qualities that this world has. Orissa's greatness lies in the fact that, though the other provinces of India submitted before the Muslims to lose their independence early, Orissa has been able to hold on to her independence for a longer period. In terms of natural beauty, Orissa is eternal."[86] Krupasindhu believed that Orissa was the land of freedom.

Bārābatī Fort was the symbol of Orissa's defence for freedom, for Bārābatī always provided the mighty rulers and the fighters of Orissa necessary morale to guard this freedom.[87]

In the field of literature also Orissa had achieved the height of excellence during the Gajapati rule for which Pandit Mishra had preferred to call this age as the Augustan age of Orissan history.[88] This was because the greatest literateur of Oriya literature, Jagannath Das, has immortalised himself by his literary accomplishments which none of the later writers could do.

As regards Orissa's military might Pandit Krupasindhu writes that during Mukunda Deva's rule the mighty ruler Akbar was the emperor of Delhi. Taken aback by the independent mililtary might and the valour of the Oriya soldiers, Akbar did not dare to include Orissa in his empire. Instead he chose to win his friendship.[89]

In the field of art and architecture, Orissa holds a special place in Indian history. In his respect also Pandit Krupasindhu Mishra spoke highly of the greatness of Indian architecture in general and Orissan art in particular.

Above all, Orissa contributed significantly to Indian history with orderly administration during different periods of her history. There were always the efforts to present efficient and orderly administration to the people of Orissa.[90] In another place he writes that the administrative system followed in India continued from the very earlier days and this was recognized by our shāstrās' and the people were acquainted and well accustomed with this rule. The system was so orderly and efficient that even the Moghuls did not think about bringing about any change in the system. Merely changing a few names, they continued with the same old traditional method of administration.[91] In his arguments Pandit Krupasindhu sharply contradicted the imperialist hisotrian's main point of attack on Indian history. The imperialist historians, namely Vincent Smith and others, justified the British rule in India by arguing that the lack of proper administration in India in any period of her history has justified their stay in India. Their main contention was that the Britishers only provided orderly administration in India. This imperialist concept had motivated and affected their history writing and their writings were thus rightly considered as publicity campaign for the British rule in India. In sharp contrast to this, the nationalist historians of India seriously viewed this notion of British historians and traced the greatness of Indian civilisation in their historical works. The nationalist historians of India had thus the motive of counteracting the imperialist viewpoint. Like the nationalist historian, Pandit Krupasindhu was prompted to take this imperialist notion on Indian history to task and presented a glorified account of the history in Orissa, regional considerations notwithstanding. His views on the administration in Orissa in the past and its mighty culture are in the nature of a direct challenge to the imperialist notions.

Inspite of the overdose of nationalism Pandit Krupasindhu admired the efforts of the British historians for making the initial attempt to write the comprehensive history of our region and have been somewhat able to help us in understanding our glorious past. But their writings cannot be accepted as our national history. For he feels that despite all their love for serious historical research, their personal tasks and perceptions cannot be accepted as the yardstick for our nationalism. As such their writings cannot be accepted as complete historical truth.[92]

And here comes Pandit Krupasindhu's concept of the purpose of history. He believed that history is vital for building a nation and imbibing the sense of nationalism amongst the people. History is the record of the life of a nation. History helps a nation in achieving fulfilment. It enlivens the memory of the past and saves the way for the future. In the preface to the book *Bārābatī Durgā*, Pandit Krupasindhu candidly spoke about the purpose and use of history.[93] History, according to him, is a necessary component of nation building activity. This equally explains his conception that people are actors of history and with them only the sources of our history are deeply rooted. Talking about the value of historical monuments as the lifeblood of a progressive civilisation, Pandit Krupasindhu argued that the present day sociologist might not give any importance to historical monuments as these monuments are not utilitarian in character. Utilitarianism in the progress of a nation is absolutely necessary, argues Pandit Krupasindhu.[94] The present and the future character of a nation is only determined by this monumental heritage and in a larger context by the history of a nation. He rightly quoted Mazzini, the great Italian nationalist, to prove his point. "I remember all these kings and bow down in reverence before the image of your past. We ought to be working the greatness of our father and seek in their tombs a pledge for the future."[95] The value of an ancient stone will be more than that of gold. Pandit Krupasindhu was categorical that it is only the past that determines the character of the future. National life cannot move without addressing itself to the past.

The above discussion presents the idea that according to Pandit Krupasindhu Misha, "history has a definite purpose. The purpose is to provide the backdrop for the progress of the nation and mankind. As such history writing has to be national and national history can only be written by its own people. Since this effort has not been made either by the Indians and the Oriyas, the foreigners wrote on India with their misconceptions where the truth of history got completely lost."[96]

In history writing, what ails the real presentation of a national character is the 'historian's individual social perception. This prevents any neutral assessment of the nation's true character. Indirectly he feels that the proper presentation of the source materials without any personalised interpretation is the right way. According to him "personalised interpretation results from the comprehension of the self by the historian with others. In other words the man measures others in his own yardsticks. If some characteristics fall into his own, then it is discarded. History writing will fail if these personalised conceptions and pure regional considerations determine the character of history writing. If this has to be national and devoid of any personlised outlook, be it guided by the time or situation prevailing".[97] Amidst this nationalistic historical writing of Pandit Krupasindhu Mishra, another aspect that is clearly perceived in his presentation of Orissan history is the social harmony he wanted to project during different periods of Orissa's history. This is more or less inherent and was in tune with the nationalistic conception of Indian history which for the sake of explaining India's internal stability had to argue that Indians had maintained high traditions of social harmony in different periods.

V. BIRUPAKSHYA KAR (1893-1968)

A historian and litêrateur, Birupakshya Kar was born on 15 Setpember 1893 in Damapada near Banki in the present Cuttack district.[98] Because of his physical troubles, he started his early education rather late. During his student days he was highly studious and completed his matriculation with a first class in the year 1912. In 1916 Birupakshya graduated in the humanities from Calcutta University with a distinction to this credit. Since his student days he evinced a keen interest in history. His devotion to the cause of truth helped him in becoming a historian. After completing graduation he decided to go for in legal studies and on the completion of his degree he joined the bar as an advocate. After some time, he was appointed by the king of Madhupur as Dewan and in this capacity he showed his potential by handling the court affairs with great dexterity. While practising law at Jajpur, he devoted himself to social reform and different philanthropic activities. Birupakshya's contribution to the expansion of higher education at Jajpur was phenomenal. He was the first principal of Narasingh Choudhury College at Jajpur. He also contributed significantly to protecting the historical monuments in and around Jajpur area and actively associated himself with different socio-cultural organisations. He died on December 26, 1968.

Birupakshya Kar was a devoted researcher. His famous historical essays are now lying scattered and missed in old magazines. Those are published in different Oriya magazines like *Uṭkal Sāhitya, Prachi,* and *Satyavadi*.

Birupakshya's historical writings can be broadly classified into three categories.

(1) Articles on Ancient Orissan history;

(2) Articles on Indian culture;

(3) Articles based on myths and legends and intended to create a sense of national consciousness.

His articles falling into the above three categories are:

(a) Gaja Siṁha and Kesari dynasty (1918)[99],

(b) Maritime History of Ancient Uṭkala (1920)[100],

(c) History of Buddhism in Ancient Uṭkala (1921)[101],

(d) Kesari dynasty (1925/26/27)[102] and,

(e) Ancient Jajpur (1960).[103]

All these articles have been written in Oriya language. Of these, only the first four writings were of vital interest for historiographical study. Birupakshya presented the article *"History of Buddhism in Ancient Uṭkala"* in the Uṭkala Sāhitya Samaj in 1921 and this also bagged him the "Hindol Award" the same year.

The greatest contribution of Birupakshya Kar to Orissan historical research has been his investigations into Orissa's maritime trade in the ancient days. He systematically traced Orissa's maritime history and the glorious tradition of sailing in the high seas. In the articles "*Prāchina Uṭkalare Jala Yātrā*" running into over 50 pages Birupakshya has tried to elaborately trace out Orissa's maritime trade by the sea route. He put forward sufficient historical evidences to prove his own hypothesis on the maritime trade of ancient Uṭkala (Orissa) and her contact with different countries of South-east Asia and the Indian Archipaelago. Though most of his observations in this essay are now out of date still the article provided sufficient data on Orissa's maritime trade. Excavations have of late revealed new historical evidences in this regard and have drawn the attention of many historians to work on Orissa's maritime glory.

The article "*Prāchina Utkalare Jala Yātrā*" is written in two parts. The first part deals with the identification of Odra, Uṭkala, Kosala and Kalinga. For this Birupakshya dealt with all available source materials, namely, the *Mahābhārata*, the *Rāmāyaṇa*, the *Purāṇas*, Buddhist literature, Kalidasa's *Raghuvaṁśa*, Yuan Chwang's *Si-Yu-ki*, inscriptions and local legends. He also consulted the works of Babu Rajendra Lal Mitra and Pyarimohan Acharya before arriving at his conclusions. The second part of his article dealt at length with the history of Orissa's maritime trade. In setting his hands upon this aspect of Orissa's history Birupakshya seems to be nationalistic. For he feels that "the greatness of a country and her civlisation depend upon her prowess in the maritime activity and that one of Orissa's major aspects of greatness lies in her great maritime tradition".[104]

Birupakshya Kar has tried to establish the ancestry of Orissa's maritime history to the very early times. For this he relied upon mainly the Buddhist literature and Kauṭilya's "*Arthaśāstra*". Taking clues from legends and folklore which suggest Orissa's maritime contact with Bali, Java, Sumatra, Malaya, Srilanka and others, Birupakshya had tried to bring forth more evidences from different sources to substantiate their historical truthfulness. He also studied in detail Ptolemy's "*Geography*" and "*Periplus of the Erythraen Sea*" by an anonymous author and identified many ports of Orissa. Similary he ananlysed the iconographic representation of the boats in the temple art of Orissa to vouchsafe the maritime trade activity during the ancient and medieval period of Orissan history. The legend of "*Kañchi Kāverī*" and the "*Taapoi*" tradition have been beautifully analysed by him. The article in toto has drawn a complete history of the maritime traditions of Orissa down to the 18th century. It is indeed a remarkable contribution of Birupakshya Kar towards Orissan historical research.

The article "*Gajasiṁha and Kesarī dynasty*" has delineated in greater details the heroic activities of Kesarī kings and the iconography of Gaja Siṁha. Birupakshya writes that "Shiva Gupta had performed a number of Yajñās at Jajpur and re-established Vedic religion in Uṭkala. According to the name of the Puranic King Jajāti who performed many Yajñās, Shiva Gupta renamed himself as Yajāti. Since Yajāti conquerred Uṭkala, we find the icons of lions of the elephants in the iconography of architecture everywhere in Uṭkala only as a mark of this *Digvijaya* of Yajati. From that day only the dynasty of Shiva Gupta or Yajāti has become popular as Kesarī dynasty."[105]

In analysing Orissan history Birupakshya relied solely on the facts of the ages, the gravity of the episodes and the contemproray socio-cultural enviroment. He made a logical synthesis of all kinds of historical sources on "Orissan history available to him. He took onus from legends, myths, purāṇās, manuscripts, copper-plates, inscriptions and other archological sources to arrive at his conclusions. He did not take any particular source material for granted and never absolutely depended on legends. In two of his writings "*Ālochanā*"[106] and "*Māgha Amābasyā*"[107] he has tried to establish history from folk legends. The article "*Ālcochanā*" is indeed a brave attempt to present the historicity of Kālāpahāḍa from the extant folklore. Similary "*Māgha Amābasyā*" puts forward an interesting hypothesis on Orissa's glorious martial tradition.

The degree of erudite excellence Birupakshya has achieved in the articles cited above gives a fair amount of value judgements historigraphically accounts for his merit as a historian. He had certainly believed that Indians did not lack the sense of history. Rather they had this consciousness right from the dawn of Indian civilisation.[108] Nevertheless he studied Orissan history as a backdrop of greater Indian consciouness and only as a part of Indian civilisation. He pronounced in the beginning of the article "Buddhism in Ancient Uṭkal" that Uṭkala (Orissa) has always accepted the messages of Indian civilisation very much as a dutiful son and without any disgrace.[109] It has not rejected any message or faith, rather had woven it either in distant Janapadā or dense forest.

At another place, explaining the reasons for the absence of urbanisation in India he writes that "Indians thrive mainly on agriculture and not commerce. That is why the rise and fall of Indian civilisation are intermixed with the development of villages. This rule which is applicable to India, Uṭkala cannot just be excluded from it."[110]

Though written during the period of national movement Birupakshya's writings did not have any inclination or tendency to serve any political purpose. We certainly find trace of his deep sense of love for his country but the same did not drag his conclusions to blindly eulogise the character of our civilisation. Anything national in his approach towards Indian history is that he considered India as one and integrated civilisation.

In Birupakshya we find a sincere attempt to trace out the different aspects of Orissan history and culture, its originality and Orisssa's contirbution to the mainstream of Indian culture. The article "*History of Buddhism in Ancient Uṭkala*" is indeed a brilliant piece of work and had the touch of a professional historian. He did not merely take the sources for granted at their face value and tried to corroborate them from other contemporary source materials as far as practicable.

He, however, neither criticised nor accepted any thought without proper explanation or justification. He did not simply blame the British for considering Orissa as a part of Bengal. To him the British considered Orissa as a part of Bengal only because they inherited Orissa from the Muslims as a part of Bengal.[111]

Birupakshya's sense of nationalism rather lies in interpreting the history of Orissa from the angle of Orissa's culture itself. We do not find anything that would present a glorious picture of the effect of the British or foreign rule on Orissa's society and culture. Nor do we find any counteraction to the foreign analysis of Orissan history in his writing except, of course, for the fact that Birupakshya considered Orissa merely as a part of greater Indian civilisation. He, however, looked at the art and architecture of Uṭkala in the backdrop of artistic heritage of the Oriyas' excellent artistic thought, imagination and extraordinary skill. He says "Indian and Orissan architecture are not a mere imitation of the west. No trace of western hand has been found in this. The artists' 'birth' intellect and death can be studied in the art itself. The shoe worn by the man depicted in the Udayagiri hill cannot said to be western. It is simply an example of the Buddhist dress prevelent during the Buddhist age in ancient Uṭkal. The same is repeated with description of costumes, tradition prevalent in contemporary Uṭkal those days."[112]

Birupakhshya Kar has thus succeeded in achieving his objective of looking into Orissan history from the point of view of Orissa's individuality as a distinct culture. In an article "*Ama Sanskruti*" *(our culture)* he had delineated the features of Indian and Āryan culture and the necessity for presentation of cultural traditon. He writes that "culture presents our national character and individuality. Love for culture most of the time helps in counteracting the attack of foreign influences and unite different religious societies and human beings. This is more than true for only culture, any nation or any individual or society. Even though some bad elements do enter our cultural habits in course of time, we have been polished by the development of culture based on religion and human behaviour. Whatever influences we have been affected by these days, we must keep and preserve the glory and individuality of our ancient past."[113]

Birupakshya is an honest onlooker of Orissa's past and had a sense of history inbuilt in his thoughts and actions. He observed that "Orissa had a distinct cultural tradition of her own which she preserved in her traditions. Orissa's art was indigenous. Ancient Orissa respected the Buddhist culture for a long time as if the religion was our own. It had great influence on Orissa's national life."[114]

It would then be proper to identify Birupakshya's approach to Orissan history as regional than national but only implanted in the greater national concept. No semblance of chauvinistic nationalism is traceable though he wrote during the matured phase of India's freedom struggle. He rather analysed the British interpretation of Indian history in its own objectivity and only from the point of veiw of dry and objective history as it explained the nations's true character.

One of the most important factual errors he had in the interpretation of Orissa history was that he considered emperor Kharavela, the greatest emperor of Uṭkala, as a Buddhist even though he was a Jaina. He might have tried to consider Kharavela as a Buddhist[115] because Buddhism had flourished in Orissa during the ancient period.

References

1. Refer to Biography of Pyarimohan Acharya by Shri Sk. Matlub Ali in 3rd Edition of *Pyarimohan Achary's Odissā Itihāsa*, 1991, Orissa Book Store, Cuttack.
2. Pyarimohan Acharya, *Odissā Itihāsa,* 1879, 3rd Edition (rep.) 1991, p.16.
3. Preface to the 1st edition of *Odissā Itihāsa* by Pyarimohan Acharya, 1879.
4. Paramananda Acharya "Odissāra Pratnatatva o' Anyanya Prabandha", Bhubaneswar, p.384-85.
5. Pyarimohan Acharya, *op.cit.*, p.46.
6. Refer to preface of the first edition of *Pyarimohan Acharya's Odissā Itihāsa*, 1879.
7. Pyarimohan Acharya, *Odissā Itihāsa*, 1879 (rep. 1991), p.49.
8. *Ibid.*, p.51.
9. *Ibid.*, p.59.
10. *Ibid.*, p.104.
11. *Ibid.*, p.171.
12. *Ibid.*, p.176.
13. *Ibid.*, p.177.
14. *Utkal Dipika*, 8.5.1880.
15. Jagabandhu Singh's *Prachīna Uṭkal* first published in the year 1929 from Puri press, has seen three editions so far. Two other editions of the book have appeared in 1964 and 1982 under the auspices of Orissa Sahitya Academy.
16. Pundit Mililani Mira's introduction to the third edition of Prāchīna Uṭkal 1982 and Jagabandhu Singh Prāchīna Uṭkala, 1929 (rep. 1982), Bhubaneswar, p.6-24.
17. Chapter Raja Vamsanucharita in Jagabandhu Singh, *op.cit.*, p.223-318.
18. Pandit Nilamani Mishra, *op.cit.*

19. Jagabandhu Singh, *op.cit.*, p.84.
20. *Ibid.*, p.1 .
21. *Ibid.*, p.1.
22. *Ibid.*, p.1.
23. *Ibid.*, p.2.
24. *Ibid.*, p.283.
25. *Ibid.*, p.3.
26. *Ibid.*, p.3 & 4.
27. *Ibid.*, p.4.
28. *Ibid.*, p.4.
29. *Ibid.*, p.4.
30. *Ibid.*, p.4.
31. *Ibid.*, p.4.
32. *Ibid.*, p.4.
33. *Ibid.*, p.4.
34. *Ibid.*, p.4.
35. *Ibid.*, p.4.
36. *Ibid.*, p.4.
37. *Ibid.*, p.4.
38. *Ibid.*, p.4.
39. *Ibid.*, p.4.
40. *Ibid.*, p.4.
41. Ibid., p.4.
42. *Ibid.*, p.4.
43. *Ibid.*, p.4.
44. *Ibid.*, p.4-5.
45. *Ibid.*, p.6.
46. *Ibid.*, p.8.
47. *Ibid.*, p.46-47, also the intoduction to the volume by Pandit Nilamani Mishra, 1982.
48. N.K. Sahu, *"Jayadeva, the Poet of Gita Govinda – His Date and Place"* in Souvenir on Sri Jayadeva, Bhubaneswar, 1968; K.S. Behera, *"Sri Gita Govinda: Cultural background and influence"* (in Oriya) in Utkalara Kavi Jayadeva, 1992, p.35-47; S. Rajguru, *"Kenduli Copper-Plate Grant of Narasimha Deva-IV of Saka 1305"* in *Orissa Historical Research Journal*, 1957, V, 4, p. 179-182.

49. *Ibid.*, Vol.2, p.54.
50. We also find the same kind of opposition to evolutionary hypothesis in the writings of Chintamani Acharya a historian of nationalist group.
51. Jabandhu Singh, *op.cit.*, p.62.
52. *Ibid.*, p.63.
53. *Ibid.*, Vol.II, p.29.
54. *Ibid.*, p.199.
55. *Ibid.*, p.199.
56. *Ibid.*, p.199.
57. Of the many works available on the life and times of Pandit Nilakantha Dash, *"Manishi Nilakantha"* (in Oriya) 1959 by Narasingha Mohapatra, *"Pandit Nilakantha: his life and times"* 1989 by Lila Ray, and "Manishi Nilakantha" (in Oriya) 1982 by Professor Chintamani Das are found to be most comprehensive. The portion dealing with the biography of Pandit Nilakantha Dash and the concept of National School at Satyavadi is based primarily on these works.
58. Pandit Nilakantha Dash *"A Brief Short Review of the History of Kalinga"* in *Journal of Andhra Historical Research Society*, 1927, II, 1, p.12-33.
59. Pandit Nilakantha Dash "Visva Sanskrutiku Odissara Dana" in Naba Bharat, 1,1,1946,p.1-10.
60. Pandit Nilakantha Dash "Bharatiya Sanskrutiku Odissar Dana" in Jhankar, X, 2, 1958, p.191-197.
61. Pandit Nilakantha Dash "Ārya Jīvan" in Satyavadi, 1921.
62. Pandit Nilakantha Dash *op.cit.* (1927).
63. *Ibid.*, p.12.
64. *Ibid.*, p.12.
65. *Ibid.*, p.12.
66. *Ibid.*, p.12.
67. *Ibid.*, p.12.
68. *Ibid.*, p.13.
69. *Ibid.*, p.13.
70. *Ibid.*, p.14.
71. *Ibid.*, p.15.
72. *Ibid.*, p.12.
73. *Ibid.*, p.15.

74. In *Satyavadi*, 1921.
75. Chintamani Dash, Manishi Nilakantha, 1982, p.137.
76. *Ibid.*, p.141.
77. *Ibid.*, p.141.
78. *Ibid.*, p.145.
79. Krupasindhu Mishra, *Uṭkala Itihāsa*, 1929, Cuttack (rep. 1979).
80. Krupasindhu Mishra, *Bārābatī Durgā*, 1913, Cuttack Trading House, Cuttack (rep. 1955).
81. Krupasindhu Mishra, *History of England*, Cuttack.
82. Krupasindhu Mishra, *Bārābatī Durgā*, *reprint*, 1955, p.3.
83. Krupasindhu Mishra, *Uṭkala Itihāsa*, *reprint*, 1979, p.60.
84. Krupasindhu Mishra, 1955 (rep.) *op.cit.*, p.41.
85. *Ibid.*, p.41.
86. Krupasindhu Mishra, 1979 (rep.) *op.cit.*, p.4.
87. Krupasindhu Mishra, 1955 (rep.) *op.cit.*, p.15.
88. *Ibid*, p.22.
89. Krupasindhu Mishra, *op.cit.*, 1979 (rep.), p.III.
90. *Ibid.*, p.85.
91. *Ibid.*, p.161.
92. Krupasindhu Mishra, 1955 (rep.), *op.cit.*, Preface.
93. *Ibid.*, Preface.
94. *Ibid.*, p.60.
95. *Ibid.*, p.41.
96. *Ibid.*, Preface.
97. *Ibid.*, Preface.
98. For a brief biography of Birupakshya Kar, refer to Asit Kabi and Bauribandhu Kar (ed) "*Uṭkalare Baudha Yugara Itihāsa O Anyanya Prabandha*", 1981, Cuttack.
99. *Uṭkala Sāhitya*, Vol. 22, No. 10, 1918.
100. *Uṭkala Sāhitya*, Vol. 24, No.7, 1920.
101. *Uṭkala Sāhitya*, Vol. 25, No. 4, Vol. 25, No. 5 & Vol. 25, No. 6, 1921.
102. *Uṭkala Sāhitya*, Vol. 29, No. 3, Vol. 29, No. 4, Vol. 29, No. 5, Vol. 29, No. 6, Vol. 29, No. 9, Vol.29, No. 12 (1925), Vol. 30, No.3 (1926), Vol. 31, No. 8, Vol. 31, No. 10, Vol. 31, No. 12 (1927).

103. Published in Pandit Gopabandhu death anniversary special issue of *Samāj*, 1960.
104. Uṭkalare Baudha Yugara Itihāsa O' Anyanya Prabandha, Cuttack, 1981, p.106-07.
105. *Ibid.*, p.67.
106. *Ibid.*
107. *Ibid.*
108. *Ibid.*, p.1.
109. *Ibid.*, p.1.
110. *Ibid.*, p.25.
111. *Ibid.*, p.107.
112. *Ibid.*, p.33.
113. *Ibid.*, p.63.
114. *Ibid.*, p.1.
115. *Ibid.*, p.18 & 21.

7

Some Biased Historical Writings on Orissa

With the gradual domination and consolidation of their position in the British civil administration in India, some social elite from Bengal started a concerted campaign against the independent existence of the Oriya language during the 1870s. Orissa then remained a part of Bengal and was under the administration of the Bengal Presidency. They tried all their best to argue against the administrative separation of Orissa from Bengal and the Oriya language became the target of their attack. Babu Rajendra Lal Mitra, who despite all his extraordinary scholarship and talent that resulted in his monumental work '*Antiquities of Orissa*', however, led this movement and thus became the major exponent of this anti-Oriya bias. The other scholar (non-professional) in this category was Bijoy Chandra Majumdar who was appointed by the ruling chief of Sonpur in Orissa to write a eulogy of the said ruling family. Like Mitra, he was highly critical of, and biased against, the Oriyas.

I. RAJENDRA LAL MITRA (1822-1891)

Babu Rajendra Lal Mitra was born on 16 February, 1822. His life and times were synonymous with the modern Indian renaissance of the 19th century which brought in its wake the socio-religious reform movements. He was the Assistant Secretary and Librarian of the Asiatic Society which brought about a collaboration among the western and Indian scholars in the task of unveiling India's past. A hardworking youngman with ciritical acumen and commendable knowledge of Persian, Sanskrit, Hindi and Urdu, Rajendra Lal Mitra, proved his academic mettle within a couple of years of his joining the Asiatic Society. He wrote a brilliant paper on an inscription from the Vijay Mandir, Udaipur, which was published in the Society's journal in the year 1848. On seeing the wealth of the source materials and the galaxy of scholars around him in the Asiatic Society he decided to devote himself to the study of early Indian society and culture. Although for financial reasons he left the Society and accepted the Directorship of the Ward's institution in 1856, he continued his researches with unflagging zeal. In recognition of the outcome of these sustained researches he became the first Indian to hold the prestigious office of the President of the Asiatic Society. Rajendra Lal Mitra died on 26 July, 1891.

As a young researcher, Babu Rajendra Lal Mitra acquainted himself with the western methodology of historical study. He knew how to separate the grain from the chaff and how to integrate the literary evidences with archaeological data. His approach to the core material necessary for the reconstruction of the distant past was predictably two fold: First, the publication of the old texts as well as preparation of notices of different collections including that of the society and then, the study of the archaeological objects such as coins, inscriptions and monumental remains.

His approach to literary materials is demonstrated by his critical editions of several texts including the '*Kamandakiya Niti Shastra*' the *Agni* and *Vāyu Purāṇas* and a nine volume catalogue of Sanskrit manuscripts.

Babu Rajendra Lal Mitra was, however, not satisfied with the existing collection of manuscripts of the Society but was always in quest of new ones. A distinguished scholar of later days, Mahamahopadhyaya Haraparasad Shastri, received his training in the preparation of the descriptive catalogues from Rajendra Lal Mitra.

Initially a language expert, Rajendra Lal Mitra had acquired sufficient knowledge in archaeological field work and study later. But his knowledge of archaeology was only rudimentary. The "*Antiquities of Orissa*" published in two bulky volumes in 1875 and

1880 respectively established him as a historian and embodied the results of this intensive study of temples, sculptures and allied relics of old cities like Bhubaneswar, Puri, Konark and Jajpur. As the name suggests, the '*Antiquities of Orissa*' should have been a survey of Orissan architecture only but he very often made departures from the original theme and spoke on different historical issues.

The other book the "*Sanskrit Buddhist Literature of Nepal*" published in the year 1882 is based on an analytical study and detailed contents of 85 year old Sanskrit manuscripts relating to Buddhism which were presented to the Asiatic Society by Bit Hodgson. Since its publication it has been of use not only to scholars but also creative writers including Rabindra Nath Tagore who chose three of its anecdotes for his poems and musical plays.

Among the other notable works of Babu Rajendra Lal Mitra are "*Bodh Gaya : The Hermitage of Śakyamuni*" (1878) and the two volumes of "*Indo Aryans*" (1881). In the former Rajendra Lal Mitra largely drew the results of the investigations of his predecessors like Cunningham and modestly admits that his task has been more of a summarist and compiler than that of an original inquirer.

The '*Indo Aryans*' is a collection of essays written on different occasions on a variety of topics such as the use of beef and spirituous drinks in Ancient India. Apart from those garnered in this book, there are still numerous articles lying scattered in periodicals and mainly in Society's journals and proceedings. Although most of them deal with inscriptions, ancient literature and monumental remains, some of them centre on numismatics and philology. Most of these monographs and papers were published between the 70s and 80s of the nineteenth century.

Babu Rajendra Lal Mitra's enormous output, on which his eminence rests, is in English. Yet as he belonged to the most elite and privileged class of renascent Bengal, he was necessarily conscious of his own Bengali identity and of the need for reaching the major chunk of his countrymen in their mother tongue. With this end in view, Rajendra Lal Mitra started in 1851 a monthly Bengali Journal called "*Vividha Sangraha*", the first penny magazine of India. Apart from papers on history and antiquities, it carried articles on science, art and literature. Every issue of the magazine also carried excellent illustrations. Scholarly yet popular, '*Vividha Sangraha*' was a landmark in the periodical literature in India and was held in great esteem by Gurudev Rabindra Nath Tagore. It continued till 1861. In 1863, Rajendra Lal Mitra took the responsibility of another illustrated monthly journal "*Rahasya Sandarbha*" and edited altogether six volumes of the journal. Collectively through these Journals—he disseminated general knowledge and historical awareness to the average man.

The other aspect of his elitist Bengali consciousness was reflected in the role he played in the campaign against the separate existence of the Oriya language. This has not only its reflections in the "*Antiquities of Orissa*" but also all the greatness of this monumental work was overshadowed by the role he played in their elitist Bengali campaign, for the abolition of Oriya language in the 60s and 70s of the last century. The concerted campaign by the Bengali employees working in the government office in Orissa (of whom most were teachers) was greatly helped by the government mismanagement during the devastating famine of the sixties in Orissa. Babu Rajendra Lal Mitra has been critcised by his contemporary Oriyas for leading this concerted Bengali intellectual campaign for the abolition of the Oriyan language. He has been severely blamed for capitalising on the simplicity of the Oriyas who rendered him untiring help during his antiquarian survey during 1867/68 in Orissa.[2] In an article in *Utkal Dipika* dated 05 September, 1868 entiled "Survey of Antiquities" the editor of the weekly had appealed to all the Oriyas to help Babu Rajendra Lal Mitra with all information available since he was working on the antiquities of Orissa. But Babu Rajendra Lal Mitra misused this simplicity of the Oriyas and conspired to abolish the Oriya language. In December, 1868 delivering a speech at Cuttack Debating Society, Rajendra Lal Mitra said[3] that any wellwisher of Utkal must try for the introduction of Bengali in place of Oriya. Until and unless Oriya language is abolished this country could not prosper. Rajendra Lal Mitra argued that since in Orissa population is merely 20 lakhs, literature and language cannot prosper independently. That is why if Bengali language would be introduced, the problem of the scarcity of the Oriya books would be over and Bengali language would be introduced as the medium of instruction and the people of this country would largely benefit by that. But Babu Rajendra Lal Mitra's statement only created confusion as he meant the population of the '*Moghulbandi*' as the population of entire Orissa. Mitra also helped Mr. Kanti Chandra Bhattacharya in producing the book "*Odia Ekta Swatantra Bhasa Noy*" (Oriya is not an independent language.). Kanti Chandra Bhattacharya not only dedicated the book to Rajendra Lal Mitra but also acknowldeged the help Mitra rendered in writing the book.[4] This book created a sort of a language agitation in Eastern India. Later at a seminar, Babu Rajendra Lal Mitra defended his arguments against the independent existence of the Oriya language. In his speech he said[5] that we found many differences of opinion as regards linguistic diversity and this term was largely misunderstood by the teaching community. In reality Bengali, Oriya and Assamese are only one language and are wrongly differentiated. The Bengalis did not feel this as offending because they are capable of protecting their own language. But the Oriyas and the Assamese because of their small population were not capable of protecting their language. When they would learn to read Bengali language they could easily absorb themselves in Bengali fraternity in a short time. They could realise all benefits the Bengalis had achieved. If these were kept as separate languages, they would still remain as small social and linguistic fragments and would face a deplorable situation. All his arguments against the independent existence of Oriya language was strongly refuted by the famous British philologist of the time John Beames, who was also a historiographer of some recognition.

This approach of Babu Rajendra Lal Mitra against the independent existence of the Oriya language had its obvious reflection in the "*Antiquities of Orissa*" wherein he had very often tried to disprove the indignity of Orissan art and architecture. This aspect we are going to dwell upon while discussing the "*Antiquities of Orissa*" during the course of this chapter. No doubt Babu Rajendra lal Mitra was an antiquarian of repute. The two volumes of "*Antiquities of Orissa*" have made him immortal as a historical researcher but he was always being considered an enemy of the Oriyas for the role he played in the anti-Oriya campaign.

At the present instance we need have to look Rajendra Lal Mitra as an historian and critically examine his "*Antiquities of Orissa*".[6] The book was the result of his diligent labours in connection with the mission that was deputed to Orissa by the British government in the year 1868-69 for the purpose of obtaining casts of some of the more important sculptures of ancient India and Babu Rajendra Lal Mitra accompanied this mission as an archaeologist.

In writing the "*Antiquities of Orissa*" Rajendra Lal Mitra depended on the spot survey and examination of the Orissan monuments. And for historical descriptions, therefore, he drew upon the materials embedded in literary sources like "Ekamra Purāṇa", "Swarnadṛi Mahodaya", "Kapila Saṁhita" and also local traditions. The monograph contained detailed descriptions. Its copious lithographic illustrations and excellent line drawings have remarkably enhanced its value.

A critical outlook on "*Antiquities of Orissa*" would reveal that Babu Rajendra Lal Mitra depended on the temple traditions including "*Madāla Paṅjī*" or the traditional documents relating to the Jagannath Temple at Puri as well. But like a true historian he accepted these traditional data only after a careful scrutiny of Madāla Paṅjī. Rajendra Lal Mitra says, "For the history of Orissa our best guide is the Madāla Paṅjī or the annals of the Temple of Jagannath at Puri. It begins with an enumeration of the kings of "Satya Yuga" or the age of purity and brings down the record day by day and year by year to the present time noting every remarkable occurrence that has taken place in the province in connection with the history of the idol and of its chief adorer, the sovereigns of Khurdha. Such a record for such a length of time as an authentic and reliable source would have been of utmost importance (sic), but unfortunately there is nothing to show that the Annals were really taken in hand at any very extraordinarily early period or regularly kept up from time to time when it was first undertaken, judging from the language in which it was written and its character in general. We believe that the writing of the *Paṅjī* was first commenced six centuries ago. That it has ever since been regularly written up is questionable. The political vicissitudes of Khurdha during the last five hundred years tend to show that there must have been many discontinuances and interpolations. We are also loathe to vouch for strict accuracy of the large benefactions of the former Rajas of Orissa and of their martial services over sea and land as recorded in the *Paṅjī*. On the whole, however, it was a valuable document and contains a pretty fair account of the later Rajas of Orissa. The Pāñjīas of the almanac makers of the provinance have also their chronicles of extraordinary events and a few "*vaṁśāvalīs*" in Sanskrit, giving the genealogies of royal dynasty but as these have already been analysed by stating on the history of Orissa by Bhavani Charan Bandopadhyana in his '*History of Puri*' we need only to refer to them here."[7]

That he was conscious of the limitations of the traditional sources will be evident from his rebuttal of the remarks of James Prinsep that if the rationality of a story be a fair test of its genuinenss which few will deny, the Pāli record will bear away the palm.[8] Opposing James Prinsep, he described the Pāli fictions as legendary and as full of romantic fables. He argued that plausibility is no proof in law nor can it be history. If we admit the reverse of the position we have to accept all the Society's novels and stories of the day as history. Similarly on historical consciousness in Indian literature Rajendra Lal Mitra writes in the introduction to "*Antiquities of Orissa*" that neither Ganesh, the Hindu patron of wisdom, nor Saraswati, the goddess of learning, seems to have paid any encouragement to history and as a consequence Indian literature is almost void of all authentic historical records. Twice ten thousand on at least the literary activity of Indian divinities and almost every branch of ancient learning has had its earnest and most devoted cultivators. Nor are the works we allied to, bearing in mind their age, in any way wanting in value as monuments of antiquity, profound erudition and superior intelligence. In antiquity, the *Samhitā* of the '*Ṛg Veda*' holds a higher rank than even the oldest writing of the Jewish race. In general, the excellence of the '*Rāmāyaṇa*' yeilds not the palm of superiority to the *Illiad* of Homer and in depth of knowledge and subtility of argument. *Darshanas* (sic) of India bear no favourable comparison to the greatest philosophies of ancient Greece. The grammar of Pāṇiṇi stands unrivalled and unique in its own time and in astronomy, mathematics, logic and rhetoric, romance and legends, law and civil polity, in medicine, in music and dramatic composition, there is an extent of ancient literature still existing, the likes of which can nowhere be met with, except perhaps in Rome and China. Yet India never produced a Xenophan or Thucydides and her heroes, her greatness and the early civilisation where they live, live but in song."[9]

Rajendra Lal Mitra had attributed a number of factors for the absence of proper historical literature in ancient India. "The ravages of time, the hostility of rival sectaries and government and iconoclastic zeal of Muslim fanatics have swept away most of them from the face of the earth and the few that remained can ill tell their tale with sufficient precision and clarity to meet the requirements of the historian."[10] The prospects thus for the historians of India is far from promising. There is, however, no limit to human enquiry and much may be done by diligence and industry even in the fields which appear at first sight to be gloomy and forbidding. Moreover every literature, however fabulous or mythical may be its character, has a historical value and that of India cannot be an exception. Tales, traditions and romances, the ordinances of kings and mandates of lawgivers, the rituals of religion, misusing of poems must all take their tone and character from the state of society in which they have developed and cannot but serve imperfectly though it to be, the annals of civilisation. In the same way almost every monument or carved stone, every ornament or utensil, however rude or monstrous or grotesque may be its design, bears its face and the index to the intellectual condition of some individual community and be made with proper care, to yield an acceptable contribution to the cause of history."[11]

On myths and mysticism in ancient Indian literature, Rajendra Lal Mitra writes, "associating Bhakti with Vedanta doctrine of relation of human to the divine soul, the *Bhagabat* have particularly developed a system in which the passions of affection and love are brought together to bear upon the divinity more permanently and earnestly than religious devotion and the God head is represented in such mystic allegorical language as to appear to the thinkers of the present fastidious age highly unbecoming, insulting, licentious and even blasphemous in which the substituion of the impassioned eloquence of the poet addressing his mistress for the sober language of respectful adoration with reference to a deity is held most sacred. This is the result of the hypertrophy of religious feelings which envelopes the religious sentiment with the changes and imagery of mundane life of an excessive favour of adoration which rising above all amenities of sober society, longs to hold communion with the god-head in a manner of which sexual love is the most perfect type known to man. Poets of ancient time indulged in variety of fanciful and voluptuous imageries in describing matters celestical and a too lateral or materialistic or spiritual interpretation of their allegorical language led either to the formation of myths or the development of mysticism of various types. The allegories of the Vedas have without a single exception been elaborated in myths in after ages and not a few of them form the basis of mystical dogmas."[12]

Of the Orissan historical records and antiquities, Babu Rajendra Lal Mitra says that "cut off from the rest of India by ranges of hills and inhospitable wilds on the one side and hemmed by the sea on the other site", Orissa enjoyed perfect immunity for a long time from the records of Mohemmedans and even in its worst days did not suffer as much as the rest of India. Commerce it had next to none and its people lived happily and contented for ages under a national government with every opportunity to cultivate arts of peace and to promote posperity of their fatherland. The ancient monuments, it contains are, therefore, more authentic than what are to be met within most other parts of India and as such have a peculiar interest and significance for the antiquarian. The greater part of the ground is all but terra incongnita for oriental explorers but few comparatively had ventured upon its borders as it were to conform a foregone opinion or indulge in a momentary curosity so that the important questions of its archaeology remain for all practical purposes unanswered to this day.[13]

Two volumes of "*Antiquities of Orissa*" certainly established Rajendra Lal Mitra as an archaeologist. As he wrote in the Preface to the book that he accompanied the British government of India's mission to Orissa as an archaeologist to secure some historical and descriptive account of the several monuments of the region of which the mission would make casts, Rajendra Lal Mitra largely succeeded in his endeavour more than what was expected of him as a member of the expedition. This enduring work speaks eloquently of Rajendra Lal Mitra's intensive study of the archaeological remains of India particularly the temples and sculptures of Orissa for which he conducted explorations. In the two volumes of the 'Antiquities of Orissa' that resulted from these labours he gave, first, a general observation on the nature and character of the objects noticed and second, a detailed description of those objects, the former embracing only those characters which are common to the particular classes and the latter, the peculiarities of individual relics. In the brief introduction to the book he put together the information available regarding Orissa in ancient authors and reserved notices of particular localities for treatment under respective heads. Excellent line drawings and lithographic illustrations of different elements of the temple complexes heightens the importance of the work as a source book for history, art and architecture of Orissa. To this, the learned author appended a critical study of the architectural, religious and social history of Orissa on the basis of the objective interpretation of sculptural materials which must have been influenced by the prevailing social conditions and the religious speculation current at the time. This work alone would have been sufficient to rank him high among the Indian historians.

Before discussing the antique remains of Orissa, Rajendra Lal Mitra discussed the characteristics of Indian architecture obviously with an intention to trace out the status of Orissan antiquities vis-a-vis the antiquities of other parts of India and in general, its position in the mainstream of Indian architecture. In this exercise he discussed the opinions of Wheeler, Fergusson and Ms. Manning on the antiquity of Indian architecture and the reasons of its absence at a remote age. Stating that their arguments are not conclusive because of the fact that the Grecian architecture and the pillars of Asoka pretty well indicate the existence of architecture before the time of Asoka and that in ancient texts the 'Rāmāyaṇa', the 'Mahābhārata', the 'ṚgVeda' and the works of Pāṇiṇi, we find notices of architecture. Analysing the untenability of Bacho-Grecian, Egyptian, Assyrian and Persian theories, he discussed Wilson's opinion on conventionalism in architecture and possible Tamilian origin of Indian architecture. Babu Rajendra Lal Mitra also made a detailed classification of Indian architecture on the basis of the Sanskrit works extant on architecture in ancient India.

After giving a detailed general background of Indian architecture, Babu Rajendra Lal Mitra went also to delineate the Orissan architecture from its minutest details. In this exercise a linear development of Orissan architecture, its origin, development, its form, quality, shape, style, design, aesthetic appeal, nationality and ethnicity of the architects, minute details of works in all the structures and scriptures including the materials used, financial aspects have been given a minute delineation. He also drew upon the peculiarities of the Orissan School of the architecture. His study also went beyond the 'merely descriptive' level since his discussions on the social condition of the contemporary temple builders as depicted in the relevant sculptural materials and the several religious systems influencing the growth of Orissan art were much above the ordinary.

A critical overview of this work notably the '*Antiquities of Orissa*' reveals the following hallmarks of Rajendra Lal Mitra as a historian. An unflinching thoroughness in the treatment of the subject is noticed in Mitra's writing, be it the cultural past of Orissa or the literacy landscape of Nepal. In "*Antiquities of Orissa*" he spared no pains as he stated in the preface to the book to secure "an accurate description—illustrated by plans, measurements, drawings and photographs and by copies of inscriptions of such remains as most deserved notice, with the history of them so far as it may be traceable and a record of traditions that are retained regarding them, and in the second place to notice permanently such points in them as were calculated to throw any special light on the social history of the ages which they were referred."[14] Indeed he was the first Indian to underline the importance of the documentation of monumental remains.

Similarly, he was careful about the methodology of historical enquiry. This is evident from his explanation of the absence of prominent marks of Buddhism in Khandagiri caves which are to be met with elsewhere in the country. On this reference Rajendra Lal Mitra writes that "these arguments at first sight appear very strong but they are nevertheless quite fallacious. They accept as majors what have no right to be considered as such and assume as such what cannot be accepted. Doubtless there are some caves which have Buddhist emblems carved on them but we have no more right to conclude therefrom that all Buddhist caves should bear such emblems carved on them. A religion founded on athesim which recognised no necessity for worshipping images can well exist – nay flourish – without its sanctuaries bearing emblems of its sectarial or specific character. It is very probable though it is not quite certain that in the time of Aśoka emblems and images had become common but there is literally no evidence whatsoever to show that in a country before his time, emblems and images were held in the same estimation and Buddhist monasteries were invariably built or excavated with prominent emblems of faith fixed on them and in the absence of such evidences it is futile to accept the hypothesis, for it is no better, as a universally accepted major and to argue upon it. The hypothesis besides takes for granted the present absence of emblems and relics as equivalent to the absence thereof in former times. It is true that in law the scotch verdict of 'not proven' is in criminal cases, as far as the prisoner is concerned, tantamount to 'not guilty' but in history absence of evidence at one point cannot be taken as proof of no evidence having ever existed."[15]

At another place, Rajendra Lal Mitra said "in the place of the hermit, an image of the God or a rude stone or a grave, or a sacred relic, suddenly rising into repute for working miracles or for some other cause, produces the same effect. In the first fervour of devotion, wealth flows rapidly towards its endowment and embellishments edifices rise over round it and a sacred place is completed. All this takes but few short years and the life time of a single generation is generally enough to take consumption. A different feeling next comes into play that of respect for antiquity which develops a strong spirit for conservation and its main objects are to give firmness to and perpetuate existing customs, practices and observances and to prevent changes and innovations. Devotion then leads to the erection of minor edifices around the principal building in order to secure for them a share of the reflected sanctity of the original shrine. Hence, it is in India at least that the richest and the most elaborate shrines are the oldest temples and the other structures around them are of comparatively recent dates."[16]

Rajendra Lal Mitra has equally given a brilliant analysis of the role of festivals in human life. Considering the festivals as inevitable social engagements, he said, no system of religion designed for the community at large can prosper without festivals. A dull routine of everyday life soon begins to pall – to blunt the age of enthusiasm and the festivals are the whetstones which take that bluntness away. The character of the festivals might vary with reference to the intellectual condition of the people for whom they are intended. But in the system of religion which recognises the festivals and there is none that does not – there is an attempt to bend, to descend from the lofty chain of the solemn and the venerable, to take the lower orders of the people by the hand and to make them partake of the solace of religion sweetened with honey or entertainment. They serve not only to keep the hold of religion on the masses and to familiarise them with the history but also to ensure a steady income for the exchequer of the clergy. The necessity for them is so absolute that even the atheistical Buddhists could not forego the opportunities for them and in our times there is not a sect whether deistic, theistic, atheistic or positivist which has not its festive gathering of some kind or other. Periodical festivals arise either from astronomical causes or from a desire to perpetuate the memory of some notable event in the history of a particular religion. The former are universal and the latter local and particular."[17]

These are the few examples which clearly explain how Rajendra Lal Mitra treated his subjects in his works. He maintained that historical evidence should be studied in the seat of a judge and not that of a counsel. He felt that a true historian should be above all kinds of prejudices like chauvinism and parochialism and should not write anything in a preconceived pattern. For instance, he once said, "it is not for me to plead in favour of Indian methodology nor am I its apologist."[18] In another occasion he averred, "if patriotism means an insinuate love of everything that is ours, good or bad, away with such patriotism."[19] This attitude of Rajendra Lal Mitra is clearly evidenced in "*Antiquities of Orissa*" itself. Alluding superiority and sanctity to Orissan architecture, he writes "Orissa was well-known to the Indian Aryans from a very early period but only as an abode of primitive non-Aryan or a fallen race. It had no reputation for sanctity and never was thought of as a holy place for pilgrimage for Hindus. It was first selected by Buddhists as a very promising field for their operations for the aboriginal races of India doubtless offered, better and more pliant subjects for proselytism than the Aryans. The fact is that even as Buddhism rose mainly by working on the religious sentiments of the people, so did modern Hinduism where it was responsible to appropriate a Buddhist temple to Hindu worship, rival temples were erected in its close neighbourhood and services and ceremonials were so moulded and adopted as to leave nothing to the former to maintain its prominence in the estimation of the people. The Hindu temples of Orissa and their superior sanctity are evidentally due to this policy, for it is from the seventh century onwards that we find the province noticed in Hindu writings not as the abode of outcastes and barbarians but as the chosen home of Gods," there are peculiarities which may be more or less products of Orissan art but at the same time there are points of excellence in it which are not to be met with in other ancient schools. The conventionality of form which is so marked in this prevails to some extent eveywhere in India. It resulted from indolence combined with a desire to initiate art instead of nature under circumstances which were particularly favourable mannerisms untouched by extraneous influences, art in Orissa successively rose, became stationary and declined with the civilisation of the people very much in the same way which marked its course in Egypt and elsewhere and its characteristics to some extent must be alike."[21]

Rajendra Lal Mitra considers the Orissan School of Architecture as belonging to the Indo-Aryan group. In this also he showed exemplary mark of neutrality. He rejected any argument to allude to either Bengali or Tamilian origin of the Orissan School of Art. He says, "the features are though not of Hindu of the Bengal type. There is nothing in any of the details in the eyes, the nose, the cheekbones and from those features where ethnic peculiarities are least indicated to show a trace of aboriginal Tamilian characteristics and the circumstances may be taken as a strong proof in favour of Indo-Aryan origin of the works. Had the temples and their decorations proceeded from Dravidian artists, these characteristics would have been entirely different. Even English painters of the present day at least those who had come to Calcutta but too often find a European character to the native portraits they paint, and it is but natural to suppose that South Indian artists, had they been employed in Orissan temples would have given them a strong Tamilian cast."[22]

From his deep erudition stemmed a suave self-confidence that prompted Rajendra Lal Mitra to challenge a western scholar of the stature of Fergusson. He challenged Fergusson's remark that Indians learnt architecture, the decoration of the buildings with carved ornaments and mouldings after their contact with the Greeks. Rajendra Lal Mitra argued ably and boldly that the Indians knew that art of building long before the time of Alexander's invasion of India until Fergusson was forced to concede.

A breadth of vision enabled Rajendra Lal Mitra to go beyond Orissa while studying her old relics and to compare the products of what he called 'Urya school' with those of Daedalian, Aeginetan, Etnescan, Egyptian and Assyrian School of ancient Europe and western

Asia despite chronological gaps. Although some comparisons have not always been fruitful, the fact that he wanted to compare the Orissan products with those of the foreign lands certainly deserve praise and in this sense, he is a pioneer, initiating the comparative study of art.

Rajendra Lal Mitra believed in a unilinear development of Orissan architecture. This is evident from his analysis of the characteristics of Orissan architecture. He says, "untouched by external influences Orissan architecture successively rose, became stationary and declined with the civilisation of the people. Very much in the same way which marked its course in Egypt and elsewhere and its characteristics must to a certain extent be a like."[23]

Above everything else Rajendra Lal Mitra was a great visionary and showed deep insight into historical analysis which is rarely seen among professional historians. It was this vision the '*Prajña*' of the Indian tradition which enabled him to make some pronouncements which subsequently came to be true. When he controverted Fergusson he had no solid fact at his disposal. It was three decades after his death that his theory regarding the indigenous origin of the Indian architecture was confirmed by the discoveries of Indian civilisation.

Similarly as early as 1880 Rajendra Lal Mitra pronounced, though without any tangible evidence that the colossal lingam of the Bhaskareswara Temple, Bhubaneswar,was the remnant of the Asokan pillar. For some time his view was not shared by many. But of late a close examination of this phallic emblem and other objects such as the railing pillar and a colossal lion near the temple conducted by late Dr. Krushna Chandra Panigrahi and subsequently by Dr. Kalyan Kumar Dasgupta favours the endorsement of Rajendra Lal Mitra's theory.[24]

All such statements were matters of the inner eye of an historian who was otherwise a down-to-earth man. Rajendra Lal Mitra was indeed an historian of this genre to whom factual foundation was more important than its conceptual superstructure. The reason for this perhaps is that he was a historian of the 19th century which was a great age for oriental investigation based on facts. Historians could hardly dream of applying a pound of interpretation to an ounce of fact.

Guidelines of the research undertaking of Rajendra Lal Mitra may be summarised as follows :

1. Exploration and exposition of source materials in a faithful and accurate manner.
2. Critical and comparative study of the materials in their proper historical setting.
3. Rational and logical analysis and interpretation of the relevant data, throughly disinterested in spirit but fully reflecting the cultural state of a given people in a given period.
4. Presentation of the historical facts in a lucid form but maintaining a balanced judgment and objectivity of outlook.

In his treatment of epigraphic and numismatic materials or for that matter archaeological remains, Rajendra Lal Mitra adopted the same prinicples of scientific objectivity in bringing out their true import and historical bearing. It is indeed a matter of satisfaction that most of his findings born out of logical marshalling of facts, had ground still to this day. If, however, some of his conclusions came to be improved upon or reversed subsequently, it has to be remembered that Rajendra Lal Mitra's efforts were those of a pioneer. The plan and methodology that he prescribed for himself in his great work '*Antiquities of Orissa*' is itself a strong example of his keen sense of historical perspective. The comprehensive character of the project is evident from his frank statement that Sir Gardiner Wilkinson's learned work '*Ancient Egyptians*' served me for a guide."

It is because of his steadfastness to facts and eye for details that even now some of his books and papers are deemed valuable. In the case of the temples at Puri and Konark and some shrines at Bhubaneswar for example, his descriptions enable us to get an idea as to what they looked like when he visited them.

Viewed from all these, both qualitatively and quantitatively, the enormous output of Rajendra Lal Mitra was marked by flashes of rare insight, apart from the hallmarks of a historian such as adherence to facts, analytical acumen and academic detachment and judged by any standards of scholarship he is undoubtedly and avant-grade historian of India. Even after a century after his death he is striding like a colossus.

Despite all his greatness in the oriental studies of the school of architecture, for which he undertook the mission to Orissa and the "*Antiquities of Orissa*" resulting from these efforts, Rajendra Lal Mitra made significant departures from the main theme of his works and spoke on the history, culture, society and language of Orissa. In all these discussions he is heavily biased against the Oriyas. We have discussed at the beginning of this chapter the vigorous campaign he led for the abolition of the Oriya language and for the merger of Orissa with Bengal. Besides that in "*Antiquities of Orissa*" itself he made a number of fallacious and biased conclusions which seem to be largely due to his malicious attitude towards the Oriyas. Rajendra Lal Mitra did not at all mind to campaign in favour of proving Bhatta Bhava Deva as the founder of the Ananta Vasudeva Temple[26] at Bhubaneshwar in view of the mysterious implanation of an inscription which did not at all belong to the temple. Similarly he dwelt upon a Popperian logic to attribute a Buddhist origin to the Konark Temple. He says, "the five leading forms of Hinduism including those of the Śaktās, the Śaivas, the Vaiṣṇavās and the Gaṇapatyās had already long since obtained good currency in the 5th and 6th centuries and at the revival of Hinduism in Orissa about that time it is but natural to suppose that each sect should select one of the principal Buddhist seats of the province for its respected system of religion. Accordingly we find the Śaivās at Bhubaneswar, the Vaiṣṇāvās at Puri, and Śaktās at Jajpur, all unquestionable places of Buddhism, still possessing vestiges of former Buddhist domination and Konark and Darpana, the places for Sūrya and Gaṅeśa may be fairly supposed to have been Buddhist. The evidence available is certainly exceedingly meagre and unsatisfactory but without the assumption of previous sanctity and celebrity, it becomes difficult to account for the selection of a sea beach for the dedication of so costly and magnificient a temple as Black Pagoda."[26]

Rajendra Lal Mitra had presented a very detestable picture of the car festival of Lord Jagannath at Puri. Explaining his points in the "*Antiquities of Orissa*" he said, "No Indian divinity had the enviable notoriety in English literature than Jagannath. Alike in poetry and prose, in the works of imagination, as in sober history, he forms a never dying illustration of all that cruel, all that is horrible, all that is most revolting to every sense of humanity. The cretan Dionysisus at which little children were immolated in honour of Dionysisus, the Draidical wicker cage which is burnt alive, the Mexican Tezcatlepoea with his annual pile of hundred thousand captive heads, the Peruvian Priloucon with its mounds of human flesh every year offered to pacify the wrath of an irate divinity, pale before this hideous Moloch whose terrible car through bloods and bones ploughs its dreadful path. Has the orater to excite in his audience a feeling of revolting abhorence against any hated object? – he cannot do it better than by denouncing it as a car of Jagannath, the preacher subserves the cause of religion by indulging in the same metaphor and the statesman holds it as one of his most potent invections fit to be hurled at everything that he thinks the most detestable. It is certain nevertheless that the human conception has never realised a more innocent and gentle divinity than Jagannath and the tenets of his votaries are very reverse of sanguinary or revolting. In fact never was opprobrium cast on an inoffensive object than in this instance and none merited it less."[27]

Similarly he took the reference in *Ain-I-Akbari* about the construction of the nine-storey palace at Bārābatī Fort by Raja Mukund Deva as highly exaggerated, "To me the description appeared on the face of it to be incorrect. I would not well believe that any sensible person would build a nine storeyed palace—would locate his artillery and guards in the second storey of the residence or his kitchen just under his public reception room and his artificers below his kitchen. The retinue of the Raja must have numbered in thousands and it was difficult to believe that they were all accommodated in the several storeys of one building. I referred, therefore, to the original text of '*Ain-I-Akbari*' and it at once solved the difficulty. The words used in it are, Raja Mukund Deva built a palace of *asianahs* (Blochman's text). Now asianah in Arabic means a nest, a suit of rooms, a layer and the sense in which it was used in the passage is that of dwellings ranged side by side and not in storeys. The word in common use for a courtyard in India is *mahal* and ordinary respectable houses include two such, one forming the outer apartment for men and the other the inner apartment for ladies. Houses for rich men include four, five or more such courtyards and the Kaiserbag Palace of Oudh comprised eighteen. In the *Toy Card,* written two thousand years ago, a description is given of a rich courtesan's house which comprised seven such court. Indian works on architecture commend this arrangement as the best for rich houses and it is obvious that the palace of Mukund Deva had nine such courtyards. Mr. Gladwin mistook the word '*asianah*' and by using the English word storey produced the confusion and Mr. Fergusson by appealing to dubious analogies has given it an air of resemblance. No vestige of the palace is, however, traceable and no conclusive evidence can be collected on the subject."[28]

Above all, Rajendra Lal Mitra did not leave any arguments to attribute a Greek origin to Orissan architecture. This, he did, only because Orissan architecture had a distinct identity and greatness of its own. He argued "but to pass from the inferential to the evidence – for it can be shown that the architecture of Orissa bears unmistakable stamp of their Greek origin all a priori arguments on the subject must be thrown away. The difficulties, however, which beset this branch of enquiry are very great and they have been multiplied by personal predilections, want of knowledge, fallacious logic and other causes to an extent which render attempts to overcome them almost hopeless. I nevertheless feel bound to note the salient points of the question in order that my readers may have it in a tangible form and be enabled to draw their own inferences."[29] At another place Rajendra Lal Mitra says that in judging sculpture, its general appearance is what we have first to deal with but it is at the same time the most misleading. It is uncertain in quantity, liable to be diversified under different circumstances and the knowledge and predilections of the observer and what may be supposed to be decisively similar, may be pronounced by another as radically different in every line and feature."[30]

All these are examples of how Rajendra Lal Mitra's shortsightedness and parochial attitude towards Orissa is explicitly expressed. These are merely a consummation of his arguments against the independent existence of the Oriya language which he vigorously cultivated with his expertise in liguistics. This consummation is evidenced in the parts of the "*Antiquities of Orissa*" where he discussed things other than art and architecture. Because of these preconceived ideas, he had before writing the book, "*Antiquities of Orissa*" proved to be heavily biased against Orissan history and culture, notwithstanding the oriental scholarship we trace in his dealing with the antiquities of Orissan monuments.

II. BIJOY CHANDRA MAJUMDAR (1861 – 1942)

While practising as an advocate at Sambalpur during 1911 and 1916 Bijoy Chandra Majumdar also served as advisor to the Garjat rulers of Sambalpur. He served mainly as an advisor in the courts of Maharaja Sir Bir Mitrodaya Singhdeo '*Dharmaniddhi*' '*Jñāana-gunakāra*', the ruling chief of the Sonepur estate. Under the patronage of the ruler of Sonepur he wrote his major historical works. In 1911, 1916, and 1925 Majumdar wrote a series of essays on Mayurbhanj based mainly on legends and local tradition. In 1916 he wrote his first major work "*Sonepur in the Sambalpur Tract*". In 1925 while serving as a lecturer in Anthropology, comparative philology and Indian vernaculars in the University of Calcutta as well as practising law at Calcutta High Court he wrote "*Orissa in the Making*" which was published by the University of Calcutta under the patronage of the Maharaja Sir Bir Mitrodaya Singhdeo, the ruling chief of the Sonepur estate. The same year Bijoy Chandra Majumdar brought out three volumes of "*Typical Selections from Oriya Literature*" in which he compiled famous literary compositions and traced out the development of Oriya language and literature. These volumes were also published by Calcuttta University under the patronage of the Sonepur Maharaja. During these years at Sambalpur, Shri Majumdar spent sometime in Bolangir as well. While he was at Sambalpur and Bolangir, he got sufficient opportunity to know about Sambalpur and the entire Western Orissan tract more than any one else. The two works that emerged out of this processs, namely, "*Sonepur in the Sambalpur Tract*" (1911) and the "*Orissa in the Making*" (1925) were acclaimed as scholarly works though they were highly of a parochial nature.

In fact Bijoy Chandra Majumdar's personal efforts to present the history of Orissa in a highly parochial degraded manner was just part of the the campaign by some Bengali elite who were out to scuttle the efforts of the Oriyas to regroup themselves and claim a separate identity of their own. On those few Bengalis who spearheaded this concerted campaign against a separate identity of the Oriyas for more than half a century, Bijoy Chandra Majumdar played a significant role. These Bengali elite starting from Rajendra Lal Mitra in 1860s and 1870s till Bijoy Chandra Majumdar in 1920s, dwelt upon some references made by William Wilson Hunter in his "*Orissa*" to ascribe a Bengali identity for the great Orissan monuments like the Konark and Bhubaneswar Temples and for the Gaṅgā rulers of Orissa.[31] References are replete in his works where Majumdar tried to distort completely the facts of Orissan history. In the '*Typical Selections from Oriya Literature*' Majumdar writes that "the Gaṅgās in order to keep up the language of their remote forefathers utterly disregarded Telgu which was the language of all the people who surrounded them at Mukhalingam and did not care either to the language of the people of their dependency of Orissa. Orissa has nothing to regret for it as this state of thing made the people of Orissa to resort to their own resources to develop an altogether new form of literature even though in the matter of language Oriya bore and still bears an intimate relation with Bengali."[32] The next point of importance, Majumdar argues is the script of the text. A good many texts of the Gaṅgā time including stone inscriptions prove unmistakably that the very Bengali script which is now in use in Bengal, was in use in Eastern Orissa at least till the middle of the 14th century. Again the script which is met with in the records of the Kośalā Guptās and of the early Bhanjās is exactly the script which was in use in Bengal in those days.[34] Majumdar also spoke much about the relations that subsisted between Orissa and Bengal and referred to his "*Orissa in Making*" for his elaboration in this regard. To substantiate his arguments he tried to trace all kinds of cultural union of Orissa with Bengal in the early times. Orissa retains in her popular tradition (as it is done in Bengal) the mythical names of '*Khana*' and '*Dak*' as the authors of some popular proverbs and homely adages. Sabhamkara is held both in Orissa and Bengal to have been the progenitor of the system of arithmetic which is taught in all primary schools. It is of great interest to note that most of the symbols for many fractional numbers are alike in physical form in Orissa and Bengal. Majumdar also suggested to the Calcutta University to take up a comprehensive thesis on the subject for execution by research scholars connected with the Indian vernaculars.[35] All these explain to what extent Majumdar engaged himself in professing his bias against Orissan history and culture. His two works on Orissan history, namely, "*Sonepur in the Sambalpur Tract*" (1911) and '*Orissa in the Making*' (1925) are clear proofs of Majumdar's professed bias against Orissan history.

'*Orissa in the Making*' is more or less an enlarged edition of his earlier work '*Sonepur in the Sambalpur Tract*'. After the former book was published in the year 1911, Majumdar did many studies on the Bhanja rulers of Mayurbhanj and wrote a number of articles in the *Journal of Bihar and Orissa Research Society*. For this he had studied a number of copper-plate grants. These studies, Majumdar included in the '*Orissa in the Making*' which he got published in the year 1925 while serving as Lecturer of Anthropology, Comparative Philology and Vernacular studies at Calcutta University. Otherwise this book presents a carbon copy of the earlier book. This book is entirely silent on the Muslim rule in Orissa (1568-1750 A.D.), Marhatta rule in Orissa (1750-1803 A.D) and British rule in Orissa (1803 onwards) but it has elaborately dwelt upon the history of Sonepur right from the middle of the 16th century A.D. The Sonepur royal family has been taken as the main theme of the book. This royal family has also been considered by Majumdar as among the makers of modern Orissa. The geographical account of Orissa as written in the '*Sonepur in the Sambalpur Tract*' has been entirely copied down in the '*Orissa in the Making*'. similarly the descriptions of the royal families and ruling chiefs of Sonepur, Bolangir and Sambalpur have also been copied down.

In writing these two books, otherwise scholarly works, Majumdar had been very choosy in selecting the sources for use. This might as well have been done with an ulterior motive to substantiate his preconceived notions on Orissan history so as to relate the Bengali superiority and at the same time satisfy the requiremts for his eulogy of the Sonepur royal family. He heavily relied upon one *Madhya Pradesh Gazetteer* published by Sir A. Grant in the year 1867 but whose real existence has seriously been doubted.[36] As a result of this he came out with so many erroneous conclusions so much so that the book '*Orissa in the Making*' came to be considered as one full of errors.[37]

In both these books Shri Majumdar has only made comparative studies of some ruling families of the state instead of presenting a complete history of the Province. Taking the help of '*Orissa Feudatory Gazetteers*', Shri Majumdar has confusingly described the rulers of Mayurbhanj. At one place he referred to one Raja Jai Singh who was a relative of the Raja of Jaipur in Rajputana[38] and at another place he described the same man as the son of the celebrated Raja Man Singh of Jaipur. At another reference he took the same man as a foreigner of the United Provinces who came to Orissa at the time of the invasion of Orissa by Raja Man Singh.

Similarly he described the early Bhanja rulers as historical and at the same time stressed upon the legends to explain the historicity of the Chauhan rulers. He has tried his best to prove categorically that the modern Bhanja rulers did not have any relation to the early Bhanja rulers. For establishing this he studied many copper-plate grants and published articles in the *Journal of Bihar and Orissa Research Society* in the year 1916. This was differently explained in the earlier book '*Sonepur in the Sambalpur Tract*' wherein he had described the modern Bhanja rulers as the successors. But when Majumdar became conscious that this conclusion might not be liked by the Chauhan family, he somehow dragged himself to prove the contrary.[40] For proving this conclusion, he deliberately depended on falsehoods. In order to disprove any relationship between the early and modern Bhanja rulers, Majumdar noted that the royal insignia of the Bhanja family was the lotus[41] which in reality was the peacock and not the lotus. He equally confusingly studied and translated the copper-plate grants of Kanka Bhanja. All these clearly indicate that one cannot expect just an iota of truth from the person who misinterpreted the official records.[42] Further he has given many vague explanations to prove that the Bhanja rulers were feudatories of the Chauhan rulers. Majumdar also tried to prove that the rulers of Mayurbhanj and Keonjhar submitted before the Chauhan rulers. According to Majumdar, the Chauhan rulers of Patnagarh and Sambalpur issued taxation decrees on the rulers of Mayurbhanj and Keonjhar. These documents are not available. The writer of the *Madhya Pradesh Gazetteer* or his responsible assistants might have seen these papers before 1861 A.D.[43]

Similarly confusing and biased are his descriptions of the acceptance of suzerainty of Sambalpur by eighteen Garrjat states. This reference has been dealt with in a different manner by historians. Though the references of Kittoe, Richard Temple and Grant speak firmly to the contrary, Majumdar carefully avoided these references and notes. He even manipulated these documents to prove his point. He also quite erroneously included Mayurbhanj and Keonjhar among the eighteen Garrjat states for which he did not extend any kind of substantial proof or evidence.

While Majumdar brought substantial changes in his earlier conclusions while writing '*Orissa in the Making*' and particularly in reference to the Bhanja rulers, he was however more careful to keep his history of the Sonepur royal family intact in both the books. He even tried to prove that the Chauhan rulers of Sambalpur maintained their independence during the Moghul and Marhatta rule which is absolutely wrong because the rulers of Patnagarh, Sonepur and Sambalpur of the Sambalpur tract had already accepted the suzerainty of the Moghul rulers. During the Marhatta rule also the Sambalpur tract was very much under the suzerainty of the Marhattas. This is evident from Mr. Motte's report of 1766.

All these deliberate references in '*Orissa in the Making*' and the '*Sonepur in the Sambalpur Tract*' are sufficient to describe these two books as a total eulogy of the Sonepur ruling Chiefs of whom he was the advisor and under whose patronage he wrote both the books.

But while justifying the title of the book'*Orissa in the Making*' Bijoy Chandra Majumdar bacame conscious of his Bengal with Kosala and Trikalinga country, he described Yajati Keshari of the Somavaṁśī dynasty as a Bengali. The Murarijamura copper-plate grant of Yajati refers to Dutta and Ghosh titles as the employees of the royal court and Majumdar took this for granted that the ruler who issued the grant was a Bengali. He also wrongly interpreted the word '*vaṁśa*' as '*baṅga*' and thus did not hesitate to call the ruler as Bengali. Considering Yajati Kesari as a Bengali Majumdar depended upon the logic to explain that the Somavaṁśīs who were Bengalis, were the makers of Orissa.[44] In his '*Lists of Northern Indian Inscriptions*' Professor D.R. Bhandarkar of Calcutta University accepted the readings of Majumdar and went on to accept that the Kesari rulers described in *Madāla Pañjī* were synonymous with the Somavaṁśīs. As a result of this distortion, the Ganga rulers also came to be dubbed as Bengalis by Majumdar who deliberately tried to prove home this point.

'*Orissa in the Making*' thus came out to be a historical writing with clearcut preconceived conclusions. Any preconceived conclusion always needs the manipulation of source materials. Bijoy Chandra Majumdar quite naturally manipulated his source materials in order to satisfy his royal patron, the ruling chief of the Sonepur states. He also exhibited the Bengali complexity and bias against the separate identity of the Orissan people. Thus by manipulating the source materials to determine preconceived historical conclusions, Majumdar fell far short of objectivity. Though the book presents a somewhat connected account of the history of Orissa, the conclusions of Majumdar are heavily biased and are at odds with the known facts of Orissan history. He has certainly put in lots of labour for his work which is out to denigrate the Bhanja rulers. Paramananda Acharya says "*Orissa in the Making*' was not written to provide any historical information. Whatever historical information has been provided in the book is merely a comparative picture of the Bhanja and Chauhan rulers, largely intended to explain the greatness of the Sonepur kings. In the book '*Sonepur in the Sambalpur Tract*' he has tried to describe the ancient Bhanja rulers as the predecessors of the modern Bhanja rulers. In this effort when he came to know that the greatness of the Chauhan rulers cannot be easily proved, he tried to forcefully change this conclusion and did not hesitate to alter the historical records. From such individuals like Majumdar historically trusted conclusions cannot just be expected. '*Orissa in the Making*' cannot be described as anything more than a royal eulogy of the Sonepur ruling chiefs."[45]

It might as well be that his bias against Orissan history proper was largely prompted by the language movement current in the then Bengal to prove that Oriya was not a separate language and did not qualify for being so. Thus Bijoy Chandra Majumdar took extremely parochial, regional and biased considerations while writing the history of Orissa. He also took a stand to put Orissan history and culture in a highly degraded manner vis-à-vis the complexity of the Bengali superiority. In both these processes Bijoy Chandra Majumdar completely overlooked the scientific character of history writing and lacked objectivity.

References

1. The detail of the Life and Times of Babu Rajendra Lal Mitra is based on K.K. Dasgupta's article on Rajendra Lal Mitra in the Statesman, Calcutta dated 01 March, 1992 entitled "*Historical Man*."
2. *Utkal Dipika*, 05 September 1868, p.142.

3. Bansidhar Mohanty, *Odia Bhasa Andolan*, Cuttack, 1989, p.27.
4. Odia Ekta Swatantra Bhasa Noi, Text reproduced in Oriya translation in Bansidhar Mohanty, *op.cit.*, 1989, Cuttack.
5. *Utkal Dipika*, 8/9, 3, 1873, p.34.
6. Rajendra Lal Mitra, *Antiquities of Orissa*, Vol.I, 1875 & Vol.II, 1880, Calcutta.
7. Rajendra Lal Mitra, *op.cit.*, Vol. I, p.ii.
8. K.K. Dasgupta, *op.cit.*, 1992.
9. Rajendra Lal Mitra, *Antiquities of Orissa*, Vol. I, Introduction.
10. *Ibid.*
11. *Ibid.*
12. Rajendra Lal Mitra, *op.cit.*, p.243.
13. Rajendra Lal Mitra, *op.cit.*, Introduction.
14. Rajendra Lal Mitra, *op.cit.*, Vol I, Preface, 1875.
15. Rajendra Lal Mitra, *op.cit.*, 1880, Vol II, p.66-68
16. *Ibid.*, p.73.
17. *Ibid.*, p.213.
18. Rajendra Lal Mitra quoted in K.K. Dasgupta, *op.cit.*, 1992.
19. Rajendra Lal Mitra quoted in K.K. Dasgupta, *op.cit.*, 1992.
20. Rajendra Lal Mitra, *op.cit.*, Vol I, 1875, p.5.
21. *Ibid.*, p.9.
22. *Ibid.*, p.85-86.
23. *Ibid.*, p.7.
24. K.K. Dasgupta, *op.cit.*, 1992
25. Rajendra Lal Mitra, *op.cit.*, 1875, p.84-87.
26. Rajendra Lal Mitra, *op.cit.*, 1880, p.243.
27. *Ibid.*, p.167.
28. *Ibid.*, p.268.
29. *Ibid.*, p.26.
30. *Ibid.*, p.78
31. Paramananda Acharya, *Odissara Pratnattva O Anyanya Prabandha*, Bhubaneswar, 1969, p.372.
32. B.C. Majumdar (Ed) *Typical Selections from Oriya Literature,* Vol. II, 1925, University of Calcutta, Introduction, p.xiii.
33. *Ibid.*, p.xiii.
34. *Ibid.*, p.xiii.

35. *Ibid.*, p.xix.
36. Paramananda Acharya, *op.cit.*, p.234.
37. B. Singhdeo "*Majumdar's Memorable Works on Orissa*" in *Journal of Andhra Historical Reserch Society*, 2, 384, (1927), p.300-02.
38. B.C. Majumdar, '*Orissa in the Making*' 1925, Calcutta, p.239.
39. *Ibid.*, p.217.
40. Paramananda Acharya, *op.cit.*, p.236.
41. B.C. Majumdar, in *Journal of Bihar and Orissa Research Society*, Vol. II, 1916, p.356.
42. Paramananda Acharya, *op.cit.*, p.236.
43. P Acharya, *op.cit.*, p.232.
44. B.C. Majumdar, '*Orissa in the Making*', 1925, Calcutta, p.173 and 175.
45. P. Acharya, *op.cit.*, p.237.

8

Some Sober Historical Writings on Orissa

Besides the colonialist, nationalists biased historical writing on Orissan history before independence, some historiographers made a modest attempt at presenting sober historical writings on Orissa. Two notable features are identified in the case of the historian of this category. Most of them, excepting Rakhal Das Banerjee concentrated only on the studies of the art and architecture of Orissa and made a somewhat sober presentation of historical ideas. Again excepting Rakhal Das Banerjee who was an archaeologist and Beni Madhab Barua who was a Professor of Pali and Ancient Indian History—none of them were professional historians. While Bishen Swarup and Manmohan Ganguly were engineers and Professor Nirmal Kumar Bose was an anthropologist and Manmohan Chakraborty was an administrator. Pandit Binayak Mishra was a Lecturer in Oriya. Of these Rakhal Das Banerji presented the most comprehensive and complete history of Orissa in two volumes.

I. MANMOHAN CHAKRABORTY (1863-1919)

Manmohan Chakraborty's association with Orissa was as an administrator of the British government. He was serving in Orissa during the last two decades of the nineteenth century when many scholars including William Wilson Hunter, John Beames, Rajendra Lal Mitra et al. were engaged in serious historical research on Orissa at this time. Dwarikanath Chakraborty, the father of Manmohan

Chakraborty, was the Superintendent of Schools in Orissa and had a better rapport with the then European scholars in Orissa. This association might pretty well have attracted Manmohan Chakraborty toward historical research on Orissa. This administrator historian, who was born in the year 1863, had his earlier education in Cuttack. Later he went to Kolkatta to pursue higher studies. He joined the Provincial Civil Service in the year 1886 and had his initial posting at Cuttack. For many years he served as an administrator at Cuttack, Jajpur, Puri, and other important places of Orissa. He had thus years of close association with Orissan life and culture. He was elected a fellow of the Royal Asiatic Society of Bengal in the year 1912. He had been a member of this scholarly institute since 1890. He regularly contributed research articles to the *Journal of the Asiatic Society*. His area of research was Orissa and Bengal and he wrote three dozen scholarly articles and books on various aspects of the history, language and culture of Orissa and Bengal. Most of these writings were published in the Asiatic Society's Journal. He died on September 15, 1919 rather at an early age of fifty-six. Some of his articles on different aspects of Orissan history and culture are listed below:

(1) 'Weights of the Gold and Silver Currencies of ancient Orissa' in *Journal of Asiatic Society of Bengal 1892.*

(2) 'Essays on the Oriya script' in *Proceeding of the Asiatic Society of Bengal,* 1892.

(3) 'Oriya Script in 15th and 16th centuries' in *Proceeding of the Asiatic Society of Bengal,* 1893.

(4) 'Two Copper-Plates of Kulasthamba Deva' in *Proceeding of the Asiatic Society of Bengal,* 1985.

(5) 'Two Copper-Plates of Narasimha Deva of Orissa' in *Proceeding of the Asiatic Society of Bengal* 1897.

(6) 'Oriya language and literature' parts I&II in *Proceeding of the Asian Society of Bengal,* 1897.

(7) 'Oriya language and literature' parts III & IV in *Proceeding of the Asiatic Society of Bengal,* 1898.

(8) 'Inscriptions of Kapilendra Deva' in *Proceeding of the Asiatic Society of Bengal,*1990.

(9) "Script of the Inscription of the Jayapala Deva"in *Proceeding of the Asiatic Society of Bengal,* 1900.

(10) "Khandagiri and Udayagiri Caves'' in *Proceeding of the Asiatic Society of Bengal,* 1900.

(11) "Chronology of the Eastern Gangas of Kalinga'' in *Journal of the Asiatic Society of Bengal,* 1903.

(12) Portion on history of *Balesore and Cuttack Gazetteer,* Government publication, 1906.

(13) "Historical geography of Orissa in 16th century'' in *Journal of the Asiatic Society of Bengal* 1916.

(14) "One Oriya Script from Konark'' in *Journal of Bihar and Orissa Researcn Society,* 1917.

His main approach to Orissan history was directed toward a proper assessment and interpretation of the original sources of Orissan history so that an accurate chronology of Orissa's political history could be determined. Thus his attention was obviously drawn towards determining the historicity of the temple chronicle '*Madāla Pañjī*' on which almost all his predecessors like Stirling, Hunter, Rajendra Lal Mitra and many others heavily relied upon. As has been noticed earlier, these writers accept '*Madāla Pañjī*' as their primary source material. But Manmohan Chakraborty doubted the historicity of this document and justifiably pointed out as to whether it should be accepted as a reliable historical source material. In an article in the *Journal of the Asiatic Society of Bengal*, Manmohan Chakraborty writes, "the medieval history of Orissa is still in the dark. '*Madāla Pañjī*' or Jagannath Temple chronicle is the only source material of this period of Orissan history. But this cannot be accepted as reliable until this is totally corroborated". His doubt was confirmed when he came across two copper-plate inscriptions belonging to King Narasimha Deva IV of the Gaṅgā dynasty. Being an epigraphist of some distinction, he thoroughly studied these copper-plates and pointed out the discrepancies in the names of the Gaṅgā kings as found in the '*Madāla Pañjī*'. When corroborated with those mentioned, Manmohan Chakraborty came out firmly with his statement regarding the reliability of '*Madāla Pañjī*' as a source material for writing a sober and scientific history of Orissa. Addressing the members of the Asiatic Society in 1882 Manmohan Chakraborty said, despite researches by Hunter, Stirling, Prinsep, Rajendra Lal Mitra et al.Orissan history still remained in the dark, because their main source for research the '*Madāla Pañjī*' is unsatisfactory, incomplete and based on confusing and contradictory details. In many of his articles and writings on Oriya language and literature he seriously focussed his attention on the minute examination of source materials for their historical accuracy as well as reliability for this purpose, Manmohan Chakraborty extensively studied Oriya literature and the available inscriptions. Though at that time John F. Fleet was considered to be an expert on epigraphical studies, Manmohan Chakraborty's efforts to decipher the inscriptions was no less praiseworthy since he was interested in collecting the accurate information for his historical writings on Orissa. This is more explicit from his final statement on '*Madāla Paṅjī*'. He says "the historical value of '*Madāla Paṅjī*' has been highly exaggerated. In this the basic facts have not been correctly stated. Besides this, since the historical matters were written on palm leaves these were copied three to four times within a space of only one hundred years and naturally incorrect evidences crept in during the copying. Lastly because of continuous Muslim invasion, this work was completely stopped for a long time. During this period many of these manuscripts might have been destroyed. As such there are many incorrect evidences in these manuscripts. And without sufficient proof these cannot be accepted. Later scribes have been utterly confused on their writings on one particular dynasty. This is because there are five or six different manuscripts of the '*Madāla Paṅjī*'. There might be historical facts in one or the other of these manuscripts. What problems have been faced in fixing chronologies is evidenced from the dynastic chronologies we have on Khurdha dynasty."[3]

Thus in all his efforts to study the inscription and the grants was inherent the idea to corroborate the evidences of '*Madāla Paṅjī*'.On that basis he challenged many conclusions of his predecessor historians and contemporaries including John F. Fleet. In all these exercises of Manmohan Chakraborty was also implicit the idea to fix an accurate chronology of Orissan history which at that time was in a state of utter confusion. In an article in the *Journal of the Asiatic Society of Bengal* in the year 1899 on an inscription of Kapilendra Deva found from Gopinath Pur in Cuttack district, he had drawn a detailed chronology based solely on inspirational evidences and rejected the chronology based on '*Madāla Paṅjī*.

In 1903, Manmohan Chakraborty brought out another brilliant article on the 'chronology of the eastern Gaṅgās of Kalinga' in the pages of the Asiatic Society's Journal. For this rather long essay running into over fifty pages Shri Chakraborty laboured for about a decade and it is indeed one of the masterpieces of historical research on the subject. Shri Chakraborty fixed the chronology of the Gaṅgā rulers of the Kalinga in this article which is mostly followed by the historians down to the present day. In these painstaking pieces of historical research he studied all the inscriptions available on the Gaṅgā period and fixed the chronology of this period in an accurate, scientific and objective manner. He drew the chronology of over 700 years of the history of Orissa starting from the rule of the eastern Gaṅgā till the British conquest of Orissa in 1803 A.D.

After1903, Manmohan Chakraborty did not concentrate more on Orissan history and shifted his attention towards the history of Bengal and Mithila, and wrote a number of books and articles on these two areas.

In historical studies, Manmohan Chakraborty entwined cultural history with political history and, for this, he gave more attention towards the study of historical geography. His article 'Historical Geography of Orissa in the 15th and 16th centuries appeared in the year 1916 in the *Journal of the Asiatic Society of Bengal*. In this article he made a detailed analysis of the places of Orissa and listed the names of the temples of Orissa with necessary details. He had tried his best to give the correct Oriya version of the names of the places of Orissa mentioned in *Ain-I-Akbari*. He collected the names of the temple and necessary detail from the '*Madāla Pañjī*' and utilized them for his purpose after proper scrutiny.

Manmohan Chakraborty's contribution to Orissan historiography lay in his attempt to present the history of Orissa based on the scientific interpretation of the source materials. His main thrust on historical research was thus concentrated on the interpretation of the source materials, rather than writing history proper. His writings on the historical geography and culture of Orissa was of secondary importance since he was more interested in reconstructing the political history of Orissa on the basis of surer historical evidences. His competence as an epigraphist helped him in this task and through his compositions he presented a somewhat sober historical account on Orissa.

II. BISHEN SWARUP

Bishen Swarup belongs, historiographically speaking, to the school of architecture. Like many of his contemporaries he concentrated his attention on the historical monuments of Orissa and particularly Konark, the finest specimen of the Kalinga style of temple-building art and, the culmination of sustaining art activity stretching over several centuries, and the manifestation of superior workmanship of the artists of Orissa. It is obvious on the part of every visitor to Konark to look at this great monument from his own angle, and, thus, every writer starting from Smith to Fergusson and other modern art historians describe the images of Konarka from their artistic angles.

Amongst the host of writers who threw light on Konark, the name of Bishen Swarup finds a special mention. An engineer in the Public Works Department, he evinced keen interest in temple architecture and tried to study Konark from an altogether different angle. He did not forget to highlight the religious and other cultural aspect of the monument. He paid better attention to this edifice in his work and admitted any mistakes that might have occurred in this exercise. He wrote in the preface to the book *'Konark: The Black Pagoda of Orissa'* published in the year 1910,[4] that the subject "is very interesting and requires better attention that I could give, as the book was written amidst numerous other official works. The same I hope will be accepted as an apology for any mistakes that might have crept in."[5]

Bishen Swarup highlights the different aspects of the temple namely, topography, description, sanctity, date, religion, architecture, sculpture, engineering and causes of the collapse of the main temple. He describes the temple and the engineering detail of its portion in an immaculate manner. Since he observed everything from his professional point of view i. e, engineering, hardly any architectural aesthetics is discussed in the book.

In writing the book, Bishen Swarup drew materials from his own excavation of the site (of course this was restricted only to the discussion of architectural engineering of the Temple). He also heavily referred to the works of earlier writers like Fergusson, Blochman, and Rajendra Lal Mitra and literary accounts like the Vedas, the Buddhist Jātaka stories, the Purāṇās, and the local legends to discuss the religion of the Konark Temple and the festivals celebrated by the people around and, more so, the ones connected with the temple itself.

Bishen Swarup writes that with all projections and recesses of the Konark Temple with which the walls are ornamented, the squarish chapter and design of the temple is fully visible, unlike the *Jagamohana* at Puri or Bhubaneswar which lost their form in these projections. The arrangements of different parts of the body of the temple as also their design and the moulding are the same as in the plinth or the walls of the *Jagamohana*. But being of a bigger scale here, the modellings are deeper and broader. The different scrolls and flora designs are neater and clearer. He further goes on to explain the advantage of such a bigger scale and says that it has been taken not in saving labour but in bringing out a finer work and showing richer details which are not possible in the smaller plan.

While explaining the engineering of the temple Swarup admits that is not much to say on the engineering of the Orissa temple no calculations were made of the stability and proportionate size of each part of the temple which was fixed only by experience. Writing the book mainly to describe the works of the Public Works Department, of which he was an engineer engaged in excavating the ruins of the Konark Temple, Bishen Swarup considered the length and breadth of walls, roof, balconies of the existing structure of the temple to determine the possible height of the structure when in complete state at 45 feet from the plinth.[9]

Bishen Swarup was in all praise for "plinth of the Konark Temple which, being of suitable height and leaving a regular form all round, gives the structure an appearance of solidity and stateliness. This necessary portion of temple architecture has been omitted in many of the temples. The Lingraj Temple has not got it. At Puri there is a plinth but so irregular and broken up as to be useless."

In order to study the character of architecture of Konark Temple, and more so, to present a comparison, Bishen Swarup gave a general outline of the evaluation of the temple in northern India and considered the Konark as built in the style of northern Hindu temples. Presenting a comparative picture of the Orissan temples with other temples in northern India which bear close resemblance to each other, Bishen Swarup made some generalization on temple architecture particularly for determining the antiquity of different temples. He says that the considerations of the evolution of conical form of shaft in upper India from that of northern Hindu temples and also the tapering form help in determining to a certain extent, the relative antiquity of these temples. On the same consideration it may not be out of place to say that the taller a temple proportionately is as compared to the one stunted, taking, of course, that the art is in progressive stage. But as regards the very origin of the temple architecture in Orissa, Bishen Swarup remained highly speculative. He says, "the question however get more difficult when we come to think of how the temples of Orissa came into existence, what the original was, that has been improved upon in form.

There are no older temples or other structures bearing resemblance to guide us. Bishen Swarup's analysis of the temple, its iconography, sculpture, religion as well as fall are based on logical arguments and precision as the engineering of the temple, though all his conclusions can not be totally accepted for their intrinsic value. He has tried to analyse the antiquities of the temple and the worship, the festival celebrated there, the Chandravaga River nearby, on the light of local traditions and interpretations of different inferences. But in most cases he relied heavily upon sheer mathematical calculations, which do not have any historical value as such.

Discussing the art and architecture of the Orissan temples, he drew heavily from Rajendra Lal Mitra and Fergusson but did not agree with them particularly on their opinion on decay in art. "Rajendra Lal Mitra is evidently with the view that the temple of Konarka is a later construction than that of Puri and does not accept the theory of decay in art and assigns a comparatively inartistic look of the latter. It is true that the plaster and the white wash have done a good deal towards making the building look ugly but that cannot account for the want or grace, solidity and stateliness, nor for the appearance of clumsiness in structure. These are architectural defects, defect of design of working out its essential parts, as distinguished from ornamentation and minor sculptural detail and so inferiority of architecture".

Bishen Swarup has made very little discussion on the erotic sculptures of the Konark Temple but describes them as real work of art. "Amongst the human figures the fairer sex is much better shown than the male and some of those figures are real works of art. The Hindu idea of beauty may differ in certain respects from that of other countries but does not make much of a difference in a really beautiful carving".

At another place he discussed the opinions of Fergusson and Rajendra Lal Mitra on this aspect of Konark sculpture and says that even if we take these indecent figures as giving indication of the religious views of the builder, it points to the mystic '*Bama Marga*' or 'Left handed shaivism' rather than to the Vaishnava doctrine of bhakti of love. It is generally supposed that the 'Bama Marga' form of the tantric worship is a later form of the Shaivism but it is inculcated even in '*Atharva Veda*' through Buddhism gave an impetus to it."

He however lead under preconceived notions to portray Konark Temple as a Buddhist temple. He had perhaps the predetermined conclusion to arrive at, which prompted him to argue that way. He, of course, analyzed the rituals in the Konark Temple in this direction. He considered the temple of northern India owing a Buddhist origin since his intention was to study the Konark Temple, he examined the Orissan temples that way starting with the first premise that the Orissan temple belonged to the northern India group of temples. He says, the temple of the Hindus started in the revived religion did not discard everything of the religion it was gradually displaying but assimilated with it. The monasteries or the mathas which so much abound in different parts of India, especially in Orissa are copies of Buddhist Viharas. As the architecture can vary but slightly by the change of religion, it is quite safe to conclude that form of the temples was also taken by the Hindus from the religious structure of the Buddhist Viharas. The plan of temple, the Amla, the topes, the rail etc., have been taken from the Buddhist religious (chaitya) caves and modified to suit the mystic worship early saivism.

On the fall of the temple again, Bishen Swarup was convinced of the "structural failure of the temple i.e. the removal of the Shikhara as being responsible for the fall of the temple. He was, however, sure that the disintegration leading to the present state of the temple was gradual. He again interestingly explained the tradition to study the down of the temple seems to be on the double meaning of the term *'kumbha'*. It means a water jar and it is synonymous with the kalaśa. Also 'kumbha pathar' stand for a loadstone. We know the Mohammedan invaders carried away the kumbha or kalaśa of the temple after a long time had passed and the real facts (sic) of the event had been forgotten, their booty was taken to be a loadstone. The rest of the story it required no genius to frame.

Whatever be his myopic intention to trace out the Buddhistic origin of the Konarka Temple, Bishen Swarup was no less patriotic for he takes a great pride in this great Oriya monument. He does not believe in any attribution of the external influence on the evolution of the Konark Temple through he lightheartedly blames the sculptures for certain defects as muscle showing on human body, etc. These defects are mainly due to the sculptures for purely copying nature instead of making their own ideal from her best production.

His gratitude and nationalistic spirit is revealed in his own words. "It deserved heartfelt thanks of the Indians in general and people of Orissa in particular for bringing out and presenting at a great expense one of the finest works of their long forgotten art."

Bishen Swarup's '*Konark : the Black Pagoda of Orissa*' published in the year 1910 stands contemporaneous with the monumental work 'Orissa and her remains' by Manmohan Ganguly though the latter book was published in the year 1912. The work, though relatively smaller in volume compared to Ganguly's, certainly is a useful contribution to the study of Orissan architecture, despite all limitation, for Bishen Swarup was a non-professional art critic rather than a serious art historian. The book is devoid of any proper study of the aesthetic aptitude of the architecture of the temple basically from the point of view of engineering and thus remained as a useful addition to the study Konark Temple in particular and Orissan art and architecture in general.

III. MANMOHAN GANGULY (1882-1926)

Manmohan Ganguly's introduction into Orissan history is a matter of accident as he himself admits in the preface to his monumental work "Orissa and her remains"[27] published in the year 1912. "When some six years ago, sitting by the side of the Taj Mahal one moonlit night I decided on writing a systematic history of Indian architecture, I little knew that the first scene of my labours would be enacted in Orissa. I was led there by a mysterious dispensation of providence and had accordingly to choose my line of action."[28] Once he introduced and engaged himself fully to the study of the Orissan architecture he convinced himself that Orissan architecture and art represent the pure form of Indo-Aryan style of architecture. Like many other European and Bengali historians Ganguly chose to concentrate on the art of Orissa in particular and that of India general.

In that process Manmohan Ganguly came out with perhaps the first ever scientific and systematic study of the art and architecture of Orissa. In his foreword to the book 'Orissa and her remains', J.G.Woodruff writes "the present book, so far as I am aware, is the first work by an Indian author in which an attempt has been made to treat the subject from a scientific order of view."[29]

The contemporary work which Manmohan Ganguly chose to refer before setting himself upon the task of writing 'Orissa and her remains' include, Sterling's articles in *Asiatic Researches*; Rajendra Lal Mitra's '*Antiquities of Orissa*'(1875 &1880); and William Wilson Hunter's *Orissa*. He had also consulted the writing of Prinsep and Major Kittoe who had in the early thirties of the 19th century brought to light new antiquities and inscriptions. He had also read Bishen Swarup's '*Konark*' which was published before Ganguly's '*Orissa, Her Remains*'.

The importance of his book 'Orissa and her remains', lay in the efforts to study and investigate the magnificent monuments and other architectural remains of Orissa which testified to India's past glory. According to Sir J.G. Woodruff, "ever since 1834 when Ram Raz wrote his remarkable essay on Indian architecture until Manmohan Ganguly wrote this book, no Indian, with the lone exception of perhaps Dr Rajendra Lal Mitra in the 70s of the nineteenth century, concerned himself with any such investigation of the profound interest of the west in the east which has been measured reflect in this country. If the interest aroused here was yet, it has something that it had risen at all oppressed as it was on the one hand by indifferent and, on the other, by progressive industrialism and by other of similar narrow outlook. Given this opposition such work either literary or by way of collection as had been recently done by P.C. Majumdar, Bishen

Swarup, Nagendra Nath Basu, Kumar Sarat Chandra Ray and Manmohan Ganguly had the greater merit."[30]

In presenting the monuments and more in writing the book, Manmohan Ganguly depended solely on investigation of *in situ* monuments existing in Orissa. Generally, ground plans are shown from measurements taken by Ganguly himself, such as, the ratio of the height of the Vimana to the length of base. The direction of the temples which was generally eastwards had been determined and the author then deals in greater details the basement (pabhaga), the temple wall (vada) and toward (shikhar). Ganguly puts forward formulas for the thickness of the walls relative to the height of the edifice to be raised, and the other details of the temple architecture. All these explain that Manmohan Ganguly had presented the original material on the monument of Orissa. Though his main approach was to write a systematic study of the Indo-Aryan style of architecture as seen in the Orissan monuments, nonetheless he has given a brief note on the political history of Orissa. This is because he feels that the development of architecture in a country is inseparably entwined with the political developments.That is why a knowledge of the political history of a region becomes imperative for a sincere and proper study of the development of architecture of a region.

Before going on to study the historical idea of Manmohan Ganguly as perceived from his study of Orissan architecture, it would be worthwhile to present a brief note on the content of his magnum opus : 'Orissa and her remains'.

In the second chapter of the book Ganguly has attempted to present a brief outline of the political history of the province. Chapter v, vi and vii form the most important portions of the book. In these chapters Ganguly had presented original material for the first time and enunciated there is in the principle of the Indo-Aryan architecture and sculpture. The last two chapters of the book are just illustrative of chapters v and vi. Chapter v deals with the main features and subsidiary parts of the Orissan temple and relative of the different section in the general ground plan. Chapter vi classified Orissan decorative program and contain very useful information and observation as to the Devtas represented in the temples of "Shiva, Vaiṣṇava and Sūrya division of Hindu worshipper's the rhythm of spacing, ornaments and its character, and the relative proportion of the representation of the human body as ascertained by actual measurement and compared with those given in the 'śukranīti' which Ganguly has believed, to be more in accordance with Orissan sculpture than 'manasara' used by Rajendra Lal Mitra. Ganguly gives a tabular statement with great care on the relative proportion of the navatala and the "saptatal" images. Chapter vi deals with the building material used and the author has made an analysis of these and the metal beams such as those found in Konark.

The remaining chapters of the book give interesting details personally examined by the author of the celebrated temple of Bhubaneswar, Puri and Konark.

The way Ganguly deals with this topic in the book reveals that due to professionally being an engineer in the Public Works Department, he was more careful about the technical details of the temple architecture than pure aesthetic appeal, and we are thus completely devoid of having a chronological study of architecture and sculpture in his monumental work "Orissa and her remains".

Before going on to discuss the historical trends and approaches in the work of Manmohan Ganguly, it would be worth while to trace first of all his particular aim in writing history and reason why he chose to write on Orissa even though he restricted himself to the study of work and architecture only. Nevertheless he talked about the political history of the Orissa with which the development of the art and architecture is intimately connected. In fact Manmohan Ganguly made his intention clear that he tried "*Orissa and her Remains*" to give a scientific exposition to the principle of the architecture and sculpture obtained from Orissa.[31] In the process he came out with the first ever systematic and comprehensive work on the subject in India. By scientific exposition he would mean the exact representation of architectural and art remains as found from the *in situ* examination of monuments. Accordingly he did not spare any effort to take measurement of the temple and other architecture and sculptural remains and dealt in all their parts and sections, main and subsidiary. He also classified Orissan decoration and gave very useful information and observation of the sculptural aspects of Orissan monument. About the presence of various erotic figures in Orissan sculpture, Ganguly raised an interesting question. He was not prepared to accept the 'ādhyātmik' or spiritual explanation normally given for the presence of erotic figures. This is because he felt 'adhyatmik' explanation is not scientifically convincing. Modern sentiments not to speak of sentimentalists, are of no use for the understanding of ancient realism. Probably no one particular theory can adequately explain the presence of such figures as are found as Dr Materlink has shown an old gothic cathedral as an Indian temple though in the former case the images are not too numerous and are more grotesque.[32]

In analysis of Orissan architecture Shri Ganguly has followed John Ruskin's model of architecture. This arranges itself in five heads as devotional, memorial, civil, military and domestic. The statistical equilibrium, as he explained of an Orissan temple, was simple due to the combined action of the simple vertical action and reaction.[33]

There are quite a few reasons why Shri Ganguly chose to write on Orissa for this scientific exercise. In fact he started with the premise that the purest form of Indo-Aryan architecture and art was prevalent only in Orissa,[34] a point contested by the historians.[35]

It is a patent fact that Orissa form peculiar interest of her own alike from an archaeological and architectural point of veiw not shared in common by the other Indian provinces. It is important by reason of its being the seat of Indo-Aryan style in the present form".[36]

Shri Ganguly was convinced from his analysis that not even the last vestige of the foreign influence is found in Orissa.[37] The fusion of religion and its influence on art is prominately traceable in Orissan art forms. The cosmopolitan character of Buddhism is still traceable at Puri."[38]

Above all, Shri Ganguly was convinced of the greatness of the gloroius tradition of Orissa. "Taking everything into consideration I am convinced that Orissa has far glorious tradition of past history than Bengal may possibly claim and that she occupied a more prominent place than Bengal in the hierarchy of Indian nation."[39]

Amidst all his scientific explanations of Orissan architecture was an attitude inherent to find out the indigeneity of Orissan architecture in particular and in Indian architecture in general.

Attention here is drawn to the foreign influence on our architecture. Like most of his contemporary historians from Bengal who mainly laid the foundation of historical reaserch in India during the pre-independence days, Ganguly was critical of the British historian's approach towards the Indian history which has been termed as colonialist. It was inherent in the Indian mind as they wrote during the year of India's struggle for independence and the approach to Indian history by these two groups of scholars is sharply divided.

It is thus quite natural that Manmohan Ganguly took the conception of the European scholar on Indian history and culture as his first premise and then chose to explain scientifically the nature and characteristics of the Indian civilisation to prove their indigeneity so that Indian history could be explained in a realistic manner with all the true characteristics.

Writing on the political history of Orissa, Ganguly writes, "my attention was struck by the remark of an English scholar that our sacred dialect Sanskrit has been forged by the Brahman after the fashion of Greeks and that the two great national epics, the *Rāmāyaṇ* and the *Mahābhārat,* have been composed on the basics of Homer's *Illiad* and *Odyssey.* I had really to pause a while before I could proceed. In a most inconspicuous moment did Sir William Jones made the startling discovery that the Standrocote was Chandragupta and Pallibothra was Pataliputra, for since then the natural tendency of our oriental scholars have been to trace the growth of everything of our culture and civilisation to the Greek and Roman influence".[40]

Manmohan Ganguly was a bit conscious of his Bengali identity when he identifed himself distinctly with those scholars from Bengal like Rajendra Lal Mitra, Narendra Nath Basu et al. In claiming that Ananta Vāsudeva Temple of Bhubaneśwar is a Bengali monument. These scholars took exception to the presence of an inscription belonging to one Bhāvdeva Bhaṭṭa of Bengal and did not hesitate to ascribe the temple to the Bengalis. Manmohan Ganguly supported this stand of Rajendra Lal Mitra and other Bengali scholars.[41] He took this inscription to be a copy of the copper-plate grant composed by Raghavendra Kavi Shekhar, which stated that Harī Vermādev was King of Bengal and that the place of issue of this grant was Vikrampur.[42] Manmohan Ganguly in fact did this to prove that the Rameśwar Temple at Bhubaneśwar was built by this Bengali ruler.[43] Indeed for a long time, Rajendra Lal Mitra and other scholars like him subscribed to this stand about the Ananta Basudev Temple where the presence of Bhāva Deva Bhaṭṭa inscription provided them such an oppportunity. This position continued till Paramānanda Acharya proved that this controversial inscription did not originally belong to the Ananta Basudev Temple and that this was brought from Vikrampur near Dhaka and was implanted on this temple.[44]

Manmohan Ganguly outrightly rejected the concept of evolution as a method of historical interpretation and enquiry which was veritably followed by the European scholars with the ulterior motive of dating same archaeological remains to the comparatively recent period. He says "some European scholars and a few Indians in their train committed egregious blunder in thinking that the elaborate caves belong to a comparatively recent period. These scholars discovered the process of evolution. The term evolution, I am sorry to remark, has acquired some sort of notoreity by reason of its application in and out of season. The historian, the sociologist, and the cosmologists all cut their gordian knot at one stroke and it is evolution. Most aptly did Professor Huxley remarked in his "Science and culture" that some truths begin as heresies and end as superstitions. The theory of evolution is an apt illustration of this vivid apotheosis."[45]

Ganguly apprehended that the ulterior motive in discovering the gradual growth of the process of evolution in Udayagiri caves was to place the elaborate carved caves at a comparatively recent perlod and to prove conveniently that they are products of extraneous influences and that the stone architecture proper was introduced by the Greeks.

Manmohan Ganguly was convinced that religious zeal first manifested itself in charitable works and in the process of transmission to posterity became envascent or conventional. Hence, more conventional religious spirit must have manifested itself in conventional work of art and, accordingly, some of the caves at Udayagiri became nothing more than a dog's kennel. This does not necessarily warrant the application of evolutionary hypothesis. Similarly he argued that from the intercomunion existing between the Greeks and Indians, it cannot safely be ascertained which of the two nations copied from the other. If we admit that the Indians copied the boots from the Greeks what avails it to prove that Greeks necessarily influenced the architecture of Orissa.

On the other hand, Ganguly has given a cogent argument in favour of the indigenity of the Orissan architecture. For this also he presented a comparative picture of the Orissan and the Graeco-Roman architecture to obviate the difficulty posed by the absence of any extant old stone building in order to counteract the European scholars' Graeco-Roman Theory of Origin of Orissan architecture.

Not only that, following John Ruskin's model of architecture to study and analyse Orissan architecture under five heads viz devotional, memorial, civil, military and domestic, he explained that the statistical equilibrium in an Orissa temple is simply due to the combined action of the simple vertical action and reaction. As regards religious instinct present in the Orissan architecture Manmohan Ganguly strongly believed that in this respect Orissan temple architecture would be far superior to that of the Greeks, not to speak of the Romans.

"Though historically speaking India may be a land of paradoxes, for, to settle the civilisation's historical chronology, one has to lose himself amidst many conjectures given rise to many hypotheses and theories. None the less the ancient Indian concept of historical knowledge began with the rise of religion of Buddha. Before its rising, Indian civilisation had no authentic historical record worth the name but since the advent of Buddha, the Indians' historical knowledge stared gaining definite shape and we have definite historical records to vouch for India's history."[46] Ganguly says that though it is inexpliciable why everything was carefully recorded since the advent of Buddha, the product of the great India synthesis and the authentic record would be missing previous to this. The religion of Buddha brought about a revolution in Indian history. From the time of the advent of Buddha, the great religious reformer, historical data began to be collected to supply the material for a connected history.[47] He was convinced that Indians in the ancient past did not lack historical knowledge and that their interest in history was as old as the rise of Buddhism.

Ganguly believes that history, more particularly the history of architecture, is the index of a nation's life and character. It is complex in nature and this complexity increases in accordance with the nation creating it. The nation which has imbibed the spirit of beauty to a great extent has its architecture commensurate with it. The spirit became reflected in the book of art that the nation produces. History bears testimony to this.[48] Manmohan Ganguly thus took the nation as the main theme and purpose of history. One cannot thus reasonably expect uniformity of architectural style in all countries for that matter even in all provinces of India. A nation's character is thus reflected in the work of art which the history furthers.

Since the work of art to him bears testimony to the character of civilisation and culture, it is quite natural that Manmohan Ganguly laid much stress on the importance of decoration in art. In this respect he rejected the concept of utilitarianism because this concept divests life of much pressure and renders it dull and insipid. Ganguly outrightly rejected those who do not attach importance to the values of decoration in art and science, condemn it as superfluous serving no specific end. He does not blame them either, for he feels that this is in the nature and spirit of rank utilitarianism that everything falls short of these standards stand rejected.[49]

At the same time Manmohan Ganguly lamented at the sad want of application of the fundamental canons of architecture in the present age. Compared to the present age, the ancient artisans had much aesthetic sense and carried the idea of decorative art to the farthest extreme. A retrogression has already set in the trends created in the past. Since then the constructive idea has eclipsed the decorative one and we have come to the other end of the diameter. Thus Manmohan Ganguly considers absolutely true nemesis action.[50] The present tendency of the age is to cofine the remains of architecture within the narrow compass of set formulas. There is a marked tendency at having this style stereotyped which is not uniform in all ages but varies under different conditions. The pediments, the metopes, the tryglyphs of the Grecian temple would be very poor substitutes in an Indian one or kalaśa, karpuri and amla of an Orissan temple would certainly spoil the beauty of a cathedral.[51] In other words Manmohan Ganguly feels that imitation destroys the very individuality of a nation's arts in appreciation of beauty of which the synthetic and analytic mental process is deeply involved. Explaining Indian art in this respect, he describes the lotus as of pan-India interest from the decoratve point of view. Delving deep into the concept of imitation which he otherwise also termed as deceit, he describes architecture as the petrified religion of the people.[52] For as religion degenerates into cant and hypocrisy, architecture also shows the sign of convention, deceit and falsehood. Architectural deceit, according to Ruskin, are three fold; constructive colour and deceit, by reason. The last, M.M. Ganguly says, is not found in Orissa.[53]

In this regard going to explain the individuality of the Indian architecture, Manmohan Ganguly described Indian architecture as completely idealistic. The Hegelian principle of 'divine is the centre of the represention of art' has been followed by the Indian artists. The Indo-Aryan and the Greek and Roman artists had altogether different starting points. The Greek and Roman school is imitative, Indian is suggestive, creative and idealist. From the earthly point of view, ours did not aim at perfection and from the point of view of eternal, hereafter of which the present is a glaring mockery, the art of Graeco-Roman school is a miserable failure. While the European artists represent realism to the last drag of reality, Indian architecture is idealistic.[54]

At this point Manmohan Ganguly considered idealism as Indian national character deeply ingrained in the minds of the oriental people. To understand rightly the Indian art one must attach importance to that trait of national character. This idealisation in Orissan architecture make it too intellectual to be easily understood.

Manmohan Ganguly's scientific exposition of the Orissan architecture presents the individuality of Orissan architecture in particular and Indo-Aryan architecture in general. In search for this national individuality, he could strongly identify the concept of idealism as the national character of Indian art and architecture. Moreover that trend in architecture always conforms to the change in national character to which history always bears testimony.

IV. RAKHAL DAS BANERJI

Judged by any standard of scholarship, Rakhal Das Banerji was one of the front-ranking historians and archeologists India has ever produced. This great intellectual who attained world fame by his discovery and excavation of the Mohenjo-daro city site of the Indus Valley civilisation was born at Baharampur, in Mursidabad district of Bengal in the year 1886. Having his early education at Baharampur,

Rakhal Das Banerji graduated from Presidency College, Calcutta in the year 1905 and received his master's degree from Calcutta University in the year of 1909. At the Presidency College he learnt Sanskrit from no less a Sanskrit scholar than Mahamahopadhyaya Haraprasad Shastri. This provided him with an enviable linguistic ability to read and decipher ancient records. Dr. Rajendra Prasad and Sarat Chandra Bose were his classmates. Close association with these national patriots might have enhanced his respect for the country and imbibed in him a high spirit of national feeling. Apart from Harprasad Shastri, D.R Bhandarkar, Theodor Bloch and R S Trivedi, the famous historians of the time seem to have left an impression on Rakhal Das Banerji. Collectively all of them appear to have inspired him to write on different aspects of the history and cultural heritage of India

No sooner than Rakhal Das Banerji completed his M.A degree than he got an appointment in India Museum as an archaeological assistant in the year 1910. In 1911 he also served for some time as Honorary Professer of History at Calcutta University. Later he got appointment in the Archaeological Survey of India and took over charge of Superintendent of the Western Circle in the year 1917. In 1924 he took over as Superintendent of the Eastern Circle at Calcutta. In 1928 Rakhal Das Banerji resigned from the government service to join Banaras Hindu University as Professor and Head of the Department of Ancient Indian History and Culture. He held that post till his premature death in 1930.

Rakhal Das Banerji's short span of life was more than compensated for by his rich academic output including his archaeological undertaking. He was primarily an archaeologist and his title to fame rests chiefly on his epochmaking discovery of Mahenjo-daro in the year 1922-23 which pushed back the antiquity of the Indian civilisation by over three thousand years before Christ. Apart from the achievement in the field of archaeology, Rakhal Das Banerji showed his expertise in epigraphy, numismatics, palaeography, inconography and art history of India. He started his epigraphical work by editing the Madhainagar copper-plate grant of Laxman Sena in the *Journal of the Asiatic Society of Bengal* in the year 1909. Later he edited a number of inscriptions from different parts of the country. His knowledge of epigraphy was based on a sound knowledge of paleography and apart from his notes and comments on paleography of inscriptions he edited, he brought out two monographs, namely, Origin of the Bengali script (1919) and Paleography of the Hāthigumphā and Nānāghāt inscriptions (1929).

In the field of art and iconography he made on-the-spot study of important monuments like temples of Bhimasa (Madhya Pradesh) and Gandhardi (Orissa). He also made a detailed study of the architectural and sculptural remains of Tripuri region of the period of the Haihaya kings as seen in his '*Haihayas of Tripuri and their Monuments*' published posthumously in the year 1931. The labour and erudition of Rakhal Das Banerji in this field is perhaps best evident in his monumental work '*Eastern Indian School of Medieval Sculpture*' published posthumously in the year 1933.

Apart from analysing archaeological and historical data, Rakhal Das Banerji succeeded in synthesizing the facts at his disposal. His '*Age of Imperial Guptas*' (1924) published posthumously in the year 1931 and two volumes of '*History of Orissa*' (1930-1931) bear testimony to this remark. Divided into six chapters, *Age of Imperial Guptas*' not only gives a readable account of the Gupta rule in India but also deals with the art, architecture, the religious life of the people, the literature, the coinage of their period. Two volumes of the '*History of Orissa*' are comprehensive and monumental in nature. There are as many as thirty chapters and several appendices. The work is remarkable as a wealth of information on Orissa based on sound interpretation and presentation from a veriety of sources.

Of the genre of the above two works is the two volume 'Banglar Itihas' (in Bengali). The other works of general nature by Rakhal Das Banerji include *'Palas of Bengal'*, '*History of Orissa*' (1915) and *'Prehistoric Ancient and Hindu India'* published posthumously in the year 1934.

Rakhal Das Banerji was primarily an archaelogist and the archaelogist was preponderantly present in the historian. The approach to investigations in archaelogical explorations, excavations and interpretations being always scientific and objective, he was not prepared to accept anything as sober history which was not corroborated or confirmed by inscriptional, numismatic or monumental evidences. Not unreasonably he considered literature as a source of secondary importance.

A comprehensive list of his writings on Orissa is given below:

(1) Patiakala Grant of Maharaja Svaraj Gupta (1907-8).[55]

(2) Parikuda Plates of Madyamarajadeva, 1911.[56]

(3) Talcher Grant of Kulastambha 1913-14.[57]

(4) Two Baudh Grants of Ranabhanja Deva 1913-14.[58]

(5) Inscriptions in Udayagiri and Khandagiri Caves 1915-16.[59]

(6) Talcher Grant of Gayadatungadeva 1916.[60]

(7) Bhanja Dynasty of Orissa 1917.[61]

(8) Notes on the Hathigumpha Inscription of the Kharavela 1917.[62]

(9) Neulpur Grant of Subhakara 1919.[63]

(10) Dhauli Cave Inscription of Santikara 1928.[64]

(11) Kara of Orissa 1928.[65]

(12) Baud Plates of Kanakabhanja 1928.[66]

(13) Temples of Orissa, 1928.[67]

(14) Non-Budhistic Cave Temples 1928.[68]

(15) The Temples of Orissa 1928-29.[69]

(16) Antiquities of the Baudh State 1929.[70]

(17) Patna Museum Plates of the Rana Bhanja 1929-30.[71]

(18) Kharavela's Personal History 1930.[72]

(19) History of the Orissa Earliest Time to British Period 1930-31.[73]

(20) Palaeography of Hathigumpha and Nanaghat Inscription 1931.[74]

(21) Notes on the Puri Plates of Dharamraja 1932.[75]

(22) Tekkali Plates of Satrubhanj 1932.[76]

Rakhal Das Banerji was brought by Maharaja Pratap Chandra Bhanj Deo the king of Mayurbhanj to write a comprehensive account on the Bhanja rulers of Mayurbhanj. This was more or less parallel effort of the ruling chief of the Sonpur, under whose patronge Bijay Chandra Majumdar brought out *'Sonpur in Sambalpur Tract'* in the year of 1911. Banerjee was entrusted with the job with virtually the same intentions. During this time Rakhal Das worked with some eminent epigraphist such as R.P.Chanda in the Museum at Khiching.

Though finally R.D. Banerji brought out a phenomenal work in '*History of Orissa*' (1930-1931) in two volumes, obviously he devoted a good chunk of this work on the Bhanja ruler of the Mayurbhanj. He also went to the extent of describing his royal patron, the ruling chiefs of the Bhanja dynasty as undoubtedly the oldest representation of the royal dynasties of ancient Orissa.[78] According to him, they are much older than Gaṅgā or Somavaṁśīs and as such the modern states ruled over by them are far more important for the study of the ancient and medieval history of that country than any of their neighbours.[79]

"History of Orissa" in two volumes by Rakhal Das Banerji came to light in the years 1930 and 1931 and are considered the first ever complete and comprehensive writing on the history of Orissa from the earliest times to the British period. An archaeologist himself, not surprisingly he started the work with a full chapter on the prehistoric culture of Orissa as unearthed till then. The volumes have dealt at length on different periods of Orissan history, and the historical sources he used have been treated with all scientific precision to arrive at nearly objective historical conclusions.

Starting from the descriptions of the geography of Orissa till the treatment of history, society, religion and politics of Orissa in the book we find real scientific treatment of source materials. Instances are replete in the entire text where Rakhal Das Banerji has tried to co-relate inscriptional sources to arrive at conclusive historical truth. In one instance he says that "the problem of the history and chronology of the early Gaṅgās of Kalinga and the era started by them is still far from being solved and unless a record is discovered in which Gaṅgā era is used simultaneously with another, it will not be possible to override the difficulties which still beset our path. In short the solution of the problem depends on the discovery of the initial year of this era in which the majority of the inscriptions of the kings of this dynasty of Kalinga are dated".[80]

Very much consonant with the requirement of sober history Rakhal Das Banerji took upon the tasks of the descriptions. He did not accept blindly any other conclusion to suit his own theories. We found in him saying in the very beginning of the book that "it is impossible to agree with Mr. Hiralal in thinking that Madhya deśa is the border district between south-west Bengal and northern Orissa.

Whatever be the traditional value of the word Madhyadeśa in modern Orissa, nobody can deny that up to Musalman conquest of nothern India, Madhyadeśa meant the central portion of the United Provinces."[81] Similarly describing the geography of Orissa Rakhal Das Banerji emphatically argued that the border district of Orissa where hybrid Oriya is spoken were civilized by the people of Orissa and Kalinga proper.[82] On Bhuiyan of Bihar and Orissa he said that "beyond the similarity in name there is no other similarity not even of language between the Bhuiyans and the Bhumijas. The idea of the social intercourse between the Bhanja kings and the Murundas is absurd."[83] We do not find much in him the attitude and sentiment apparent among a section of the Bengali elite who spearheaded a campaign against the separate existence of Oriya as an independent language and demanded the regions around Medinipur, Baleswar bordering Bengal as parts of Bengal. Contrary to this attitude, Rakhal Das Banerji writes that the "country of Kalinga originally extended up to modern district of Medinipur and Howrah in Bengal. In the Mughal times the Subarna Rekha river now in south western part of the district of Medinipur was regarded as the northern boundary of Orissa. Even now the title of the majority of the Hindu jamindars of Medinipur prove that they were landholders and feudatories of Hindu kings of Orissa at no later date.[84] Rakhal Das Banerji says that the people of West Bengal, northern Bengal and Kalinga therefore regarded in the time of the Sutras as being altogether out of the pale of Aryan civilisation and among them the people of Kalinga obtained a slight preference. So while the people of Bengal were regarded as untouchables and were not spoken to or touched by the Aryans, the people of Kalinga were not so. We have no means to determine for what reasons the Aryan lords condenscended to confer this distinction on the dark Dravidians of Kalinga but it is there in the Sutra literature and cannot be denied."[85] At another place talking about the sulkis Rakhal Das Banerji says that the sulkis belonged to northern Orissa which once contained the modern district of northern Orissa.[86] This explanation refutes the arguments given by the Bengal scholars as regards the geography of Bengal vis-à-vis Orissa.

As Rakhal Das Banerji approached the political history of Orissa, his historical concept came to be clearly discernible. We can first of all trace out the aspects that are attributed to the nationalist historians in his analysis of the political history. First he regarded the people of Kalinga who have been proved to be poineer colonists of India, Indonesia and Oceania are probably the very same people whom the modern barbarian of the pacific and the Indian ocean regard with awe and wonder as people from the sky who civilised them and taught them the rudiments of culture.[87] This concept of colonisation by the Indians we see variety among the nationalist historians of the calibre of K.P. Jayaswal, R.C. Majumdar, Rakhal Das Banerji et al. Intrinsically, this seems to be a contradiction as far as the nationalist history of India is concerned particularly because these historians' major point of attack was the British colonization of our country. But the nationalist historians seem to have committed that same mistake rather unknowingly. This contradiction cropped up mainly because of their effort to glorify India's past. Rakhal Das Banerji does not seem to have separated himself from this line of nationalist thinking, whatever contradiction might there have been.

Rakhal Das Banerji has clearly toed the line of thinking of Ramesh Chandra Majumdar who followed a distinct Hindu nationalist stand. He clearly interpreted the battles and the imperialist movements in terms of the Hindu-Muslim divide and position. Very often we come across sentences that clearly speak of such tendencies. Some such sentences are:

"The scared Hindu religion did not seem to have entered into the conception of Hindu king and statesmen of northern India in 12th century A.D. The grandson of Anangabhimadev II received and met Musalman aggression with equal vehemence, but for the time being, Rajaraj III was completely paralysed by the Musalman raid into Orissa on account of the supineness of his father."[88] "It is quite probable that Narsimha I of Orissa took advantage of the stupid indolence of the Musalman officer of Bengal and advanced toward Gaud...."[89]

"An invasion from Orissa against the common enemy of all Hindus must have been welcome by them. Moreover an invasion of Hindu territories in south and Central Bengal would not have affected the Musalman nobels and officer of western Bengal."[90]

Similarly, on Narasimha I's fight with Muslims Rakhal Das Banerii writes that "the statement of Minhajuddin in this regard does not bear any stamp of truth." No victory is recorded for the Musalman army and not a word of praise is bestowed upon governor showing that the Hindu army of Orissa plundered the Musalman districts thorughly and then returned to their own country on the approach of the monsoon.[91]

"An exceptionally brilliant and active governor like Yuzbak might have launched campaign after campaign against Narasimha I but the general effect of a forward policy on a Hindu state was magical in the 13th century. Till Bengal obtained autonomy under the descendants of Balban, Orissa practically remained unmolested; not only so, the southern districts of West Bengal such as Medinipore Howrah and Hoogly became a part of the Medinipore or Orissa."[92] Similarly, at another place he says that in the first place, Mahamad III had really retired from the capital of Orissa after receiving 25 elephants, then it was to be admitted that he was compelled to turn tail by a superior force. No victorious Musalman army had ever set off a defeated Hindu king at such a small cost."[93] The last statement thus seems to explain the strength of the adversaries i.e. the Hindu kings and the Muslim emperors of the time. But nevertheless Rakhal Das has tried to prove that the Hindu rulers of medieval Orissa were certainly powerful forces to reckon with by the Muslim encroachers and adversaries.

From this we can safely infer the reasons, Rakhal Das attributed for Prataprudra Deva seeking help from a Muslim to fight a Hindu adversary i.e. King Krishna Deva Raya of Vijaya Nagara empire. He says "the acquisition of help from a Musalman neighbour to fight with a Hindu adversary involved a moral and political depredation in the Hindu world which can be easily understood by those who are famililar with Rajput history but this was not the only occasion when Prataprudra Deva employed mercenaries against the Hindus."[94]

Despite this clear Hindu nationalist stand, which he professed more as a nationalist historian, Rakhal Das considered Chaitanya's Vaiśṇavite movement in Orissa as the principal cause of the political decline of the Gajapati empire and the people of Orissa. He believed that the acceptance of Vaiśṇavism or rather neo-Vaiśṇavism was the real cause of the Musalman conquest of Orissa 28 years after the death of Prataprudra Deva. His arguments in this regard can be summed up as follows:

"Even if we accept only one-tenth of what the Sanskrit and Bengali biographies of the Saint Chaitanya state about his influence over Prataprudra and the people of his country, even then we must admit that Chaitanya was one of the principal causes not only of the political decline of the empire and the people of Orissa but also the Musalman conquest of Orissa 28 years after the death of Prataprudra."[95]

The influence of Chaitanya was so much ingrained in the royal behaviour that "at the time when any nation needed the services of every honest and capable man for the defence of her political independence, prestige of the empire. Ramananda Ray betrayed his trust to the people of his own empire by returning from his position on the weakest frontier of the country."[96]

"The advice of Chaitanya was sufficient to cause the cowardly and his religious minded king to desist from a proper defence of his own territories."[97]

"With the death of Prataprudra Deva the pall of dense darkness descends upon the medieval history of Orissa to be lifted only with the Moghul conquest of Orissa half a century later."[98]

"The next important step in the decline of Orissa was the religious superiority of Jagannath and its hierarchy of temple priests."[99]

"The decline of the power and prestige of Orissa is solely due to the national adoption of the sublime Bhakti Marg of Chaitanya. The effect of the conditions of the provinces of Orissa may be gauged by the Garjat Chiefs of the present day who worship shakti images in secret and subordination to Vaiṣṇava deities."[100]

These arguments of Rakhal Das Banerji are certainly the fall out of his pro-Hindu nationalist bias. This is evident from the fact that he considered Bhakti cult of Chaitanya Deva as radically different Hindu theology proper. He candidly spoke about this implication of this Bhaktimārga on India's political history. He said "considered as a religion, Indian Bhaktimārga is sublime but its effects on the political status of the country or the nation which accepts it, is terrible. The religion of equality and love preached by Chaitanya Deva brought in its train false faith in men and thereby destroyed the structure of society and government in Bengal and Orissa, because in reality no two men are born equal and government depends upon brute force especially in a country like India in 14th, 15th and 17th centuries. A wave of religious fervour passed over the country and during this transformation, Orissa not only lost her empire but also her political prestige. The effect of Vaiśṇavism on the society and government of Orissa was far more destructive than in Bengal because in the latter country militant śaktism was not destroyed totally and the effect of neo-Vaiśṇavism was beneficient to the extent of bringing within the pale of society a number of decadent Buddhists who had been outcast by orthodox Brahmanism. In Orissa, on account of its acceptance by royalty, neo-Vaiśṇavism became fashionable and powerful officers of Prataprudra like Ramananda Ray were the most notable converts after the king himself. The result was corrosive though Tārānāth, the Buddhist historiographer has recorded that some form of Buddhism lingered in Orissa till the end of the 16th century gradually stamping out all other sects of Hinduism from the country."[101]

Rakhal Das Banerji's ideological approach to history of Orissa in particular can be summed up as follows:

Himself an archaeologist of repute, Rakhal Das Banerji adopted a strong scientific approach to historical research. His works thus tried to bring about a perfect synthesis among the archaeological source materials, and, perfect corroboration of all literary sources by coins, inscriptions and other archaeological source materials.

He was a pro-Hindu nationalist of the genre of Professor Ramesh Chandra Majumdar. This is clearly perceived from the Hindu-vs-Muslim approach he took upon in the study of the most volatile period of Orissan history, i.e. the medieval age that saw the resurgence as well as decline of real imperialist power in Orissan history. The rise and fall of the Hindu empires during this age have been delineated on the backdrop of their strength and weakness against their Muslim adversaries.

The fall of the medieval Hindu empire in Orissa was largely due to the excessive state involvement in Bhaktimārga which Rakhal Das took to be a marked departure from the strict line of Hindu ideology. So much so that he alleged Chaitanya's Bhaktimārg for preaching a false sense of truth that contributed largely to the degeneration of society and culture not only in Orissa but also in Bengal.

Though Rakhal Das comprehensively dealt with the history of Orissa in all its aspects, his notes on the art and architecture of Orissa have been presented like an archaeologist's report on the architectural monuments of Orissa and deal more with the architectural designs of sections than any subjective analysis of aesthetic appeal of sculptural remains even though he dwelt at length on the evolution of art and architecture including that of plastic art in Orissa. In this also, he made some objective analysis while rejecting some opinions of earlier writers on the subject like Manmohan Ganguly and others.[102] He attributed a distinct and separate style for Orissan architecture disregarding arguments for giving it a Nāgara representation.[103] He said that during the six centuries of existence of Kalingan type temples, new features were added and older ones metamorphosed in form but remained constant factors.[104] He also rejected Manmohan Ganguly's arguments on the Gupta influence on Orissan art on the basis of the historical fact that Orissa was never conquered by the Guptas politically.[105]

Along with originality Rakhal Das also attributed superiority to Orissan art. He says that the railings of the Udayagiri caves are exactly like the great railings around the Buddhist shrine at Bodh Gaya, Bahrut and Sanchi.[106] The carvings at Ananta Gumphā show the polish of the Maurya caves at Barber and Nāgārjuṇa hills.[107] Describing the greatness of Orissan architecture he writes that in this period there was practically no naturalism, want of equipoise or provincial mannerism. Therefore the majority of the scholars on the subject have hailed the art of the Mukteśwar very highly.[108] Similarly the image of the Sun on horseback in the Konark Temple has been described as a rare example in Indian iconography.[109]

Like some present day historians Rakhal Das felt the necessity of writing history from bottom up and produced regional histories like *History of Orissa* and *History of Bengal* (in Bengali) for better understanding of general pattern of Indian history. In writing such regional histories he kept himself alive to the fact that the history of any region in India is but an integral part of the history of India. Thus in the preface to the *'Bangalar Itihasa'* he clearly avers that the author of the history of Bengal should write his narrative in tune with that of the different periods of India without losing the main thread. This is equally in tune with his nationalistic stand accepting the fundamental unity of India as a reality.

Though apparently a *dry dust* historian, Rakhal Das was not concerned exclusively with bare facts. As a historian he was perfectly aware of the art of correlation of facts which make history meaningful and lively. In advance of many of his contemporaries he was aware of the anthropological roots of Indian history.

Strict adherence to facts, scientific disinterestedness and critical acumen are the hallmarks of Rakhal Das as an historian. According to K.K. Dasgupta "if he is seen on occasions as a patriot or nationalist he has proved once more that history, when it goes beyond a mere catalogue of facts, becomes subjective and individual, conditioned by the interest and the vision of the historian and that history, consciously or semiconsciously, allies itself with literature when it becomes true history."[110] As a serious researcher of his profession, Rakhal Das spared no pains to collect facts from every possible source. After gathering his primary data he selected and classified them and made generalisations and finally tried to present facts and his view in a readable manner. In general Rakhal Das Banerji was on guard against being swayed by extra historical considerations—regional, religious or otherwise—and tried to take his stand on the terra-firma of facts and to uphold the historical truth. A considerable progress in researches notwithstanding, *'Age of Imperial Guptas'* and *'History of Orissa'* are still indispensable works in the relevant fields.

His largest contribution to Orissan historiography lay in the fact that he presented the first ever complete and comprehensive book on the history of Orissa from the earliest time to the British period. In fact his was the first attempt to divide and discuss Orissa's history under distinct parts, chapters and titles maintaining the perfect sequence of chronology and subject matter. That is why for a long time Banerjee's *History of Orissa* remained a standard work on the subject and was widely cited by authorities.

V. BENIMADHAB BARUA (1888-1948)

Benimadhab Barua was a well-known figure in the field of epigraphic and ancient Indian studies. He was born on 31st December, 1888. For long, he served as Professor in the Department of Pali as well as in the Departments of Sanskrit, Ancient Indian History and

Culture in the prestigious Calcutta University. For some time, he also served as a Government of India scholar in Pali. Benimadhab Barua was actively associated with the *Indian Historical Quarterly,* which was one of the most scholastic and highly acclaimed indological research journals of the country. The journal which was devoted mostly to the researches on Indian history and culture was published without any interruption till 1963. Benimadhab Barua associated himself with this journal mainly as an author by contributing many scholarly articles on epigraphy and on the different aspects of ancient Indian history and culture. His endeavour in the field of epigraphic studies was widely acclaimed in academic circles. Benimadhab Barua says that he was initiated into the study of Indian inscriptions in the year 1912 by Late Rakhal Das Banerjee, then Superintendent of Archaeology Section of the Indian Museum at Calcutta.[111] He achieved perfection in the study of epigraphy when he was teaching at Calcutta University. Benimadhab says that by conviction he feels himself toeing the line of D.R. Bhandarkar in his study of inscriptions particularly because of his analytical than subjective treatment of historical sources.[112] One aspect of this acclamation was realised when Benimadhab Barua adorned the Presidentship of the Ancient India Section of the Indian History Congress, the premier organisation of the historians of India, in its annual session held at Annamalainagar in Tamilnadu in December, 1945. In his address as Sectional President, Benimadhab Barua made a scholarly presentation of facts connected with ancient Indian history by relying upon epigraphic as well as archaeological sources. In this address, which provides an outline of the history of Ancient India from the pre-historic periods, he made an effort to present a continuous chronological account of the history of India. It bears an imprint of his ideas and approaches towards ancient Indian history. Benimadhab Barua breathed his last on 23rd March, 1948.

Benimadhab Barua exhibited phenomenal expertise in linguistic studies, particularly the ancinet Indian languages like Pali, Prakrit and Sanskrit. This linguistic expertise which was then considered a rare achievement, helped him to study the Old Brahmi inscriptions based on Pali and Prakrit languages in a more accurate manner. In studying these epigraphic records of mainly the Asokan periods and the inscriptions of King Kharavela and other Brahmi inscriptions of this period, Benimadhab Barua utilised his expertise on linguistic studies. He not only differed in his conclusions with the then authorities on the subject like D.R. Bhandarkar, Rakhal Das Banerji, Kashi Prasad Jayaswal and others who contributed significantly to these studies, but also on many counts, countered their readings, interpretations and hypotheses with cogent and reliable arguments. His works are replete with such arguments and counter arguments. Benimadhab Barua produced two phenomenal works namely, *Old Brahmi inscriptions in Udaygiri and Khandagiri Caves* (1929)[113] *and Ashok and his Inscriptions* (1946).[114] He contributed a number of scholastic articles on epigraphy and other aspects of studies on sources of ancient Indian history. Some of his noteworthy articles are listed below :

(1) Message from Bharut Jataka labels- 1925.[115]

(2) Stupa and tomb-1926.[116]

(3) Multiplication of Jatakas-1926.[117]

(4) Inscriptional excursions- 1926.[118]

(5) Maskari as epithet of Gopala - 1927.[119]

(6) Old Brahmi inscriptions in Udayagiri and Khandagiri-language-1928.[120]

(7) Old Buddhist Shrines from Bodhgaya - 1930.[121]

(8) Kharavela's personal history - 1930.[122]

(9) Bodhgaya image inscriptions- 1933.[123]

(10) Estimation of the people of Orissa - 1934.[124]

(11) The Sohgaura Plate- 1934.[125]

(12) Old Brahmi inscriptions of Mahasthana - 1934.[126]

(13) Minor Old Brahmi inscriptions in the Udayagiri and Khandagiri Caves- 1938.[127]

(14) Hathigumpha Inscription of Kharavela (revised edition)- 1938.[128]

(15) Kharabela as king and builder - 1947.[129]

(16) The scribe engravers of Indrapala's second copper-plate and Prakrit of pre-Ahom times - 1947.[130]

Most of his works relate to the intensive studies on old Brahmi inscriptions particularly those related to the periods of Ashoka and king Kharavela. *'The old Brahmi Inscriptions in Udayagiri and Khandagiri Caves'* is fully devoted to the study of the Brahmi inscriptions engraved in the Khandagiri and Udayagiri hills where the well-known Hathigumpha inscription of Kharavela has been engraved. Benimadhab Barua looked into these inscriptions in an holistic manner wherein he not only devoted his attention to the historical aspect of the period of the inscriptions but also about their authors, the symbols, letter forms, palaeography, the language, the style, the contents, the relative chronological position, the geographical allusions, the king's personal history, the city of Kalinganagari, the caves, shrines and the pillars of the Khandagiri and Udayagiri hills. He also analysed the opinion of the then authorities extensively on the Khandagiri and Udayagiri inscriptions. In discussing the inscriptions, Benimadhab Barua also drew clues from sources like the '*Jātaka*' stories, and the '*Arthaśāstra*' of Kauṭilya while writing the history of the kings as well as analysing the relative merit of these inscriptions as potential historical source materials. Born of these scholastic labours 'Old Brahmi Inscriptions' turned out to be a highly authoritative work on the inscriptions of the Chedi rulers as found in Khandagiri and Udayagiri hills and particularly on King Kharavela.

Another significant aspect or rather an extraordinary feature of this work is that Benimadhab Barua presented Sanskrit transliteration of all the Brahmi inscriptions he had studied. This was certainly the result of his expertise in Sanskrit language and it was of considerable help to the scholars of ancient Indian history as well as Orissan history.

Benimadhab Barua, in the preface to the book, has outlined his very intentions for making an holistic study of the Old Brahmi inscriptions. He says "realising that the study of the important Hathigumpha inscription would be incomplete without that of other old Brahmi inscriptions in the Udayagiri and Khandagiri caves I thought it would be worthwhile also to carefully examine their readings and renderings published by Princep, Cunningham, Indraji and finally by Rakhal Das Banerji. Examining and re-examining these shorter inscriptions as they appeared on original stones, plaster casts and fascimiles, I was able to detect certain palpable mistakes in previous publications standing badly in need of correction. This in itself, as I believed, was sufficient justification for venturing a fresh undertaking."[131] It seemed to be no less a justification, he says, that Kharavela's inscription in the Hathigumpha and the remaining old

Brahmi inscriptions in Udayagiri and Khandagiri caves were not studied before in their inter-connection as well as in their connection with the table of Brahmi alphabet in the first Tattva gumphā on the Khandagiri hill.[132]

Benimadhab Barua has treated all the shorter inscriptions together with the table of Brahmi alphabet, as appendices to the Hathigumpha inscription while the Hathigumpha inscription itself has been treated as the main text serving as a complete *Kharavelacharita*. He observed that the inscription was "anyhow a Prakrit panegyric (prasasti) of King Kharavela in ancinet Indian epigraphy composed by some unknown Harisena or Bana in an elegant prose diction clearly anticipating the prose style of the Pali Milinda Panho".[133]

Benimadhab Barua was humble enough not to accept his readings of old Brahmi inscriptions of Khandagiri and Udayagiri hills as conclusive and fullproof [134] and yet he was sure and convinced largely because of his expertise that "if the readings proposed (by him) stand the test of time they will serve to lay many ghosts for ever and to convince the reader once for all that

(1) there is no statement in the Hathigumpha inscription as to the population of Kalinga;
(2) that there is no allusion to Rsi Khibira;
(3) that it contains no statement as to the Greek King Dimita-Demetrios retreating with his troops and transports to abandon Mathura;
(4) that there is no mention of Avaraja;
(5) that there is no statement as to Pithunda being ploughed with an ass plough;
(6) that here is no statement as to the existence of a league of the Tamil powers;
(7) that here is no mention of the Maurya era;
(8) that there is no reference to the corpus of the Jain canon with its various divisions; and lastly
(9) that there is no such epithet of Kharavela as Bhikuraja."[135]

Besides, Benimadhab Barua came out in his analysis of the Hathigumpha inscription with some brilliant, erudite and highly scholastic conclusions.These were considered highly reliable and historically dependable as regards the Hathigumpha inscription and the rule of King Kharavela.

As regards the reference to the construction of 117 caves in the Udayagiri hills by His Majesty Mahameghavahana King Kharavela, Benimadhab Barua writes that the total number of inscriptions in the Udaigiri hills must have stood far below that of the caves.[136] "Further it has been wrongly assumed that the inscriptions of Kharavela were meant to refer exclusively to one cave, namely the Hathigumpha on the Udaigiri hills. It is far from being the case. It is not distinctly stated in the record of Kharavela's thirteenth regional year how many out of the 117 caves were excavated by His Majesty, how many by his queens and how many by his relatives. We shall bring injustice to him to suggest that the inscription standing in his name was meant to relate exclusively to a cave which is of little importance as a work of art. To suggest this is to leave the widely acclaimed and excellent works of art and architecture accomplished by him altogether unexplained. The so-called Hathigumpha inscription of Kharavela was indeed meant to refer not to one cave but to all the works of art and architecture done by him on the twin hills of Khandagiri and Udaigiri."[137]

At another place speaking about the scribes of the Hathigumpha inscription he writes that "we are prepared to entertain R.D. Banerjee's hypothesis in so far as it leads to believe that the scribes employed to incise Kharavela's inscriptions represented different localities. In examining the letter forms of the Barhut inscriptions we found some clear data compelling us to think on similar lines to feel that certain carvings and inscriptions were the workmanship of a particular group of artists and others those of other groups."[138]

Benimadhab Barua attributes a unique position to the Hathigumpha inscription of Kharavela as regards its contents. He says that "this inscription presents a systematic record of all the notable achievements of Kharavela including all the works of art and architecture done under his auspices. And this too will be but an imperfect and inaccurate characterisation of the contents of this inscription. The Hathigumpha inscription appears to be a very systematic record of Kharavela's personal history and glorious achievements. The recorded facts are presented in the garb of an autobiographical sketch. The concluding paragraph is so designed as to make the record appear as closed with the name of Kharavelasiri, that is to create the impression that the record is written and signed by the king with his own hand. The invocation formula with which the record begins is meant to indicate the nature of religious faith of the king."[139]

The highest quality of the epigraph, Benimadhab Barua writes, is that it contains all the principal qualities specified by the *Arthaśāstra* of Kauṭilya as regards a composition.[140] The composition of the Hathigumpha inscription of Kharavela is free from all the defects and is bright with the required qualities.

Benimadhab Barua made an equally brilliant analysis of the chronology of the events described in the inscription as well as reference to the Nanda King of Magadha as well as the geographical allusions made in this extremely important epigraph of ancient Orissa.

Refering to the personal history of His Majesty Kharavela, Benimadhab Barua says that the Hathigumpha epigraph does not lack any information as regards the possession of enormous wealth in the shape of a large amount of ready money, vast stores of foodstuff, precious stones, rich apparels, horses, elephants and other livestock which give a test of the high fortune and prosperity of a king overlord.[142]

Besides analysing the old Brahmi inscriptions of Kharavela, Benimadhab Barua devoted a number of pages in the book to determine Kharavela's place in history and to identify the city of Kalingānagarī with the data available from the Hathigumpha inscription and other sources. Finally, he has given from Marshall's opinion on chronology of the Khandagiri and Udaigiri caves.

Chronology seems to be his foremost concern. This is because, in the study of the old Brahmi inscriptions in the Udaigiri and Khandagiri caves, his main aim was to present an holistic analysis of the dynasties to which the inscriptions belonged. And, thus, he equally devoted his attention to draw a definite chronology for the royal dynasty. For Benimadhab Barua, chronology forms the backbone of history.[144] And to reconstruct this historical chronology which can be relied upon, Benimadhab found the inscriptions to be extremely reliable historical source materials. In fixing this chronology he considered the traditional accounts and stories as only of supplementary value to inscriptions. He says, the traditional stories are entitled to serious consideration not only for the additional historical data by which these supplement the inscriptions constituting the direct source of information but also for their suggestiveness. These also help in the clarification of certain knotty and obscure points in the inscriptions and the correct interpretation of the historical bearing of certain statements in them.[145] Stating that these traditional accounts are of secondary value.[146] Benimadhab Barua makes his final statement on his endeavour to the study of inscriptions and says that to evaluate properly the inscriptions is not only to trace through them the successive stages of the working and outpourings of the king but also to consider them cautiously and critically in their manifold bearings on the contemporary, earlier and later Indian as well as world civilisation.[147]

Side by side with chronology Benimadhab Barua sets out the importance of the knowledge of geography for the historian. He says that "if we agree to understand by the history of the country its collective life movement shaping the course and determining the character of a distinct form of culture and type of civilisation within certain territorial limits and a definite period of time, it becomes incumbent on the historian as much to define spatially the territorial limits as to make a clean chronological set-up of events in terms of time. In other words, the knowledge of geography in the widest possible sense of the term is to be used as an indispensable aid to the historian's duty of conceiving the collective life movement in its manifold bearings on the different branches of culture and represent it in terms of facts and sequence. The facts collected from all available sources of information are to be tested, classified and interpreted in the workshop of history before these are sent to the next department for preparing a workable framework or superstructure. When such a framework is ready, the master historian with his constructive imagination and proceeding in the light of problems can sit to his work clothing it with flesh, making it function as a living organism and having a clear vision of the collective life movement passing through the various phases, junction and stages."[148]

In this endeavour in the study and knowledge of epigraphy and palaeography, literature and its language play a vital role. "With a mere knowledge of palaeography indispensable to decipherment and of the dictionary meaning of the words employed was not in itself sufficient for either a correct interpretation of the epigraphs or a thorough grasp of their importance as historical documents. A first-hand knowledge of contemporary literature and its language was as much a decideratum as the historical training and intellectual equipment for proper assesssment of their evidentiary value. In other words the mere epigraphist or the mere linguist was incompetent to fulfil this task."[149]

This intellectual endeavour of Benimadhab Barua in attempting a holistic, analytical as well as scientific treatment of inscriptions as historical source material at last resulted in the study of inscriptions gaining adequate currency as an independent branch of historical study. His expertise and linguistic ability in Sanskrit, Pali and Prakrit was certainly of great help in achieving for him the position of a front-ranking epigraphist of India. As far as the historiography of Orissa is concerned, his erudite interpretation of the old Brahmi inscription in Khandagiri and Udaigiri hills not only helped the later historians in reconstructing the history of Orissa of the period but also brought for Benimadhab Barua a place of distinction among the historiographers conducting research on Orissa history.

VI. PANDIT BINAYAK MISHRA (1894-1971)

A great Sanskrit scholar and epigraphist, Pandit Binayak Mishra was born on 2nd September 1894 at Sarankul in the present Nayagarh district (earlier Puri district). He was initially a Sanskrit Pandit but his appointment as lecturer in the post-graduate Department of Oriya in Calcutta University provided him the important breakthrough. He had attained mastery over both Oriya and Sanskrit languages and this helped him in deciphering old epigraphs and in becoming an epigraphist of distinction. Pandit Mishra published a number of books in Oriya, the notable among them being *'Oriya Bhasara Itihasa'* (1927), *'Oriya Shityara Itihasa'* (1929) (both literary works), *'Mahamanya Gandhiji'* (1948, Biography), *'Oriya Sahityara Parichaya'* (1950, criticism). He had also two notable historical works to his credit. These are *'Orissa under Bhauma kings'* (1934) and *'Dynasties of Medieval Orissa'* (1936). These two works give us first-hand information of the epigraphic sources on the different dynastics of Early and Medieval Orissa. Pandit Binayak Mishra died on 05 August 1971. Long after his death, his descendants brought out a volume on the cult of Jagannatha supposed to have been written by him. This volume is a collection of some essays by Pandit Binayak Mishra on all and sundry topics on Orissa and is mostly a repetition of his earlier writings.

Among the scholars of Orissa in the early 20th century, who made attempts to decipher the epigraphic records for arriving at a more reliable and fairly acceptable chronology of the history of Orissa, the name of Pandit Binayak Mishra would find special mention. True to the nature of historical research of his time, Pandit Binayak Mishra, who was primarily a Sanskrit scholar, concentrated more on the study of the epigraphic records of the early medieval period of Orissa. His two brilliant works *"Orissa under Bhauma Kings"*[150] published in the year 1934 and the *'Dynasties of Medieval Orissa'*[151] published in the year 1936 were aimed to analyse the most vital source materials for the reconstruction of the history of the Bhauma-Karas, Bhanjas, Sulkis, Nandas and Tungas. Besides Pandit Mishra wrote a number of articles on different inscriptions and grants of the early medieval period in Orissa. A comprehensive list of his writings is given below:

(1) "A note on the Kangoda Country", 1926.[152]

(2) "Note on the Time of Kara Dynasty", 1926.[153]

(3) "The Area of Orissa in Hiuen Tsang's Time", 1927.[154]

(4) "Trikalinga country", 1928.[155]

(5) "Hindol Plate of subhakaradeve", 1930.[156]

(6) "Copper-Plate Grant of Netabhanja", 1931.[157]

(7) "Sailodbhava Rulers of Kangoda", 1931.[158]

(8) *"Orissa under Bhauma Kings"* 1934.[159]

(9) "Narasimhantah Stone Inscription of Vijaladeva" 1936.[160]

(10) *"Dynasties of Medieval Orissa"* 1936.[161]

(11) "Maurya Chandragupta and Mayurbhanj rulers", 1937.[162]

(12) "Initial Year of Ganga era", 1938.[163]

(13) "Identification of Indradyumna", 1939.[164]

In *Orissa under Bhauma Kings* Pandit Binayak Mishra brought the Bhaumakara dynasty to limelight by a careful compilation of the inscriptions issued by the rulers of that dynasty. The *"Dynasties of Medieval Orissa"* has attempted to give a fairly reliable chronology of some minor dynasties of early medieval Orissa after a comprehensive and careful coroboration of facts from epigraphic sources.

In fact the 19th century historians who attempted writing the history of Orissa, depended entirely on the most unreliable *Madāla Pañjī* for the chronology of Orissan history. Later in the beginning of the 20th century many learned historians and epigraphists like J.F. Fleet and Manmohan Chakraborty challenged the reliablility of '*Madāla Pañjī*' as historical source material; still their works covered the history of Orissa from beyond the 12th century. When Rakhal Das Banerji attempted to write the history of Orissa right from the prehistoric period, it suffered, at some places, from a paucity of historical source materials. The chronology of Orissa thus fixed by R.D. Banerji could not be accepted as complete and correct. Pandit Binayak Misha tried to arrange all the information available from the epigraphic sources of early medieval Orissa to fix the chronology of different dynasties and more particularly the Bhauma-karas, Professor Rama Prasad Chanda wrote in the foreword to the *"Dynasties of Medieval Orissa"* "this book is a useful supplement to the late Professor R.D. Banerji's *History of Orissa* so far as it relates to the dynasties that held sway in Orissa from about 600 to 1100 A.D."[165]

Pandit Mishra did not interpret the epigraphic records at their face value but with extreme ingenuity and erudition, his main aim being the reconstruction of the chronology of early Orissan history. He explained the epigraphic records as extremely reliable historical source material. Analysing the number 2 grant of the Sailodhava rulers Pandit Binayak Mishra writes that "if Aranabhitta of the chronological table be not accepted as the son of Ayasobhitta to further generalisations namely, Aranabhitta and Ayasobhitta would be supposed again to have preceded Aranabhitta of the given chronological table. This supposition seems to be untenable because 75 years reign of three supposed generations put the initial year of Dharmaraja's reign in 820 A.D when Trivarnadeva was certainly not alive. It therefore appears that the supposition of one generation is sufficient."[166] Explanations of this kind by Pandit Binayak Mishra testify to the fact that he did not prefer to subscribe any historical conclusion unless backed by sufficient epigraphic evidence.

At the same time to make his works potentially valuable he goes further to identify the places mentioned, in the epigraphic records as far as practicable. However, in doing so, he exemplified extraordinary academic honesty and erudition when he says "Rai Bahadur Hiralal identifies Khinijali with Keonjhar which is locally called Kendujhar. This identification seems untenable phonetically. I, therefore, identify this with Injili in angul. This is certainly not opposed to phonetic rules. In this manner I corrected the identification previously made either by myself or others. However, the credit for the identification of the places mentioned in the copper-plate records of the Bhanja rulers does not belong to me but goes to Rai Bahadur Hira Lal who first undertook this tedious task.[167]

Pandit Mishra's treatment of the chronology of some dynasties of Orissa is undoubtedly a valuable contribution to the existing stock of historical knowledge on Orissa.

Both the works *"Orissa under Bhauma Kings"* and *"Dynasties of Medieval Orissa"* are so replete with mere descriptions and bare analysis of the inscriptions that these do not give a picture of complete historical works. But nevertheless the epigraphic talent of Pandit Mishra is amply manifested in both the works. So much so that both the works give the impression of being excellent compilations of inscriptions rather than complete historical works. These two works are extremely helpful for future researchers on the subject particularly since both his works mainly dealt with inscriptions, one of the most authentic, reliable and valuable historical source materials for the reconstruction of history.

VII. NIRMAL KUMAR BOSE (1901-1972)

An eminent anthropologist and social worker Nirmal Kumar Bose was born on 22 January 1901. He served most part of his career as Professor of Anthropology in Calcutta University except for the brief stint of four years he served as Secretary to Mahatma Gandhi, the father of the nation. Thus, whatever contributions he made to Indian historical research was part of his research as an anthropologist. But that was no less extraordinary. For his *"Canons of Orissan Architecture"*[168] continue to remain as one of the master-pieces of research on Orissan architecture. As the caption reveals itself, his works on Indian history remained restricted to the study of architecture.

"Canons of Orissan Architecture" first came to light in the year 1932. Besides, he conducted the first archaeological excavation of the pre-historic sites in Orissa Kuliana in Mayurbhanj on a scientific basis. The results of this excavation have been reported in the monograph *"Excavations of Mayurbhanj"*[169] published in the year 1948. Nirmal Kumar Bose died on 15 October 1972.

Professor Nirmal Kumar Bose belonged to the primary phase of research on Indian architecture. As such, his contributions to this field of research were undoubtedly original. He certainly had to begin where his predecessors had left off. As he himself claims, "My *"Canons of Orissan Architecture"* may be taken as a continuation of the work which Manmohan Ganguly began on Orissa."[170]

Introducing himself to the study of Orissan architecture Bose first of all identified four methods followed by his predecessor historians on Indian architecture. The studies of Fergusson, Prasanna Kumar Acharya, Manmohan Ganguly and E.B. Havel may be considered as the representative works of these four methods.

The earliest researchers like Fergusson and Rakhal Das depended principally on personal field observations. Almost all our knowledge on Indian architecture has been learnt through this process, Bose claims. Still this method suffers from an important limitation in the past. "The workers from the west as well as their Indian disciples were trained in the schools of Europe and as they were not in touch with the Indian craftsmen they lost the vital means of gaining an insight into the traditional point of view in regard to Indian architecture. What was essential and what was secondary according to the local science of architecture was not known to them. This is the reason why in some historical reconstructions of Fergusson school, primary matters have been given secondary importance. Such a shortcoming was inevitable in view of the fact that Indian scholars generally followed tracks of western pioneers instead of trying to restore the original science on Indian architecture which they might more profitably have undertaken."[171]

Eminent Sanskritists like Ganapati Shastri and Prasanna Kumar Acharya succeeded in restoring the texts on the architecture of about a dozen ancient books but their labours have not yielded the results which were expected of them. These canonical books of the śilpīs are of the nature of menmonic notes and are consequently unintelligible to one not belonging to the caste of the śilpīs. This has been the reason why inspite of the great labours of the scholars our knowledge of the Indian architectural science has not advanced as has been expected.

The third approach to Indian architectural study was first initiated by Ram Raz in the year 1835 in an essay entitled '*Architecture of the Hindus*.' Ram Raz read the Sanskrit texts of the '*Śilpashāstra*' with the help of local craftsmen and employed the knowledge so gained in analysing the architectural forms extant in the Deccan. A combination was thus effected between the çraftsman's traditional knowledge, field work and Sanskrit learning, and the results yielded thereof were correspondingly of a very valuable character. In the year 1912, Manmohan Ganguly, an engineer by profession, a Sanskritist and a wide traveller applied the same method to an even analysis of Orissan architecture. Manmohan Ganguly had secured an Oriya Manuscript on architecture but having no parallel reading in his possession he had failed to make proper use of it. He, therefore, analysed the forms with the help of local craftsmen and also applied his knowledge of western architecture to the task.. In this manner he succeeded in restoring a large part of the traditional knowledge of ancient Orissan architecture.

Then comes Bose's own approach towards the study of architecture. This, he admittedly considered as the continuation of the works of Manmohan Ganguly. In other words, Nirmal Kumar Bose began where Manmohan Ganguly had left off. Several readings of Orissan architecture as was secured and sustained with the help of local craftsmen were made use of. Professor Bose supplemented these by the field works done by him in different parts of Orissa and the neighbouring provinces. "A workable restoration of the science of architecture in Orissa has thus been studied. When similar restorations are available and the existing examples are studied in their light, it will be possible to reconstruct the history of Indian architecture with some degree of certainty."[172]

Bose believed that historical research on Indian architecture moved in a unilinear direction. Works of a particular group of historians were certainly developments upon the works of their predecessors.

This was because the earlier group of historians who worked on Indian architecture were Britishers who had got severe limitations of their own. They were conversant with the European method of architecture and could not properly comprehend the local science of architecture in India. Without a proper and detailed study of this local science of architecture, researches on Indian architecture would certainly be incomplete. The attention of the successive scholars were to unearth the details of this local science on Indian architecture from different ancient texts and *śilpaśāstras* restored from time to time. The descriptive notes of these texts were later properly scrutinised and confirmed by the extensive field work undertaken at different sites of ancient monuments.

The main idea behind this exercise was to establish the science of Indian architecture with a fair degree of certainty. This is equally necessary to understand the artist's expression of thought in his works.

Forms, methods and approaches to study the Indian architecture cannot thus be complete at any particular point of time, believes Nirmal Kumar Bose. Forms are employed by the artists to express certain thoughts and the students of Indian architecture may either be interested in the history or the forms or in that of the ideas which they are meant to convey. In one case, he is like a student of literature. Havel, unlike Fergusson, was interested in the latter aspect. To him, architectural history becomes a means of investigation into the history of Indian thought and civilisation. But the profund penetration for this task is not only rare but also the results are not acceptable to scientific verification. "We, therefore, have to be content with a scientific study of the outer forms of architecture alone and rest satisfied with the light which it may throw upon the development of Indian history," Bose candidly observes. An expert in anthropology, Bose thus revealed the anthropological researches on Indian history and would like that any work on Indian architecture should be open to scientific enquiry, no matter even if for this work we have to contend ourselves to the study of the outer forms alone. Further, whatever forms, methods or approaches might have been applied this should throw light on the development of Indian history.

The historical ideas of Nirmal Kumar Bose, as far as his studies on Orissan history are concerned, can be summed up as follows:

(a) Professor Bose believed that researches on Indian architecture had a unilinear form.

(b) Establishing the history of Indian architecture with some amount of certainty and accuracy would need the restoration of texts on the local science of architecture, their study and interpretation and confirmation by sufficient fieldwork and experiments.

(c) Any work an architecture should be subject to scientific enquiry and investigations even if this sets a limit to the study of the aesthetic part of architecture. And for this again, the study of the outer forms of architecture is only warranted.

(d) Forms, methods and approaches on the study of Indian architecture are not complete at any particular point. It is progressive with time and cannot be subject to any kind of limitations.

But very much like all other non-professional historians of architecture as he himself was, Nirmal Kumar Bose concentrated only on the study of the outer forms of architecture, the rather scientific details like measurements, construction style, etc., of the architectural monuments. This seems to be a relatively easier design and attempt than going to discuss the artistic details, iconographic representations, etc., which normally should be within the scope of the work of an art historian.

Nirmal Kumar Bose did never go into any such finer details of art in his study of Orissan architecture. Moreover, we do not have a complete chronological study of Orissan art and architecture in *"Canons of Orissan Architecture"*.

References

1. Manmohan Chakrabotry, '*Two Copper-Plate Grants of Barsimha Deva*' in *Journal of Asiatic Society of Bengal*, 1895, p.128.
2. Manmohan Chakraborty in *Proceedings of the Asiatic Society of Bengal*, 1892, p.140-41.
3. Manmohan Chakraborty, *Oriya Language and Literature*, part iii & iv, 1898, Calcutta, p.379.
4. Bishen Swarup, Konark: the black pagoda of Orissa, 1910, Reprint 1980, Ramananda Vidya Bhawan, New Delhi.

5. *Ibid.*, Preface.
6. *Ibid.*, p.17.
7. Peferences=VI
8. *Ibid.*, p.23.
9. *Ibid.*, p.27.
10. *Ibid.*, p.52.
11. *Ibid.*, p.46.
12. *Ibid.*, p.47.
13. *Ibid.*, p.47.
14. *Ibid.*, p.75.
15. *Ibid.*, p.56.
16. *Ibid.*, p.57.
17. *Ibid.*, p.63.
18. *Ibid.*, p.48.
19. *Ibid.*, p.49.
20. *Ibid.*, p.99.
21. *Ibid.*, p.99.
22. *Ibid.*, p.99.
23. *Ibid.*, p.99.
24. *Ibid.*, p.99.
25. *Ibid.*, p.99.
26. *Ibid.*, p.104.
27. Manmohan Ganguly, *Orissa and her Remains*, 1912, Calcutta.
28. *Ibid.*, see Preface.
29. J.G. Woodruff in foreword to '*Orissa and her Remains*', 1912, Calcutta.
30. *Ibid.*
31. See Preface to Orissa and her remains, Calcutta, 1912.
32. Manmohan Ganguly, *op.cit.*, Preface.
33. *Ibid.*, p.155.
34. *Ibid.*, Preface.
35. R D Banerji, *History of Orissa*, vol.ii, Calcutta 1912, p.335-38.
36. *Ibid.*, p.1.
37. *Ibid.*, p.2.
38. *Ibid.*, p.3.

39. *Ibid.*, p.4.
40. *Ibid.*, p.5.
41. *Ibid.*, p.379-80.
42. *Ibid.*, p.379.
43. *Ibid.*, p.380.
44. Paramananda Acharya, *Odissara Pratnattva o Anyanya Prabandha*, Bhubaneswar, 1969, p.135-36.
45. Manmohan Ganguly, *op.cit.*, p.63.
46. Manmohan Ganguly, *op.cit.*, p.6.
47. *Ibid.*, p.6.
48. *Ibid.*, p.161.
49. *Ibid.*, p.161.
50. *Ibid.*, p.162.
51. *Ibid.*, p.162.
52. *Ibid.*, p.199.
53. *Ibid.*, p.199.
54. *Ibid.*, p.226.
55. *Epigraphica Indica*, ix (1907-8), p.285-88.
56. *Epigraphica Indica*, xi (1911), p.281-87.
57. *Epigraphica Indica*, xii (1913-14), p.156-59.
58. *Epigraphica Indica*, xii (1913-14), p.321-28.
59. *Epigraphica Indica*, xiii (1915-16), p.159-67.
60. *Journal of the Proceedings of the Asiatic Society of Bengal*, xii, (1916), p.291-95.
61. *Journal of Bihar and Orissa Research Society,* 111, 3, (1917), p.319-23.
62. *Journal of Bihar and Orissa Research Society,* 111, 4 (1917) p.486-507.
63. *Epigraphica Indica,* xv, (1919), p.1-8.
64. *Epigraphica Indica*, xix, 4 (1928).
65. *Modern Review*, xliv (1928), p.636-40.
66. *Journal of Bihar and Orissa Research Society*, xiv, 1(1928), p.114-26.
67. *Indian Antiquary*, lvii, (1928), p.235-39.
68. *Modern Review*, xliv, (1928), p.9-16.
69. *Indian Antiquary,* lvii, (1928-29) p.235-39.

70. *Journal of Bihar and Orissa Research Society*, xv, (1929), p.64-84.
71. *Epigraphica Indica*, xx, (1929-30) p.100-04.
72. *Proceedings of Indian Oriental Conference*, v, 1, (1930), p.364-85.
73. *History of Orissa from Earliest Times to British Period*, Calcutta (1930-31).
74. *Memoirs of Asiatic Society of Bengal*, xi, 3 (1931), p.132-45.
75. *Journal of Bihar and Orissa Research Society*, xviii, À (1932) p.383-85.
76. *Journal of Bihar and Orissa Research Society,* xviii, À (1932), p.387-90.
77. R.D. Banerji, *History of Orissa*, Vol.I & II, 1930-31, R. Chatterjee & Co., Calcutta.
78. *Ibid*, Vol.I., p.161.
79. *Ibid*, Vol.I., p.161.
80. *Ibid*., p.226.
81. *Ibid*., p.9.
82. *Ibid*., p.15.
83. *Ibid*., p.29.
84. *Ibid*., p.2.
85. *Ibid*., p.58.
86. *Ibid*., p.196.
87. *Ibid*., p.108.
88. *Ibid*., p.256.
89. *Ibid*., p.263.
90. *Ibid*., p.263.
91. *Ibid*., p.265.
92. *Ibid*., p.304.
93. *Ibid*., p.304.
94. *Ibid*., p.325.
95. *Ibid*., p.330.
96. *Ibid*., p.332.
97. *Ibid*., p.333.
98. *Ibid*., p.335.
99. *Ibid*., p.336.

100. *Ibid.*, p.336.
101. *Ibid.*, p.330.
102. *Ibid.*, Vol.II. p.337-38.
103. *Ibid.*, p.335.
104. *Ibid.*, p.335.
105. *Ibid.*, p.337-38.
106. *Ibid.*, Vol.I, p.85.
107. *Ibid.*, p.86.
108. *Ibid.*, Vol.II, p.350-51.
109. *Ibid.*, p.387.
110. K.K. Dasgupta, 'R.D. Banerjee' in S.P. Sen (Ed)- *Historians and Historiography of India*, Calcutta, 1973, p.25.
111. Benimadhab Barua, *Ashok and his Inscriptions*, 1946, Calcutta, p.4.
112. *Ibid.*, p.4.
113. Benimadhab Barua, *Old Brahmi Inscriptions in Udayagiri and Khandagiri Caves* (1929), University of Calcutta, p.324.
114. Benimadhab Barua, *Ashok and his Inscriptions* (1946), New Age Publications, Calcutta, p.472.
115. *Indian Historical Quarterly*, i-1, 2, 50-58, 245-49.
116. *Indian Historical Quarterly*, ii-1, p.16-17.
117. *Indian Historical Quarterly*, ii-3, p.1-31.
118. *Indian Historical Quarterly*, ii-1, 87-128.
119. *Indian Historical Quarterly*, iii-2, 235-61.
120. *Indian Historical Quarterly*, iv-3, 511-29.
121. *Indian Historical Quarterly*, vi-1, 1-31.
122. *Proceedings of Indian Oriental Conference*, 15th Session, Lahore 1928, Lahore (1930), v, 1, p.364-85.
123. *Indian Historical Quarterly*, ix-2, 417-419.
124. *Indian Culture*, 1,1,p.126-127.
125. *Indian Historical Quarterly*, x-1, p.54-56.
126. *Indian Historical Quarterly*, x-1, p.57-66.
127. *Indian Historical Quarterly*, xiv-1, p.158-166.
128. *Indian Historical Quarterly*, xiv-3, p.459-85.
129. *Journal of Indian Society of Oriental Art*, xv, p.45-61.
130. *Indian Historical Quarterly*, xxiii-3, p.242-47.

131. Benimadhab Barua, *Old Brahmi Inscriptions in Udayagiri and Khandagiri Caves,* (1929), Calcutta, Preface.
132. *Ibid.*
133. *Ibid.*
134. *Ibid.*
135. *Ibid.*
136. *Ibid.*, p.40.
137. *Ibid.*, p.140
138. *Ibid.*, p.152.
139. *Ibid.*, p.176.
140. *Ibid.*, p.179.
141. *Ibid.*, p.180.
142. *Ibid.*, p.250
143. *Ibid.*, p.252.
144. Benimadhab Barua, *Ashok and his Inscriptions* (1946), Calcutta, p.5.
145. *Ibid.*, p.4.
146. *Ibid.*, p.4.
147. *Ibid.*, p.4.
148. Benimadhab Barua, *Presidential Address to the Ancient Indian* Section of Indian History Congress, Annamalainagar, 1946.
149. *op.cit.* (1946), Preface.
150. Binayak Mishra, *Orissa under Bhauma Kings*, Calcutta, 1934.
151. Binayak Mishra, *Dynasties of Medieval Orissa*, Calcutta, 1936.
152. *Journal of Bihar and Orissa Research Society*, xii, 4(1926), p.585-86.
153. *Journal of Bihar and Orissa Research Society*, xii, (1926), p.289.
154. *Journal of Bihar and Orissa Research Society*, 13, 1, (1927), p.86-89.
155. *Journal of Bihar and Orissa Research Society*, xiv, 1, (1928), p.144-46.
156. *Journal of Bihar and Orissa Research Society*, xvi, 1 (1930). p.1.
157. *Journal of Bihar and Orissa Research Society,* xvii, 1(1931), p.104-18.
158. *Indian Historical Quarterly*, vii, 3, (1931), p.665-68.

159. *Orissa under Bhauma Kings*, (1934), Calcutta, p.98.
160. *Indian Historical Quarterly*, xii, 3, (1936), p.485-88.
161. *Dynasties of Medieval Orissa,* (1936), Calcutta, p.111.
162. *Indian Historical Quarterly,* xiii, 3, (1937), p.418-31.
163. *Journal of Orissa Academy,* ii, 1, (1938), p.39-43.
164. *Mayurbhanj Chronicle,* viii, 4, (1939), p.20-22.
165. Refer to foreword by Prof. R.P. Chanda in *'Dynasties of Medieval Orissa'*, Calcutta, 1936.
166. *Ibid.*, p.8.
167. *Ibid.*, p.43.
168. Nirmal Kumar Bose, *Canons of Orissan Architecture*, Calcutta, 1932 (*reprint*, 1980).
169. Nirmal Kumar Bose, *Excavations of Mayurbhanj*, Calcutta University, Monograph, 1948.
170. See Preface to the book *"Canons of Orissan Architecture"* Calcutta, 1932.
171. Nirmal Kumar Bose, *op.cit.*, 1932, Introduction.
172. *Ibid.*, Introduction.

9

Conclusion

The centrality of the Raj in the British empire rendered the Indian undertaking very attractive. The conquest of Bengal in 1757 reinforced British culture with a renewed interest in militarism, royalty, national heroes, cult of personality, racial ideas of differences amidst similarities, racial superiority and a contrived sense of Christian mission. The Raj became an essential part of British social and political history. It hastened the development of the core culture of imperialism and fashioned the dominant ideology of the British society. The determination to hold India at all costs led to the improvisation of a series of imperial myths and legends. The British mission in India was providential in character, which was upheld on the grounds of lofty moral principles. By the middle of the nineteenth century they had already become masters of the enormous territory. This conferred on the British character a sense of imperial pride and it had also engineered a set of prejudices. Despite the British liberal traditions of freedom and justice, the maintenance of an arbitrary rule over India was sought to be cushioned by widely circulated racial stereotypes. Kipling gave the Raj a wide ideological umbrella.

India, according to British statesmen, was a geographical expression, inhabited by various ethnic stocks and held together by British imperial hegemony. It had been held that the empire was necessary at certain stages of civilisation and for the world's progress. A Christian sense of superiority was grafted on to that imperial mission. Christianity and progress according to the imperial ideologues were interdependent as a universal law for all times, all states and all societies.

In the historiographical discourses, the British encountered in the mid-eighteenth century India a varied, complex and highly developed civilisation, which was very different from that of contemporary Europe. The British administrators in their attempt to understand this complex reality developed paradigms, which emphasized the difference rather than the similarities between the two cultures. It is interesting that the conceptualisation of India as one of Europe's proto type, quintessentially different from the west since the beginning of time, belongs to the high noon of the empire.

By then Britain and Western Europe were convinced of their inherent superiority, the result of cultural evolution somehow similar to the evolution of species. Utilitarian philosophy, which inspired the early 19th century projects of reform and development in India, were inspired by the same ideology. One of its progenitors, James Mill, was convinced that Indians were inferior to the nobler animals. The orientalists who took a much more sympathetic view of at least the Indian past were believers in the simple dichotomy of the East and the West.

The British colonialist historiography consisted of a coherent set of ideas. That India's past had to be explained and made subservient to the needs of the Raj. The technological prowess of Britain had provided it with the moral right to explain Indian history. Technology was accepted as the appropriate measure for judging the worth of cultures and to mark out differing levels of achievement between itself and India. While similarities demanded by the Aryan theory were accommodated, the differences in terms of decline or of invincible mobility were accentuated. These were shaped to insure a space in India for the Raj.

The historiography of Orissa during the entire period of the British rule in Orissa was also moulded in the same line. William Bruton and Thomas Motte belonged to the mercantilist phase of Orissan historiography. Bruton was very keen in securing space for free trade for the British in Orissa. He described the land of Orissa as debased and people as idolatrous, ignorant and backward. Lockean Mercantilist thought guided Thomas Motte's intentions. He studied the communication system, and market forces in greater detail. Very often he had mentioned about the backwardness and barbarity of the people. As the expansion of the British empire in Orissa was his essential motive, so he frequently mentioned about the lawlessness and anarchy of the country and the necessity of the establishment of British rule in Orissa.

James Princep, Andrew Stirling, Markham Kittoe, J.R.Ouseley, James Fergusson, etc., during the first half of nineteenth century were mostly guided by the Victorian philosophy of ordering and classifying India's difference according to the scientific system of 'knowing'. Princep's contributions as an epigraphist and historian were enormous. He provided one of the finest phases of Indological studies undertaken by the Asiatic Society of Bengal. Himself a genius, Princep had the rare gift of enthusing others with his love of learning, so that they bore all kinds of hardships. Princep provided a sound footing for the study of archaeology and numismatics and discovered several important kings and dynasties of ancient India. His greatest achievement was the decipherment of the Asokan inscriptions, without which Asoka would have remained unknown to Indian history.

Stirling's *Account of Orissa* was the first comprehensive study of the state. He described its physical features, giving details of the soil, products, rivers and towns, and also dwelt on the population, the castes and customs, political institutions and the land tenure system. The most important was his account of the history and antiquities of Orissa. Because of the legendary nature of the sources he had taken into consideration, Stirling's account conveyed an idea of Orissa's past before its ancient history began to be discovered. The superiority of the British over their Indian subjects, Orissan architecture lacking universally valid principles, the decline of Indian culture, timidity, backwardness, short-sighted attitude towards the Hindu faith had remained the general characteristics of Stirling's magisterial readings.

Markham Kittoe was the most indefatigable coadjutors of James Princep. He had investigated the ruins in Orissa and discovered an important series of inscriptions on a rock at Dhauli, (then in Cuttack). Those discovered by Kittoe at Dhauli proved to be identical with those received from Girnar in Gujrat, being a series of inscriptions of King Asoka. Kittoe had acknowledged that Orissa possessed more temples, sacred spots and relics than any other province in Hindustan. Besides being a sober orientalist, colonialist knowledge had also its imprints on his work. He described the people as troublesome, timid, superstitious. Besides, he had pointed out the defects of Indian architecture.

J.R.Ousley's *Tour diary* was replete with mismanagement tyranny and lawlessness existing in the northern and western part of Orissa.The existence of dirt and disease in the countryside had encompassed his knowledge. His primary motive was to advance arguments in favour of amalgamation of Sambalpur tract into the British territory. So at every stage of his report, imperial bearings were explicitly clear.

Fergusson being a hard core colonialist tried to accentuate the differences between the British and India. He wanted vehemently to establish and justify the superiority of the Britons over the Indians.

W.W. Hunter was highly complacent about the imperialistic achievements of the British people. He opined that the main reason for the success of Europeans in the East was the national character of their attempts. His historical works conformed to the modern lines of historiography. Hunter's "*Orissa*" displayed a curious admixture of both colonialist and liberal historiography.

John Beames' approach to the administration was extremely critical. He had on many occasions challenged the un-British character of the rule of the British in India. Simultaneously he had spoken of the civilising missions of the British in India. He had demarcated the areas, which contained the modern elements of British culture. He had also mentioned about the efficacy of the British laws and regulations in Orissa. He considered the British always superior to the Indians. So Beames' scholarship combined in itself a magisterial sentiment and oriental scholarship.

The discovery of India's past had left an indelible impact on the course of modern Indian history. It led to the evolution of historical consciousness in its people. Another most important effect of the discovery of a rich past was that it fostered a sense of nationalism and patriotism among the Indians. It was one of the long-term ironies of history that it was the British rule that led to the renaissance in India, consciousness of her identity and her past, the ultimate emergence of nationalism. Orissa provided one of the bright examples of the growth of consciousness among the Oriyas regarding their social, cultural and linguistic identity. In this context the racial history of Orissa constructed by Hunter and Beames philological analysis had a major role to play. The controversy regarding the individuality of the Oriyas had gone to such an extent that the Oriya delegates had no independent political identity in the Indian National Congress till the early years the of twentieth century. They were either known as delegates from Bengal or the Madras Presidency. With the new province coming into being from Ist April, 1936, the dream of years at last became a reality giving the Oriya-speaking people a separate and distinct political identity. It marked the culmination of a long period of peaceful and constitutional struggle in defence of linguistic and cultural homogeneity which later formed the basis of reorganisation of states in independent India in 1955. Thus the people of Orissa had played the pioneering role in the formation of linguistic the states in India.

Indian historians had always been eager to hang the British historians on the lamp posts of the Raj Syndrome without seriously analysing their works and their 'crimes'. They had just been given a bad name. Indian historians were more earnest in accepting the glory of India's past as revealed by the British historians, but the historians themselves were rejected as biased and motivated. So it would be right, if we help on highlighting the fact that many of the British historians were scholars in the true sense of the term for the history of Orissa.

The nationalist historians of Orissa, on the other hand, took up the challenge thrown at them by the Orientalist-colonialist historians and adopted a more regional approach where a nationalistic view of Orissan history was attempted. These nationalist scholars also tried to unearth many historical source materials and interpreted them in their own way only to arrive at some conclusions which suited their objective of glorifying Orissa's past. They were amateurish and were devoted squarely to the cause of the amalgamation of Oriya-speaking tracts and the formation of a separate province for Orissa on linguistic basis. Their writings influenced some writers and future historians even after independence.

Though Rajendra Lal Mitra took a partisan bias against the Oriyas, still he set the foundation for the study of the antiquities and architecture of Orissa on scientific lines. Bijoy Chandra Majumdar, who also had certain reservations against the Oriyas, wrote his works to glorify the past of his patron, the Sonepur Raj family, and to denigrate the lineage of the Bhanja ruling family.

The last group of historians proved themselves as trend setters for the scholars of the post-independence period. The works of Bishen Swarup, Manmohan Ganguly and Nirmal Kumar Bose on the monuments and architecture were widely quoted and referred to by art historians like Vidya Dehejia, Stella Kamrisch, Charles Fabri, Sarasi Kumar Saraswati, Vasudev Saran Agrawala and others. Similarly the inscriptional works of Manmohan Chakraborty, Benimadhav Barua and Pandit Binayak Mishra influenced many scholars like Paramananda Acharya, Kedarnath Mohapatra, Satyanarayan Rajguru, Sushil Chandra De, Dinesh Chandra Sircar, Nabin Kumar Sahu et al. who tried to unearth many new historical source materials and utilized them in their writings on the different aspects of Orissan history and culture. Rakhal Das Banerjee's "*History of Orissa*" in two volumes happened to be the only systematic and comprehensive work on Orissan history before independence and it served as a model for future scholars who worked on the different aspects of Orissan history and culture in the post-independence years. Because of the sincere efforts of these scholars a fairly reliable chronology of the political history of Orissa has been fixed and a fair idea about her art treasures has been formed.

These sober historical writings set the model of historical research for many historians of the later generations. By their scientific approach towards writing history, these writers remained a source of inspiration for future writers. Banerjee's works on the history of Orissa has often been quoted as a standard historical work on Orissa. The influence of Rakhal Das Banerjee's trend of research is clearly perceived on many historical works of the later generations.

Bibliography

PRIMARY SOURCES

Acharya, Pyarimohan

1981 *Odissara Itihasa*, Orissa Book Store, Cuttack, *reprint* of 1880;1981, 181 pages.

Banerjee, Rakhal Das

1907 "Patiakela Grant of Svaraj Gupta" in *Epigraphica Indica,*IX, p.285-88, 1907-08.

1911 "Parikuda Plates of Madhyamarajadeva" in *Epigraphica Indica,* XI, p.281-87.

1913 "Talcher Grant of Kulasthamba" in *Epigraphica Indica*, XII, p.156-159.

1913 "Two Baudh Grants of Ranabhanja Deva" in *Epigraphica Indica,* XII, p.321-28.

1915-16 "Inscriptions in Udayagiri and Khandagiri caves" in *Epigraphica Indica,* XIII, p.159-167.

1916 "Talcher grant of Gayadatungadeva" in *Journal of Proceedings of the Asiatic Society of Bengal,* XII, p.291-95.

1917 "Bhanja dynasty of Orissa" in *Journal of Bihar and Orissa Research Society,* III,3, p.319-23.

1918 Notes on the Hathigumpha inscription of Kharavela" in *Journal of Bihar and Orissa Research Society,* III,4, p.486-507.

1919 "Neulpur grant of Subhakara" in *Epigraphica Indica*, XV, p.1-8.

1924 *Age of Imperial Guptas,* Calcutta.

1928 Dhauli cave inscription of Santikara" in *Epigraphica Indica,* XIX,4, p.263.

1928 *"Kara of Orissa"* in *Modern Review*, XLIV, P.636-640.

1928 "Baud plates of Kanakabhanja" in *Journal of Bihar and Orissa Research Society,* XIV,1, p.114-26.

1028 "Temples of Orissa" in *Indian Antiquity*, LVII, p.235-239.

1928 "Non-Buddhistic Cave temples" in *Modern Review*, XLIV, p.9-16.

1929 "The Empire of Orissa" in *Indian Antiquity*, LVII, p.235-39.

1930 "Antiquities of the Baudh State" in *Journal of Bihar and Orissa Research Society*, XV, 1-2, p.64-84.

1929-30 "Patna Museum Plates of Ranabhanja" in *Epigraphica Indica*, XX, p.100-04.

1931 "Kharavela's Personal History" in *Proceedings of Indian Oriental Conference,* Lahore, VI, p.364-85.

1929 *History of Orissa from Earliest Times to British Period,* R. Chatterjee & Co, Calcutta, Vol.I 351 pages and Vol.II, 481 pages.

1930 "Paleography of the Hathigumpha and Nanaghat inscriptions" in *Memoirs of the Asiatic Society of Bengal*, XI,3, p.132-45.

1931 "Notes on the Puri Plates of Dharmaraja" in *Journal of Bihar and Orissa Research Society*, XVIII, 3-4, p.383-85.

1932 "Tekkali Plates of Satrubhanja" in *Journal of Bihar and Orissa Research Society,* XVIII, À, p.387-90.

Banerjee, R.D. & K.P. Jayaswal

1917 "Hathigumpha Inscription of Kharavela" in *Journal of Bihar and Orissa Research Society,* III, 4, p.325-72.

Barua, Benimadhav

1925 "Message from Bharut Jataka Labels" in *Indian Historical Quarterly,* 1-1-2, p.50-58 and 245-49.

1926 "Stupa and Tomb" in *Indian Historical Quarterly,* II-1, p.16-27.

1926 "Multiplication of Jataka" in *Indian Historical Quarterly*, II-3, p.1-31.

1926 "Inscriptional excursions" in *Indian Historical Quarterly*, II-1, p.87-128.

1927 "Maskari as Epithet of Gopala" in *Indian Historical Quarterly,* III-2, p.235-61.

1928 "Old Brahmi Inscriptions in Udayagiri and Khandagiri Language" in *Indian Historical Quarterly*, IV-3, p.511-29.

1929 *Old Brahmi Inscriptions in Udayagiri and Khandagiri Caves,* University of Calcutta, 324 pages.

1930 "Old Buddhist Shrines from Bodhgaya" in *Indian Historical Quarterly,*VI-1, p.1-31.

1930 "Karavela's Personal History" in *Proceedings of Indian Oriental* Conference, 15th session, 1928, Lahore (1930), V,1, p.364-85.

1933 "Bodhgaya image inscriptions" in *Indian Historical Quarterly,* IX-2, p.417-19.

1934 "Estimation of the people of Orissa" in *Indian Culture,* 1,1, p.126-27.

1931 "The Sohgaura Plate" in *Indian Historical Quarterly,* X-1, p.54-56.

1934 "Old Brahmi Inscriptions of Mahasthana" in *Indian Historical Quarterly,* X-1, p.57-66.

1938 "Minor Old Brahmi Inscriptions in the Khandagiri and Udayagiri Caves" in *Indian Historical Quarterly,* XIV, p.1158-166.

1938 "Hathigumpha Inscription of Kharavela" in *Indian Historical Quarterly,* XIV-3, p.459-85.

1946 *Ashoka and his Inscriptions,* New Age Publications, Calcutta, 472 pages.

1947 "Kharavela as King and Builder" in *Journal of Indian Society of Oriental Art,* XV, p.45-61.

1947 "The Scribe Engravers of Indrapala's Second Copper-Plate and Prakrit of Pre-Ahom times" in *Indian Historical Quarterly,* XXIII-3, p.242-47.

Beames, John

1871 "The Ruins of Kopari; Balasore District" *in Journal of Asiatic Society of Bengal,* X, p.247-50.

1872 "More Buddhist Remains in Orissa" in *Journal of Asiatic Society of Bengal,* XLI, I, p.7-8.

1872 "Jungle Forts of Northern Orissa" in *Indian Antiquary,* I, p.33-76, 74-76.

1872 "Folklore of Orissa" in *Indian Antiquary,* I,7, p.168-220, 21-212.

1874 "Query on the Mode of Dating in Orissa" in *Indian Antiquary,* I, 2, p.64.

1875 "The Altai Hills in Cuttack" in *Journal of Asiatic Society of Bengal,* XLIV, p.19-23.

1883 "Notes on the History of Orissa under Mohemmadan, Marhatta and English Rule" in *Journal of Asiatic Society of Bengal,* LII, 1, p.231-58.

1896 *Memoirs of a Bengal Civilian*, reprint 1984, Manohar Publications, New Delhi.

Bose, Nirmal Kumar

1929 "Some Ancient Remains from Bhubaneswar" in *Journal of Bihar and Orissa Research Society*, XV, 1-2, p.259-62.

1931 "Odissake Mandir" in *Vishal Bharat*, VIII, I, p.99-109.

1932 *Canons of Orissan Architecture*, R.Chatterjee & Co, Calcutta,194 pages, reprint 1982, Cosmo Publications, 211 pages.

1939 "An Illustrated Manuscript from Orissa" in *Modern Review*, LXV, p.95-97.

1940 "Prehistoric Researches in Mayurbhanj" in *Science and Culture*, VI, p.75-79.

Chakraborty, Manmohan

1895 "Two Copper-Plate Inscriptions of King Narasimha Deva IV of Orissa" in *Journal of Asiatic Society of Bengal*, LXIV, p.128-54.

1897 Notes on the Language and Literature of Orissa" in *Journal of the Asiatic Society of Bengal*, LXIV & lxvii.

1898 "The Date of the Jagannath Temple in Puri" in *Journal of the Asiatic Society of Bengal*, LXVII, p.328-31.

1900 "Inscriptions of Kapilendra Deva" in *Journal of the Asiatic Society of Bengal*, LXIX, p.173-89.

1903 "Chronology of the Eastern Gangas of Orissa" in *Journal of the Asiatic Society of Bengal*, I, p.97-147.

1908 "Certain Unpublished Drawings of Antiquities in Orissa and Northern Circars" in *Journal of the Proceedings of the Asiatic Society of Bengal*, IV, p.299-325.

1916 "Notes on the Geography of Orissa in Sixteenth Century" in *Journal of the Asiatic Society of Bengal*, XII, p.29-56.

Dash, Nilakantha

1927 "A Short Review of the History of Kalinga" in *Journal of the Andhra Historical Research Society*, II, 1, p.12-33.

1946 "Visva Samskrutiku Odissara Dana" in *Nav Bharat*,1,1, p.1-10.

1958 "Bharatiya Samskrutiku Odissara Dana" in *Jhankar*, X, 2, p.191-97.

Ganguly, Manmohan

1912 *Orissa and her Remains: Ancient and Medieval*, Thacker and Spink, Calcutta, 540 pages.

Hunter, William Wilson

1872 *Orissa or Vicissitudes of an Indian Province under Native and British Rule*, Vol I & II, Thacker and Spink, Clacutta, Vol I, 330 pages and Vol II, 278 pages.

Hunter, W.W., Andrew Stirling, John Beames and N K Sahu

1956 *History of Orissa*, Vol. I & II, Sushil De & Co, Calcutta.

Kar, Birupakshya

1920 *Utkalere Baudha Yugara Itihasa O anyanya Prabandha*, reprint in a compiled form in 1981, Grantha Mandir, Cuttack.

Majumdar, Bijoy Chandra

1911 *Sonepur in the Sambalpur Tract*, University of Calcutta.

1920 "A Brief Historical Sketch of Orissa" in *Journal of Bihar and Orissa Research Society*, VI, 3, p.348-60.

1925 Orissa in the making, University of Calcutta, 247 pages.

1925 *Typical Selections from Oriya Literature*, Vol. I, II,III, University of Calcutta.

Mishra, Binayak

1926 "A Note on the Kangod Country" in *Journal of Bihar and Orissa Research Society*, XII,4, p.585-86.

1926 "Note on the Time of Kara Dynasty" in *Journal of Bihar and Orissa Research Society*, XII, p.289.

1927 "The Area of Orissa in Hiuen Tsang's Time" in *Journal of Bihar and Orissa Research Society*,13,1, p.86-89.

1928 "Trikalinga Country" in *Journal of Bihar and Orissa Research Society*, XIV, I, p.144-46.

1927 "Hindol Plates of Subhakaradeva" in *Journal of Bihar and Orissa Research Society*, XVI,1, p.71.

1928 "Copper-Plate Grant of Netabhanja" in *Journal of Bihar and Orissa Research Society*, XVII, I, p.104-18.

1931 "Sailodbhava Rulers of Kangoda" in *Indian Historical Quarterly*, VII, 3, p.665-68.

1934 *Orissa under Bhauma Kings*, Calcutta, 98 pages.

1932 "Narasimha Stone Inscription of Vijaladeva" in *Indian Historical Quarterly*, XII, 3, p.485-88.

1936 *Dynasties of Medieval Orissa*, K.N. Chatterjee, Calcutta, 111 pages.

1937 "Maurya Chandragupta and Mayurbhanj Rulers" in *Indian Historical Quarterly*, XIII, 3, p.418-31.

1938 "Initial Year of Ganga Era" in *Journal of Orissan Academy,* II, 1, p. 39-43.

1933 "Identification of Indradyumna" in *Mayurbhanj Chronicle,*VIII,4, p.20-22.

Mishra, Krupasindhu

1912 *Barabati Durga,* Cuttack Trading Co, 62 pages.

1929 *Utkal Itihasa,* Cuttack Trading Co.

1934 Konark, Cuttack Trading Co, 425 pages.

Mitra, Rajendra Lal

1873 *Antiquities of Orissa,* Vol.I & Vol.II, Calcutta, reprint Mukhopadhyaya & Co, Calcutta, 1961-63, 252 pages and Vol. II 269 pages.

Mottoe, Thomas

1786 "A Narrative of a Journey to the Diamond Mines at Sambalpur", *Asiatic Miscellaney,* Vol. II (reprinted in the *Orissa Historical Research Journal,* Vol. I, 3, 1952).

Risley, Herbert

1915 *People of India,* London (reprinted Delhi, 1969).

Singh Jagabandhu

1928 *Prachina Utkala,* Puri Press, reprint 1964, Vol. I & Vol. II, Orissa Sahitya Akademy, Bhubaneswar, Vol I, 318 pages and Vol. II 248 pages.

1929 "Kalinga" in *Journal of Andhra Historical Research Society,* II, p 196-203.

Stirling, Andrew

1822 *An Account Geographical, Statistical and Historical of Orissa Proper or Cuttack"* in Asiatic Researches, XV, p. 163-338.

1846 *Orissa: Its Geography, Statistics, Religion and Antiquities,* John Snow, London 416 pages.

Swarup, Bishen

1909 *Konark: The Black Pagoda of Orissa,* Star Press, Cuttack, 104 pages, reprint 1980, Ramananda Vidya Mandir, Delhi,110 pages.

Toynbee, G.

1874 *A Sketch of the History of Orissa 1803-1828, Calcutta.* reprinted in *The Orissa Historical Research Journal,* Vol. IX (1&2), 1960 and Vol. X (1&2), 1961.

SECONDARY SOURCES

BOOKS

Acharya, Paramananda

1935 *Two Centuries of British Connection: A Chapter from History of Mayurbhanj,* Mayurbhanj State press.

1969 Studies in Orissan History, Archaeology and Archives, Baripada.

1969 *Odissara Pratnatatva O anyanya Prabandha,* Orissa Sahitya Akademi, Bhubaneswar

Acton, *Lord*

1904 The Study of History, London.

1905 *Lectures on Modern History,* reprint, 1960, with an introduction by Trevor Roper, London.

Allan J. (et al)

1933 *The Cambridge Shorter History of India,* New York.

Alvares, Claude

1991 *Decolonising History*, New York.

Ambasthya, B.P.

1976 *Beames Contribution to the Political Geography of the Subahs of Awadh, Bihar, Bengal and Orissa in the Age of Akbar,* Patna.

Arendt, Hanna

1951 *Origin of Totalitarianism*, New York.

1988 *Imperialism*, New York.

Bellamy, Richard

1990 (ed) *Victorian Liberalism,* London.

Bloch, Marc

1954 *Historians' Craft,* Manchester.

Chakraborty, Suhas

1989 *The Raj Syndrome,* New Delhi.

Chandra, Bipan N.D.

Colonialism, Stages of Colonialism and Colonial State, Monograph.

Chaturvedi, Badrinath

1992 *Dharma, India and World Order,* Edinburgh.

Cohen, Benjamin J.

1973 *The Question of Imperialism: The Political Economy of Dominance and Dependence,* New York.

Cromer, Earl of

1910 *Ancient and Modern Imperialism,* London.

Dash, Chintamani

1962 *Aitihasika Krupasindhu,* Samaj, Cuttack.

1982 *Manishi Nilakantha,* Bhubaneswar.

Dasgupta, K.K.

1976 *Indian Historiography and Rajendra Lal Mitra,* Calcutta.

Devahuti

1980 (ed) *Bias in Indian Historiography,* Delhi.

Ganguly, Dilip Kumar

1975 *Historiographical Geography and Dynastic History of Orissa,* Calcutta.

Geyl, Peter

1955 *Debates with Historians*, London.

Gottschalker, Louis

1952 *Generalisation in Writing of History,* Chicago.

1957 *Understanding History*, New York.

Grant, Charles

1870 *Gazetteer of the Central Provinces of India,* Nagpur.

Habib, Irfan

1963 *Agrarian system of Moghul India*, Bombay.

1985 *Interpreting Indian History*, North-Eastern Hill University, Shillong.

Haque, M.A.

1981 *Muslim Administration in Orissa,* Calcutta.

Hegel, G.F.W.

1979 *Phenomenology of Spirit,* Oxford.

Jones, Stanley

1925 *The Christ on Indian Road,* London.

Joshi, V.

1946 *Problems of History and Historiography*, Allahabad.

Kant, Sashi

1970 *The Hathigumpha Inscription of Kharavela and Babhru Edict of Ashoka,* Delhi.

Kipling, Rudyard

1967 *Kim,* London.

Kosambi, D.D.

1956 *An Introduction to Indian history*, Bombay.

1957 *Exasperating Essays,* Peoples Publishing House, New Delhi.

Kulke, Herman & Dietar Rothermund.

1991 *A History of India,* New Delhi.

Lal, K.S.

1966 *Studies in Medieval Indian History,* Delhi.

Ladurie, Le Ray

N.D. *Territory of the Historian*, n.p.

Mahatab, Harekrushna

1947 *History of Orissa,* Vol. I & II, Cuttack.

Majumdar, Ramesh Chandra

1934 *Outline History of the Bhanja Kings of Orissa*, Dacca University Studies.

1967 *Indian Historiography: Some Recent Trends*. Presidential Address at the 6th Annual Conference of the Institute of Historical Studies held at Srinagar.

1968 *Historiography of Modern India,* Calcutta.

Maltby, T.J.

1882 *Ganjam District Manual*, (ed) G.D. Lemon, Madras.

Metcalf, Thomas R.

1995 *Ideologies of the Raj*, Cambridge.

Mishra, Pramila

1979 *(ed) Gangavamshanucharitam Chamou Kavyam* by Vasudeva Ratha Somayaji, Bhubaneswar.

Mohanty, A.B.

1969 (ed) *Madāla Pañjī,* Utkal University, Bhubaneswar.

Mohanty, Bansidhar

1989 *Odiya Bhasa Andolan*, Cuttack.

Mohapatra, N. and Madhusudan Das

1983 *Manishi Nilakantha*, Bhubaneswar.

Morris, James

1973 *Heaven's Command: An imperial Progress,* London.

Mukhia, Harbans

1976 *Historians and Historiography during the Reign of Akbar*, New Delhi.

Mukhopadhya, S.K.

1980 *Evolution of Historiography in Modern India* 1900-1960. Calcutta.

Pathak, V.S.

1966 *Ancient Historians of India*, New Delhi.

Pavlov, V.I.

1979 *Historical Premises for India's Transition to Capitalism*, Moscow.

Ranga, N.G.

1986 *Pandit Nilakantha Dash: A National Leader and Father of Modern Orissa State*, Utkal University, Bhubaneswar.

Ray, Lila

1984 *Pandit Nilakantha: Life and Achievements*, Bhubaneswar.

Raychoudhuri, Tapan

1996 "The British Raj: A Story of an Empire which had no Qualms" in Peter Marshall (ed) *Pictorial History of British Empire*, Cambridge.

Sahu, L.N.

1944 *Orissa* in 1912-1942, Cuttack.

1945 *History of Orissa*, Poona.

Said, Edward

1985 *Orientalism*, London.

Sarangi, K.C.

1982 *Madāla Pañjī Kala O Kala*, Cuttack.

Sarkar, Jagdish Narayan

1977 *History of Historical Writing in Medieval India*, Calcutta.

Schweinitz, Jr Karlde

1983 *Rise and Fall of British India: Imperialism as an Inequality*, London.

Seal, Anil

1968 *The Emergence of Indian Nationalism*, Cambridge.

Sen, S.P.

1973 *Historians and Historiography of Modern India*, Calcutta.

Sheikh Ali, B.

1980 *History: Its Theory and Method*, Madras.

Stokes, Eric

1958 *English Utilitarians and India*, Oxford.

Subramanium, N.
1973 *Historiography,* Madras.
Subudhi, Umakant
1978 *Bhaumakaras of Orissa*, Calcutta.
Thapar, Romila
1979 *Ancient Indian Social History*, New Delhi.
1980 *Past and Prejudice*, New Delhi.
1984 *From Lineage to State: Social Formations in Mid First Millennium B.C. in Ganga Valley,* Bombay.
1992 *Interpreting Early India,* New Delhi.
Thapar, R, H. Mukhia and Bipan Chandra
1981 *Communalism and Writing of Indian History*, New Delhi.
Tripathy, G.C. and Herman Kulke
1987 *(ed)Kataka Rajavamsavali*, Allahabad.
Weinberg, A.K.
1935 *Manifest Destiny: A Study of Nationalist Expansion in American History,* John Hopkins University.

ARTICLES AND JOURNALS

Acharya, Paramananda
1938 "Odissa Itihasare Bibhrata" in *Navabharat*, IV,10, p.685-91 and 12, p.843-850.
1943 "Historical References Relating to Orissa in Sandhyakara Nandi's Ramacharitam" in *Journal of Bihar and Orissa Research Society,* X, p. 49-55.
1961 "Bruton's Account of Cuttack and Puri" in *Orissa Historical Research Journal,* X, 3, p. 25-30.
1967 "Account of Travels of Fray Sebastian Manrique" in *Orissa Historical Reearch Journal,* XV, p.72-94.
Aiyangar, S.K.
1921 "Orissa" in *Journal of Andhra Historical Research Society,* II, 1, p. 1-11.
Arnold, David
1985 "Cholera and Colonialism in the British India" in *Past and Present,* 113, n.p.
Basu, K.K.
1959 "Tour Diary of J.R. Ousley" in the *Orissa Historical Research Journal,* Vol 5, 3 &4, Bhubaneswar.
Dash, Gaganendra Nath
1961 "Madalapanjira Aitihasika Pramanikata" in *Dagara*. 25, 4, p.16-18.

Dev, Arjun

1993 "Distorting History to Suit Political Ends" in *New Wave,* 22,28, p.8-13, New Delhi.

Ewer, W.

1955 "Correspondence of the Settlement of the Khoordah in Pooree, 13th May, 1818" in the *Orissa Historical Research Journal,* III (4), Iv (3&4).

Fink, Carale

1971 "Marc Bloch: A Life in History" in *Journal of Modern History,* 44,4, p.447-539.

Gopal, S.

1962 "Writing History in Reverse" in *Proceedings of the Seminar Held on 21-25 January 1963 at India International Centre,* New Delhi.

Guha, Ranjit

n.d "Dominance without Hegemony and its Historiography" in Ranjit Guha (ed) *Subaltern Studies* VI, Delhi.

Kosambi, D.D.

1951 "On a Marxist Approach to Indian History" in *Bhandarkar Oriental Research Institute Journal,* XXXI.

1952 "Studying of Ancient Indian Tradition" *in Indian Historical Research Institute Silver Jubilee Commemoration Volume.*

Lorenzen, D.

1982 "Imperialism and Historiography of Ancient India" in S.N. Mukherjee (ed) *India: History and Thought,* Calcutta, p. 84-102.

Mishra, S.K.

1993 "John Beames *O Odissara Itihasa*" in *Paurusha,* p.51-55.

Mitter, Partha

1972 "Western Bias in the Study of South Asian Aesthetics" in *South Asian Review,* Vol 6, n.p.

Mukherjee, Ashutosh

1924 "Historical Research in Bihar and Orissa" in *Journal of Bihar and Orissa Research Society,* X, 1&2, p.1-20.

Sarkar, *Sir* Jadunath

1916 "History of Orissa in the 17th Century as Reconstituted from Persian Sources" in *Journal of Bihar and Orissa Research Society,* 11, 2, p.153-65; 3, 238-249; VIX,1, 53-56.

Index

❑❑❑